PRAISE FOR

# WHAT THIS PLACE
# MAKES ME

"You are going to face here the web of cultural quandaries of family, home, place, and most of all, Being. Multisensory and multivocal forces will drag you across the immigrant and stage universe. Bilingual breath will surround you—India, Africa, Middle East, Korea, and the triturating screams of river-crossing water in its borderland phantasmagoria. You are going to be loved, and pulled, teased, blurred, mud-mashed, and sculpted by stories, longings, losses, and migrant-soaked river blood. A new grammar, a new rhythm of writing, speaking, performing, sounding, movement, and Queer speakers will thrash you—is this the immigrant experience? Is this America? Arrival? Accommodation? Is this Transcendence? Or is this Immigrant Liberation? Fractured spaces, cultures, and the gone shackles of true persons call for a new Freedom. Wait until you meet La Sirena, the border river, freakish Mermaid riding your back—part Virgen de Guadalupe, part Llorona, part Mouth-spirit of the migrant drownings, howling through the fences of 'Fascist' Border Guards. I bow to these brave writers. Each play and voice steps toward Humanity, Unity, Deep Reality, Borderland-Talk, the Unknown that America fears. We have been waiting for such Enlightenment, Art & Love. We are not 'Invaders.' Bravissimo, a Miracle, a groundbreaking, prize-winning set and chorus of Truth."

—JUAN FELIPE HERRERA,
POET LAUREATE OF THE UNITED STATES, EMERITUS

"This groundbreaking anthology shows us the people we are becoming: a nation of multilingual intimacies, our hearts split between homelands. The bold, visionary playwrights in *What This Place Makes Me* shatter stereotypes, and reveal the deep and beautiful human truths inside the immigrant experience."

—HÉCTOR TOBAR,
AUTHOR OF OUR MIGRANT SOULS

"This vibrant and thrilling collection of groundbreaking plays explodes well-worn twentieth-century tropes around immigration to show that movement across borders is central to the story of humanity. These plays make us feel, make us think, open up new worlds, and exemplify some of today's best dramatic writing."

—DAVID HENRY HWANG,
TONY AND GRAMMY AWARD–WINNING PLAYWRIGHT

"This extraordinary assembly of plays speaks to the range of brilliant writing on the many meanings of being an 'American.' Each text projects a unique voice and a revelatory vision of immigration, belonging, and what it means to make a home in this nation. Stavchansky's selections resonate off of each other, and lead to a luminous portrait of how the theater can tell the stories that make us who we are, and help us see each other more clearly."

—MELIA BENSUSSEN,
ARTISTIC DIRECTOR OF HARTFORD STAGE

# WHAT THIS PLACE MAKES ME

*Contemporary Plays on Immigration*

# WHAT THIS PLACE MAKES ME

*Contemporary Plays on Immigration*

Introduction by Luis Valdez
Edited by Isaiah Stavchansky

RESTLESS BOOKS

NEW YORK · AMHERST

*The Hour of Feeling* by Mona Mansour. Copyright © 2022 by Mona Mansour. Published in *The Vagrant Trilogy: Three Plays* by Mona Mansour, published by Bloomsbury Publishing Plc. Used by permission of Bloomsbury Publishing Plc.

*Sojourners* by Mfoniso Udofia. Copyright © 2025 Mfoniso Udofia.

*Coleman '72* by Charlie Oh. Copyright © 2025 Charlie Oh.

*Public Obscenities* by Shayok Misha Chowdhury. Copyright © 2024 Shayok Misha Chowdhury. Published by Theatre Communications Group. Used by Permission of Theatre Communications Group.

*Sanctuary City* by Martyna Majok. Copyright © 2021 by Martyna Majok. Published in *Ironbound & Sanctuary City* by Martyna Majok. Copyright © 2023 by Martyna Majok. Published by Theatre Communications Group. Used by Permission of Theatre Communications Group.

*Wolf Play* by Hansol Jung. Copyright © 2021 Hansol Jung. Published in *Wolf Play* by Hansol Jung, published by Bloomsbury Publishing Plc. Used by permission of Bloomsbury Publishing Plc.

*a river, its mouths* by Jesús I. Valles. Copyright © 2025 Jesús I. Valles.

Introduction Copyright © 2025 Luis Valdez
Editor's Note Copyright © 2025 Isaiah Stavchansky

Restless Books and the R colophon are registered trademarks of Restless Books, Inc.

First Restless Books Paperback edition December 2024

Paperback ISBN: 9781632062277
Library of Congress Control Number: 9781632062277

This book was made possible in part thanks to the generous support of Edwin Cruz.

Cover design by Sarah Schulte
Text design by Tetragon, London

Printed in the United States

1   3   5   7   9   10   8   6   4   2

RESTLESS BOOKS
NEW YORK · AMHERST
www.restlessbooks.org

# Contents

# INTRODUCTION

## LUIS VALDEZ

This remarkable collection of twenty-first-century plays about global immi-gration belies the stereotypes of emigrants from all corners of the earth. The post-colonial world is still smarting from the impositions of white supremacy throughout the British Empire, as well as from the hegemony of Spanish, French, and other past European imperialists. Clearly, a new category of global citizenship is needed to deal with the contradictions left by centuries of ignorant assumptions about the superiority or inferiority of disparate ethnicities and cultures. I hesitate to call it a world problem of race, as there is only the human race, yet the color of skin, the shape of the eye, and the kink of hair continue to provoke fear and fascination around the marked differences of "others." This anthology goes a long way toward defining the universal similitude of all immigrants.

As a Chicano playwright born and raised in California, my lifelong struggle with nationality and identity has centered on the US–Mexican borderland. How long does it take for generations of hyphenated Americans to feel at home? In my case, well over one hundred years. My grandparents took the big leap and crossed over from Sonora, Mexico, at the turn of the twentieth century, though they were born just south of the border. In fact, my father was born right on the border in Nogales, just six days after the Arizona territory became the forty-eighth state of the union. Eight years later my mother's birth was registered in nearby Mammoth, but she always claimed she was born in El Sasabe, one of the key entry points for documented and undocumented immigrants to this very day. My parents were both American citizens, but as migrant farm workers, they identified as Mexicans.

In the fall of 1965, I joined Cesar Chavez, Larry Itliong, and Dolores Huerta, the leaders of the Great Delano Grape Strike, to organize El Teatro Campesino on the picket lines of what became a protracted five-year struggle.

In those early days, I had no idea that my farm workers' theater would survive and continue to pursue its mission for four generations. For over half a century, our home has been the California mission pueblo of San Juan Bautista, whose foundation stones were laid in 1797, while George Washington was still serving as our first president. Before that, San Juan Bautista had been the native home of the Ohlone people for thousands of years. Notwithstanding the imperialistic US–Mexican War that ceded the Southwest to the United States, I feel at home in America. Not just the USA, but the continent as a whole.

As with the playwrights in this collection, the theater for me has been the search engine for my basic human rights—which is why I can relate to the acute experiences of displacement and alienation detailed here. All the dramatists have found their own truth in their own words, notably some in their own languages apart from standard English. The reality of bilingualism (or multilingualism, for all that) has sculpted the dialogue in my own works since the 1960s. There is no other way to fully express the authenticity of my Chicano experiences without using interlocking Spanish and English dialogue. In this compendium of dramatic works, we are gloriously regaled with an array of scenes in Arabic, Nigerian Ibibio, Bengali, Korean, and Spanish counterposed with translations, but not all with staged supertitles, as if English were the "foreign" language here.

Inherent in all these plays, regardless of their individual dramaturgies, are the aspirational values of immigrants striving to achieve stability, freedom, and independence. On the one hand, these values are direct outgrowths of the struggle in their home countries to achieve the self-determination emblematic of democracy in a post-colonial world. On the other, they reflect the personal accommodations of sojourners in the supercilious society of their former colonial masters. As it turns out, the critical pivot in this regard is literacy in the English language.

*The Hour of Feeling* by Mona Mansour is a case in point. Opening on the eve of the Third Arab–Israeli War (also known as the Six-Day War), a young Palestinian scholar named Adham is invited to London to lecture at University College about the syntactical meaning of a specific poem by Wordsworth. It is an enticing offer. So he accepts, taking his young newlywed wife Abir with him, despite the looming danger of war to both their families at home. To meet the challenge before him, Adham must interpret Wordsworth with all the acumen of a British scholar. He succeeds, finding Anglophile comfort in the collegial company of his university sponsors. As he ponders the possibility of a permanent residency as an academic in England, Abir suddenly questions their future together. Speaking Arabic and almost no English, she is not happy in London. The start of the war in the Middle East decisively settles the issue, motivating her to head home to be with her family while Adham stays on in London.

The dilemma of abandoning one's homeland in favor of another country, be it in Europe or America, is embedded in the twenty-first-century immigrant experience. Obviously, it has shaped the infra-history of the United States since its founding, as wave after wave of newcomers have adapted to a new way of life predicated on their political, economic, or religious fears and hopes. In the play *Sojourners* by Mfoniso Udofia, we meet Abasiama Ekpeyong, "a privileged paragon of Nigerian femininity" who is nonetheless a struggling immigrant in Houston, Texas. In her early twenties, she is eight months pregnant and speaks English with an Ibibio accent. While working at a gas station, and during the painful prolonged labor before she delivers her baby, Abasiama gets to know Moxie Wilis, a streetwise African American teenager, as well as Disciple Ufot, an intelligent dreamer who is also an immigrant without a tether. Weighing her future, Abasiama decides to separate from her husband Ukpong, "a man-child with effortless and magnetic charisma," sending him packing back to Nigeria with their infant daughter. Given her traditional tribal role as an African woman, Abasiama's choice to strike out on her own is a powerful step toward her empowerment and self-determination.

Hanging on an existential hyphen connecting the old country identity with the new is the conundrum that afflicts an entire Korean-American family in Charlie Oh's *Coleman '72*. In order to facilitate their assimilation into the United States, the parents deliberately fail to teach the kids their mother tongue, slyly speaking Korean only when they don't want their children to understand what they are saying. This is a sad but familiar stratagem among immigrants that often only results in later tragic resentments. *Public Obscenities* by Shayok Misha Chowdhury offers a different take on the emotional complications of those who are circumspectly living neither here nor there. Two filmmakers, Choton and Raheem—one Bengali, one African American—arrive in Kolkata to shoot a documentary about queer culture in that country. They interview and film various characters as Choton deals with his complex reactions to being back home after living in New York, while his boyfriend Raheem is warmly welcomed by his family. Written bilingually in Bangla and English, some scenes are boldly sexual, but not out of context. The contrast between the differences in the acceptance of the LGBTQ+ community in Bangladesh and America is an essential point of the play. Ironically, race is not a problem. Rather than a stigma, the color of Raheem's skin is attractive in Bengali eyes.

*Sanctuary City* by Martyna Majok and *Wolf Play* by Hansol Jung also touch on LGBTQ+ relationships, though they primarily address the experience of working-class children of immigrants, whether they qualify as DREAMers or not. The former play entertains the notion of gaining American citizenship by marriage. Though the deep friendship between two migrant children, G and B, does not mature into adult love as they grow up in Newark, New Jersey, G offers to marry B anyway to legalize his status. But B's undocumented status comes between them, isolating him from G just as another lover might. By contrast, *Wolf Play* deals with the adoption of a Korean boy by an American couple, one of whom is AFAB and a boxer. The foreign-born adoptee is Jeenu, portrayed by a puppet boy carried by an Asian actor who howls and speaks for him, identifying as Wolf. As the action unfolds, the boy/Wolf cryptically comments on the emotional complexity of his adoption as he perceives it through his wild animal insights. This fanciful actor/puppet device effectively underscores Jeenu's profound isolation as a stranger in a strange new world.

The varied theatrical styles utilized by all the foregoing playwrights to frame their plays are rich in imaginative and dramatic invention, yet they are rooted in the unrelenting realism of the immigrant experience as captured in their settings, characters, and dialogue. Our last play, *a river, its mouths* by Jesús I. Valles, takes this realism to the hyper-symbolic limits bordering on surrealism. The playwright even issues a warning: "This play depicts violence against migrants, the drowning of migrants at the US/Mexico border, depression, suicide ideation, and suicide." To tell his story, he introduces us to YOU, a law school dropout, who returns to his border town next to a river one must assume is the Rio Grande in South Texas. All the other characters are called MOUTHS.

This is a play about drowning, so the image of mouths is more than symbolic. It is visceral and intrinsic to the meaning of the river, and to the violence that is a direct result of the desperation that drives immigrants to try and cross into Texas from Mexico only to drown midstream. In another powerful sense, it is the MOUTHS of the living and dead that give powerful testimony for the world's immigrants. A FINAL PROVOCATION from the playwright spells it out: "Imagine this play is a spell. Imagine all language is just skin, Spanish, English, just a thin film of sound covering all that we actually are; water." As one Mexican-American playwright to another, I salute Isaiah Stavchansky for editing this astonishing collection of plays about humanity in transit all over the world.

# EDITOR'S NOTE

## ISAIAH STAVCHANSKY

For as long as America has had stages, as long as its doors have been open to new communities, immigrants have made important contributions to theater. Over the last decade, in particular, the number of immigrant writers bringing work to American stages has grown tremendously.

This collection of seven twenty-first-century American plays showcases the most exciting of those theatrical explorations. The playwrights have diverse origins—Lebanon, Korea, Nigeria, India, Mexico, Poland—but what unifies their work is the ways in which they shed light on immigrants' challenges and dreams. While each playwright approaches immigration from a distinct perspective, their stories form an unmistakable collage of America, one that reflects a narrative in which immigration is intrinsically connected to every major issue of our time. Their plays raise crucial questions about assimilation, the meaning of borders, dreams deferred, and the ever-evolving American experience—both the range and the interconnectedness of immigrant communities across generations and backgrounds. As a whole, they underscore the profound influence of immigrants on the fabric of the nation and its theater, emphasizing the importance of sharing these stories to foster empathy and understanding in the broader context of American society.

I wish that I'd had a collection like this when I began reading theater. Like many students in America, I didn't grow up reading plays beyond Shakespeare and Arthur Miller. I had three actor grandparents, two of whom were active in the United States, and one in Mexico, so I saw quite a bit of theater as a child. My first memory of watching a theater performance was at about nine years old, when I went to my grandmother's performance of *The Vagina Monologues* by Eve Ensler, a celebrated series of monologues about sex, menstruation, and reproduction, among other subjects. Even with that unforgettable early exposure, I remained unfamiliar with playwriting.

I spent all of 2016 in the UK, seeing plays and studying the medium as literature. Amid the exhausting political landscape of that year, something clicked and I decided that I wanted to spend my life in the theater. Theater is the place where I could feel most engaged and inspired. Theater examines the way societies function and how that impacts the individual. In a world dominated by short narratives on social media that disappear as quickly as you've seen them, the stage allows for an unavoidably dynamic storytelling. As an audience member, I couldn't hide from the actors in front of me or from my fellow theatergoers. I was part of a singular communal experience.

After that, I wanted to explore American plays that reflected my multicultural upbringing. I had no idea how challenging it would be to find them. Upon my return home to Amherst, Massachusetts, I visited my public library and found plays by Shakespeare, Chekhov, Albee, and Shepard, but almost nothing from the twenty-first century. At my local independent bookstore, I stumbled upon the invaluable *Norton Anthology of Drama*. Although it provided a broad perspective on Western drama, its most recent play was *The American Play* by Suzan-Lori Parks from 1994.

As a result, I had to create my own reading list of contemporary plays. I decided I would read every Pulitzer Prize–winning play to date. The prize, which had been continuously awarded for nearly a century at that point, prided itself on championing a "distinguished play by an American author . . . dealing with American life." Immigration is fundamental to my understanding of American life. As I read through many of the most esteemed plays of the last century, I hoped to encounter the contemporary narratives I craved.

I discovered that much of the conversation only lightly touched on immigration. I encountered comic plays I'd never heard of, such as 1944 production Mary Chase's *Harvey*, plays that I only recognized as movies, like Jason Miller's 1972 production *That Championship Season*, and plays whose brilliance left me astonished, such as Robert Schenkkan's 1991 production *The Kentucky Cycle*. While these works are innovative and depict aspects of American life, they don't fully encompass the multitudes of the America that I knew. I couldn't help but feel disappointed that there were few plays by Latinx writers, few plays by or about immigrants, and few plays addressing cross-cultural identities.

Theater exploring the immigrant experience—love, despair, triumph, failure, and perseverance—has always existed. But of the nearly one hundred Pulitzer winners, there were only a few that touched on these themes directly.

In the honorable mentions for the Pulitzer Prize for Drama, I found a treasure trove of immigrant writers, such as Stephen Karam, Rajiv Joseph, and Kristoffer Diaz. I could only assume that, like most immigrant contributions in America, their brilliance has gone largely uncelebrated, often because of the color of their skin, the cadence of their English, or the language in which they write.

And then I encountered another equally significant issue: even if I could identify the playwrights I wanted to read, I couldn't access their plays unless I bought copies online.

The root of the problem rests in how plays are published in the US. The extent of reader-focused theatrical publishing in America is dwarfed by that of other countries. Most plays are made available largely in actor's editions, typically recognizable as Samuel French paper booklets. These prints are designed for practical use, to be carried during rehearsals, marked up, and so on. They are tailored for theater artists. The majority of these books never find their way onto the shelves of local bookstores.

In my now-local bookstore in Fort Greene, Brooklyn, home to a diverse community of theater artists, most of the plays I can find premiered before the turn of the century. The store manager explained to me that they rely on an advisor who suggests books that are likely to sell, and stock their shelves accordingly. Unless plays are specifically requested by customers, they don't appear in the bookstore.

Public libraries acquire books similarly. Book publishers submit their titles to various publications that review and recommend them. Librarians read those publications and decide which books to include in their collections. Most publishers of plays do not submit their books to these reviewers, which means that plays aren't on the average librarian's radar.

The most recent anthology of contemporary American theater is the second volume of *The Oberon Anthology of Contemporary American Theater*, published in 2018. I learned that many library systems do not carry even a single copy of it. The Los Angeles Public Library, one of the largest public libraries in America, had two copies of the first volume, published in 2012, but none of the second. How is it possible that some of our largest public libraries lack a single copy of the most recent anthology of contemporary English-language plays?

We find ourselves trapped in a self-fulfilling prophecy. Lower book sales and fewer people reading than ever before has resulted in fewer purchases.

As a consequence, each year, booksellers allocate less and less shelf space to plays. The American publishing industry views publishing theater as unprofitable. Without readership, plays don't end up on library shelves either.

With the concentration of professional theater in urban settings (not to mention soaring ticket prices), books can be a powerful tool to inspire interest in theater among the general readership. Books offer a more affordable and accessible medium. In collaboration with public libraries across the nation, they could even be made available for free.

The act of reading plays offers a distinct opportunity to peer into the minds of playwrights. While any performance is an interpretation of the written word, a play serves as an artifact that provides insight into how a storyteller crafts a narrative. To read a play is to partake in a shared experience of the text.

American playwrights from decades past are already included in high school curricula. Playwrights like Arthur Miller, Sophie Treadwell, and Lorraine Hansberry reside on our library shelves alongside authors like Jhumpa Lahiri, Viet Thanh Nguyen, and Chimamanda Ngozi Adichie. We include them because we believe these plays should not only be performed, but read. If we don't make contemporary plays accessible to readers, tomorrow's immigrant children outside our major cities may not have the chance to discover our thriving theatrical tradition. It is high time our contemporary immigrant playwrights be read as literature.

# WHAT THIS PLACE MAKES ME

# The Hour of Feeling

## MONA MANSOUR

*"Politics is the family at breakfast. Who is there, and who is absent and why. Who misses whom when the coffee is poured into the waiting cups. Where are your children who have gone forever from these, their usual chairs?"*

—MOURID BARGHOUTI,
*I SAW RAMALLAH,*
TRANSLATED TO THE ENGLISH
BY AHDAF SOUEIF

Please note that the Arabic dialogue has been romanized with the actors and not standardization in mind.

## PART ONE: THE HOUR OF FEELING

*The cast for the entire trilogy assembles onstage. Hopefully, before they enter, we've been hearing a range of Arabic music. However you can make the theater feel warm and alive, do it. The ensemble members speak as themselves, in their own voices/dialects, up top. Which is to say they aren't acting in any discernible way. It should feel welcoming. Except where indicated, ensemble lines can be divvied up in any way we see fit. It's okay if there is overlap.*

ENSEMBLE  This is a trilogy

This is the first part of the trilogy

The character of Adham

This fictitious character

Makes a choice at the end of this first part, the other two are alternate realities.

SOMEONE IN THE ENSEMBLE  Choice implies you have agency!

SOMEONE ELSE IN THE ENSEMBLE  History comes for him!

ENSEMBLE  A global event turns our lives in another direction—

A decision—

Followed by two alternate realities.

Two different roads Adham could have taken.

Like *Sliding Doors*?

I love that movie.

*The panels start coming in, the play starts pulling them in.*

ENSEMBLE  It's a trilogy

This is part one, it's 1967.

\* \* \*

ENSEMBLE  Lights up on a hill above a small village.

*A panel: Somewhere in the Middle East*

ENSEMBLE  A young man stands on a hill above a small village outside Ramallah. In what used to be called Palestine.

*Panel: In what used to be called Palestine*

*Panel: But now is Jordan*

*Panel: It's complicated*

ENSEMBLE  Below him is the village where he grew up

And where he has returned, for a visit.

THE ACTRESS PLAYING BEDER  Below, in the village, his mother smokes angrily, having prepared food for a party for him.

*A flash of a moment from moments ago:*

ADHAM  I'm going for a walk.

BEDER  You can't leave, it's your party!

ENSEMBLE  He walks.

And walks.

*Adham walks. Someone throws him a book. He catches it and keeps walking—*

ENSEMBLE  As he walks, we see his world.

*Men run in with posters and "paste" them all over the city.*

*Panels: cartoons of 1960s Arab/Israeli figures—Dayan, Eshkol, Nasser—framed by Arabic or Hebrew.*

*Beder dances for a split second.*

ACTOR PLAYING JUL  He has just graduated college. It's 1967.

*Panel: Lulu's "Shout"*

He goes to the top of the hill, where he can think.

ACTRESS PLAYING ABIR  A young woman, also from the village, also walks—

*She now is Abir.*

*And now everyone leaves except Adham.*


## THE CITY—A VILLAGE OUTSIDE JERUSALEM (APRIL 1967)

ADHAM  Meeting someone?

ABIR  Oh. Hello. No. I'm just taking a walk.

ADHAM  It's a long way up from the village.

ABIR  Clears my head. So.

*She reaches into a small cloth bag, pulls out a pack of cigarettes, takes one out and lights up.*

ADHAM  Wow!

ABIR  Want one?

ADHAM  Are you allowed to do that?

ABIR  No. But I don't ask anyone for permission.

ADHAM  All right then.

*She holds up a cig for him. He reaches to take it.*

ADHAM  Your hand is shaking.

ABIR  No.

ADHAM  Okay.

ABIR  It's cold up here.

ADHAM  Okay!

> *They light up; smoke in silence for a beat.*

ADHAM  If you're going to transgress, at least enjoy yourself. I don't know why it's considered shameful anyway. The prophet never saw a cigarette. If he had, who knows? Maybe he'd have liked Gauloises.

ABIR  You shouldn't be talking that way about the Prophet.

ADHAM  Says the girl who's sneaking a smoke.

ABIR  I'm Abir.

ADHAM  Abir, yes. We met at some point, yes? Sorry. I've been away for school . . . So why are you not at my party? Everyone in the village was invited.

ABIR  Why are you not there? You don't like parties?

ADHAM  —I don't like smiling and pretending to be gracious.

ABIR  Even if the party is for you?

> *He laughs.*

ADHAM  You think I need a new suit?

> *He models for her. She studies him for a second.*

ABIR  Yes. And those shoes are worn out.

ADHAM  I see! And they say the village girls have no taste!

ABIR  Who says that? I know what looks good! I read magazines. I see movies. I have taste. I speak French fluently and some English.

ADHAM  And Arabic, of course, with a bit of a peasant accent.

ABIR  I'm not ashamed of being a villager.

ADHAM  You shouldn't be.

ABIR  We had a farm. But I bet I'm more educated than most city girls. I learned how to design irrigation tunnels from my father. How many people can say that?

ADHAM  No one I know. —So let's hear some English.

ABIR  What?

ADHAM  You said you spoke English.

ABIR  I mean, some phrases. Here and there.

ADHAM  Such as?

ABIR  *(caught)* Tosir Widloh.

ADHAM  What?

ABIR  *(hedging)* Toh. Sir. Widloh. The song? You know that one. Lulu.

ADHAM  *To Sir, with Love?*

ABIR  Yes!

ADHAM  So that's your English.

ABIR  And a few lines from a movie. The new Julie Christie one. I see all her movies.

ADHAM  Hm.

ABIR  You don't go to the movies?

ADHAM  Honestly, I'm a boring academic.

ABIR  Are you really going to speak at Oxford?

ADHAM  No. Where did you hear that? University College. London. A conference on Romantic Literature. Every year they highlight one speaker from abroad, and this year it was me.

ABIR  Praise to God.

ADHAM  I'll keep the praise for myself.

ABIR  You don't believe God had a hand in this?

ADHAM  I don't believe he has a hand, a face, an arm, a tooth; I don't think he exists.

ABIR  *(challenging, a little)* Do you pray at least?

     *Beat.*

ADHAM  Not for years. Do you?

ABIR  Of course. It's habit.

     *Beat.*

ABIR  So . . . what happens after you go to London?

ADHAM  You become well known in Cairo, you teach in Cairo. You become well known in London, you can go anywhere.

ABIR  So that's what you want, to teach?

ADHAM  Well, I've finished my Masters, so that's done. Then when you complete the PhD, teaching is the next step. But then, anyone can do that, you know? It's another thing to be—sought after. To have other scholars, people you respect, say, "Yes, I've heard of you. I've read your work." It's an imprimatur, you see. You keep building your reputation, and eventually you chair a department, and then . . . you go to any great city, and they ask you to do a talk, that's how it goes—You think I'm too much?

ABIR  I think that, to get anywhere, one must have a lot of confidence.

ADHAM  So what do you want?

ABIR  I studied civil engineering in secondary school.

ADHAM  And now?

ABIR  Now I'm supposed to wait at home for a husband.

ADHAM  How's that going?

ABIR  I don't like any of them. It feels forced.

ADHAM  Hm. It should feel natural, no?

   *Beat. They both smoke and look out.*

ABIR  So you don't believe in any god? Not ours, no one's?

ADHAM  I believe in Fate. If anything.

ABIR  Yes?

ADHAM  When we were forced out of the Galilee, we ended up at a refugee camp in Southern Lebanon.

ABIR  I'm sorry.

ADHAM  I was five, barely remember it. Anyway, my mother grabbed me and got us here, somehow. My father—thought things would get better.

ABIR  So he stayed? In the refugee camp?

ADHAM  He and my brother never left.

ABIR  Do you talk to them?

ADHAM  My father's not alive anymore. But my brother and I? No, not really. It's very strange.

ABIR  What's his name?

ADHAM  Hamzi.

ABIR  Hamzi . . . So what does Fate have to do with all that?

ADHAM  My mother put all her energies on me. Demanded I be her equal. If it hadn't been just us two, I might not have achieved a thing.

   *Beat.*

ADHAM  You think I'm strange.

ABIR  I think you say strange things.

   *Beat.*

ADHAM  So why did you come up here?

ABIR  You saw. To smoke. Why did you?

ADHAM  *(he barely understands this himself)* I had to get out of there! The apartment, my mother, the no air inside. You ever get that feeling? That you have to escape?

ABIR  Not really.

ADHAM  I can't imagine that.

   *She approaches him.*

ABIR  I saw you walk up the hill. And I thought, if I don't talk to him now, I'll never get to talk to him.

   *They are both on some kind of precipice.*

ADHAM  How does it feel? Talking to me?

ABIR   Not altogether good.

ADHAM   Oh.

ABIR   And not altogether bad.

> *They want to be all over each other, but is 1967, and they are out on a hill, in the open. He reaches for her hand.*

ADHAM   You look like your actress, like Julie Christie.

ABIR   No.

ADHAM   More beautiful.

ABIR   I'm not supposed to think that.

> *She looks at him. She leans in. They kiss very lightly, very slowly.*
>      To Sir, with Love *starts playing:*

> *"If you wanted the sky I would write across*
> *the sky with letters, that would soar a*
> *thousand feet high."*


## AT HOME (MAY)

> *Beder's apartment.*
>      *She turns a panel, revealing: a giant picture of Adham, 14, looking very serious, holding a certificate. She then sits down next to Abir, who has come in with a plate of food on her lap. Adham stands, leaning against the door frame.*

BEDER   That's him getting the Jowett.

ABIR   Oh.

BEDER   *(overlap)* He's the youngest recipient in the history of the award.

ABIR   / So impressive.

BEDER   Then the Partington. That got him into university. That one was from the Catholics, they made him do some of these—

> *She waves her hands carelessly in the air, doing something resembling the Sign of the Cross.*

BEDER   —and write a letter to the Pope, but I didn't care. They want to pay for his education, we do what they want.

ADHAM   It's this.

> *He does it the right way.*

ADHAM   Left to right. Father, Son, Holy Spirit. *(Teasing her)* Get it right, Mother.

BEDER   And this is his graduation picture.

> *Beder hands her a small Polaroid photograph.*

BEDER   Careful.

> *Abir looks at the picture, anxiously, balancing her plate. Adham reaches his hand out to take the picture.*

ADHAM   I'll take that.

BEDER   More food?

ABIR   Oh. Yes. It's delicious.

BEDER   It's passable.

ABIR   I don't agree.

BEDER   Keep eating.

> *Mini-beat as they all eat the passable morsels.*

BEDER   Did my son tell you what I did for him as a child?

ADHAM   Of course / I did!

ABIR   You made him read to you. And uh, you tested him . . . ? Right?

BEDER   That's what he said?

ABIR   Well. / I mean—

BEDER   That's one-tenth of what I did. After al-Nakba . . .

ADHAM   Oh no . . .

BEDER   You want to tell the story?

ADHAM   Of 1948? I'll pass. She knows, anyway. The Israelis took her family's farm. Her father died.

BEDER   They killed him?

ABIR   No, not from that. It was all the smoking. His lungs. He smoked a couple packs a day.

BEDER   *(her mind is made up)* They killed him. What about the rest of your family?

ABIR   I live with my brother, and my sister and her husband. And my mother lives with my other brother. In Detroit, Michigan. America.

BEDER   What does he do there?

ABIR   He makes cars.

BEDER   Hm.

ABIR   For the Ford company. Automobiles.

BEDER   I got that.

ABIR   Adham told me you were from the Galilee.

BEDER   Before they cleaned out every village.

ABIR   And then . . . Lebanon?

BEDER   It wasn't a pleasure trip. We get there, and we sit in a refugee camp.

A shithole! I realize: This isn't temporary. This place is Death. I grabbed my son, and came back here. With nothing but my education, that's it. Did he tell you I had started a degree in philosophy?

*Loud explosions are heard in the distance. Everyone jumps. Beder gets up.*

BEDER  God help us.

*Another explosion, and now light bursts through the window.*

BEDER  The war is on? It's happening?

*Beder moves to go look outside. A beat.*

BEDER  It's just fireworks.

ADHAM  Disappointed, Mother? Did you expect to see Egyptian jets, here to liberate us all?

ABIR  That's not funny.

ADHAM  We hear about it every day. War at any moment. We have to laugh / sometimes!

BEDER  Independence Day fireworks. How can they call it Independence and not choke on the words? They celebrate forcibly removing people from their homes? Killing men, women, children?

ADHAM  Let's not get political.

BEDER  Who's getting political? Anyway—did he tell you what I did for him? He was a nervous child. No shame in that, he was born that way. But it was a problem. I took him to the Quaker school, first time, and he starts crying.

ABIR  Aww.

BEDER  I said listen, NO. You can't do this. Remember this?

ADHAM  Would it matter if I said / no?

BEDER  So I made it a game. I pointed at the pathway. Here, each tree on the side is a great poet, okay? And each tree is here to greet you. You know what he says? He says, Tell me their names. And I thought, Shit. He's genius. So I had to play along. This wasn't my style, this sort of whimsical approach.

ADHAM  Really.

BEDER  So I scramble, I say, uh this tree is, Al-Mutanabbi, the great poet. This one, Al-Yaziji. Al-Barudi. Aristotle. Shakespeare. And then? He goes. On his own.

ABIR  That's a beautiful story.

*Beat. Adham waits it out, displaying a rare show of sensitivity.*

ADHAM  So. I don't want to have to ask your blessing. We're not traditional that way.

BEDER  So don't ask.

ADHAM  I've already talked to her brother, and we spoke to the sheikh.

BEDER  Oh.

ADHAM  But I'm giving you the chance.

　　　　*Beder looks right at Abir.*

BEDER  My son is too young to make his way with a woman.

ADHAM  / What?

BEDER  In ten years or so, when he's established, that's when he starts looking for a wife. And then, he'll be at a higher level, you understand.

ABIR  I should . . . go.

ADHAM  Mother, stop.

BEDER  We've discussed this. I said the same thing about your Egyptian girlfriends.

ADHAM  She's the smartest girl I've ever met. She's your match.

BEDER  Oh really.

ABIR  I'm leaving.

ADHAM  You are unbelievably insulting.

BEDER  I'm insulting? I waited with you for your passport for hours, begging them to issue it to you. They're suspicious of every Palestinian these days, and I'm standing there, pulling out my birth certificate from the British Mandate! Telling them lies, that your father died! Performing the sad widow act! Bribing them! You have your mind made up? Then why go through the motions? You're making a mistake if you go with her! I know what mistakes are! So even though you really don't want to hear my opinion, I'm giving it. This is my house!


## STRAND PALACE HOTEL, LONDON (JUNE)

　　　　*Summer, late afternoon. Panels have turned to reveal 1967 London, with parts of the original ancient city still showing.*

　　　　*Adham and Abir enter their hotel room—not huge, but well appointed. A desk with a lamp. Two chairs and a table, on which has been placed a tea service, and a bottle of champagne. A bed.*

　　　　*They close the door behind them and take in the room.*

ABIR  This is—

ADHAM  Nice.

　　　　*Adham carries the suitcase into the room. Leaves it by the window. He peers through the sheer curtains.*

ABIR  What's out there?

ADHAM  Theaters. Lots of things.

ABIR  Can anyone see in?

ADHAM  I don't think so. I don't think anyone cares.

>  *Abir goes into the bathroom. Adham opens the window. Sounds of the street come in. Abir comes back.*

ABIR  So many towels.

ADHAM  Yeah?

>  *She giggles a little bit.*

ADHAM  *(smiling)* What's going on?

ABIR  Nothing. We just haven't been. Alone. What was the man talking about, something "downstairs"?

ADHAM  Oh, bomb shelters. During the war.

ABIR  He talks so fast.

>  *Abir opens a cabinet.*

ABIR  *(excited)* A television set.

ADHAM  All the nice hotels have them now.

>  *Abir turns it on. It's Tom Jones on the BBC, singing "Show Me." We see it projected on one of the panels behind them.*

TOM JONES  *(V.O.)* Show me a man that's got a good woman. I'll show you a man that goes to work hummin'. He knows he's got some sweet love comin' at the end of his working day.

>  *It's Tom Jones, so it's kind of amazing/sexual, obviously. Abir shuts off the TV. Closes the cabinet. Awkward beat.*

ADHAM  You like that?

ABIR  Yes.

>  *She scans the room, sees something on the tea service. Exhausted, fluttery, she sits on the bed. Bounces back up. Grabs the champagne off the tea service.*

ABIR  Let's have some of this.

ADHAM  You can't have alcohol!

ABIR  A little. With my husband.

ADHAM  A little, huh? You read that somewhere?

ABIR  No. I know it.

>  *She impulsively starts to open the bottle.*

ADHAM  Do you know what you're doing?

ABIR  No one did, the first time they did it.

>  *The cork goes flying. Hits a painting on the wall.*

ABIR  Oh no.

*Adham walks over to look.*

ABIR  Do you think anyone could hear it?

*Adham checks the painting.*

ADHAM  I don't think so.

*Abir pours some into a glass, drinks.*

ABIR  It tastes . . . sour. Hm.

*She pours some for him, holds it out.*

ABIR  Go.

*He takes it, drinks it quickly.*

ADHAM  It's good.

*She stands and looks at him. He goes over to her, puts his arms on her, runs his hands up her back. This is new for both of them. His grip gets tighter.*

ABIR  Ouch.

ADHAM  *(letting go)* Shit.

ABIR  No. It's okay.

*She takes his hands, places them on her waist. The hands stay there, still firm, but not going anywhere. He stalls. Breaks off.*

ABIR  Did I do something wrong?

ADHAM  No, no. You. You're beautiful.

*He goes to the window. Looks out. Takes a big breath.*

ADHAM  This is my chance, you know? This, here. Tomorrow I meet the professors. Maybe I'm no one to come here and tell them what their poetry is.

ABIR  What? No. You're everyone.

*She walks up behind him, places a hand on his back. He turns. She kisses him quickly, almost surprising herself. She takes his face in her hands, looks at him. He kisses her back. Wraps his arms all around her body.*


## THE LUNCH

*Lights up. Two English scholars, George and Theo, open the panels to reveal a domed building above the words: University College. They sit down at a table and hold up teacups to Adham.*

GEORGE  To the next wave of literary criticism.

THEO  You're embarrassing him.

GEORGE  But he is. You are. Don't you feel it's so?

ADHAM  I do believe I'm finding an interesting angle in my approach.

GEORGE  You're far too humble.

ADHAM  No one's ever called me that before.

>  *They laugh.*

GEORGE  And funny.

THEO  I think we needed it frankly. A fresh infusion.

GEORGE  Will you tackle Tennyson as well?

ADHAM  I don't find his work particularly engaging.

GEORGE  But have you read Tennyson, actually? Everyone loves to malign Tennyson but most haven't actually bothered to read him.

ADHAM  No, I have. I appreciate the imagery in *(confidently, but hitting the T hard, and following it with the Arabic H sound)* Tet-HO-nus.

GEORGE  Which one?

>  *They don't seem to know what he's talking about.*

ADHAM  *(faking confidence, slowing the word down)* TET-honus

THEO  Tithonus!

GEORGE  Of course. Sorry.

THEO  Adham, we've been looking forward to meeting you.

GEORGE  Oh! Forgive my manners!

>  *George reaches onto the seat next to him and pulls out a paper bag. He pulls out a large towel-like thing with an old painting on it.*

GEORGE  To our most esteemed guest of the international language exchange.

>  *He hands the thing to Adham, who holds it up appreciatively.*

ADHAM  Oh this is, it's perfect.

GEORGE  He hasn't a clue as to what the hell it is. It's a tea towel.

THEO  It's hideous!

ADHAM  Oh.

>  *George points to the figures on the towel.*

GEORGE  Ah, but this is a University College tea towel. These are our founders, Jeremy Bentham et al, fighting our blood enemies from King's College.

ADHAM  Who's winning?

GEORGE/THEO  We are, of course.

ADHAM  What's the fire?

GEORGE  The pits of hell. Into which our rivals will fall.

THEO  I for one won't be insulted if you leave it in the hotel when you go.

ADHAM  I will treasure this. Thank you.

THEO  Now give him the real gift.

GEORGE  That old thing?

>  *George pulls out a book. Hands it to Adham.*

GEORGE   Your Wordsworth. Third edition. It was the oldest one we could find.

ADHAM   Thank you. I don't know how to thank you.

*He opens the book. Amazed.*

ADHAM   Thank you.

*He closes the book and sets it down carefully.*

GEORGE   I must ask, how did you find your way to the English Romantics?

ADHAM   Find my way?

GEORGE   I can't imagine you woke up every day hearing Wordsworth.

ADHAM   My mother decided I should be a scholar. It was this or Cicero.

GEORGE   You chose right! Was she a teacher?

ADHAM   No. Just full of opinions.

GEORGE   And she grew up in, uh, Israel? Or . . . um, of course. Palestine.

ADHAM   Yes.

THEO   The landscape there is splendid. Mountains and the sea, yes?

ADHAM   I don't know. I never get out that way.

THEO   Really? The famous road down the coast, on the way to Jerusalem. I'm dying to try it one day. The Romans, the Phoenicians . . .

ADHAM   I've heard that. The road is cut off now, so.

GEORGE   What do you mean?

ADHAM   We can't go back there. It's off-limits. To—us.

THEO   Sorry.

ADHAM   No, no. It's. You can't miss it if you don't know what you're missing.

*Abir approaches. She speaks to Adham in Arabic.*

ABIR   Eish akul? (What should I eat?)

*All of the following is in Arabic. Adham is jarred; immensely embarrassed to be speaking in his native tongue.*

ADHAM   Eish? (What?)

ABIR   Il akil. BaArafish shu deen hal akil. (The food. I can't tell what anything is.)

ADHAM   Koli mitl inniswan ettanyat. (Eat what the other wives are eating.)

*She makes a face.*

ADHAM   IHzaree, maashi? (Just take your best guess, okay?)

THEO   Everything all right?

ADHAM   *(to Theo, in English)* Yes.

ABIR   BaArafish shu lazem aAmel. (I don't know what I'm supposed to be doing out there.)

ADHAM   *(to Abir, in Arabic)* Wala ana bAaraf. Ana asif. Ana dayman Aimilit hay il ishya' la Hali. Biseer bas takli 'ay ishi o toAdi daqeeqa. Ma bazon il shaghleh hatawil. (I don't know either. I'm sorry. I've only done these things by myself. Can you just eat something and sit for a minute? It won't be long I don't think.)

*Abir, trying to make it work, goes.*

THEO She doesn't like the food?

GEORGE Can't blame her for that!

ADHAM Oh. No. No no. She's fine.

THEO But she did mention food? Bad food?

ADHAM Yes.

THEO *(to George)* See? I'm not as hopeless as you think.

GEORGE Hurray, hurray, you understood one sentence.

ADHAM You speak Arabic?

THEO I try.

GEORGE Very hard sadly. Actually, Theo here is a bit of a pan-Arabist.

THEO An Arabist. But this pan-Arab phenomenon is fascinating. Nasser seems rather inspiring.

GEORGE Would you agree?

ADHAM He's very charismatic. Sweats a lot.

GEORGE *(enjoying Adham's assessment)* Brilliant.

> *George offers Adham a cigarette. He takes it. All three men light up, looking back toward where Abir went.*

GEORGE You've been married a long time?

THEO That's rather a personal question, isn't it.

ADHAM Not at all. We're just. Married.

GEORGE Just?

ADHAM Three weeks ago.

GEORGE My God.

> *They look at Adham.*

THEO Oh. It's very new, then.

ADHAM Yes. We barely know each other. So. Here we are.

> *For some reason he starts to laugh. As do Theo and George. A moment of some understanding.*

GEORGE Sometimes that's best. Sometimes you need to just jump in. Don't look at how high the cliff is, or that you might hit the rocks on the way down.

THEO So cynical.

GEORGE How so? I love women.

> *Abir returns, and this time sits down next to Adham.*

ABIR  Ana Ijeet kul hal masafeh. Bidii 'akoon MaAk. (I came all this way. I
    want to be here with you.)

GEORGE  *(to Abir)* Would you care for a cigarette?
    *He holds up a cigarette to her.*

ABIR  Thank you.
    *He lights it. She inhales, exhales. Smiles at Adham.*

THEO  I can't imagine how difficult it must be right now, down there. In
    your homeland, I mean. I mean, politically.
    *(re: Abir)* I feel terrible leaving her out.
    *(in Arabic, to Abir)* bHiss inno da ma'sah . . . lam nushrikuki fil hadith.
    (I feel terrible . . . leaving you out of the conversation.)

ABIR  Ashkuru qawloka hatha! (Thank you for saying that!)

THEO  al Aarabi bitaAi, taAban, mish kida? (My Arabic is terrible, isn't it?)

ABIR  la'. (Not at all.)

GEORGE  Can she understand a word he's saying?

THEO  Of course she can.
    *(to Abir again, in Arabic)* mabastaAmilhash kiteer. bi ged mish battal?
    (I get to use it so infrequently. It's really not bad?)

ABIR  la'. btiHkee ka annak min masr. haada il ishee il waheed il ghareeb.
    (No. You sound like you're from Egypt. That's the only strange thing.)

THEO  *(to Abir)* ma kansh Aindee ayy fikra. kunt faakir inno huwa da al
    mustawa? (I had no idea. Imagine that. I suppose that's the standard?)
    *Abir shrugs.*

THEO  She's absolutely unimpressed with me. She's very beautiful if you
    don't mind me saying.

ABIR  *(she understands this)* Thank you.
    *Abir smiles.*

ADHAM  You understood that! So we can speak in English.

ABIR  Aal aqal asHaabak Habbounee. amma anniswaan in the "dining
    room," kullhum khataayreh w la'eemat. (At least your colleagues like me.
    The women in the dining room were all old and mean.)

THEO  I agree! The women back there are old and mean.
    *He and Abir laugh.*

THEO  Beer, anyone?

ADHAM  Oh. Yes, thank you.

THEO  Certainly. Would your wife . . . ?

ADHAM  She's fine.
    *Theo leaves.*

GEORGE   You ready for your talk tomorrow?

ADHAM   Oh, yes. Yes.

GEORGE   Some of our colleagues have got pretty worked up about the poem on which you're speaking. They take issue with Wordsworth's way of seeing. He sees something, then he doesn't.

> *Theo returns with three beers.*

THEO   Oh no. Is this your "hardly hedgerows" discussion again?

ADHAM   Let me hear it.

GEORGE   Early on in "Lines Composed a Few Miles Above Tintern Abbey, on Revisiting the Banks of the Wye During a Tour, July 13, 1798"—you'll forgive me if I don't abbreviate—Wordsworth mentions the hedgerows he sees. But then in the same line, backs off from the observation: "hardly hedgerows." He who is the master observer of nature backs away from what he sees.

ADHAM   *(not sure where it's going)* Um-hmm . . .

THEO   That's what I say! "Um-hmm."

> *Abir reaches for the beer glass, but Adham stops her.*

GEORGE   It's been said—not by me—that these hedgerows are a sign of enclosure, and, and, rural impoverishment.

THEO   By one neo-Marxist historian! Not even a Romantic specialist.
*(to Adham)* Should I get her a beer?
*(to Abir, in Arabic)* BEDIK tarabeiza?

> *Abir laughs and shakes her head.*

THEO   Oh no. What did I say? What've I done?

GEORGE   What did he say?

ABIR   *(in Arabic)* ult "tarabeiza."

ADHAM   *(in English)* You asked her if she wanted a table.

THEO   Oh dear. Just when I think I've made progress.

GEORGE   *(resuming his argument)* Do you feel this is way off the mark?

ADHAM   I don't understand.

GEORGE   That Wordsworth backs off from an indictment of the landed class!

THEO   So now it's an "indictment"? / That reading isn't supported!

GEORGE   Wordsworth sees this sign of social stratification, of the subjugation of the peasant, and then dismisses it. It bears some investigation.

> *Abir sneaks in another sip of Adham's beer.*

ABIR   *(to Theo)* Habbetha kteer haadi. Hatta law kaanat tarabeiza. (I like whatever this is. I don't care if it's a table.)

> *She laughs, as does Theo.*

ADHAM   Wordsworth says, "Once again I see these hedgerows, hardly hedgerows, little lines of sportive wood run wild." He sees the structures, the outlines of them, but then he reflects on what he's seen, almost instantaneously, and amends it. "Hardly hedgerows." Not because he's disturbed by the implication. But for the simple reason that the hedgerows have become overgrown with grass. He's giving himself license to let things fade in tableaux as they fade in the mind.

THEO   Ah. I like that!

GEORGE   Hm. What about the vagrant then?

ADHAM   From "The Ruined Cottage"?

GEORGE   No, from the same poem we're discussing. "Tintern Abbey." What about him?

ADHAM   Forgive me, but what about him? I don't understand the question.

GEORGE   My dear man, you need to be ready for this kind of textual interrogation.

ADHAM   I am. Oh I am.

THEO   You're making him feel unwelcome.

GEORGE   Not at all. We're having a discussion. Exchange of ideas. You don't feel I'm making you unwelcome do you?

ADHAM   (overcompensating) Me? No. No no. I feel, uh, welcome. Yes.

GEORGE   So, yes, in this same poem. Wordsworth suggests this life, this vagrant is there, but he clearly finds it distasteful, moves on.

ADHAM   "Vagrant dwellers in the houseless / woods." That's it.

GEORGE   There are readings that imply that the vagrant is deliberately tucked away, something marring the poetic vision.

ADHAM   What more did Wordsworth need to say about the vagrant?

THEO   Right!

ABIR   Wattee sotak. (Don't yell.)

ADHAM   ana mneeH. (I'm fine.)

THEO   (to George) George, did you want a bloody epic poem about the bloody vagrant? Sorry, Madam.

>   Abir smiles. She hasn't understood, but decides to respond anyway, in English.

ABIR   It's all right. Where is my table?

GEORGE   I'm saying no discussion of Wordsworth should be considered complete without an acknowledgement of this unseemly underbelly. Our friend Adham is in a perfect position to understand.

ADHAM   I am? I don't know how.

GEORGE  As a Palestinian, a, a, refugee.

ADHAM  I see.

GEORGE  Your world. Where you live. I mean, what's going on now. The Egyptian army building up in the Sinai . . .

THEO  Some of that is / overblown.

GEORGE  And the Israeli generals panicking, taking the reins from the Prime Minister. We have been hearing about how dire it is, all over the Middle East.

ADHAM  I've never known things not to be dire.

    *Beat.*

THEO  There was an, uh, interesting article in *The Times*. Saying that basically Nasser is bluffing, with no intention of going to war. But Moshe Dayan, who says he won't go to war, is actually readying the rifle, so to speak.

ABIR  *(alerted)* Dayan kazzab. (Dayan is a liar.)

    *Adham tries to quiet her.*

ADHAM  All right, all right.

GEORGE  What'd she say?

THEO  She believes Dayan's a liar.

GEORGE  Well he may be, Madam, but he's saddled with the task of protecting his country. Israel is surrounded by those who wish them extinct. They must fight back if provoked. Clearly you grant them that?

ABIR  eish? Aam beedaafiA Aan el israa'eeliyyeen? (What's he saying? He's defending the Israelis?)

ADHAM  *(to Abir)* La'!

    *(to the men)* I'm sorry.

GEORGE  No need to apologize. I like the passion.

ABIR  eish Haka? (What did he say?)

ADHAM  Khallas. (Don't worry about it / Enough)

ABIR  *(in Arabic)* Dayan kul shughlo wisikh. O Eshkol saaket Aamel Haalo ma ilo dakhal bishee. haada kullu mukhattateenlo Aashaan ybeinoo abriyaa' mustafazzeen. (Dayan is the one doing the dirty work, while Eshkol gets to sit back and pretend he knows nothing about it. It's all part of their plan to look innocently provoked.)

THEO  What's all that?

ADHAM  I guess this is an area she has strong feelings about.

ABIR  Lazim ennas tiAraf. Khalleehum yismaAou la Dayan. Bas tisAa w tisAeen bil miyyeh min Hakyo kullu kizib b kizib. (People should know.

You can listen to Dayan, but ninety-nine percent of what comes out of his mouth is lies.)

ADHAM   IHna ma ijeenaa hon Aashan niHkee bi haada elmawdouA, mashi? (We didn't come here to talk about this, all right?)

ABIR   *(to George)* Bas ibtiAraf Eish, iza biddak itdal jaahel, khalleek jaahel. Shu aAmelak? (But you know, if you want to stay ignorant, stay ignorant. What can I do?)

ADHAM   uskutee! (Shut up!)

THEO   What's she saying?

ABIR   eish? leish ibteHkee maAee heik? Ma tihkee maAee heik. (Don't talk to me like that. Why would you talk to me like that? Don't talk to me like that!)

ADHAM   I think the vagrant is, is, Wordsworth sees him, as much as he sees everything else in the poem! And I don't feel any affinity for the, uh, vagrant in that poem, or any other. Is what I think.

*Adham takes the beer away from Abir again, and downs the rest.*


## REHEARSAL

*Adham enters, turns a panel, revealing: "Adham's rehearsal." A beat of panic upon seeing this title, then he takes his place behind a podium, leans into a microphone, and starts his lecture.*

ADHAM   Wordsworth's poem—

*Adham backs away. There's a tremendous echo, almost surreal.*

ADHAM   —begins with the mention of time passing: "Five years have passed." Is this the way it's supposed to sound?

*The others are heard but not seen.*

GEORGE   That's this hall. You have to fill it up or you get swallowed.

*Adham looks supremely uncomfortable.*

THEO   You okay up there?

GEORGE   It's just a rehearsal.

ADHAM   It's uh—yes.

   *(he laughs)* It's so big in here. What's the word—

   *(in Arabic)* WasiA. (Cavernous.)

   I don't know it in English.

   *(laughs again, nervously)* Oh well. WasiA. Leave it at that.

   *He wipes sweat from his face.*

THEO   Take the coat off, you'll feel better.

ADHAM  Yes, thank you. *(starts to take his coat off, stops)* I'll be all right.
> *We hear the low sounds of Fairuz's song "Dabke Libnan." Adham adjusts his coat.*

GEORGE  Just a few more words.
> *Adham begins again, but he's fighting the need to get the fuck out of there. It's a full-on fucking panic attack. As he speaks we hear Fairuz's "Dabke Libnan" rise up under him. He fights it, until it drowns out his words.*

ADHAM  As the poem says, uh:
> "I have owed to them
> In hours of weariness, sensations sweet
> Felt in the blood, and felt along the heart,
> Feelings too
> Of unremembered pleasure: such, perhaps
> As have no slight or trivial influence
> On that best portion—"
>> *Lights out.*


## ADHAM CONFRONTS HIS MEDIOCRITY

> *Early evening. Adham, in some kind of torment, enters the hotel room. Rain has come through the open windows, drenching the curtains. Adham doesn't seem to notice. He takes off his jacket, throws it on the floor.*
>> *Starts to unbutton his sweat-stained, wrinkly shirt. Lays on the bed.*
>> *Abir, adventure-happy, slightly buzzy from the beer, enters. Switches on the light.*

ABIR  The old man—the clerk? He wanted to show us the pictures of when Omar Sharif stayed here. Did you know there was a movie called *Genghis Khan*? We didn't get that one—
> *Abir notices the windows open, the jacket on the floor.*

ABIR  What's wrong?

ADHAM  Nothing.
> *She picks up the jacket, shakes it out. Takes the cigarettes out of the pockets and sets them on the desk. Hangs the jacket in the closet, looks at Adham, who goes to look out the window.*

ABIR  You're tired. I'll make you a cup of tea.

ADHAM  I don't want anything.
> *She studies him.*

ADHAM  I failed.

ABIR  Failed? At what?

ADHAM  Today. With the scholars. They looked at me, like—"Who is this idiot?" "Why did we bring him here?"

ABIR  What? No one thought / that.

ADHAM  I was an embarrassment. Scrambling for an answer, coming up with mishmosh, nothing.

ABIR  It didn't sound like that!

ADHAM  You don't speak the language, my dear.

ABIR  Some. I saw them talk to you. They liked you. I wish you could see that.

ADHAM  Why are you not disgusted with me? You should be disgusted with me. I stood in that hall, and looked out . . . My legs couldn't hold me. I can't do it. I can't.

ABIR  Wait, wait . . . It was just practice.

ADHAM  Your husband was flailing. They ask me to defend my point of view, and what do I give them? Theories that took fifteen years to trickle down to us. Old thoughts, old theories. I'm useless.

ABIR  By God, that's not true.

ADHAM  By god, it is! We're backwards! While we've been fighting over this and that scrap of desert, crying over the last assassination, they've been living with the great thoughts. We've wasted so much time.

*He looks like he might cry, but he holds it together. She goes to him, touches his back.*

ABIR  You have a great mind.

*Adham laughs.*

ADHAM  Is that right.

ABIR  He said that.

ADHAM  Who?

ABIR  What was his name, Theodore. In Arabic. He said that.

ADHAM  He just wanted to get close to a beautiful woman.

*Beat.*

ADHAM  Flirting. You didn't know he was doing that? Men will say anything to look into a woman's eyes.

ABIR  So what? It doesn't matter why he said it. He also said you have a unique scholarly voice.

ADHAM  Because it comes with an accent.

ABIR  I don't know why you've forgotten how smart you are. The man I met—was sure of himself, and didn't care about what anyone thought.

ADHAM  Well, maybe that wasn't me.

    *He looks at her.*

  Maybe this is me.

    *Beat.*

ABIR  Then I want them both.

    *She reaches for his head, touches it.*

  I can handle both.

    *She takes his hands.*

  Your hands are shaking.

    *He pulls his hands away. She places her hands on his head, runs her hands through his hair, trying to fix it.*

  I don't know what happens with this hair.

    *He relaxes, just a little. She takes his cigarette from him, smokes, studies him . . .*

ADHAM  Wondering what you got yourself into?

ABIR  No.

ADHAM  You lie.

    *She goes and grabs his Wordsworth book.*

ABIR  Tell me what it says.

ADHAM  You'll be bored.

ABIR  You're so insulting, you know that?

ADHAM  It's in a different language!

    *She starts reading it, in English. It's barely recognizable:*

ABIR  "Thus by day" . . .

    *She stops, but keeps her eyes on the page, nodding as if she's reading and comprehending it.*

ADHAM  *(teasing her)* You don't understand it!

ABIR  I get some of it. I'm very smart, too.

ADHAM  I know.

    *She hands the book to him.*

ABIR  Go. Read.

    *He shrugs. She watches intently. He takes a beat, then reads, speaking in English:*

ADHAM  "Thus, day by day, / Subjected to the discipline of love—"

ABIR  Translate.

ADHAM  Into what?

ABIR  Into classical Arabic.

ADHAM  FusHa.

*Adham shakes his head at first. Abir waits. He then translates it into Arabic, haltingly. This feels very unfamiliar to him.*

wa haakadha maA el waqt, wa huwa khadiAan li qaaAidati lHub.

ABIR  More.

ADHAM  "His organs and recipient faculties / Are quicken'd, are more vigorous—"

*He looks at her. Translates again, into Arabic.*

Aada'uhoo wa quduraatuhu lHissiyya tatasaaraA, tatazaayadoo nashaatan.

ABIR  I like this poet. He's not boring.

ADHAM  It doesn't translate well.

ABIR  I disagree.

ADHAM  You're not supposed to disagree with your husband.

ABIR  I thought you weren't traditional.

ADHAM  Sometimes I am.

*Abir gives him a look.*

ABIR  More.

ADHAM  Ordering me about!

ABIR  Go.

ADHAM  " . . . his mind spreads / Tenacious of the forms which it receives."

*And translates again:*

Aaqluhu yatafataH. Yatamasak bil ashkaal alati yatalaqaaha.

*As he finishes translating this last part, Abir moves closer to him.*

*Both of them are on the bed now. She kneels, places her hands on his hipbones.*

*Leans in, kisses him there.*

*Lights shift: early morning light.*


## RIGHT AT EXETER STREET

*Abir is gone. It's raining again. We hear a shower. As Adham says the following, he gets out of bed very slowly, in his underwear.*

ADHAM  No flinch, no fear. Hands, still. Hands, still.

*He puts on his shirt.*

ADHAM  Shirt? Pretend it's nice. Pretend it's dry.

*He breathes in and out, fast.*

ADHAM  Remember why you're here.

*He puts his pants on. His jacket.*

ADHAM A proper gentleman. A scholar.

*He leaves the room and goes "outside," into and through the panels/London.*

ADHAM On his way to do his work: Right at Exeter Street, left at Wellington Street, Bow Street, Long Acre, Endell Street, High Holborn, Shaftesbury Avenue, Gower Street. The Darwin Lecture Theater, University College.

*Inside. A simple washroom. A single sink, and a mirror. He takes a towel hanging there, and dries his hands.*

ADHAM A clean towel. With letters. England's letters.

*He hangs the towel. Looks in the mirror.*

ADHAM Vain.

*He fixes his hair for a second. He likes what he sees.*

ADHAM Not bad.

*He walks away from the mirror, goes through the vast hallways of the building.*

ADHAM New shoes. Clean shoes. Tight. On marble. Solid. History in this floor. Scholars buried here. This history. Scholars underneath, learned men. Here. Shoes click above the great scholars. The poets. The poetry. And me. And me walking past, and through, and history, and honor, and great thoughts, and those that abide by language. Its laws, and its mandates. Me above, moving through.

*He arrives at the door that takes him backstage.*

ADHAM Last breath. Hands, still.

*He finds a folder, his folder.*

ADHAM Folder.

*Checks his zipper.*

ADHAM Pants zipped.

*Opens the door and steps into darkness, into the backstage area.*

ADHAM Darkness.

Breath. Last big breath.

Dust. Old air. A small light on a table. How are you sir? Do you have everything you need, sir? Glass of water for you sir? Glass of water for the scholar, for the man, for me. No smile, no thanks, this is expected, this is how it goes.

*And now he takes his place at a podium, stepping into a very bright light.*

ADHAM Stand still. Paper. Light. Light.

*We hear very faint, muffled clapping. He looks out over the audience:*

ADHAM Glasses. Hair. No one I know. Glasses, hair. Small, easy breath.

Easy. You know how to talk. No rolling R's. No attack. The British, the English, they don't attack the language.

You know this: In England, the words are like water. One false sound, and a man is exposed. We Arabs? Our words are like hammers, hitting nails.

A thousand breaths, waiting for me. For this man, this scholar, ready to do the Work of God.

> *Adham stands at the podium, the lights go as bright as they can, and then blackout.*

> *Music: Joni Mitchell, "Night in the City."*

## THE PARTY

> *Lights up at a party in an apartment. Theo is there, as is George, as is a very beautiful English woman, Diana, 20s, who sits languidly on a couch next to Theo. Adham and Abir, having just arrived, stand and look at the group, awkward.*

GEORGE  *(to Adham)* Have you met Diana?

DIANA  I'm George's girlfriend.

> *(re: George)* How he hates that word. He flinches, don't you George?

GEORGE  Not in the least.

> *Staying on the couch, Diana reaches her hand out to shake Adham's.*

ADHAM  Pleasure to meet you.

DIANA  Actually, we spoke for a moment right after your talk.

ADHAM  I'm sorry—

DIANA  It's all right. There were loads of people. As well there should've been.

THEO  And this is Adham's wife, Abir.

DIANA  Oh! My goodness. Yes. They said you were married.

ADHAM  Sorry—yes.

DIANA  *(to Abir)* You sat in front of me. I admired your dress.

ABIR  Hello.

> *Beat.*

ADHAM  She doesn't speak English.

DIANA  Sorry.

> *(now waving to Abir, as if to make it clear)* Hello.

ABIR  Hi.

THEO  *(to Abir, in Arabic)* ana Hakoon mutarjimik illeileh. (I'll be your translator tonight.) ana bHeb etkallem Aarabee. (I love speaking Arabic.)

ABIR seret kteer aHsan. (You've gotten better already!)

ADHAM ah, sar. aHsan. (He has.)

THEO shukran. (Thank you.)

*Beat. They realize they are leaving the others out.*

DIANA *(re: hearing the language)* Marvelous. Don't stop.

GEORGE I think we all need more of whatever we're drinking. Adham, can I get you started?

*Adham nods. George goes.*

DIANA So, she couldn't understand any of what you said tonight?

ADHAM No, not so much.

DIANA Tragic.

ADHAM Maybe it was a relief. She has to listen to me a lot.

DIANA Ridiculous!

*(to Abir)* Your husband did very well.

*(to Theo)* Tell her that.

*(to Abir)* Could you see how well he did?

ADHAM *(to Abir, in Arabic)* bid ha tiAraf keef shufteeni illeileh. (She wants to know how it was to watch me tonight.)

ABIR *(to Adham, in Arabic)* kunt mbayyan kteer mirtaaH. (You were the most comfortable I've ever seen you.)

DIANA What did she say?

THEO She—

ADHAM *(cutting him off)* She enjoyed it.

DIANA And how does she find London?

ABIR *(to Adham, in Arabic)* aysh? (What?)

ADHAM bid ha tiAraf keef Habbeitee London. (She wants to know how you like London.)

ABIR hiyyeh aalat inni hilweh? (Did she say I was pretty?)

THEO *(to Abir)* naAam. (Yes, she did.)

ADHAM *(to Diana)* Oh. Uh . . . she likes London very much.

ABIR *(to Theo)* hiyyeh hilweh. mish mbawzzeh, hon. (She's beautiful. Not angry, here . . .)

*(points to her mouth, pouty)* . . . mitil ba'ee anniswaan al engleeziyyat. (like so many of your English women.)

DIANA What did she say?

*Theo starts to translate.*

THEO She says you're beautiful, not like—

ADHAM *(cutting him off)* We both like London very much.

DIANA  Well. You should both stay. Finish your studies here. I think Adham
would do well. Don't you, Teddy?

THEO  *(feigning nonchalance)* Eh.

DIANA  *(to Theo)* Stop it.

*(to Adham)* They're so gruff, these academics. No wonder I had to drop
out.

THEO  Diana was halfway through her literature course.

DIANA  I met George, and that was it. He seduced me, and I couldn't con-
centrate anymore. I wasn't cut out for it anyway, though. Focus your whole
life on one poet, or one bloody poem? I need variety.

THEO  Really? According to whom? Your fortune teller?

DIANA  She's been right about a lot of things.

*She smiles at Adham. George returns with a fresh bottle of wine and two
glasses. He fills everyone's glasses, and pours for Adham and Abir.*

GEORGE  To a great speech!

THEO  Hear, hear!

ADHAM  You're too kind.

DIANA  No kindness. We're impressed.

THEO  Don't start being humble now, my dear chap.

GEORGE  You were good.

ADHAM  I mentioned your vagrant.

GEORGE  I noticed.

THEO  Funny that. The vagrant made it in. Satisfied, Georgie?

GEORGE  Surprised.

ADHAM  The vagrant had his place. Just a smaller place than you'd have liked.

DIANA  I heard all that. But I didn't remember a vagrant in the poem. I'm
sorry.

THEO  Aw, Georgie, that's got to be hard to hear.

DIANA  I mean, it was really just about Wordsworth, this man. The individual. Oh God. You're afraid I'll massacre your point.

ADHAM  I'm not worried.

THEO  You haven't read her work, Adham. / Maybe you should be.

GEORGE  Let's hear it.

DIANA  Well, really, it was all sort of ironic, wasn't it? The way you put it.
Old William was sort of going on and on about Nature, but in the end, it's
not the things he sees at all. Or even the place . . . It's the imprint it leaves.
He could be anywhere.

THEO  See? People were listening.

ADHAM  *(to Diana)* Maybe you should go back into academics.

DIANA  Right.

THEO  *(to George)* Maybe she had the wrong teacher.

DIANA  Maybe.

GEORGE  I admit. It's a very close reading of the text. Not accounting for the socioeconomic underpinnings . . .

THEO  Oh no . . .

GEORGE  But it worked. In your hands, the poem was vital. Alive.

DIANA  *(to Adham)* Did I get it right, though?

ADHAM  Well, it's the paradox of . . .

> *He stops himself.*

ADHAM  I don't want to go on too much. She . . . *(meaning Abir)* . . . doesn't understand any of this.

> *Everyone looks at Abir, who's been listening, smiling, not getting any of it.*

DIANA  Isn't she a dear? She must be bored out of her mind.

ABIR  *(in Arabic, to Adham)* eish? (What?)

ADHAM  *(in Arabic)* Wala ishee, ma biddi itDallik laHaalik kteer. (Nothing. I don't want to leave you out for too long.)

ABIR  la'. ana mirtaaHa. haadi leiltak. (No. I'm all right. This is your night.) *(she takes his hand, moves close into him)* Talk.

> *Adham smiles. As he speaks, we see his passion for the work unleashed.*

ADHAM  For Wordsworth, this, uh, this meaning of home, it comes to him only after leaving. His tie to this part of Nature, uh, paradoxically helps him transcend the specific place itself. Line sixty-three:

> The picture of the mind revives again:
> While here I stand, not only with the sense
> Of present pleasure, but with pleasing thoughts
> That in this moment there is life and food
> For future years . . .
> Essentially it's—Should I go on?

DIANA  Yes!

ADHAM  It's—the paradox is: Wordsworth, great poet of nature, comes to know himself as part of the grand scheme of Spirit only when he lets go of his attachment to the very landscape that inspired him to write in the first place.

DIANA  And then he forgets all about it?

ADHAM  No. It stays here.

> *Points to his head.*

ADHAM  And here.

> *Points to his heart.*

> *Beat.*

GEORGE  Bravo.

ADHAM  Can I have another drink?

> *He holds up his glass.*

GEORGE  I can do even better.

THEO  I think we've rattled Georgie!

GEORGE  *(as he goes)* Nonsense!

ADHAM  I don't mean to cause any problem.

DIANA  George deserves a little trouble. He's got another girlfriend, you know. I'm not the only one.

ADHAM  I see.

THEO  You're the most important.

DIANA  He said that?

THEO  It's clear.

DIANA  That's too bad. Poor Theo's being forced to lie! What do you think, Adham—should a man be confined to one woman?

ADHAM  Yes.

DIANA  Ha!

ADHAM  If it's the right woman, of course.

> *Abir, exhausted from the day, slowly falls asleep on Adham's shoulder. He takes her glass.*

DIANA  Sweet. I wish I could fall asleep like that.

ADHAM  I think she's just tired.

THEO  Been a long day for both of you.

> *George returns with a rolled-up joint.*

GEORGE  Here we go. *(sees Abir)* Oh look at that. We've bored her.

THEO  No different than some of your first-years.

GEORGE  I've taken a fair amount of beating tonight.

THEO  Aw. Did you bring something to ease the pain?

GEORGE  I did. Adham, will you join us? It's good stuff. From Morocco, I believe.

> *George lights up, takes a hit. Passes it to Theo.*

> *He passes it to Diana, who takes a long drag, then passes it to Adham. After Adham smokes:*

ADHAM  That is strong isn't it.

THEO  It is! Well done George.

GEORGE  I didn't make the stuff.

>   *They laugh. Beat. It is strong stuff.*

DIANA  I went out with a man from Morocco.

THEO  Oh ho!

DIANA  Claimed he was some kind of royalty.

GEORGE  I'm sure he was.

DIANA  Spoke six languages . . . My flatmates adored him. I found out later he was selling hash to everyone.

THEO  And none to you?

DIANA  It's not really my thing!

>   *Realizes she's holding the joint. Laughs.*

DIANA  God, present circumstances excluded. Adham, you must think we're all so decadent.

ADHAM  No.

DIANA  You know, the children of the faded empire / and all that.

THEO  "Faded empire"? / Good god.

DIANA  Hong Kong, Rhodesia . . . Our empire is on its last legs—and rightfully so!

GEORGE  Let me have that.

>   *He takes her hand, wrestles the joint from her. Leans in and kisses her.*

DIANA  Fine, shut me up.

GEORGE  Never.

DIANA  *(to Adham)* When do you go back?

ADHAM  To the hotel?

DIANA  No! You're so funny. Home. To your, to your country. Oh god, I've messed it up. It's not really a country, is it?

THEO  Not for twenty years.

ADHAM  Uh, day after tomorrow? Yes, yes.

DIANA  You should stay longer.

ADHAM  Why? To go to more parties?

DIANA  To see London. Didn't you just get here? Why are we sending him off so quickly?

THEO  That's how the university works these things out. They rush you in, pat you on the back, and rush you out.

GEORGE  Seriously, Adham. You can't want to go back home now?

ADHAM  After meeting all of you?

GEORGE  After hearing the news.

ADHAM  What news?

GEORGE  The war is on. You didn't hear? The *Evening Standard* said the Israelis destroyed the entire Egyptian air force this morning.

ADHAM  What?

DIANA  No.

THEO  But that's not confirmed. Radio Cairo is saying Egypt took down Israeli jets.

GEORGE  Where did you see that?

THEO  I heard it on the Home Service. They say there was dancing on the streets of Damascus.

DIANA  So who's lying?

GEORGE  And it commences. The muddle of wartime rubbish begins promptly on schedule.

THEO  I didn't realize we were getting our news from the *Standard*.

GEORGE  I don't. / Normally.

DIANA  It's half past midnight.

ADHAM  Do you have the paper here? / Can I see it?

GEORGE  Downstairs.

THEO  Adham, you shouldn't put any credence in the *Standard*. It's biased.

GEORGE  Not always.

DIANA  Isn't tomorrow's *Guardian* out?

GEORGE  And they're not biased at all.

THEO  Yes! Let's nip down to Euston station for the first edition. Adham?

*Adham gets up, the slightest bit wobbly.*

THEO  You all right?

ADHAM  Yes.

THEO  *(to Diana)* Be right back.

*They leave. Beat. Abir sleeps, Diana watches, stretches . . .*

DIANA  Hm.

*Abir, feeling Adham gone from next to her, wakes up, slowly. Sees Diana.*

DIANA  Oh. Sorry. They'll be right back.

ABIR  wein zoji? (Where's my husband?)

DIANA  Oh. Em.

ABIR  Où est mon mari?

DIANA  Oh, dear. No parlez vous pas. I mean, beyond that. So sorry. I'm sorry.

*Abir gets up, looks around. Diana gets it.*

DIANA  He left. Just for a moment. They left. Just to get the newspaper. They'll come right back.

*Diana smiles, trying to reassure.*

DIANA  I promise, it'll be all right.

ABIR  heloo shaArek. (I like your hair.)

DIANA  Sorry?

*Diana doesn't seem to understand. Abir reaches over, touches Diana's hair lightly.*

DIANA  Oh! I like your hair. I mean, it's beautiful.

*Abir seems to get this. They smoke, and smile at each other appreciatively.*

DIANA  Yes? God. I'm afraid they left you with the most illiterate of the bunch . . . Studied ancient Greek of course. Ancient Greek? "Thalassa! Thalassa!"

*Beat.*

DIANA  You. Like. It. Here?

ABIR  (*shy*) Tosir Wid Loh?

DIANA  What's that—*To Sir, with Love*? You like that film?

*Abir nods.*

DIANA  It is rather good, isn't it.

*Abir smiles. Emboldened, throws out:*

ABIR  Julie Christie.

DIANA  You like her? I love her. God, did you see her in *Darling*?

*Abir nods.*

DIANA  Wasn't she fabulous?

ABIR  Three times.

DIANA  Really?

*Diana does a bit from the film—Julie Christie, of course, furious:*

DIANA  "A pound's not enough! A pound's not enough!"

*And another moment:*

DIANA  "We're not married! At least not to each other!"

ABIR  So good.

*The men return, each holding newspapers.*

THEO  It doesn't look good for the Arabs.

*Adham scans the newspaper. It's hard to tell how it's affecting him.*

ADHAM  It doesn't, does it?

GEORGE  Well, then. They overplayed their hands, didn't they? They had to have known Israel would take their threats seriously.

*Theo shakes his head to shush George. Abir has been intently studying Adham.*

ABIR  eish haada? (What's this?)

ADHAM  akhbaar. (News.)

ABIR  eish bito'ol? (What does it say?)

ADHAM  kullo zift. baHkeelik baAdein. (It's all bad. I'll tell you later.)

ABIR  La'. halla'. (Tell me now.)

ADHAM  ma ba'dar. (I can't.)

ABIR  shoo esseereh b masir? (What's that about Egypt?)

ADHAM  silaaH aljaww. shiklo kullo raH. (The air force. Apparently it's gone.)

ABIR  Byom? Fakkaret kullu kan kizib. (In a day? I thought the whole thing was a bluff.)

ADHAM  shikloo inkashfat. (The bluff got called, apparently.)

    *Abir, upset, grabs the paper from Adham, scours it.*

THEO  I'm so sorry. I thought you knew.

ADHAM  Not today. We've been preoccupied. *(recovers)* The news is always bad. We learn not to jump at every rumor.

DIANA  That's understandable. One hears so many things.

ADHAM  The Israelis have been digging trenches for months, getting ready. But no one thought anything would really happen.

THEO  We can put the wireless on if you want. / I'm sure they're still covering it.

ADHAM  No no, not now.

GEORGE  Egypt's jets were parked in the open air. No hangars or sandbags, even. Shocking.

ADHAM  *(trying to keep panic down)* Yes, it is.

THEO  I didn't think Israel would move first without getting the green light from Johnson.

GEORGE  America can't be seen as giving a green light—

THEO  Not explicitly!

DIANA  *(cutting them off)* God. It's all so confusing. How can one keep track of any of it?

ADHAM  No one does.

DIANA  That settles it. You have to stay. Couldn't we work something out, with Adham's visa?

GEORGE  I suppose so.

THEO  Would you even want to?

ADHAM  Uh—

DIANA  Of course they would. Why wouldn't they?

ABIR  eish hadi essoura? (What is this a picture of?)

THEO  With the war happening, we could try to get the department heads to push through a fellowship.

ABIR  weinhum? (Where are these hostages?)

ADHAM  I wouldn't quite call it a war.

ABIR  masr? (Egypt?)

THEO  The reporters are. Most assuredly.

ADHAM  How long would a fellowship last?

THEO  Depends. Six or seven months?

GEORGE  One term.

ABIR  wein bi masr? (Where in Egypt?)

DIANA  At least wait for things to calm down before you go back.

> *Abir stands up.*

ABIR  yallah. (Let's go.)

ADHAM  Well. There's a lot to think about. *(repeats this to Abir, in Arabic)* Bas lazem infaker bi kteer ishya'.

ABIR  *(in Arabic)* fakker wa iHna mashyeen. (You can do that as we walk.)

> *Abir stands up, looks at Adham: Time's up.*

ABIR  yallah. (Let's go.)


## SEVEN DIALS

> *Outside. Midnight. It's dark. Panels reveal a London intersection where a large monument stands. Adham's a combination of cocky, drunk, and stoned mixed with a rising panic he tries desperately to push down.*
>
> *Adham sits down on the steps in front of the monument, lights a cigarette.*

ADHAM  Come here.

ABIR  Why?

ADHAM  It's a nice night. Come sit for a minute.

ABIR  I don't want to.

ADHAM  You don't recognize this place? We saw it yesterday. Seven Dials. We can listen to all the bad news when we get back to the hotel, okay? It'll be waiting for us, okay? I promise it won't forget about us.

> *From Adham, a slight laugh at the situation.*

ABIR  It's not funny.

ADHAM  I didn't say it was.

ABIR  How much alcohol did you have?

ADHAM  I'm happy. I spoke in front of people. I succeeded. They listened to me, a foreigner, tell them about their Poet Laureate. What he meant, what he didn't mean, why he used a comma, a semicolon, a dash.

ABIR  I know!

ADHAM  No you don't. Not really. *(challenging her)* You barely understood it.

ABIR  I don't speak English! You want an Englishwoman, is that what you want?

*Adham's stunned she even asked, speechless.*

ADHAM  No! —No . . . I want you. You can't tell? *(softens, takes her in)* My love.

Beat.

ADHAM  They offered me a fellowship.

ABIR  What?

ADHAM  Well, they didn't offer. But they think it can be arranged. It can be pushed through, maybe, they said. There's a lot to work out, but. *(almost pleading)* Why are you in such a rush?

ABIR  I want to hear the news.

ADHAM  I told you all of it.

ABIR  On the radio.

ADHAM  Paper, radio, it's all bad. You want specifics? Egypt lost its air force. And uh, I'm not sure about Jordan, but I think they fired a few rounds and are making, what do they say in military terms, a hasty retreat? The Arabs lost. We lost. The whole thing's a bust.

ABIR  Oh god. What's going to happen? There was so much talk about the Egyptians being superior.

ADHAM  Yes, yes, talk. Talk talk talk, bullshit bullshit bullshit. It's all bullshit, my dear.

ABIR  You talk like an old man.

ADHAM  That's what I'll be if we go back!

Beat.

ADHAM  Please. Listen to me. We have, we have here, I have, this window of opportunity. You see? We should leave, just leave, our so-called lives and stay where we're wanted.

ABIR  We know no one here!

ADHAM  Sometimes that's preferable!

ABIR  You're crazy!

ADHAM  Please, come sit. Just for a minute.

*She relents, goes and sits next to him. He puts his arms around her.*

ADHAM  See? Monmouth, Mercer, Earlham, Shorts Gardens: All the world connects here.

*He takes her in, caresses her hands . . .*

ABIR  If the Israeli army goes into Jerusalem—

ADHAM  They won't. They can't. It's their "holy place." Everyone's "holy
    place." It's so "holy," they don't want to destroy it.
ABIR  But if they do? What will happen to my family? What will happen to
    your mother?
ADHAM  I'd say the old bat can fend for herself.
ABIR  You talk about her this way? At a time like this?
    *Adham shrugs, laughs. Beat as she just watches him.*
ABIR  Some of the things you say . . . You joke now, but one day—
ADHAM  What? God will punish me?
    *Beat.*
ABIR  At least, let's go get her, bring her here / to live with us!
ADHAM  A man, his wife, and his mother!
ABIR  Everyone lives like that.
ADHAM  Not here! Not here! These are civilized people!
ABIR  Everything she's done, she's done for you! To advance your career!
ADHAM  YES. Which brought me here!
ABIR  You would leave her there to die?
ADHAM  She's always had a flair for the dramatic.
ABIR  I know you don't mean that. You wouldn't be here if not for her. I'm
    thinking of her safety. We have to go home and wait for the situation to
    stabilize.
ADHAM  Stabilize! Stabilize? Where? Where? Where are you talking about?
    When have we ever known stability, you stupid peasant girl?
    *Abir is shocked. It's as if he's slapped her.*
ABIR  You—
ADHAM  Shit.
ABIR  —really mean that.
ADHAM  Goddammit.
ABIR  When you look at me. That's what you—
ADHAM  I didn't mean it. I'm drunk, don't listen to me!
ABIR  That's what you think I am? I'm a village girl you rescued, some girl
    with the smell of shit on her boots—
ADHAM  Okay, okay . . .
ABIR  —and dirt on her hands, who you get to show the world, and feel
    superior to, is that how you think of me?
ADHAM  No.
    *He tries to comfort her.*
ABIR  Don't touch me! Don't you ever touch me again!

*She bursts into tears. Goes. Stunned, he stands, watching her. Long, long beat. He doesn't know what to do with himself. Suddenly looks very lost. He paces, there in that public space.*

*On the panels around him, we see: a silent film, dated June 6, 1967.*

*No sound, a handheld camera, almost a home movie, of bombs going off, civilians running through the streets, soldiers. This is Jerusalem. The War. Adham just sits there in these images for a couple minutes.*

*We see Abir in the hotel room, the same images hitting her face. Adham comes through the door:*

## THE RUINED COTTAGE

*The hotel room. It's very very late. Lights are off. The television is on, volume down—we see the images of the ground war in Jerusalem reflected on Abir's face. Adham enters.*

ADHAM  I was almost hoping I would fail. I was! If I failed, it's not complicated. I go home, fade into obscurity. No choice. Where we come from, we get one chance. You know that right? That's it. We're not, uh, designed for success, we. Arabs. From Palestine. We're good at packing up, and leaving places, and waiting.

ABIR  I shouldn't have left my family with a war coming. I was foolish to come.

ADHAM  *(gently)* If we stayed every time a war seemed near none of us would ever leave the house. I know I behaved badly.

*He turns a light on. Sees on the floor a packed suitcase.*

What's this?

ABIR  I'm leaving.

ADHAM  No, no, no, you're not. It's been a big day, okay? I talk sometimes, I don't know what I'm saying.

ABIR  Oh, I think you do.

ADHAM  Why are you doing this?

ABIR  I'm leaving you. Don't you understand?

ADHAM  And going where?

ABIR  Home! My home. I tried calling my family—I couldn't get through. All the lines are down. I don't know where they are.

ADHAM  Chaos. Wherever they are.

ABIR  We have to go back. I want to be with them.

ADHAM  Why? So we can all be refugees together?

ABIR  You don't know that.

ADHAM  So I don't. Maybe everything will turn out fine.

ABIR  I want to be with my family! There's something WRONG with people who don't.

ADHAM  You can't even get near the country—

ABIR  I'll go to the airport, and I'll wait. I can't be with you for another minute.

ADHAM  You're being ridiculous—

ABIR  I am? You're leaving your mother to die, Adham.

ADHAM  She's not dying—

ABIR  What is that? Who does this? I don't understand a man who has no ties! Who are you?

ADHAM  She taught me to be that way! She did! Because there was nothing in her life that wasn't taken away from her at some point or another. So she taught me to love that way, easy come, easy go.

ABIR  That's love.

ADHAM  That's—

ABIR  So if I leave you now, just leave, and we, we separate, and get a divorce—

ADHAM  —She's so modern now! Listen to her!—

ABIR  —you would have no feelings about it. Would you? Would your heart break?

ADHAM  . . . I don't talk that way. Use phrases like that.

ABIR  I'm asking you. Would you have a broken heart? Because I would.

*He can't answer. She tries not to cry.*

ABIR  At least I know now. It's only been a month. I was such an idiot to come here.

ADHAM  Just slow down, okay? You can't get home now anyway.

ABIR  I don't care. I'll sleep at the Consulate until I get a ticket—

ADHAM  "Sleep at the Consulate"? You're crazy! It's going to get better.

ABIR  What is?

ADHAM  Everything. My career.

ABIR  *(stinging him)* Your "career"? You gave one lecture. That's it.

ADHAM  *(stung)* So she can be cruel, too.

ABIR  I never was before.

*Abir starts packing again, crying as she does so.*

ADHAM  Please, stop. It's okay.

ABIR  No it's not.

*He watches helplessly as she cries.*

ADHAM  I have no idea what to do.

ABIR  I do.

> *She gets up to leave. He tries to stop her.*

ADHAM  I didn't say you could walk away!

ABIR  *(wresting free)* You don't get to pick and choose your traditions!

> *She goes to the bathroom, comes back with a little makeup bag, puts it in her suitcase, zips it up.*

ADHAM  Don't tell me I don't love my mother. I LOVE her. And she loved me. She loved me in a way that— We don't need to BE with each other, you see. It's here—

> *He points to his head.*

ADHAM  *(points to his heart)*  —and here. It's all in here, you see? She made an imprint.

ABIR  If you don't come with me now, you may never get to go back. Do you know that, Adham?

> *Beat. From somewhere inside him, the answer:*

ADHAM  . . . Yes. Yes.

ABIR  Okay.

> *She packs up the last of her things, grabs her suitcase. He gets in front of her.*

ADHAM  Don't do this. Please.

> *She stands there facing him.*

ADHAM  You'll regret it.

> *Beat.*

ADHAM  I don't want you to go.

> *Beat.*

ADHAM  Come on. Look what you'd be giving up.

> *Beat.*

ABIR  This feels like Nowhere to me.

ADHAM  *(half joking?)* Well then it suits me.

> *She shakes her head, grabs her suitcase. He watches her go. Door shuts. He suddenly is completely alone.*

ADHAM  Okay. Okay. Okay. Okay.

> *Adham opens a panel that stretches the length of the room: blankness. Nothing.*

·          ·          ·

# Sojourners

## MFONISO UDOFIA

*Dedicated to Enyeneama and Paul Udofia*

### Characters

ABASIAMA EKPEYONG, early 20s. Privileged. Paragon of Nigerian femininity. Eight months pregnant. Ibibio accent.

MOXIE WILIS, 15–18 years old. Far younger in age than attitude might belie. Frayed from the harsh realities of street life. Quickwitted and hard-edged. Massachusetts-born and Southern-bred. Black American, East Texan accent (inclusive of Houston).

UKPONG EKPEYONG, early–mid-20s. Privileged. High on life and America. A man-child with effortless and magnetic charisma. Ibibio accent.

DISCIPLE UFOT, early–mid-20s. Exceedingly intelligent. Intense and driven. An acute and rabid dreamer without an emotional tether. Ibibio accent.

### Note on Nigerian Names and Ibibio Words

Previous drafts from the original productions used a phonetic spelling of Nigerian names and Ibibio words for the clarity of non-Ibibio-speaking actors and critics. This published edition uses the traditional spelling of Nigerian names and other Ibibio words.

The sole exception is the anglicized "ng" in place of the velar nasal letter "ŋ" at the end of names. "Ukpoŋ Ekpeyoŋ" would be the traditional spelling, but the pronunciation is comparable to "Ukpong Ekpeyoung," and native Ibibio speakers have recently begun more readily adopting the anglicized "ng" ending.

However, words in Ibibio (other than proper names) retain the ŋ, and have been so spelled in this acting edition.

Future credits should please reflect the correct spelling herein.

### Punctuation & Language

(".") The play is written in the language of thought, there is no need to wait for the thought to come to you. The next thought is simply right there. That said, periods should not stop the flow. Move through the language with ease.

("—") A dash is a hard shift in thought/flow. Do not smooth these over. Instead, collide into the dash, and turn quickly into the next thought.

(" . . . ") An ellipsis is a thought-breath. It is not overlong. Collect yourself during this slight break and then pick up again.

("?") Questions are never rhetorical. Please do not ask questions as if the answer is known. Dare to upward-inflect and be vulnerable.

("[ ]") Nothing in brackets is ever said. Brackets are there to aid the actors' emotional scaffolding within swallowed moments.

(SILENCE) A silence is a filled sac of time where the characters nonverbally confront someone/thing. Silences are pregnant and almost uncomfortable in length. Talking restarts after a silence only when absolutely necessary.

(DOUBLE-STACKING) A double-stacked word (i.e., thatthat, finefine, etc.) denotes the Nigerian/Ibibio way of adding extra emphasis and color. The double-stacked word means exponentially more than a singular use of the word. Triple, quadruple, etc. stacking can and does occur. Translations for Ibibio songs, words, and phrases used in the play can be found in the endnotes.

## Stage Directions

Read all stage directions carefully, including parentheticals. Stage directions are not merely suggestions. They are there to support the story. Implement the action of the stage directions to the best of your ability.

## Character Notes

Abasiama: Abasiama's pregnancy pain and her ferocious emotional life are to be demonstrated through the strategic use of breath. Abasiama swallows her emotion until all remaining internal space is overfull. The danger is to give the pain too much sound. Play in her breath, in the silence, and how things move across her face. And remember, a voice, even in the throes of abject sorrow and/or incandescent rage, can be achingly sweet.

Please swallow the bitter pill of Act One in order to discover the release of Act Two.

Also note that Abasiama does not go into active labor until sometime after Ukpong leaves in Act One.

The Nigerian Men: These men are charming; however, never conflate charm with politesse. Take up space. Do not apologize.

## Designer Notes

Please keep in mind the energy of the piece. The world of *Sojourners* is isolated and remote. Design/production should never foster comfort. Keep the world, inclusive of transitions, jagged, unpredictable, and fleet.

# ACT ONE

## SCENE 1

*Houston, Texas, April 30, 1978, almost 10:00 p.m.*

*Lights up on a tiny apartment. Rooms meld into each other without barrier; both the living room and the kitchen are effectively one and the same. The most prominent piece of furniture is a 1970s striped fabric couch centering the designated living room space.*

*A young, striking, unadorned woman (except for plain head/sleep scarf), Abasiama, stands in a small corner of the kitchen. She stares into middle distance.*

*Vacant.*

*Vacant.*

*Vacant.*

*A pain hits her stomach. Her gaze suddenly narrows.*

*Alive.*

*Abasiama, in response to the pain, closes her eyes, cocks her head against the wall, and hums "Canoe." She snuggles into her nook, seeking an embrace. Her humming soars while tears well behind her eyelids. Her closed-eye gaze is downward, focusing the song toward the swell of her belly; a smile is even possible. The humming, after a while, coalesces into a fully formed song.*

*Her voice is mighty fine. It is the most encouraging, uplifting pick-me-up Abasiama offers herself.*

ABASIAMA  mme nti usen atimme edi afit
nti ŋkpọ atimme edi menie
owo se ŋdọŋ esit nwat ubom
mi ye afo[*]

*(Spoken, on the exhale, eyes still closed.)* Abasi, sọsọnọ.

*Abasiama opens her eyes, water runs down her cheeks.*

*(Release, wiping it away.)* No more purposeless water.[†]

---

[*]  Ukpong first sang this lullaby to Abasiama when they were both still in Cross River State, before Abasiama came to America. In this play the song functions as Abasiama's way to calm the baby by conjuring the father. Always take note of which verse is being sung. The first verse of the song is a tale of loss, while the second verse is a tale of healing. (See translations in the endnotes.)

[†]  Abasiama is having a biological response to stress. These tears are not expressed as active/intentional crying. The tears are more an involuntary leaking of the eyes.

*Another dull deep pain strikes Abasiama's midsection. She closes her eyes, effectively chomping back the pain. Visually, nothing extraordinary occurs during this moment, and almost nothing is audible. But something IS happening. A release of breath marks the end.*

*(A subtle cajole.)* I think we're hungry. Usuŋ?*

*Listening for pain. No pain.*

*(Gentle smile.)* Okay. Usuŋ.

*Abasiama opens a cupboard and pulls down a yellow Bisquick pancake box. Abasiama dips in one finger and retrieves a coat of white. She inserts this finger into her mouth.*

Fufu America. Wow.

*Abasiama takes a small pot from the fridge and warms this pot (containing soup) on the stove. She then retrieves another, different pot and boils water. Abasiama pours Bisquick into the boiling water and starts pounding fufu. That same dull pain strikes again. Abasiama's gaze narrows and shutters.)*

*(Soft, firm.)* Stop. We will like it!

*Abasiama quickly finishes, washes her hands, and eats standing. She deftly molds and scoops food from pot to pot.*

Better?

*Listening for pain. No pain.*

*(Conspiratorially.)* You know, I have to read now.

*Another dull pain. Abasiama forges ahead—*

*(Rising up.)* Hm. Okay. Fine. We'll sing it one more time. Then? We read—

*Abasiama goes to her corner. Sings:*

mme nti usen atimme

edi afit nti ŋkpọ atimme

edi / menie owo se

ŋdọŋ—

UKPONG *(Offstage patter.)* mpah pah

pah cross the river

mpah pah pah

*Abasiama registers the percussive chanting and freezes.*

ford the stream

mpah pah pah

---

* Usuŋ is made from root vegetables that were not yet shipped or grown in the States. This is a critically different word than "fufu," which the playwright is using as an all-encompassing term for any variation of a starch product made to be eaten with Nigerian soup.

conquer land

mpah pah pah

round again

> *Abasiama, recognizing the owner of the voice, readjusts her head wrap, trying to restrain her thick plaits. She almost succeeds. Ukpong enters. He's a wildly attractive man in a jaunty hat and bongos.\* His singlet[†] showcases the strong lines of his body and also carries the look of partying long and enjoying much. Though slightly tipsy, he is cogent.*

. . . Wo-man. Womanwomanwoman.[‡] Beautiful womanwomanwoman. Ama, idem fo? Idem afọn? Because eke mmi afọn!

*(Playful.)* Ah! Your hair. *(Pidgin.[§])* Wettin be this? Come. Come! Kiss me.

. . .

Not yet time for that? Cool. Search me then. I never fail to bring you things. I promise, you have never ever experienced something like this—

. . .

*(Switch, childish-contrite.)* Okay. I know. I've been very—See! It's done. Pah. I've been spanked.

> *Ukpong drops to his knees before Abasiama. Abasiama deals, as best she can, with the sudden unexpected sight of her husband. Perhaps the lullaby finally worked . . . ?*

Hey, don't look that way. Say something. Anything. No? *(Threat.)* I can call your father. Tell him you're ignoring me.

ABASIAMA  Ukpong . . .

> *Ukpong latches onto the sound, and joyfully spins Abasiama around.*

UKPONG  Eh-heh! Softsoft. Hey now, my softsoft, look my way. *(Kiss.)* Let me tell you what happen. After you hear, you will totally forgive this your husband. First. I am sorry. Believe. I am.

> *Ukpong marshals Abasiama to the couch.*

Some days ago, Etuk and I, we went in that—his Thunderbird. The one his father just bought him. We were riding, like our normal okay. Testing horsepower, and then something came on network radio. AM. This—a social . . . I don't recall the correct name. A sort of gathering. A kind of

---

\*  Bongos are flare jeans.

†  A singlet is a sleeveless men's undershirt.

‡  Please refer to the notes in the dramaturgy for an explanation of stacking.

§  Nigerian Pidgin is an English-based creolized language that Nigerians across tribal/ethnic lines can use to hear and understand each other.

meeting—no—yes—wait—they call it "rally"! A rally where people come to talk about our world. It was advertised! I mean, why not? How do I pass over, Ama? *I* was the one who told Etuk to drive to the concourse, get on that freeway, and—hey! Just like the radio foretold. All of these people. People like you have never ever seen. Houston?! Hm. You couldn't imagine it. Whites. Blacks. Hispanic. Asian. Women. Poor. Rich. Who could have thought all of these sorts of people jam-packed in one room? And we rallied about everything oh. Politics? Economy? Love? No subject taboo! And then . . . This speaker! Sampson. Got up there, round midnight, to light the altar on fire on how we have to live and love and that that is the sole purpose of life. It blew my mind. The whole process blew my mind to shards. This kind of peace. This kind of living. Living initiated from a radio . . . ? Remember radio back home? Ama! An instrument of death. But here?! *(Sucks his teeth.)* Never have I seen anything like it. No guns, no thought of a shot being fired. Watch! Americans have the way of it! They have the human understanding! We didn't stop—didn't think about stopping until four—no five a.m. And then everyone went for some drink and it was cool. Nothing but cool. Listen. Even Etuk, with his impatience? Once there? That man sat entranced.

    *Silence. Ukpong finally looks at Abasiama.*

    You heard me?

ABASIAMA  . . . Mm.

UKPONG  *(Excited.)* Okay. Tell me then!

ABASIAMA  *(Confused wonder.)* Ndioŋoke. It sounds fine.

UKPONG  Just fine. All of that glory and just . . . "fine"?

ABASIAMA  Ukpong. What do I say?

UKPONG  Something! Anything! Where is the life in you?!

    *Silence.*

    *(Shift.)* So . . . what have you been doing here.

ABASIAMA  . . . Studying. We've exams and—I've been working Fiesta* and—

UKPONG  Throwing your moods at me.

ABASIAMA  Wow. Ukpong . . . hm. I don't know.

UKPONG  Ama, I was just bringing you joy! A happy story into this dank place and you are—

---

* Due to Ukpong's misconduct/irresponsibility, Abasiama has taken a job. This is an abnormality. Ukpong has been spending the money sent from home, by his parents, on entertainment and living.

ABASIAMA  It's nothing. I'm nothing. I . . .

>    *Abasiama shifts her body, and props up her legs. Dull pain. Abasiama*
>    *exhales and attempts to stabilize.*

(*Trying to joke.*) The bottoms of my feet have started holding too much water oh. It hurts even to sit. I know now to pity my sisters. It's been real pain.

UKPONG  . . . Okay . . . stop. Come. Let's dance. Like we used to. That can soften you.

ABASIAMA  I am soft enough.

UKPONG  You will jump and dance with me once you hear this.

>    *Ukpong retrieves a package from his satchel.*

It's a—

ABASIAMA  Record.

UKPONG  (*Dismayed.*) Yes—

ABASIAMA  Smokey.

UKPONG  You saw the package!

ABASIAMA  No.

>    I've just come to know a bit of you now. Motown makes you eager.
>    You've been wanting that new Smokey thing so I deduced I'd soon receive it . . . (*Chosen decisiveness.*) I don't like him, Ukpong.

UKPONG  (*Mildly defensive.*) Why not.

ABASIAMA  I just don't—

UKPONG  You can learn to like him he is—

ABASIAMA  (*Sudden and direct.*) You don't buy those records for me!

>    *Pain hits. Eyes shut. Hissed exhale. Ukpong places hand on Abasiama's*
>    *stomach.*

UKPONG  Calm yourself.

ABASIAMA  I am fine.

UKPONG  Ama . . . why this? Let's get to know each other. You can come out with me—

ABASIAMA  Are you serious?

UKPONG  Of course! It's me. Remember me? "Finefine"? Recall when I first came to your compound and you saw me. Underneath your breath you muttered, "finefine." (*Hot.*) I could not stop looking at—hm. I marveled at that space between your teeth oh.* Ah, I'll never forget. My daddy

---

* The diastema, or gap between two front teeth, is generally regarded as a beauty symbol in Nigeria.

rings me. Middle of summer school here,* saying he found someone for me. *My* turn to have a woman to make me that strong kind of man! The very second after I heard? I celebrated in the halls of that hellish Texas Southern.† Dancing and apologizing: "Excuse me ma'am. I did not mean to knock you." "Sorry, Professor ManMan. I have lost no marble. I am getting married"—I could not breathe until after I got off that plane, ran to my compound and then. You. Small. Sharp. Pretty. A mightymighty gap between your teeth. A woman! Surpassing, farfar, the height of my grandest imagining. But see? As soon I bring you here, all you do is this. This dour broken bird thing.

*Ukpong sinks. He puts the record away under couch.*

ABASIAMA  (*Negotiating.*) . . . Ukpong. I'm— . . . I am not trying to be any kind of way but the end of the school year for you is one month arriving?

UKPONG  . . .

ABASIAMA  . . . How far are you?

UKPONG  Far now. What kind of questioning / is this?

ABASIAMA  Your father said you are to be graduating soon. May. End of this month?

UKPONG  Yes—

ABASIAMA  Yes—okay—but now—because here I am. Studying and work-ing so you can buy me records I don't like with the money I make while you keep all your father's funds and ride in Thunderbirds. How many class days have you missed? And where are you when I need . . . —Then you remind me of my daddy? When I also know your father. From there to here, you are a new person for me too. I don't understand.

UKPONG  It's not your job / to—

ABASIAMA  Bet now, please. Patience because I'm not gleaning something. And, I'll do it. If that's what I have to do. I'll beg you. Please. Ukpong, we have to finish.

UKPONG  How are you to / tell me—

ABASIAMA  (*Simple.*) Goal one. Kiet. You, who always call me to remem-ber . . . remember this. Goal one: Marry well. Goal iba: Get ticket to

---

* Ukpong is older and has been enrolled in American school longer than Abasiama. He traveled home for an arranged marriage to Abasiama, in Cross River State. Ukpong should be at the end of his college tenure, while Abasiama, having come to America after marriage, is at the beginning of hers.

† Texas Southern University (TSU) is a historically Black college/university (HBCU), which, at the time, had very low tuition rates.

America. Enroll. Goal ita: Get that degree, have a baby. Last goal. Important goal. Goal number four: Return home. Go home, Ukpong. If we are stuck at point three there can be no going home.*

UKPONG  Who is stuck?!

ABASIAMA  *(Unleashing.)* You are two steps from embarrassing me in the wide-open field. And, I don't know, you have to forgive me, as I have to forgive you but—I don't—I'm trying to—but I don't understand on what kind of earth, husband, do you become so enamored by another man's speech, some free-radical White, free-lover person, a foreigner who has no idea of you, that you forget to come home to your wife. Rally?! When you have a wife, Ukpong? Have I been given to a forgetter† because / afo adi America ndien afo afre se akedi nam—"piam!"

> *Ukpong stands suddenly, rage twisting his face. His sudden anger barrels him toward Abasiama.*

UKPONG  *(Menacing.)* Who are you to call me a—

> *Abasiama shrinks. Ukpong attempts to rein himself in.*

ABASIAMA  . . . Ukpong, you are all I / have here.

UKPONG  *(Sharp.)* I am no forgetter! I am not. Why sink into this, eh? I return home for this? No! . . .

Okay.

. . . Mrs. Ekpeyong! Mrs. Ek. Pe. Yong. Ah my God! Remember after your "finefine" I whispered back "softsoft"? . . . I crave that softsoft now. Why not transform an ordered marriage into a love match.‡ I asked you that.

*(Sung.)* under the sun§

*(Spoken.)* remember me?

*(Sung.)* under the moon

under the stars

---

* Abasiama outlines a migratory movement in this speech that markedly disrupts the (particularly Western) narrative that all immigrants are coming to America to stay and plant. There were many Nigerians during this era that had no desire whatsoever to stay. The dream was to rebuild Nigeria, and if Abasiama's generation could not, they would have Nigerian-American babies who could.

† Please note whenever the word "forget" or "forgetter" is used, it is an insult of the highest order. A Nigerian who forgets the desires of the community is rendered foreigner unto himself.

‡ While Ukpong and Abasiama's marriage was arranged by their fathers, Ukpong is referring to the fact that they fell in love despite the contract. Love matches are rare and not even sought after, so Ukpong's vocabulary here is a glimpse into real chemistry and connection between the two.

§ "Under the Sun, Moon and Stars" is a song by Jimmy Cliff that hit airwaves in 1976. (See special note on songs/recordings.)

*(Spoken.)* Ama . . .

We used to sing Jimmy Cliff* and . . . then—

*(Sung.)* mme nti usen eboyo.

*(Spoken.)* . . . Smile for me? Come. Give me that your gap and—

> *Abasiama's alarm clock rings. Abasiama stands calmly and puts on her coat.*

ABASIAMA   I have to go.

> *Abasiama points to the alarm.*

Work . . .

## SCENE 2

> *April 30, 1978, almost 10:00 p.m. The alarm continues ringing.*
>
> *Lights up on Disciple's domain. This is another cramped apartment, albeit extremely precise. Disciple's walls are lined with books and pamphlets. He wears worn house pants, a threadbare singlet, and thin-rimmed metal aviator eyeglasses. His sideburns and beard are meticulously manicured. Burned down white taper candles pepper the room and incense scents the air.†*
> *A Walgreens cap and uniform hang in plain sight. Disciple, a serious man, sleeps on his typewriter. Finally, the alarm pierces Disciple's consciousness. He wakes, silences the device, wipes sleep out of his eyes, and lights a cigarette.*
>
> *Disciple stares at his typewriter, scanning over what little he has written. He pulls the sheet out of the typewriter and balls it up. He grabs the small stack of papers by the typewriter. He reads, balling up page after page.*

DISCIPLE   *(Mumbled and repeated as many times as needed.)* Uduaŋ ŋkpǫ, ata uduaŋ ŋkpǫ. *(Into the typewriter.)* Why won't you work?

> *Disciple's right hand massages his heart.‡ The massaging is soft and compulsive, almost as if pressing into the exact physical location of past trauma might*

---

* Reggae was very popular in Nigeria and Jimmy Cliff is an artist that both Ukpong and Abasiama would have known and listened to before coming to America. Other artists they would both have known include Bob Marley and the Wailers, Toots and the Maytals, Bunny Wailer, Peter Tosh, and Desmond Dekker. (See special note on songs.)

† Disciple practices an amalgamated religion. There are strains of Pentecostal Christianity, brought in by the missionaries, fused with indigenous religions. This fusion of religion is seamless and has its own logic.

‡ Please mark which side Disciple performs tasks on. The "right" side is seen as "good" while the left side is the antithesis. Disciple is trying to push "good" into his chest.

*ease that very trauma. Disciple might look around this hateful room in dismay [how did he get here?], he might look at the writing he can't seem to complete in confusion [why can't he write here?], Disciple might look to the spirits above [have they forsaken him here?]. In frustration escalating, sound hisses out from between his lips. The sound is a shout, a shout hammered and compressed into submission. Disciple's gaze finally focuses on his typewriter.*

*All the blame for his situation fixates there [that's easiest, really]. The typewriter's suddenly in danger.*

*Sweet soft humming pierces Disciple's room. Elsewhere, Abasiama has walked onstage and entered her post as gas station worker, she is the music-maker.*

*Disciple relaxes, his body sinks into the humming, completely unconscious of its source, he finds ease. He lights three white taper candles and sets them by his typewriter. He grabs some crumpled balls of paper, uncrumples them and lays them flat to reread/restart.*


## SCENE 3

*May 1, 1978, right after midnight. Graveyard shift in a small gas station. For protection, the doors are locked and workers stand behind a window. Abasiama was studying* but that same insistent pain is hitting her strong. Moxie clacks in, drinking.*

MOXIE  Charming. Charming.

Why? Be charming I can be charming.
I'm a real—I am charm!

*Abasiama lays her head on the register. Pain.*

ABASIAMA  Mm!

*Moxie reaches the window and discards the bottle. She peers into the box.*

MOXIE  Hey lady—you—you in there! Ma'am? I mean—

(*Shift.*) 'Scuse me, I got a question.

*Abasiama is unaware of Moxie. Moxie strains her neck to see inside.*

What in the hell?! You need a tissue or something? Take this—

*Moxie retrieves a tissue from her chest and pushes it against the opening. Abasiama does not notice.*

ABASIAMA  Still this?
Your daddy's back now.

---

* Abasiama studies Biology/Microbiology. Studying can happen a plethora of ways throughout the play: flashcards, collegiate-level textbooks, articles.

Huh. Just 'cause it's tattered on the edge don't mean you can't use it. (*Muttered.*) You need to take it. Sheeiiit. Boogies running all down your face. Come on! Lady!

    *Moxie bangs loudly on the glass pane. Abasiama slams her head up.*

ABASIAMA  Ah, my God! Sorry—sorry—ehm—

    *Abasiama opens the slot in the glass so she can hear better.*

Welcome to Fiesta how can I help you?

    *Moxie takes in Abasiama.*

MOXIE  Uhuh. Your manager in?

ABASIAMA  I am sure I can assist.

MOXIE  (*Simple.*) My questions'll be over your head. Where your manager be at honey?

ABASIAMA  He is not here right now so how can I—

MOXIE  Shoot! Just my luck. Look, never mind, girlie. You couldn't do nuh-thing. No-thing. Notta damn thing. Catchya on the flip, ya hear?

    *Moxie clacks off, only getting about five paces away as pain hits Abasiama.*

ABASIAMA  (*Inhaling the pain.*) Please stop—

    *Moxie spins on her heels.*

MOXIE  What you say?

ABASIAMA  Welcome to / Fiesta

MOXIE  Lady. You crazy?

ABASIAMA  No, I'm okay it's—

MOXIE  (*Looking around suspiciously.*) You ain't right. You acting real— someone here? That it? You need help? 'Cause— (*Loud, while scoping the area.*) I got what it take to put the hurtin' on any jive motherfucker who trying to run a game on a woman at night!

ABASIAMA  It was nothing—

MOXIE  (*Laser-quick.*) And, I can spot a liar a mile away.

ABASIAMA  (*Even quicker and with a smile.*) I am fine. Thank you.

    *Moxie, again, takes Abasiama in.*

MOXIE  I dunno know 'bout that. But. Since you made me walk all the way back over here, you know and turn around and shit—maybe you could. I do need / some

ABASIAMA  Of course. What can I / get—

MOXIE  I can finish my own sentences.

ABASIAMA  Okay . . . sorry.

MOXIE  I need a gig.

    *Abasiama takes in Moxie.*

ABASIAMA  (*Guileless.*) . . . You?

MOXIE  (*Curt.*) Yea. Me.

ABASIAMA  . . . Sure. Hold.

> *Abasiama retrieves an application. She slides it through the slot. Moxie looks at the application dubiously and slides it back.*

MOXIE  Okay. A pen?

> *Abasiama retrieves a pen and slides both items through the window. Moxie slides them back.*

Straight. So. My name is Moxie. Moxie Annamae Wilis. But with just one L. I was born June 9, 196—Write I was born in '56. They need an address though right? So. Tuesday I shack with Leroy and on Wednesday and Thursday with Carl. Goddamn. I can't use neither of 'em. They been real tense lately . . . Hey! Use Eddie! He real stable. He at 229 Vernon— . . . you writing this down?

ABASIAMA  What are you doing?

MOXIE  The application. I gotta repeat alla that again?

ABASIAMA  I believe you are confused. My job is not to fill in your—

MOXIE  Told you I needed your manager.

ABASIAMA  Okay. You are obviously one of these wild types. If there is nothing else / I must return to my work.

MOXIE  (*Overriding.*) There is something else. I told myself / I would—

ABASIAMA  Please. Find another (*Mispronouncing/misemphasizing.*) "sucka" / to fill—

MOXIE  (*Dry.*) Sucka? Sheeiiit. Africa, you sound funny saying sucka girl. That ain't one of your words.

> *Abasiama pushes the application and pen to Moxie.*

ABASIAMA  Here are your things. The manager's here in the daytime. If you finish drop it between ten a.m. and four p.m.

MOXIE  Your boss'll help me fill this out, right?

ABASIAMA  No.

MOXIE  Sooo . . . ?

ABASIAMA  I am not sure how you need me to dice my meaning for you.

MOXIE  (*To herself.*) I fucking bet Jesus Christ Crystal* didn't know nothing 'bout this shit right here! You know what? I gotta do it. So I'm gonna do it. Imma fill out this application myself.

---

* Crystal functions as Moxie's one real "friend" on the street. They are both young and vulnerable and in the past they stuck together for safety.

*Abasiama returns to reading, taking deep soothing breaths. Moxie takes the pen and paper and heads to a little post. She sits and writes on her lap. She is within Abasiama's eyesight.*

Imma fill this out. Ain't nothing that hard. Just gotta focus. Focus Anna-girl. Okay.

*(Muttered.)* Name. Name: Moxie Annamae Wilis . . . Add-add-dress . . . Address! Hip girl! Right on! Okay. This easy. Okay. Uh. 229 Vvverr-er-rn— Vern—V-E-R-R . . . ? Mother. Shit. Damn. Africa, spell Vernon. The street. Vernon Street. Like that street up the corner you gotta take to get to Main. Lady you been to Vernon!

ABASIAMA  V-E-R-N-O-N.

*Abasiama, rapt, watches Moxie.*

MOXIE  Well thank you, madam. Okay. Sheeiiit. Stir-eeeet-ree—S-T-E-R-E-T?

ABASIAMA  *(Corrects her, astonished.)* S-T-R-E-E-T.

*Moxie writes "street." Abasiama's brand of staring goosebumps Moxie's skin.*

MOXIE  *(Quick look.)* What in holy tarnation you staring at?

ABASIAMA  You can't—

MOXIE  I wasn't actually wanting no talking from ya. I'm in the middle of something. Hey—what T-E-L-E—

ABASIAMA  Telephone. Abasi, see this! How is this possible?

MOXIE  Good goddamn be quiet!

*Moxie crumples paper.*

I can't figure these letters with you insulting me every two seconds. How you expect me to—? *(Crumbling.)* Oh, forget it—

*Abasiama retrieves the key from the register and goes outside.*

I shouldn't have even tried this— *(Sees Abasiama's pregnancy.)* Holy hell. What on earth is going on?

*Abasiama stoops to pick up the crumpled paper. Moxie snatches it from the ground herself.*

You wanna eat cement? Don't be picking up anything looking like that—

*Abasiama takes the crumpled paper from Moxie's hands. Moxie's chatter fills the uncomfortable silence.*

*(Fast and rambling.)* I don't even know why you wanna look at it anyway. Shoulda known. Crystal told me all I had to do was walk up to a place that looked like this and be charming. She such a no-thinking fool. All pretty and shit.

ABASIAMA  Excuse me. What are you talking?

*A black Volkswagen rolls up. The lights from the vehicle throw the women in stark relief. They shield their eyes.*

MOXIE  *(In relation to the car.)* Shit. *(Whip-fast to Abasiama.)* Goon, I'm speaking plain. My premium gal told me all I had to do if I really wanted a job was to walk up to one that seemed straight and ask for the papers and they'd hire me. She didn't tell me about no jive-talking Africans and filling in no thirty-page applications. I didn't even know how much there was to fill out on something like that.

*The car beeps. Moxie starts walking toward the light.*

*(A different side of Moxie.)* Cool your jets baby. I'm coming!

*(Hard to Abasiama.)* You get your Black behind back in that station right now.

*The car horn beeps. Abasiama quickly waddles back into the station and peers out the window.*

Aww. You miss me? Baby, quit that honking. I'm right here.

*Moxie heads into the light and disappears. Abasiama stands dismayed.*


## SCENE 4

*May 1, 1978, a little past 4:00 a.m. Ukpong is at home. He is nodding off with beer bottles and magazines surrounding him. Textbooks and miscellaneous remnants of Abasiama also litter the space.*

*Ukpong wakes violently.*

UKPONG  Ama?!

*Ukpong shakes off the covers of sleep.*

Ama, where are you? Ama? I can explain—

*Ukpong races to the bedroom. He quickly returns. He stands turning in silence until he suddenly remembers.*

Fiesta. Hey! What sneaky terror. My God, Ukpong. Fiesta! Remember now. Fiesta has our wife. Fiesta has our wife and I have the night—mpah-pah-pah—

*Ukpong shakes himself awake and into comfort. He turns on the radio and a popular 1978 song like Jackson 5's "Bless His Soul" plays.* He goes to fridge and gets a Guinness.*

cross the river

mpah pah pah pah ford the—

---

*   See special note on songs/recordings.

*Ukpong settles down on the couch. A thought suddenly assails him.*
*(Playing himself back.)* . . . Fiesta has our wife while I have the . . . ? Hm.
Sese itie emi anam mien-o. Sai! What this place has made me.

*Ukpong downs the last of his Guinness and shoves that bottle and all the*
*other cans/bottles around him under the couch. He gets water, turns off the*
*radio, and retrieves a textbook from his satchel. An envelope falls out. The*
*contents further deflate him.*

Miracles have been worked from less. I can do it. It just needs focus.
Focus first then conquer.

*Ukpong shoves this envelope under the couch and opens his textbook.*
*Economics. Abasiama enters through the front door. She sees Ukpong*
*reading.*

ABASIAMA  *(Soft mock.)* Really. You. Sitting there. Reading. Is it possible?

UKPONG  *(Thin smile.)* . . . Why not.

ABASIAMA  Hm. Good.

*Abasiama takes off her light outerwear and enters the kitchen. Ukpong stands.*
No. Stay there. Continue.

*Ukpong sits, his eyes follow Abasiama.*

UKPONG  What are you doing?

ABASIAMA  I need to sleep but first, I'm hungry.

UKPONG  You know, I am hungry too . . .

*Ukpong closes his book and heads to Abasiama.*
Woman. I have better food than / that.

ABASIAMA  What is wrong with garri?

UKPONG  Were you ever a peasant? Fried cassava and sand? That's what
you're drinking. Not even hot. Not even fish. We have fish in the cupboard.

ABASIAMA  Who smokes garri with stockfish.

UKPONG  Ama, there's no taste. Unless you like drinking sour. Have you
tried the food in the—

*Ukpong points to the refrigerator.*

ABASIAMA  I'm okay—

UKPONG  Do you know what makes an adventurer?

ABASIAMA  . . .

UKPONG  *(Enthusiastic.)* Woman! Hey my woman! Do you *know* what makes
an adventurer?

ABASIAMA  *(Rote.)* Risk.

UKPONG  I asked you that question before we got here. We have so much
adventure in this place!

*Ukpong opens the fridge and pulls out a jar of pickles.*

ABASIAMA  No. No—

UKPONG  Just try it.

*Abasiama tightens her face.*

ABASIAMA  That thing is rotting, okay. A rotting green thing soaking in its own water. Mbọk, please, find someone else to disturb.

UKPONG  Who else is here with me now? Come. Let's try this together. Me and you. Simple. A pickle . . . A pickle.*

*She closes her eyes slowly.*

Good girl. Open your mouth. Stop scrunching your face. Bite down. Chew. Chew it. Stop that. It's tasty.

*Abasiama opens her eyes and chews thoughtfully.*

See? You like it! Sour garri, sour pickles. But I assure you, this is better. We also have meat in there. You can make a sandwich and fill yourself. If not for you then feed my baby.

ABASIAMA  Mm.

*Abasiama goes back to slurping her garri. Ukpong sits beside her and chomps a pickle.*

UKPONG  Foul. Foul gamer. I know you liked it—I can feel you liked it. Vinegar: the water of the gods! Was it really that bad? . . . Tell me.

*A begrudging smile lifts Abasiama's lips.*

ABASIAMA  It was a different kind of / experience—

UKPONG  Eh heh! I caught a glimpse of you oh! Behind that rock, softsoft I see you. Okay! Drink your sand water and I will give myself gas. We're making a good night!

*Moments pass. Abasiama's smile is gone.*

ABASIAMA  There's this clerk job. If you apply, I'll cut my hours. It's becoming hard to stand.

*Silence.*

UKPONG  I've been studying. Micro-macro shit. Are you going to wring my neck if my pace is different than yours?

*Abasiama starts eating again.*

I've been thinking. About what I promised when I married you, what I promised my father . . . Ama . . .

You don't look at me when I talk to you.

---

* Certain foods and thus their flavors are not present in traditional Nigerian cuisine. Vinegar, chocolate, and fresh dairy products may have provided revelatory experiences.

*Abasiama, without looking at Ukpong, continues eating.*

Is it too late to repair a damage? I'll take up occupation as a foreman and rebuild—

ABASIAMA  *(Simple reasoning.)* A magistrate's son, a foreman?

UKPONG  *(Simple reasoning.)* Yes. So a superintendent's daughter can stop Fiesta.

*Abasiama slowly puts down her spoon and looks at Ukpong. Her gaze is even and direct. There is no hope, no expectation.*

Ama. Every—. . . every time I close my eyes . . . I see him, okay? Ete mmi! Such a big man. And—and then me. I'm third son. And of how many?! I'm a spare. Never warranting any sort of—. . . anything. Then—sometimes, if I would do something well, he would train his eyes on me and—and I could become *the* son.* One son. First son. He was so proud to send me here . . . Abasiama . . . he's under my nose, behind my eyes, ringing my ears. Under sleep I saw him just now . . . shaking his head, crying over me. I dreamt of him, woke up, and you were gone.

ABASIAMA  I am here.

UKPONG  I want you to know you don't have to worry. Anymore . . . I mean it. *(Shows his palms.)* Never again.

*Abasiama looks at Ukpong. Ukpong kisses the palms of his hands, and puts them on Abasiama's face.*

ABASIAMA  *(So open.)* I've been wanting edikaŋ ikoŋ soup / but I can't find it.

UKPONG  You won't find that here. When I first came, I searched high and low. I gave in. This is why you slurp sand? . . . Hey my darling, it's not home. It's something else. The way you're holding only makes it harder.

*Ukpong lifts Abasiama out of her seat.*

Softsoft, school year is almost over, okay? The plan. First. I graduate. Then. You birth the most beautiful baby boy /

ABASIAMA  Girl—

UKPONG  Beautiful unknown, then. Watch! Our fathers will see us settled in our ekpuk. A fine upstanding couple. I'll be the head and you'll be the neck that turns me . . . I'll set myself to action! . . . But right now . . . ? I've been in love with Motown oh but there is a prince you should know. An American one.

---

* Ukpong faces the particular dilemma of being a middle son in a line of sons. His person may never acquire his father's vast land wealth and his posterity may not be as important as the brothers' before him. He is still, however, bound by a strict rule of law, albeit without reward.

*Ukpong opens his satchel and pulls out a brand-new record, like Prince's 'For You'.\**

It's a revolution.

*Ukpong goes to the record player and puts it on.*

You'll like this voice. If you don't, your ears are backwards.

*Ukpong sways. It is sexy, sweet, and ridiculous at the same time.*

Abasiama. Ama. Love of God. We are a love match. Come.

*Abasiama does not move.*

*(Joking.)* Hey! What of your training?[†]

*Ukpong lifts Abasiama's hands and wraps them around his neck.*

*(Serious.)* Abasiama Ekpeyong. Afo odo owo ekenọhọ ensọk mien. You hear me? Between my sounds please hear me. We will complete.

*Abasiama slowly lets Ukpong surround her.*


## SCENE 5

*May 1, 1978, almost 10:00 p.m. Disciple's domain. Disciple measures the space of his room with his feet. His gaze zones in on his typewriter. From a distance, he carves it out with his fingers.[‡]*

DISCIPLE   We are writing today.

*He sits, next to the flat uncrumpled sheets—remnants of last night's disaster. He begins again.*

Okay.

*(Out loud, to himself.)* Ŋyin itoho Nigeria ima ikpọŋ iduŋ ŋyin. Ŋyin isinamma ŋkpọ ntoro— *(Whispers his coherent thoughts into his typewriter.)* Mme enie akuk enọ nditọ mmọ eka iduŋ mfia owo ekekpep ŋwed mbak mmọ eda ukara. Mmọ ema ema mmọ enyọŋ eka Nigeria ekediọŋ eyuŋ ebọp Nigeria nnọ afọn.[§]

Okay . . . Thoughts? Good. Now, write. What is simple home is simple

---

\*   See special note on songs/recordings.

†   Ukpong is referring to Abasiama's breeding, which should have trained her to obey him on command.

‡   "Carving" is a gesture Disciple learned from his sister, a character we more fully meet in *Runboyrun*. This gesture helps Disciple mark out/claim "good" objects and/or people in an unstable world. The gesture is performed in *Sojourners* by outlining the object or person with the index and middle fingers.

§   See translations page.

here, so . . . *Nigerian Immigration: Reconceptualizing a Country*, a disserta-
tion by Nsikan Disciple Ufot.

*(Mumbling his thoughts out loud, while typing what he can.)* . . . Nigeria is
encountering one of the most peculiar . . . —[abnormal] . . . ? Peculiar.
Hm. Nigeria is encountering—Nigeria is *facing* one of the most peculiar
external movements—No. Migrations. There's a return as Nigeria leaves
itself to find itself—cycle migrations? Or—hm . . . Mmọ ema ema mmọ
enyọŋ eka Nigeria ekediọŋ eyuŋ Nigeria nnọ afọn. Again. Nigeria is
facing one of the most peculiar . . . wanderings of the modern African
era. Academics are wrestling—grappling. My Lord! How many words for
almost the same thing here!

> *Grabs sheet from the typewriter and crumples it.*

Mixing, mixing, mixing into nothing . . .

Okay. Okay. Okay.

> *Silence.*

*(Serious, prayer.)* In the name of the Father . . . In the name of the Father,
the Son, and the—

> *Silence.*

Not even prayer rings similar? Mbọk, why this problem. I cannot write
the right— *(Knocking his head.)* Had I known it could be this way, I'd have
stayed back. Jesus. What kind of land is this . . . Okay . . . a break. I know.
We need a break . . . But first . . . Gratitude. *(Praying.)* I thank You, Lord
for—for giving me three lines! Give me a million times that. I need it. I
command it. God You must remember your child! You hear me? In Your
name we pray. Amen.

> *Disciple slips on his shoes, grabs a set of car keys, and exits.*


## SCENE 6

> *May 2, 1978, a little past 3:00 a.m. Gas station.*

MOXIE   Yea. I'm back so. Can I get another application?

ABASIAMA   Sure.

MOXIE   I gotta do this fast 'cause—Let me hold a pen?

> *Abasiama hands Moxie the pen and application. Moxie quickly fills in her
> name and scans the document. She then painstakingly parses out a sentence.
> All the while Moxie convulsively taps her foot.*

I think this asking me if I got a license. Texas, right?

*Moxie shoves the paper against the glass. Abasiama nods.*

Yea. I don't got one. But I got a birth certificate. Annamae. Massachusetts. Real random. Don't ask. They take that?

ABASIAMA  Yes. So write no on the line and then write—ehm. *(Helpful but very quick spelling.)* M-A-S-S-A-C-H-U-S-E-T-T-S.

MOXIE  What the fuck was that.

ABASIAMA  *(Sincere.)* Spelling—I was spelling . . . for you to—

MOXIE  How in the hell, even if I wanted to—How in the hell am I supposed to hear through that.

*Abasiama retreats. Moxie tries to parse out Massachusetts on her own. She sounds it out.*

M-A-S— . . . I heard you say two Ss?

ABASIAMA  Yes.

MOXIE  *(Writing.)* M-A-S-S—

ABASIAMA  *(Quick.)* A-C-H—

*Moxie looks at Abasiama like she wants to flog her; however the completion of the application proves more important. Moxie writes.*

U-S—

*Moxie writes.*

E-T-T-S.

*Moxie writes.*

Massachusetts.

*Moxie again pushes the paper against the glass. She points at the next sentence she wants read.*

Why do you want to work for the Fiesta group of companies?

MOXIE  . . .

ABASIAMA  It—I said—it says—"Why do you want—"

MOXIE  'Cause I wanna job.

ABASIAMA  I think the application demands a more thoughtful response like—

*Moxie, frustrated, abandons the application. She folds it up and puts it in her pocket.*

Why?!

MOXIE  He coming soon and—it don't matter anyway. Look. Can I get a small one and a Snicker bar?

*Abasiama hands Moxie a nip and a bar. Moxie spots a book behind Abasiama's glass.*

*(Coarse/fast.)* What that book you reading. That big one.

ABASIAMA  . . . Biology.

MOXIE  Mind if I stand right here.

ABASIAMA  No.

MOXIE  So you a student huh.

ABASIAMA  Yes.

MOXIE  *(Serious.)* You like it.

ABASIAMA  Yes.

MOXIE  *(Looking Abasiama over.)* Cool. So, you understand it all and stuff? Like what it is? I mean I get biology. But *all* that book biology? Sheeiiit. How much biology can there be.

ABASIAMA  This is just general. I am going to focus on micro in the future. And my hus— . . . Economics.

MOXIE  *(Dry.)* That sound smart.

ABASIAMA  Yea. Daddy always told me the sciences cross over. Wherever in the world I am, I will work. Anywhere.

MOXIE  Smooth.

ABASIAMA  Bring back that application.

> Silence. Moxie's legs still shake involuntarily.

It's fine. I want to help.

MOXIE  Can I get another small one? Nah. Gimme two.

ABASIAMA  . . . How was your day, Moxie?

MOXIE  *(Sharp fear.)* You got my name? How you got my—

ABASIAMA  You told me. When you . . . yesterday when you were here and asked me to fill in your—

MOXIE  Oh yea. I did do that.

ABASIAMA  Mine is Abasiama. People who know me call me Ama. How was your day?

MOXIE  Fucked.

ABASIAMA  Why.

MOXIE  Look. I'm starved. Can I get—

ABASIAMA  But, why was it—

MOXIE  *(Suddenly explosive.)* Goddamn! None of your goddamn business, 21 questions.

ABASIAMA  My Lord! Sorry.

MOXIE  What you sorry for. You ain't done shit yet. You 'bout the only person today that ain't done shit to me.

> Moxie takes in Abasiama.

Fix your face.

ABASIAMA  Moxie. Let's finish it. Bring it out . . .

Give it to me now.

MOXIE  Fucking take it.

*Moxie uncrumples the paper from her pocket and shoves it through the slot.*

ABASIAMA  I don't know what all this is about but this must get done. Moxie, why do you want to work / for the Fiesta group of companies.

MOXIE  Africa, how the hell I write this here shit down.

*Moxie lifts her shirt, showing a series of pulsing welts framing her waist. Imprints of a rough "embrace."*

ABASIAMA  (*Quiet shock.*) Abasi, what happen!

MOXIE  The regular. John say he holding me. But damnit, if that's holding then—then holding and killing done switched places.

ABASIAMA  You need ice or—

MOXIE  I know what this is. This gonna level out and look like some of the old bruises on my back and—you should see my—

*Gestures to her legs.*

—Lady, you look like you 'bout to die.

ABASIAMA  People can do this?

MOXIE  Hell yea. They pay for it. It's part of the package. Fucking new-age hippie wannabes. They where the dough at. But I tell ya, ain't no real hippies in Texas ya hear?* You got any—something for my head 'cause—

ABASIAMA  There's Anacin here.

MOXIE  Open it. Gimme eight.

ABASIAMA  Eight?

MOXIE  Yea. And another small one.

*Abasiama hands her the pills and Moxie slings them back with her drink.*

I'll feel better in . . . 3, 2, 1 . . . Better. Look. Do me a solid, okay. I know y'all expect people like me to do this kinda shit but—I can't pay for the meds and that last bottle—bottles of—I left that guy early so. I didn't get no money or nothing. Can I spot you tomorrow? After I work some?

ABASIAMA  Where do you go at night?

MOXIE  Whatchu mean.

ABASIAMA  To sleep.

---

* The free-love movement did not wash over America evenly. Moxie is referring to the fact that while America has been ensconced in free-love, Houston has remained conservative. In fact, free-love might have been used as a guise to violate women.

MOXIE  Oh. I dunno.

ABASIAMA  Where.

MOXIE  Goddamn. Motels. If I make enough or—

ABASIAMA  Do you have a father?

MOXIE  No.

ABASIAMA  Mother?

MOXIE  No.

ABASIAMA  How.

MOXIE  I don't know.

ABASIAMA  No one? Aunties? Uncles?

MOXIE  Ain't you understand no? It's a simple ass word.

ABASIAMA  . . . Where I come from we have a compound.* / Complete extended family. A daughter would never be allowed to—

MOXIE  I ain't on no African compound am I? But I gotta . . . 'cause—I'm on the uptick if you ask me. Got this idea. I got an exit plan. (*Referring to Abasiama in her kiosk.*) I can *do* what you doing. I can stand. In there.
     *Small silence.*

ABASIAMA  Let's attack from this angle: "I want to work for Fiesta because I bring focus and determination." And, "I will be a good worker," always sounds nice.

MOXIE  (*Fast.*) I just need help 'cause sometimes I can't piece together all I know into regular, normal shit. So, when I don't know something . . . then can you—†
     *Moxie forces herself to look at Abasiama dead in the eye.*
     . . . I can read. A little bit. Letters just swim.

ABASIAMA  No problem. Do you want another Snickers?

MOXIE  You paying?

ABASIAMA  I'll cover.
     *Abasiama slides a bar and watches Moxie eat.*
     . . . You—you enjoy it . . . ?

MOXIE  Hell yea. Nougat, caramel, and nuts. Eating this right here? On nights like tonight? Fuck. On nights like this whole week? Sheeiiit. Eating this here bar give me a little bit of love.

---

* A compound is a cluster of family homes. This directly refers to the communal nature of Nigerian society. One is never far away from one's people, and therefore never truly lost.

† Along with being grade-levels behind, Moxie also struggles with what is now known as dyslexia.

*Abasiama reaches for a bar, unravels it, and starts eating. Moxie watches Abasiama tentatively bite into the bar.*

Uh-uh. You ain't never had one before?

ABASIAMA *(Bright bright excitement.)* It's—hey! Moxie, it's good oh! Creamy. Ahah. I see why you eat it. Wow!

MOXIE That's one joy that ain't gon' cause no pain. If I was you, I would eat every damn sweet in that box.

*A car beeps in the distance. The light changes suddenly. Moxie hangs her head.*

ABASIAMA You are not well. You / shouldn't.

MOXIE *(Trying to pick herself up.)* What else I got.

ABASIAMA If you want—Just for tonight—I can allow sleep in the station. Just no more eating anything. I can't fund the store. But. That way you can rest. Also you have to leave before six a.m. when Rodney comes to open or else I'll be in trouble.

MOXIE What?

ABASIAMA I don't know. It's an idea. To save you from—

*Car beeps. Moxie's focus never shifts away from Abasiama.*

MOXIE You'd do that.

ABASIAMA . . . You don't have a place.

*Moxie clacks away. Abasiama waits, peering into the light, trying to make Moxie out. Moxie clacks back fast.*

MOXIE *(Frightened.)* Quick. Open up. I mighta made him mad. *Abasiama opens the door. Both women are now behind the glass.*

*(On an exhale.)* Ah! Golly! Whoo! Fuck! I just had to do that once, once so I know I can—'cause—Ama, if I can do that one by one to alla them? If I—Damn! That right there might could make up for every one of these bruises. Ama. One motherfucker down five more to go. *(Simple.)* Listen I won't eat nuh-thing. No-thing. Notta damn thing. And Imma finish this tonight. Cross my heart. Hope to die. I won't bother you no more.

*Strong kick in Abasiama's stomach.*

ABASIAMA Mm . . .

MOXIE Damn! You okay? Your belly shaking!*

*Abasiama nods weakly.*

ABASIAMA Hm.

---

* The baby has been quiet for some time. Remember, however, that when the play began the baby was upset. This baby and Ukpong are inextricably linked. When Ukpong is away, the baby is upset. When Ukpong is about to go away again, the baby becomes agitated.

## SCENE 7

*May 2, 1978, sometime after 4:00 a.m. Ukpong holds a Guinness while chewing chewing-stick. His singlet is stained from sweat [drinking]. His economics book is open on his lap. He stares out into space. Vacant. He's been frozen like this a long time.*

*He can take no more. Ukpong downs the remaining Guinness, shoves the empty bottles and debris under the couch, dons his hat and stands to leave the apartment.*

*Abasiama jiggles her keys in the lock. Ukpong slams back onto the couch, he sits as if all is well. Abasiama's eyes never leave her husband Ukpong.*

UKPONG  Milady.* Early night?

ABASIAMA  *(Sitting.)* No. It's the right time.

*Ukpong melts into her. Abasiama pulls away, smelling Ukpong. Ukpong removes his hat completely and lays his head on Abasiama's belly.*

Lift off me. My tummy's hurting.

UKPONG  Again?

ABASIAMA  It just started. She's been calm until—On the way home it became so angry like. Killing almost.† Ukpong. Move. You're laying right where it hurts.

UKPONG  Your tummy is your magic man. What are you worrying about now?

ABASIAMA  Nothing. I don't know. Something isn't—

UKPONG  Woman be straight.

ABASIAMA  I didn't see you on campus today. I sometimes see you on my way to lab. Did I miss you?

UKPONG  Master Interrogator, I don't walk the same path everywhere every day! Are you going to fault my feet.

ABASIAMA  So you went to class wearing this singlet. You, the one who reminds me I'm not from peasants. It's stained and smells like—you smell. What was your day?

---

* Nigeria was colonized by Great Britain thus English is the national language. Ukpong and Abasiama, from time to time, use adopted "Britishisms" to subtly mock, heighten, or draw attention in specific directions.

† Please mark that there has been a substantive increase in Abasiama's pain level. The pain she suffered earlier is growing in depth and color.

UKPONG  My day was roses and winds and green and red and water. There was lots of water! And land! Paradiso! Economics!

ABASIAMA  Economics was paradise. Since when—

*Abasiama has a cramp.*

UKPONG  Shoo! That was strong oh! Woman. Okay. Still yourself.

ABASIAMA  My one and only husband, if I am in pain why are you laying on it eh? What happened?

UKPONG  I like it here. I will calm my child. We sing. I want him to hear me before he's born—Plus you may like this more than American popular!

ABASIAMA  Ukpong—

UKPONG  *(Kisses her and lays head on her belly.)* To my boy and to my woman. Wait. I have to do it right.

*Ukpong vocalizes.*

Mah-meh-mi-mo-moo

ABASIAMA  Ukpong, where are you?

UKPONG  White people! They do that to warm up a muscle that is already warm but hey, why not! I am now ready—

*Ukpong centers his energy and manages to sing extraordinarily well.*

mme nti usen eboyo

ABASIAMA  *(Dry.)* I want to know—

UKPONG  Shhh. I have to begin again now . . .

mme nti usen

eboyo afit nti ŋkpọ

eboyo

niche owo nkket se ndọŋ esit

nwat ubom mi ikpọŋ*

*The singing has temporarily sobered Ukpong. The singing has temporarily sobered the baby.*

I deserve a musical contract. My mother sang it for me. I tell you, it's good medicine for stubborn kickers.

ABASIAMA  You love yourself / too much—

UKPONG  You do too. Abasiama have you not yet learned to love your finefine?

ABASIAMA  Hm.

UKPONG  I remember how much you liked me back then. See my shoulders move up and down. You are wanting me oh . . . no matter. You cannot deny

---

* Please note that Ukpong has sung the first verse of the song, the verse of loneliness and being outcast.

the facts. See! *(Gesturing to her calm stomach.)* I am the bringer of peace! The prince of peace—

ABASIAMA   Are you Jesus? Stop in the name of hell[fire]—

   *Abasiama cramps.*

UKPONG   Ah! It hit me. I know this child's name.

ABASIAMA   Eh-eh. Just now. Are we to call it "kicks too hard" or—

UKPONG   Joker! No. "Freedom." Jah. What a high name. Mebǫkǫ.

ABASIAMA   Mebǫkǫ doesn't move like that.\* It means "flight" or, "I am going." We are not giving that name. That's what I am trying to control here.†

UKPONG   That's the closest word for—

ABASIAMA   Birds mebǫkǫ in the spring, okay? Ants know mebǫkǫ when they see my fists. I'll not name my daughter Mebǫkǫ. No. Have another inspiration than that one.

UKPONG   You must drink the name the right way! Mebǫkǫ! It's freedom if we mean it to be freedom. And it's not a girl. That is a man's name I have given. Feel the strength! Mebǫkǫ Ekpeyong! No. Jason Mebǫkǫ Ekpeyong.

ABASIAMA   Who in our history has ever been named / Jason.

UKPONG   We must make it easier on the children. How else will they fit in / here.

ABASIAMA   *(Sharp.)* No! Why?! *(Fighting for composure.)* . . . Ukpong, our life is smoother than this.‡ If we stay? We'll be like the trash this country puts on the side.

UKPONG   I hear you—but—

ABASIAMA   That's the truth! I've seen her. I've seen what this place can do.

UKPONG   *(Realizing the depth of his miscalculation, assertive.)* Ah! I have had enough of your mouth. It obviously needs a purpose. Get here.

   *Ukpong pulls Abasiama toward him and kisses her.*

   I like that you're not mad at me anymore.

   *Ukpong kisses Abasiama again.*

---

\* There is a literal translation issue here. English has many more words than Ibibio and the word Ukpong is using can literally only mean "I am going." He is trying to deviate/widen its usage, but this is not strictly allowable.

† Abasiama is referring to both her baby's desire to kick its way out of her and Ukpong's desire to spontaneously leave her.

‡ This is a direct reference to Abasiama's and Ukpong's class. Their struggle in America is meant to be temporary only. The lives carved out for them back in Nigeria have more ease and creature/class comfort.

You taste like you have finally forgotten all your anger. I've forgotten mine.

ABASIAMA  Because you forget everything.

UKPONG  *(Bristling.)* Soft woman. It's late. Time for bed now, right?

ABASIAMA  No.

UKPONG  Why. You want to spend time with me.

ABASIAMA  We can stay up. And study. You need to study. I am not yet tired.

UKPONG  You and this school sickness. Go! I am coming into bed right behind you. I know your energy is / low.

ABASIAMA  Hm.

UKPONG  Brush your teeth Ama. I will be right in.

ABASIAMA  I am / hungry.

UKPONG  Tall-tale teller.

ABASIAMA  I am!

UKPONG  Fantasy story / spinner.

ABASIAMA  Fine I'm not hungry. But you are coming in / right?

UKPONG  Where else would I go. I'm just getting a Guinness—

ABASIAMA  Why.

UKPONG  Drinking it. Looking at the ceiling for / two minutes.

ABASIAMA  I'll wait. I feel you Ukpong. Something is not—

UKPONG  *(Sharp.)* You don't like the smell of drink. Woman, I am a man. I will not be dry. Go. Catch your rest. I'll not fail to squeeze you when I get in bed.

ABASIAMA  . . . Swear to God . . . Open your mouth and promise me.

UKPONG  How many times in two days do you need / to hear me promise—

ABASIAMA  Finefine . . . please.

UKPONG  *(Sober.)* What on this wide earth can keep me from you. Softsoft? I will remain in my softsoft.

> *Ukpong kisses Abasiama. Abasiama and a calm baby reluctantly exit.*
> *Ukpong goes to the fridge, grabs a six-pack of Guinness longnecks and the jar of pickles. Ukpong immediately downs as much of a Guinness longneck as he can. He turns on the AM radio. He stands, looking outside.*
> *Ukpong closes his eyes. His father's face instantly appears behind his lids.*

Papa . . . ? Listen to it. There is a whole world [of—Hey! If you could hear you would swell oh!] I know it. I know [it]—Don't—don't be—Ete mmi, mbọk suk tie. Dry your eyes.

> *He sinks into the energy he had before Abasiama arrested him. Ukpong continues listening to the AM radio, drinking heavily.*

*(Plea.)* Please don't be mad with [me].

## SCENE 8

*May 2, 1978, hazy edges of daybreak. Ukpong is gone. On the countertop are bottles of Guinness and the jar of pickles. The AM radio still plays.*

ABASIAMA   *(Offstage.)* Ukpong where are you? My tummy is hurting again. Bad. I will take that song if you—

*Abasiama walks out into the living space.*

Ukpong?

*Silence.*

*(Knowing and yet calling out all the same.)* Ukpong?

*Abasiama sees the bottles and the mess on the counter, she hears the radio.*

Okay. Okay. Sure. Okay. Hm. *(Switch.)* Hey! Wow, Ukpong! Wow! *(Switch.)* Okay.

*Abasiama goes to her corner and lays her head on the wall. She is restless. She boils water for tea and attempts to sit on the couch. The couch scoots back and she hears the clang of cans and bottles underneath. She pushes the couch back further and Abasiama sees the extent of her husband's debauchery. Discarded magazines, Guinness, cigarettes, brand-new unopened records. Abasiama stands in the middle of it.*

My husband lived under my couch.

*She spots an official-looking letter. She opens it and reads its contents. Tears flow. Without a sound being made, and with abnormal grace (albeit pregnancy), Abasiama calmly stoops, picks up a record, and with a strong, graceful hand she opens the package and snaps it in two. Records split. Beer bottles shatter in her hands. Cans crush. Dishes chip. A very quiet woman makes a violent storm. Just as the frenzy is about to climax there is a pregnancy pain.*

*(Breaking down.)* He's gone! Stop! Why kick me, eh?! I am the one on this earth covering you.

*The tea kettle whistles.*

*(Firming up.)* Hm. Hey, this purposeless water. What can water give me? Give us?

## SCENE 9

*May 2, 1978, around 10:00 p.m. The teapot and alarm sounds bleed into one. The alarm startles Disciple out of stupor. He quickly shuts the alarm off and looks at the sheets of paper on his desk. He reads to himself silently, enraged. He crumples sheet after sheet.*

DISCIPLE  *(Escalating, to the sky.)* Aya nnọ ŋkpọ mfin sibi inyaŋa mien.

Mmeyem uwam uto fien akọnoyo emi.

Aya nnọ ŋkpọ mfin sibi inyaŋa mien.

Mmeyem uwam uto fien akọnoyo emi.

. . . Okay? Just in case you don't—let me repeat. Aya nnọ ŋkpọ mfin sibi *inyaŋa* mien!

Mmeyem uwam uto fien akọnoyo emi!

Sistah? I need you oh. God has forgotten me. He's forgotten our language. If you are up there . . . *(Correcting.)* . . . you are up there. Please, you must whisper in His ear, with your sweet voice. And you must tell Him, that I need . . . I need . . . Oh! Mbọk, please. This place must yield something good.

*He slips on his singlet, button-down, and worn brown slacks. He grabs his keys and walks out.*

## SCENE 10

*May 3, 1978, after midnight. Gas station. Abasiama hums loudly, soothing the child. Moxie clacks toward the station.*

MOXIE  Ama! I was out before six, not a single person came by, which was good 'cause—Sheeiiit. You real green.

*Abasiama suddenly exhales and sways a bit on her feet.*

Sheiiit. Stand up now Ama—What's the matter with you?

ABASIAMA  Nothing. Just a little kicking—

MOXIE  You ever been to a doctor?

*Abasiama grabs the key and goes outside.*

ABASIAMA  Keep watch for me.

*Abasiama starts walking laps around the gas station.*[*]

MOXIE  What the hell is happening? Get back in there.

ABASIAMA  I need to walk. The air feels good.

*(Sung.)* mme nti / usen eboyo

---

[*] Abasiama is following the pull of her body and submitting to the urge to walk; however, what she does not know is that walking is helping induce labor, not arrest it. From here on out, Abasiama is in the throes of delivery and does not intellectually realize any of it because of emotional stress/duress.

MOXIE  I'm gonna go / get help—

ABASIAMA  No. Don't leave here. Please—

> *(Sung.)* afit nti ŋkpọ
>
> *Abasiama's lap brings her around to cross Moxie. Moxie stops her in her tracks.*

I don't—It's never been this bad. Move now. I need to pass. But stay. Just—Let me keep walking—

> *Moxie touches Abasiama's stomach.*

Jah! Yes. Moxie, keep your hand there—

MOXIE  What?

> *Moxie removes her hand.*

ABASIAMA  Keep your hands on me please. It helps. Somehow.

> *Moxie puts her hands back on Abasiama's stomach.*

I just need to calm down. *(Re: Ukpong.)* He always does this. You'd think I'd be stone by now.

MOXIE  Listen, Imma let you go for a sec. There's a pay phone right over there. Give me a number. I'll call somebody. Your—

ABASIAMA  Daddy.

MOXIE  Okay. Gimme his—

> *Moxie slowly releases her hands from Abasiama's stomach, trying to make sure Abasiama doesn't succumb to more pain.*

ABASIAMA  011-234-87-857-6483.

MOXIE  *(Confused.)* Uh . . . okay cool—just—hold on lemme get some paper from the box so I can—

ABASIAMA  You want to use that there pay phone? You are funny! The phone just ring, ring, ring. And if someone is there, it may not even be Daddy. Someone will have to run him a message and then three more days of waiting and then more ring, ring, ring. Ring, ring, ring. And then maybe, maybe I can talk to my father.

MOXIE  In the States. Brothers? Sisters?

ABASIAMA  Nigeria.

MOXIE  Friends?

ABASIAMA  Nigeria.

MOXIE  Where the fuck is your man?

ABASIAMA  You know, I am not sure how long this time. He may return tomorrow morning. He promises a lot and sometimes he— *(Explosive.)* He could be back months from now!—

MOXIE  Easy, Ama.

ABASIAMA  (*Unleashed.*) If my father knew who he was before he sent me off he would cry. I saw the paper, Moxie! I saw it! With my eyes! This man—three and a half years in school and twelve credits?* Twelve credits! Twelve, Moxie. Lies. All lies. Look at me. How can I—

MOXIE  Ama, don't shout, it's not good for you or the—

ABASIAMA  How can someone be so careless, with a woman? Hm? How? Ow.

> On a sudden impulse Moxie embraces Abasiama.

(*Brittle laughter.*) Hm. It's like she knows. She misses him, so she wars me. I just need to calm down and—Whew. Breathe.

> Tired, Abasiama braces against Moxie and lowers herself to the pavement. Moxie assists, to make the lowering easier.

Breathe. Okay. Okay. Okay. Better. Okay. I can be. You know what? He promises— . . . so. He's probably on his way back. I cannot restrict a man's movements. In the name of God I'm okay.

MOXIE  Where your God at? I only see you and me here.

ABASIAMA  Moxie . . . God is good, He—

MOXIE  Cool. Keep your invisible man. Men. Maybe they work where you come from, but out here? You need to know how to care for yourself.

ABASIAMA  I know how to—

MOXIE  (*Teaching.*) How you get here Ama.

ABASIAMA  My daddy gave me to Ukpong. Ukpong brought me here.

MOXIE  Yuckpong your husband right?

ABASIAMA  Yes.

MOXIE  Bam. Problem numero uno. Learn this fast. No one but you got the goddamn right to bring you nowhere.

ABASIAMA  It's not the same.

MOXIE  You need to focus and do what you gotta do so you ain't standing out in the middle of a Texas gas station asking to get killed. This ain't Africa girl. You gotta—This be the free jungle!† Better than the jungle jungle.

---

* Twelve credits is a humiliatingly low number of credits to have received over the course of 3.5 years. It is so low it borders on ridiculous. There is no earthly way Ukpong can make up those credits before graduation. Somewhere Abasiama knows the implication of such a letter; whether she can allow herself to live in its reality is another story.

† Moxie is making the assumption that all of Africa is covered in jungle. She would have gotten this idea from the unforgivably one-sided stories of Africa that permeate the United States media and thus the United States consciousness.

*Abasiama has a contraction.*

Look I'm—I'm gonna go get some help. Gal, you listening to me?

ABASIAMA  Yes. It is just hurting again and there's no jungle where I'm from, Moxie. Last time I could go, the doctor gave me an exercise—Ah! Okay. Calm. One . . .

*Breathes.*

Two . . .

*Breathes.*

Three . . .

*Breathes.*

MOXIE  I got you. I got you. Four . . .

*Breathes.*

Five . . .

*Breathes.*

Six . . .

*Breathes.*

. . . how you doing?

*Abasiama relaxes.*

Better?

ABASIAMA  For now.

MOXIE  Good.

*A man walks onstage from a far distance. He carries a small red plastic gas carton.* *He wears off-brown, too-oft-washed trousers, hard bottom shoes, and a tucked-in, off-white singlet. His sideburns and beard are meticulously manicured. He wears aviator eyeglasses.*

DISCIPLE  *(From far off.)* Pardon . . .

*He walks toward Moxie and Abasiama.*

MOXIE  Come on. Imma put you in the station, then go find some help.

DISCIPLE  Hello?

MOXIE  Alright. Up. We.

DISCIPLE  Excuse . . . ?

MOXIE  Go!

DISCIPLE  Hey!

*Moxie jumps slightly. Abasiama drapes on Moxie.*

MOXIE  *(Instant defense.)* What the fuck? Where the hell you come from?

---

* Disciple simply ran out of gas and is carrying the carton to refill his tank. Assume the car is a distance away.

DISCIPLE  My car stopped. I am searching for gas.

MOXIE  We look like we can get you some gas? We look like we have gas?

DISCIPLE  Is this not a petrol station?

ABASIAMA  Yes. Excuse her. We are in the middle of a little—Welcome to Fiesta. / How may—

MOXIE  If you don't quit saying that—

DISCIPLE  Madame?

    *Abasiama suffers one last swallowed stomach cramp—*

ABASIAMA  Mm.

DISCIPLE  *(To Moxie.)* What is this now? *(To Abasiama.)* Madame?!

    *Disciple looks at Abasiama's face and takes in her features; a subtle change comes over him. His meter slows, his energy calms.*

MOXIE  Come on. We ain't got no time for—

DISCIPLE  Sistah . . .

MOXIE  You know her? This the fool Ama? Yuckpong?! You need to step back.

DISCIPLE  *(To the sky.)* For me sistah? Thank you. *(Soft, to Abasiama.)* Mbok, mmeyem uwam uto fien akonoyo emi.

ABASIAMA  Bro, nsido? Ameyem uwam akonoyo emi?

DISCIPLE  Yes.

MOXIE  Ama who in the hell is this—

DISCIPLE  I need to get you some help— *(To Moxie.)* Call the ambulance!

ABASIAMA  Lord. Are you serious?

    *Abasiama looks down.*

  *(Soft.)* Mmon idip mi abomo.

MOXIE  Huh? . . . What?

DISCIPLE  *(Subtly shaken.)* Water. She said water has come.

    *Blackout.*

## ACT TWO

### SCENE 1

    *May 9, 1978, 11:00 a.m. Sterilized white room. Disciple stands with a bunch of vibrant-hued flowers and a small, stuffed terry cloth bear in his hands. Abasiama stares straight ahead, awake yet silent.*

DISCIPLE  You look better. Not as terrible as you did when I first saw you.

    . . .

They tell me to bring flowers for cheer. So, I brought the forest. And stuffed animals. They are American symbols of comfort.

. . .

I can't grasp it. But, that's what I am finding. Do they comfort you?

. . .

And they call us backwards. I should have brought good food or fine cloth. Doll?! What for.

. . .

I see you hear me. Why aren't you talking? It makes better sense to talk.

. . .

Sistah, where is your husband.

. . .

Do you have a husband—of course you have a husband.

. . .

How can I help if you don't use your voice? Let me hear it no?

. . .

. . .

OK. I will return tomorrow. That your friend who sometimes comes here? I believe she will be here as well . . . ?

> *Disciple sets the flower bundle down, picks up his book bag, and begins to walk to the door. He stops himself.*

(*Promise.*) Eti awo wan. Ndisuk ndidi tutu afo ataŋ ikọ ye ami. You hear me?

> *Disciple gets to the door.*

ABASIAMA  Who sent you.

> *Disciple freezes.*

DISCIPLE  Eh . . . ?

ABASIAMA  What information are you looking for. I've not sent anyone any letters about anything. I've made no calls.

DISCIPLE  I'm no informant now. Swell down.

ABASIAMA  You've been buzzing around me for days. I demand you tell me who you are. Are you working for his father? My father?

DISCIPLE  Shhh—

ABASIAMA  I don't have to whisper.

DISCIPLE  My name is—

ABASIAMA  And I don't care for your fake name.

DISCIPLE  Jesus, see this! Paranoia! I am not—Nsikan. My name is Nsikan Disciple Ufot and—

*Disciple pulls out his license.*

See? I am not lying. And, I have no knowledge of your people—at least, I don't believe I know your people.

ABASIAMA You just found me then.

DISCIPLE Yes.

ABASIAMA By accident.

DISCIPLE No. Not an accident. Never by accident.

*Abasiama recoils.*

Bet. Please. I was out of gas. I walked to a station, the first petrol station I could find, and I saw you there with that woman and I tried to help. No more than that. Look at my palms I hold nothing to harm you.

ABASIAMA Let me see under your skin before we talk of trust.

DISCIPLE I am from your area. How irresponsible of me would it have been not to inquire about / your safety?

ABASIAMA I am safe.

DISCIPLE But then where is your protection, eh? A woman and child without a man in this place make a bad formula. You hear me . . . Where is he. Is there someone I should alert?

*Disciple sits down.*

You turn away dialogue. I have already shown you my hands. Look on them again. If I could lift my cover to show you my underneath without rattling your spirit . . . ? Know that I would.

ABASIAMA This is—

DISCIPLE Simple talk. I just want one name. Am I God? I can't search for a human by solely first / name.

ABASIAMA Ukpong, Okay. Now thank you and—

DISCIPLE See that! I know no Ukpongs, unless of course, your husband is my cousin's son's son. Come on! Lighten yourself! What part are you? I come from—I'm based in Uyo.

ABASIAMA . . . Etinan.*

DISCIPLE Etinan! Hey! A pretty land. The best God ever made.

*Beat.*

You know you are right to have that caution . . . because if I knew him I would report him to his father. Abasiama we should—

---

* In the 1970s Etinan and Uyo were both part of Cross River State, Nigeria. In 1987 a southeastern portion of Cross River, inclusive of Uyo and Etinan, was excised to create a new state, Akwa Ibom. Present-day Uyo is the capital of Akwa Ibom State and Etinan is a major city therein.

ABASIAMA  How do you know to call me!

DISCIPLE  Simple. I have been seeing you with that your friend, as you were sleeping for days, hooked to that dripdrip machine. And I have heard her, that girl. I've heard her butcher your name over and over and, for the pièce de résistance, there is your name on that file right there. Printed clear. I have eyes.

    *Disciple has a sudden thought while looking at the file.*

    Eh-heh. That makes him Ukpong Ekpeyong.

    *Sudden shift into calm.*

    Don't worry, I still don't know him. Listen, I can allow you the time to unearth me but first—first you should call someone. Have you been calling people?

ABASIAMA  *(Exasperated.)* Please. God help me.

DISCIPLE  Listen, I am convinced. If someone knew about this they would care. If someone knew? They would come.

ABASIAMA  Brother Disciple, I have called.

DISCIPLE  But we know that even miracles take work. We can try it again. Someone will eventually—

ABASIAMA  Leave.

DISCIPLE  Who has you.

ABASIAMA  Abasi mbọk, oh just—pass me the—

    *Disciple hands Abasiama the phone.*

    *(To operator.)* Dialing out . . . 229-3829. Thank you.

    *She waits; no answer. Abasiama hands the phone back to Disciple.*

DISCIPLE  What happen?

ABASIAMA  I called the apartment. No answer.

DISCIPLE  Okay. Try a friend of his then.

ABASIAMA  Brother. No.

DISCIPLE  Someone who knows him. Someone who may be able to relay a message?

ABASIAMA  Is that my / job?!

DISCIPLE  Swallow that pride and—

ABASIAMA  Oh, just give me.

    *Disciple passes Abasiama the phone.*

    Outside . . . 221-3177.

    Etuk? Hm. Hello. Aba die. Have you seen Ukpong? Hm. Okay. Well if he returns and you see him, please relay him this message. I'm at Sunnyside. I have been here now five—

DISCIPLE  Six days.

ABASIAMA  ... Six ... days.* Tell him, it's a girl. That's it. No. You don't
need to come. I'll be leaving here day after tomorrow. I just wanted to alert
him. Okay. Mm-hm. Sure now. Okay. Bye.

DISCIPLE  Good! See? A seed sown. Try your father now.

ABASIAMA  *(Decisive yet respectful.)* I will do that one in my time. Again.
Thank you for your care brother. I can appreciate it. I am now safe.

DISCIPLE  ... Sai! Abasiama?

We were not sent out for this. Whatever your husband is doing is not
what we were meant to do ... I don't know what your faith base was like
back home but—have you prayed about—

To God? For God to place His hand on this situation and mete out ease?

ABASIAMA  Eh?

DISCIPLE  Abasiama, believe me prayer works oh. Pray today and tomorrow
discover the way. That is my family's tongue.

ABASIAMA  I have been praying in my heart every moment of every day.
My people too taught me / prayer.

DISCIPLE  Good! Then you are prepared. We open the sky!

*Disciple prays.*

In the name of the Father the Son and the Holy Ghost—Give your hand—
*Without waiting, Disciple takes Abasiama's hand.*

Close your eyes now.

*Abasiama does. She immediately reopens them to get a good look at this
man in front of her.*

In the name of the Father the Son and the Holy Ghost, in the name of
the Father the Son and the Holy Ghost, in the name of the Father the Son
and the Holy Ghost, Thou God of Abraham Isaac and Jacob. Lord we ask
You to untie us from the path of evil. Wash these our bodies, our minds,
our spirits. Cleanse Abasiama and put her back into the arms of Your
favor. We know that not a single hair on a head shall fall without Thou
knowing the reason. We call on You and thank You for the relief You have
sent along the way. In Jesus Christ's name I pray. We pray. Amen.

---

* Six days is an abnormal time to stay within a hospital. Abasiama faced both extraordinary
physical and mental stress during her pregnancy. Physical stress accumulated during her job
at Fiesta, which demanded actual labor (lifting, standing, etc.). Mental stress accumulated
within her marriage to Ukpong. All of this stress resulted in Abasiama inducing her pregnancy.
Her baby was born at 36 weeks. Abasiama and her baby are both in the hospital stabilizing,
thus the long stay of six days.

ABASIAMA  Amen . . . Thank you.

DISCIPLE  Thank Him. I too have been in major problem. The kind where you want to disappear from life and return only if you can erase total history. I've learned to pray like that at least twice a day. Do it. It helps.

> *Disciple, too swift for Abasiama to swat his hand away, adjusts her head scarf, tucking one careless plait underneath.*

I will come back tomorrow bearing better presents. Chin-chin maybe. There is this store—

ABASIAMA  It was good meeting you but I tell you—

DISCIPLE  You are part of a great plan.

ABASIAMA  Yes. / But—

DISCIPLE  And you are my— . . . my family. I can fully understand the demands on you and you can understand me. Who on this earth knows you but your own?

. . .

I will come see you.

. . .

Just to ensure—

. . .

For positive reinforcements. Positivity and prayer and chin-chin!

ABASIAMA  Bro please—

DISCIPLE  I grant you, one day you'll want to see my face over and over. People call me strange, yes! But people also call me good . . . Tomorrow I return. And we pray. And smile . . . You are not alone.

> *Silence.*

ABASIAMA  Sọsọŋọ.

DISCIPLE  No. Thank Him.

> *Disciple exits the hospital room. As he is walking away, and out of Abasiama's sight, a sudden thought hits him.*

(*Spilling forth.*) Before 1960, there is no documentation of free-traveling Nigerians within America. However, post-independence, and after the Biafran War of 1967, a great educational migration will begin.[*] The perfect storm of: low American tuition rates, lax immigration law, and the demand

---

[*] The Biafran War, also called the Nigerian Civil War, was fought from July 1967 to January 1970. Igbos, from the resource-rich Southeast, attempted to secede from the Northern federal government. This brutal 2.5-year war led to a famine that took the lives of 500,000– 2,000,000 Southeast Nigerians (inclusive of many Ibibios).

for Nigerian wealth yields the greatest opportunity. Nigeria's talented tenth, privileged married couples from the oil-rich Niger Delta, have the extraordinary opportunity to refashion their country into a world power. As the energy of this generation is harnessed and nurtured, Nigeria can create a viable model allowing for dispossessed nation-states to rise and take their place on the global stage.

*Disciple looks in the direction he came from [Abasiama's direction] and flings his arms to the sky in joy. He silently thanks his sister, God, and the universe. He races home.*

## SCENE 2

*Next day. May 10, 1978, 11:00 a.m. Visiting hours. Just outside of Abasiama's door.*

DISCIPLE *(Aware of public space.)* Why this commotion?

MOXIE 'Cause you outta pocket!

DISCIPLE All I'm saying is—

MOXIE Back away from me—

DISCIPLE Can you unblock your ears? This is a delicate situation and she is starting to open up again—

MOXIE Whatchu mean.

DISCIPLE She's becoming lighter. More transparent—

MOXIE I don't get it. Okay. Excuse—

DISCIPLE Why do you know her!

*Moxie moves toward the room. Disciple holds her back.*

We have put up with your presence here long enough.

MOXIE We have put up with your presence long enough and get your fingers offa me.

DISCIPLE I have been here. I am starting to see progress.

MOXIE Just 'cause I missed a day, just 'cause she talking to you, you think you can get rid of me? I ain't leaving your creepy behind up in there, alone, with a vulnerable woman. *(Loud.)* Y'all hear me? Vulnerable woman in room 208! *(Quieter.)* You in there by yourself and she talk to you and suddenly you so high and hot? She woulda talked to you sooner or later. And who the hell are you again?!

DISCIPLE A fellow compatriot—

MOXIE I'm starting to think that that mean stranger. 'Scuse me.

*Moxie barges into the room.*

How you doing!

DISCIPLE  Let's maintain an order. She may not be feeling well.

MOXIE  I keep telling that nurse your feet don't need to be all low like that. We have to stop a problem before there is a problem.

You feel me? Where baby girl?

DISCIPLE  She is resting in that / other area.

MOXIE  Hey Ama. Come on now. Whatchu say? I heard you're talking.

DISCIPLE  I just told you—

MOXIE  Ama!

ABASIAMA  Moxie! I have a headache.

MOXIE  Ama, listen to you!

DISCIPLE  What kind of behavior is this?

MOXIE  Fuck you. Hey girl, you sound good.

DISCIPLE  Let's have a seat and act civilized.

*Quiet as they sit.*

MOXIE  Ama, you know this fella?

ABASIAMA  No, not really but—

MOXIE  Yup. You need to leave. Now.

DISCIPLE  Abasiama—

ABASIAMA  I wanted him to come back. I told him—

MOXIE  You wanted? . . . Whatchu do to her.

DISCIPLE  Nothing.

MOXIE  This why you be knocked up alone in a bed. You can't be allowing strange men anywhere near—

DISCIPLE  Are you one to talk?

MOXIE  Come again, Africa?

ABASIAMA  He is from my area, Moxie.

MOXIE  What kinda reason is that? Houston, Texas, big as hell. I don't let everybody near me 'cause they say they from Houston.

ABASIAMA  I know—I know that but he is here just to ensure—It is fine. I promise.

MOXIE  Go on and sit over there. I'm watching you.

DISCIPLE  It is I that is watching you.

ABASIAMA  Enough.

MOXIE  Yea. So. You leaving tomorrow! You excited?

ABASIAMA  Hm.

MOXIE  It's going to be alright, ya hear. You don't need a man. You got this!

DISCIPLE  She doesn't need a bad man.

MOXIE  They all bad—Ama you don't need one. You have yourself . . . and . . . maybe [me], especially if I get a—when I get a—
>  *Beat.*
>  . . . Hey, Ama . . .

ABASIAMA  Hm?

MOXIE  I know this ain't the right time but. I wanna drop it off so I can stop working the—Can you look it over for me.

DISCIPLE  What is this thing you all are trying to do? Instead let's go get the child and—

ABASIAMA  *(Correcting.)* I see her every day. She is fine. *(To Moxie.)* Bring it.
>  *Moxie rummages in her bag.*

MOXIE  I'm looking for it.

DISCIPLE  What is it you are about to be doing?

ABASIAMA  Don't worry it's not that important just—

MOXIE  You need to mind your business.

DISCIPLE  Abasiama. What is it now?

ABASIAMA  Mbọk, tre—Disciple, it's a simple thing.

MOXIE  English only.

DISCIPLE  I don't understand. Why this paper? Is it some sort of magic between you? How are the two of you connected?!

MOXIE  Jesus! She helping me with an application.

DISCIPLE  Why not do it yourself?

ABASIAMA  Disciple stop.

DISCIPLE  *(To Moxie.)* Why?
>  *Moxie is increasingly flustered.*

MOXIE  Cause I can't—

DISCIPLE  Can't what?

MOXIE  I can't—

ABASIAMA  Disciple.

DISCIPLE  *(Simple.)* Why do you want to fill it? You have a kind of job, right?

MOXIE  Yea, motherfucker I do—but I would like—like to live a little longer than my goddamn moth[er]—Let me go ask the nurse for a pen. Excuse me.
>  *Moxie exits. Silence.*

ABASIAMA  Bro Disciple.

DISCIPLE  Yes sistah—

ABASIAMA  I will risk sounding disrespectful so that you can hear me. That is a friend . . . Understand? . . . The one person I could talk to as big men ran scared. To say you respect me, means you respect her. The two of us are the same . . . Letters can be difficult for her. We filled that application together.

*Moxie enters holding a pen.*

MOXIE  *(Determined.)* Found one.

*Moxie beelines for Abasiama.*

Let's get this ended.

DISCIPLE  You. Hand me that application.

MOXIE  Hell no.

DISCIPLE  I won't hurt it.

MOXIE  *(To Abasiama.)* Look. This all I got.

DISCIPLE  Give it now.

ABASIAMA  Give to him.

*Moxie hands Disciple the paper while looking hard at Abasiama.*

DISCIPLE  It was my sister taught me how to read. Sometimes mothers cannot complete the duty assigned them. No fault of their own.

*Disciple drops to his knees with the paper in his hand.*

MOXIE  Whatchu doing?

DISCIPLE  Carving.

*Moxie moves to Disciple and drops down to her knees hesitantly.*

MOXIE  Give it back. That took a long time. *(Imploring to Abasiama.)* Ama . . .

DISCIPLE  *(Firm.)* Follow my hand.

MOXIE  Why?

DISCIPLE  *(Sharp.)* Keep your mouth closed and do it. *(Shift.)* I won't hurt it.

*Together they trace the outline of paper on the floor.*

*(Something he has said before.)* When you carve the space you want your spirit seeks after. The universe provides. That is the supreme rule. That job is yours. It can be none other than yours. In Jesus Christ's name it is so. Amen.

ABASIAMA  Amen.

MOXIE  Do I need to say amen . . . ? Amen.

*After Moxie's fingers finish tracing, Moxie looks at Disciple, wanting to say something. She cannot. She, instead, snatches back her paper.*

Okay. Cool. *(To Abasiama.)* Check it for me?

*Moxie hands Abasiama the application and the pen. Abasiama scans the document, quickly making corrections.*

ABASIAMA  Not bad, Moxie. I spelled some things over but not bad at all.

MOXIE  Really?!

*Moxie takes the paper back.*

I'm gonna make a clean copy and—You think they got an envelope at the desk? Imma send it out right after I clean it up. Finish it tonight! Know what, Imma be right back. Let me go see if they have one—

*Moxie turns to Disciple.*

Thank you.

DISCIPLE  Nothing.

> *Moxie exits. Disciple and Abasiama are alone. Disciple looks at her for long moments before—*

ABASIAMA  Is something the matter?

DISCIPLE  You're good to her. Even though she is not like you.

ABASIAMA  Well. That's just—why not?

> *Disciple becomes formal, steady and intent. His eyes never leave Abasiama.*

DISCIPLE  I go to Texas Southern.

ABASIAMA  Okay.

> *Beat.*

I have never seen you there.

DISCIPLE  I don't wander around. I am receiving a degree in Communications and . . . I'm developing my own thoughts for—

ABASIAMA  That is good for you.

DISCIPLE  I will be here until I obtain my most advanced degree. I've already begun writing my future doctoral thesis: *Nigerian Immigration: Reconceptualizing a Country.*

ABASIAMA  Okay.

DISCIPLE  When I return home I'll be a radio news journalist. As I'm older, teach in University.

ABASIAMA  Eh-heh. Good—

DISCIPLE  What do you study?

ABASIAMA  Biology.

DISCIPLE  Strong choice! Tomorrow start pumping that knowledge again. With or without him, education is our future.

ABASIAMA  You sound like my father.

DISCIPLE  I don't come from anything. I'm here alone. If you were to know me you could never meet my father. I have one brother. Ben Gun. He is no longer with me even though he breathes. Casualty of war.

ABASIAMA  Bro Disciple, accept my condolences.

DISCIPLE  That's the way of it. I saved for a long time to bring myself here. But I did it. I did it. I did that. I brought myself all the way to America.

ABASIAMA  Not an easy task I'm sure.

DISCIPLE  Why do you work?

ABASIAMA  I'm sorry?

DISCIPLE  Fiesta.

ABASIAMA  Oh. My husband has pigeon feet and I like to eat. I became smart quick.

DISCIPLE  Is he evil? To be this way?

ABASIAMA  No he is—

DISCIPLE  Not a man. I work. Walgreens. And in my spare moments I come to see you.
 . . . Between writing and studying and working—

ABASIAMA  I appreciate your concern but / you do not have—

DISCIPLE  My feet walk here. Of their own accord. I have a lot of work. I'm really cranking my brain. I should remain home but if I don't set my alarm to come, my mind fractures, and my studies are lost . . . You are the exact same skin color as my sister.

ABASIAMA  I am sure she is / beautiful—

DISCIPLE  She's passed on.

ABASIAMA  Wow . . . Bro. Okay. Wow.

DISCIPLE  No. Stop. I mention only because you remind me of her. Do you feel alone?

ABASIAMA  Eh?

DISCIPLE  Are you lonely here?

ABASIAMA  I don't / know.

DISCIPLE  My typewriter's my only lover. No one to marry me before I came. Are you / lonely?

ABASIAMA  I am fine.

DISCIPLE  Do you want somebody?

ABASIAMA  No.

DISCIPLE  I know you have someone.

ABASIAMA  Yes.

DISCIPLE  But everyone must have someone who is real. Reality. Real. Flesh and bone. When one is absent, God sends another. If I had been blessed with such a prize as you. Such a luck? I would not squander such bounty. Tell me about yourself. Something. Anything.

ABASIAMA  . . . Brother, nothing / Okay.

DISCIPLE  Tell me.

ABASIAMA  I don't know.

DISCIPLE  Sistah. Try.

· · ·

Please.

ABASIAMA  I come from Cross River—from Etinan—

DISCIPLE  I know this. Paint me your home.

ABASIAMA  Are you serious?

DISCIPLE  Yes.

ABASIAMA  . . . Okay. My house—my house it was big and—I don't know and . . . and white. Had blue shutters and lots of land around it. And—hey—my daddy—that man—how I miss that man . . . Well we were one of the only families to have a car in Etinan. A—this Peugeot. And a bicycle and motorcycle and—

DISCIPLE  Church?

ABASIAMA  Apostolic. You and church.

DISCIPLE  Mine was not Apostolic, but I have heard miracles happen in there. Tell me more.

ABASIAMA  More? More what?

DISCIPLE  More everything. Stories of home keep us tethered here.

ABASIAMA  . . . Secondary school . . . have you heard of Cornelia Connelly School for girls? Because that's where I went. And I loved it. Oh, I remember it. It was such a schedule. But at night. Night time there could be fun. I remember this my roommate was scared of the dark though. This mouse used to chew the skin from the pads of her feet—

DISCIPLE  More!

ABASIAMA  Okay now. And, my favorite part of—

DISCIPLE  (Almost to himself.) Yes.

ABASIAMA  When I was home? You know, I would go with all of my cousins to the river right. Hm . . .

> Abasiama closes her eyes as she slips into reverie. In the air, unbeknownst to Abasiama, Disciple's fingers outline her body. He carves her out.

We would carry water. For miles we walked and. Talking and walking. Picking the fruit and just easy fun. It took the day. Sometimes they would swim. And that's when. Hey!

> Abasiama's eyes open.

That's when I turned off, I don't like the water. I didn't want it to overpower me. I only let it touch my toes. They mocked me oh like I was a—

> Moxie barges in . . .

MOXIE  That nurse is a piece of work! Sheeiiit. So much trouble for one envelope?! Goddamn . . . Air got real thick in here people.

## SCENE 3

*May 10, 1978, early evening. Abasiama holds the baby kangaroo-style.*[*] *Moments pass as she holds her, rocking. A sudden thought hits Abasiama. Abasiama closes her eyes and holds the baby off the side of the bed. Critical seconds pass. Abasiama opens her eyes and brings the baby back from danger and back into the kangaroo hold. Rocking.*

ABASIAMA  (*Simple.*) I'm to call you Mebǫkǫ. . . . Yet you came in God's time. 36 weeks. So then, Iniabasi. Iniabasi. Iniabasi, cry.[†]

*Abasiama jostles the baby.*

Cry.

*She jostles the baby again.*

Cry your father home.

## SCENE 4

*Even later that same night. Moxie has returned. Moxie sits at the foot of the bed while Abasiama holds her child. They watch TV.*

*After moments Moxie shuts it off. She rises and drags her pillow to the floor.*

ABASIAMA  What are you doing . . .

MOXIE  It's time. We been watching for hours. And . . . it's late and. Lemme get the nurse so they can take her.

ABASIAMA  Come back.

MOXIE  Nah. You need your space.

ABASIAMA  We were fine.

MOXIE  I know but—

ABASIAMA  You like the floor?

MOXIE  No.

---

[*] Kangaroo-style is a skin-to-skin method of anchoring a baby to their caregiver. This method is especially soothing/connective for preterm babies.

[†] Abasiama does not follow Ukpong's desires and instead takes power and names her own child.

ABASIAMA  So then come back—

MOXIE  Won't you feel squished?

ABASIAMA  No.

MOXIE  But—

ABASIAMA  Okay. Take the floor then.

*Moxie tentatively lies next to Abasiama.*

MOXIE  Bed is nicer than the floor. So.

*Moxie tries to take up as little space as possible. Abasiama looks at her, mildly miffed.*

ABASIAMA  I stink . . . ?

MOXIE  Naw! I just wanna make sure you comfortable.

ABASIAMA  Eh-eh. Put your head on my pillow.

*Moxie does.*

Stretch your legs. Look! They can touch mine oh. I'm not diseased! Shamed but not diseased.

*Moxie does.*

Moxie, ease yourself. At times you behave very awkward.

MOXIE  I just. You doing a lot. This a lot. And. Thank you.

ABASIAMA  Stop the foolishness.

*Moxie looks at Iniabasi.*

MOXIE  You love her yet?

*Abasiama looks at her child and thinks. Abasiama nods, affirmative, after thinking about it.*

She hard to love?

*Abasiama nods affirmative.*

She don't look a thing like ya.

*Abasiama looks down at her baby and chuckles softly.*

(*Hard thing.*) Should have had a couple myself by now. Let 'em go though . . . What it feel like to have her?

ABASIAMA  Like having my worry on the outside of me.

MOXIE  Huh.

ABASIAMA  She *doesn't* look like me. As if I had nothing to do with any of it. Even the hair. These coiled little balls of—I don't have that

MOXIE  If I was you I don't know what I'd do / with her.

ABASIAMA  Where is he, Moxie?

MOXIE  Sure to God I don't know and why the hell you still care?

 . . .

Look. You the god-dang genius, okay.

*Moxie picks up a textbook nearby.*

Even the pictures be looking complicated. Compared to this, nothing can be that hard.

ABASIAMA  You all have been born with how to—Moxie, tree does not fall without ikwa. I don't even know how to think on how to—

MOXIE  What's your favorite color.

ABASIAMA  Yellow. Why?

MOXIE  Check. Favorite food.

ABASIAMA  Moimoi. It's a ground—a kind of ground bean with—

MOXIE  Check. Try a hamburger, it's ground up. Favorite music.

ABASIAMA  Chief Commander Ebenezer Obey. King of jùjú.

MOXIE  Three choices in three seconds and you made 'em. You know what you like. And you know what you need to do. For yourself.

*Silence.*

ABASIAMA  . . . We don't separate ourselves like that. We can't. I feel like *(Bitter laughter as she moves from plural to singular.)* . . . I feel. Hm. Hey! Hear me. My own language does not have the exact word for— . . . Moxie? I—I think of pickles and Snickers and I like the taste. Iniabasi calls out to me and I can't even—my husband, Ukpong is not—there's no word, where I'm from, for what this is.

*Silence.*

. . . I think I'm going to call my father.

. . . Wow. I— . . . I am the first child of his to be here and if I go, I go back in—oh! Abasi . . . what is this?

MOXIE  . . . You gon' leave. 'Cause. If you tell your pops, and he a pops worth his salt, he gon' make you leave. If I was him I would.

ABASIAMA  I don't know.

MOXIE  You gon' stay.

ABASIAMA  I don't know.

MOXIE  Cause if you did and you needed like a roommate? When I get this job it could be real like. I ain't never had no roommate, or a job so. We could try it out. That is if you stay, or if you can.

. . .

. . .

Your choice.

ABASIAMA  Hm. Moxie. *(Sucks her teeth.)* My choice.

MOXIE  . . . I brought you something! I'm happy you said you like 'em so much 'cause—

*Moxie gets up and rummages in her sack. She retrieves a Snickers bar and lies back down.*

Here.

ABASIAMA  Hey! My favorite American pastime. Snickers!

MOXIE  Yea. I spent my last little bit until—till I, yea but—Well. Snickers! . . . Tomorrow's the day. Imma wake up early and see if maybe I can swipe us a doughnut. You ever had one? They these cakes . . . kinda look like little toy tires. And they sweet. There ones filled with jelly and then you got others covered in chocolate and sprinkles or coconut and—

ABASIAMA  I like coconuts now!

MOXIE  Gal you is too funny. A coconut doughnut, then. Breakfast.

ABASIAMA  . . . Okay.

MOXIE  Okay! Cool. Lemme go get the nurse so she can take Iniabasi outta here. You want anything else while I'm—[out there?]

*Abasiama pulls Moxie close with her free hand and hugs her.*

Ama. Girl. I can't breathe.

. . .

. . .

You alright?

*Abasiama grabs Moxie's wrist.*

You checking my pulse . . . ?

ABASIAMA  Bimbim. Bimbim. Bimbim. That's your sound. Back home I had this one good friend named Itogowo. She should be in Atlanta now with her new husband. We used to check each other and measure. It is important to know your friend's sound. That way, when you lose her, you can always remember some path back.

MOXIE  I ain't never checked no pulse like that before.

(*Sudden, honest, and direct.*) . . . Ama? I really wanna get better. Like better-better. And I think I can do it—I can learn more . . . more words than I know . . . and then maybe, maybe once I do that—

*Uncomfortable silence.*

Once I do that we can—

ABASIAMA  Moxie, all things run through God. Ask Him for what you need, then believe. God opens the way.

*Abasiama drops Moxie's wrist. Moxie exits and Abasiama closes her eyes.*

## SCENE 5

*May 11, 1978, 11:00 a.m. Disciple arrives at the hospital carrying many bags. He walks with purpose toward Abasiama's room. Moxie enters moments after, carrying a box of doughnuts.*

MOXIE  Hey. Hey! D! Uh . . . Disciple! D! Wait up.

*Moxie runs after Disciple to reach him. Disciple may or may not hear Moxie. (Winded but finally caught up.)* Hey!

DISCIPLE  Good morning.

MOXIE  Hey brotha! You heading in there right?

DISCIPLE  Where else would I be going?

MOXIE  I was hoping—before we go in—could I ask you something? What you did to my paper? Where'd you learn that?

DISCIPLE  Carving?

MOXIE  Yea—

DISCIPLE  My sister taught me.

*Disciple re-shifts his bags and starts toward Abasiama's door.*

MOXIE  Yo, why don't you like me?

DISCIPLE  . . .

MOXIE  Know what? Forget it. It'll be alright. Men either love me or they hate me. Nature of the business.

DISCIPLE  I don't hate. Are you trying to goad me? . . . You are fine, Moxie.

MOXIE  Uh-huh . . . uh-huh. You right. I'm fine.

*Beat as Moxie tries to move into conversation.*

Look. I'm gonna get that job. You know I can feel it? My life—My life is—Man, brotha my life is gonna—

DISCIPLE  Good!

MOXIE  Hey. You like Ama? I mean, I seen the way you look at her.

DISCIPLE  She's a woman.

MOXIE  I mean, I know that. But it was too clear when I walked in that room how you—She nice right?

DISCIPLE  . . .

MOXIE  Right?

DISCIPLE  She is very—she's good.

MOXIE  She is! She was the first person who really, you know, she really . . . Like, I got this fake friend Crystal—

DISCIPLE  We should enter in there.

MOXIE  No. I swear. I am about to make sense.

*Disciple places the cumbersome bags on the ground.*

I got this fake friend Crystal. We been in the game together since we was like thirteen. She don't even think to want more—I mean—And she better than me. She came from better. She sorta knows more, you know. She knew more than me anyway. I mean not a lot more, 'cause she dumb. But. She *could* go back if she straightened out. Sheeiiit. If I had half of what y'all's parents did for you or wanna do for you. Or even what you do for each other. Except for Yuckpong. I mean. If I had that? I could be a star. I really could be. I just gotta move outta what I—You get what I'm saying right? Like, if I had parents? A compound? Ama always talking 'bout this compound shit. Like you! You musta had a groovy compound. People carving their destinies and—golly. Golly, Disciple, golly!

DISCIPLE  Ama is waiting—

MOXIE  Every kid here needs a compound and parents and—

DISCIPLE  I don't have parents.

MOXIE  Ama said all Africans have—

DISCIPLE  No.

MOXIE  Nuh-uh man. It's different over there.

DISCIPLE  Life is what you believe.

MOXIE  Huh?

DISCIPLE  What is your thesis, Moxie.

MOXIE  I don't—I don't know. I just like y'all. Y'all like my—I don't know. This probably sound stupid but—I'm Annamae Wilis from the gas station compound and I got me a family of—

DISCIPLE  Who is Annamae.

MOXIE  Me! My name Annamae! My moms named me that. She called me that before she. Anyway. One of her guys say I had moxie so. Moxie stuck. D, I don't know what the fuck I'm trying to say. Just. Ama is really nice . . . like really inside, nice . . . and you prayed on my paper so. If she decides to stay maybe you could carve us a house—she gonna be my roommate and—you know I ain't ever really asked for nothing big, but lately, shit seem to be working and . . .

DISCIPLE  She is not staying.

MOXIE  What?

DISCIPLE  . . . She was never staying.

MOXIE  She ain't decide nothing yet.

*Small silence.*

You know something? She told you something she ain't tol' me?

DISCIPLE  No.

MOXIE  Then why you actin' tight and shit?

DISCIPLE  ...

MOXIE  She made up her mind already? But—no, I saw her yesterday and she say she didn't know. Disciple, I don't get it—I don't understand—you know something!

    *Silence.*

DISCIPLE  I once knew a woman. Perhaps quite like your own mother. Whenever I asked for something, she would give the exact opposite of what I needed. My body grew trice her size, and still, I never stopped needing. Always needing. It was my sister who taught me how to survive this life. We've both tasted hunger. Our experiences make us the same. I cannot hate you. I know where you hurt.

MOXIE  You ain't know me, or my—

DISCIPLE  And I know Ama. She is different.

MOXIE  Yea. She is! I know that already—

DISCIPLE  I am not trying to cause pain, Moxie.

MOXIE  You ain't doing shit!—

DISCIPLE  Annamae. Listen now.

MOXIE  Don't call me like you know me. I don't understand what the fuck your problem is, so call me by my fake-ass name!

DISCIPLE  Moxie. I know you know this. Somewhere inside of you, where you are shoving niggling feelings into dark corners and trying to drink hope? Believe me, I know—

MOXIE  Motherfucker you are fucking pissing me off—

DISCIPLE  Please. Let me do this for you. You and I, we are the two free radicals roaming around. Right? Making life up in any way that we can. Spinning fantasies from thin air. But think. Think far into the future. If her daddy comes, can the two of you still be friends? How well do you even know her? I can at least hide under the cloak of the familiar. What of you?

MOXIE  Uh-uh. She my friend.

DISCIPLE  For now. Yes.

MOXIE  If her daddy comes—

DISCIPLE  When / he—

MOXIE  If motherfucker, IF her daddy come, Imma tell him! Imma tell him. "I'm the ace that took care of her when she felt down." And—and "Even though I'm born this way, I ain't have no intention of staying this way and—"

DISCIPLE   Moxie. What can you give her that furthers her—

MOXIE   Friendship motherfucker! And when I get my job Imma pay. I'll pay. I would never—

DISCIPLE   Okay, but how long till you are on your feet?

MOXIE   I am moving as fast as I can!—

DISCIPLE   You are becoming attached to a forever, Moxie!

MOXIE   She's my friend! That what this is? Naw! Naw! You gotta find another piece. I been waiting for somebody like her since before I even knew I needed her. She mine. You can't have her!

DISCIPLE   I've been waiting too! For forever and a day. From Nigeria to here. My own people dying and no one for me! Okay?! My brain turning into nothing here. Until I see her. I see her and I can write sentences. Full ones. Complete. It's complete! I couldn't wait anymore. The moment I saw her and realized she was good. I carved her out. For me.

MOXIE   You did what?

DISCIPLE   There will be someone soon for you. You have your paper. The person for you is coming.

MOXIE   You did what?! You a thief! You knew I needed her. More than you did. You knew it! More than—

DISCIPLE   Not more than me!—

MOXIE   Disciple, she's my—my insides are . . . inside me be breaking up and. Breaking down. D. You gotta let me have—you can untrace her and—or—

DISCIPLE   I learned a long time ago, Moxie, that no matter what, you always receive exactly what you need.

*Moxie stares at Disciple in disbelief. In these precious moments we see how young Moxie actually is.*

Moxie . . . ?

MOXIE   *(An escalation.)* Leave. Leave me alone. Leave me alone, leave me alone, leave me alone leavemealoneleavemealoneleavemealone / leave—

*Moxie drops the doughnuts. Disciple stoops to pick them up.*

DISCIPLE   Moxie! Shh now / we're in a public—

MOXIE   Motherfucker! If you don't get the fuck out my face right now—right now. RIGHT NOW. RIGHT—

*Disciple picks up the doughnuts and carries them into Abasiama's room. Moxie's breath is heaving, her world imploding 20 feet from Abasiama's door.*

## SCENE 6

*May 11, 1978. A little after 11:15 a.m., just moments after the prior scene. Abasiama is packing her small things and, even though she doesn't have to, out of respect she will fold down her bedding. Iniabasi is in a makeshift, portable bassinet, something the hospital could/would have given her.*

ABASIAMA  Where is Moxie?

DISCIPLE  ...

ABASIAMA  Disciple?

DISCIPLE  ...

ABASIAMA  Sit there. Are you sick? I thought I heard her voice outside. That nurse and her are oil and water oh.

*Disciple hands Abasiama the box of doughnuts.*

Why? We were supposed to share these together.

DISCIPLE  *(Muttered.)* She will reappear again. Reincarnate. Stronger.

ABASIAMA  Eh? I can't understand your murmuring.

DISCIPLE  I feel it. She's on her path. Her soft places will grow tough and— She's young yet—how old?

ABASIAMA  Moxie? Twenty or so.

DISCIPLE  No. Not more than sixteen. See? See that? She has time to grow past—

ABASIAMA  No. She's not that young. This air around you. What is this energy, Disciple? Where is she?

DISCIPLE  Moxie Annamae. Annamae is fine. Can I assist you?

ABASIAMA  She's not here.

DISCIPLE  No. She had a sudden realization and had to go. Don't blame her.

...

...Can I help?

ABASIAMA  ...There's nothing more to do.

DISCIPLE  My father should be my intercedent—is that a proper English word? Intercedent? ... Hey! Who knows.

*Disciple unpacks his bags. He formally and precisely lays garri, atama, seeds, smoked fish, and African lace before Abasiama. The weight of the offering thickens the air.*

In this I am very green. I have never opened my mouth this way before.

...

I don't know your mother or your father but I know them because of how you are. They raised a good girl. What my hands offer you now is not worth—If I had had more I would give; however, this is the current limit of my pocket.

. . .

Abasiama, I am asking for what is not mine. You are not mine but—and, so, I am willing to work to earn mere quarters of you.

. . .

It may not even matter. It might have been done for nothing.

ABASIAMA  What has been done?

DISCIPLE  You must tell me it wasn't for nothing—no—See? See me? I am busy. Very busy. I came to this country only to write and then go back and—

ABASIAMA  Disciple. What is done?

DISCIPLE  I am well aware that you belong to someone. But in the event—In case he is no longer for you. I offer. I will take you.

ABASIAMA  Hm. You are just lonely.

DISCIPLE  Yes. Yes no. I will take all of you—every part of you—even the the ugly parts—at your worst, you are better than me oh.

ABASIAMA  . . . You are some sort of strange—it's like you—you came right at this moment. Not one second before. Not one second after.

DISCIPLE  Yes.

ABASIAMA  Bro, I have too much swirling, and ehm—there are many women. Find one that can warm you.

DISCIPLE  Yes.

ABASIAMA  Find one.

DISCIPLE  I have. I am looking on her.

ABASIAMA  Thank you but—

DISCIPLE  No. Thank Him. Sistah, I thank Him. I thank Him for the little ease you have brought. A glimmer—a spark—a—a spark of hope, a ray of light, a smile without consequence hey—Hey! See me? You can make me poet academic.

. . .

It's the last of my dried food here. I know I should bring you fresh things but . . . Use this to make yourself a good soup.

*Disciple moves some of Abasiama's belongings toward the door. Abasiama stands in the middle of the strange movement.*

## SCENE 7

*Later that same day. Late afternoon/early evening. Ukpong, in a tight,*
*contained panic, waits on the couch. Abasiama enters into her apartment,*
*bassinet in hand.*

UKPONG  Abasiama!

*Ukpong sees the child.*

. . .

. . .

My God I— . . . Mebọkọ . . . ?

*Ukpong touches Iniabasi gently. Abasiama, proper, sits on the couch. Her*
*back straight. Her eyes on her husband. Silently, unflinchingly, she examines*
*the man she was given.*

(*Soft.*) A girl . . . Sweet . . . she looks like—

*Ukpong's gaze moves from the baby to his wife. He meets her eyes.*

(*Drops his eyes.*) Abasiama. Ama? I can explain.

*Ukpong sinks to his knees.*

Let me tell you what happened. I'll say what makes you understand.

. . .

. . .

. . . The night I left you . . . ? I had had my Guinness, heard my radio,
looked out our window, saw outside and—I wanted to—

. . .

I told myself, I was—was just going to grab some more beer. More—But.
No—I walked, okay. I walked. Watching, and trying to be how I saw these
bigheaded Texas-Americans living because—nobody chains them! They
are the owners of their own thought. I wanted—one time! to do that, one
real time before I die. Ama I didn't know . . .

. . .

Who was the Ukpong that married you, eh?

. . .

You didn't love me when you first met me. Or—no. I think we—we. No!
Our fathers made it such, that we never looked at each other and said this
love is our original. I learned here, that for some, that is a right! Then this
our whole marriage? Someone else's design! I don't know—I didn't know if
I put that baby inside your stomach because I wanted it to be there inside
you, or if it happened because the ancestors told me that that was the plan.
My life has never been my own! I wanted to—

ABASIAMA  (*Simple.*) What am I to do with that?

UKPONG  I came back! All this freedom, and you see them, and they behave like . . . like. And I've seen it. Okay—can you hear me? Our ways are better.

. . .

(*Soft.*) Our daddies experienced everything so we wouldn't have to. I cannot undo that their long history. Ama. I, Ukpong Ekpeyong, open up my mouth and say. It is you. It must be [you] . . .

. . .

(*Softest soft.*) Maybe you can go away. For— . . . for eight-nine-ten days. A month . . . however long you need. Go away and see, for your own good, if on your own, you can—

*Uncomfortable* . . .

. . . Maybe after, maybe we can start this over again. The same thing but better.

*Silence.*

*In this discomfort, Ukpong takes Iniabasi out of her bassinet and holds her, waiting. Abasiama reaches under a couch pillow and retrieves the official-looking letter.*

ABASIAMA  (*Soft.*) What is this letter? . . . Almost four years and twelve credits? You choose me with twelve credits.

*Ukpong, with hands full, gets closer, trying to soothe Abasiama. Abasiama remains firm, that letter never leaves her hands.*

First time you [vanished] I called the police. I thought you were in serious danger. Five minutes after they left this house you returned. I had to call back and apologize, sounding like another stupid, worrisome wife. Next time? I recalled every phone number in the world trying to see if I could reach you. Next time? I stood in that corner crying for you. Waiting. I'm very used to you.

. . . What a beautiful plan. I can now go away and take eight days. Hm. Ukpong. Hm . . .

. . . What if I had had the same desires as you, hm? What then. See how you wind time? Whenever you have the feeling, you move. But what of me? How would I have gone away to learn? How do I do anything? I can't just walk unburdened on the street. You can put down your father to learn yourself. My daddy is my red blood and your life swelled my belly. The pain of her? . . . constricting my breath.

UKPONG  We can change that. Take what I had. Do what I did.

ABASIAMA  Oh be quiet.

UKPONG  Yell or scream. That can make you feel better.

>*Abasiama laughs.*

ABASIAMA  Let me not be quick-oh. Maybe besides words you brought gifts to fill me. What did you bring?

>*Ukpong pulls out a record from underneath his couch. He finds the media shattered.*

UKPONG  It wasn't—I don't—I don't know what happen here—When I was here last it wasn't—

ABASIAMA  You must have something real—something sweet for me in your hands.

UKPONG  This is what I have—I thought—

ABASIAMA  Hey husband! Bid high! Once you know, as you say you know, you have to bid higher than before you knew. Taking your words and your gifts into highest regard, and without my father here, Ukpong. My most favorite color / in this world is yellow and—

UKPONG  Ama! The plan was / to—

ABASIAMA  (*Explosive.*) What plan? There can be no planning between us! Stand in your letter fully. Risk that for yourself, please. School ends for you next week? Unless you possess powerful jùjú, I don't know how you'll complete all your missing credits by then. And they've told you. They are not renewing your education. No more extensions. No more summer school. And I've never known student visa to work without institution. It's the end. May you do better back home.

>*Abasiama holds out hands for Iniabasi. Ukpong holds on to Iniabasi tightly.*

UKPONG  Wait now. Please wait . . . Ama? Are you—Ama. How long can I keep Mebọkọ / before I—

ABASIAMA  Iniabasi! Ukpong, there is no such thing as your Mebọkọ. I gave the right name. Iniabasi. In. God's. Time. She came in God's time. And you are so very late. Give her over.

>*Abasiama looks at her daughter content in Ukpong's arms.*

>(*Discovery.*) . . . Ah.

>*She looks at Ukpong and the contented baby. A sudden understanding finds words.*

>Wow. It's the exact same kind of love you had for me . . .

>(*To Iniabasi.*) Mountains of desire and a bitterbitter river of burden . . .

>*Abasiama takes her baby herself. Iniabasi cries. She places her right hand on Iniabasi's head and blesses her child.*

>Ini. My daughter.

. . . My name is Abasiama and *I* . . . *I* carried you. I am the woman who gave you your name. And . . . and I am the one who will make our line strong . . . I shall see you again soooo soon my darling. You must enjoy those people on that compound for me oh because—hey! You will dance with the multiples. Multiples of grandmas, aunties, cousins . . . all of them? Just for you. One great big fiesta.

Ukpong, she must never ever ever taste this kind of lonely.

. . . Iniabasi? Remember my voice oh.

*Abasiama kisses Iniabasi's forehead and puts the child back in Ukpong's hands. Ukpong takes the child, Iniabasi calms instantly.*

*Abasiama retrieves her coat, satchel, and textbooks and exits. She stands outside the door. What Abasiama has done and what Abasiama intends to do unmoors her. When she can, she snatches composure, shoving all that emotion somewhere deep, down and away. She breathes and looks around her. She takes in this world. She takes it all in and, when she's ready, she takes a step forward.*

*Blackout.*

•       •       •

# TRANSLATIONS

## Canoe Song

mme nti usen eboyo afit nti ŋkpọ eboyo
niehe owo nteket se ŋdọŋ esit
*very good days gone by everything passes away*
*I have nobody to comfort my soul I paddle my own canoe*

mme nti usen atimme edi afit nti ŋkpọ atimme edi
menie owo se ŋdọŋ esit nwat ubom mi ye afo
*good days return all good things have come back*
*I found somebody to comfort my soul I paddle my boat with you*

## Disciple's Monologue

DISCIPLE  *(Out loud, to himself.)*

Ŋyin itoho Nigeria ima ikpọŋ iduŋ ŋyin. Ŋyin isinamma ŋkpọ ntoro— *(Whispers his coherent thoughts into his typewriter.)* Mme enie akuk enọ nditọ mmọ eka iduŋ mfia owo ekekpep ŋwed mbak mmọ eda ukara. Mmọ ema ema mmọ enyọŋ eka Nigeria ekediọŋ eyuŋ ebọp Nigeria nnọ afọn.

We that come from Nigeria have left our country. We don't do things that way— *(Whispers his coherent thoughts into his typewriter.)* People who have money send their children to the white man's country to go learn so that they can rule. And when they're done they go back to Nigeria to make it good/build Nigeria.

## Phrases

Ama, idem fo? Idem afọn?
*Ama, how are you? Are you well?*

Because eke mmi afọn!
*Because I am doing very well!*

Afo adi America ndien afo afre se akedi nam—"piam!"
*You come to America and forget everything you're supposed to do like—"piam!"*

Uduaŋ ŋkpọ, ata uduaŋ ŋkpọ!
*Shit, pure shit!*

Sese itie emi anam mien.
*See what this place has made me.*

Afo odo owo ekenọhọ ensọk mien.
*You are the one that was given to me.*

Ete mmi, mbọk suk tie.
*Papa, please sit down.*

Aya nnọ ŋkpọ mfin sibi inyaŋa mien.
*You will give me something to help me.*

Mmeyem uwam uto fien akonoyo emi.
*I need your help tonight.*

Mbọk, mmeyem uwam uto fien akonoyo emi.
*Please, I need help from you tonight.*

Bro, nsido? Ameyem uwam akonoyo emi?
*Bro, what's wrong? You need help tonight?*

Mmọŋ idip mi abomo
*My water has broken.*

Eti awowan. Ndisuk ndidi tutu afo ataŋ ikọ ye ami.
*Good lady. I will keep coming back until you talk to me.*

## Words and References

| | | | |
|---|---|---|---|
| Aba die | *Hello* | Ikon | *Melon seed* |
| Abasi | *God* | Ikwa | *Machete* |
| Bet | *Patience/calm* | Ita | *Three* |
| Chin-chin | *Sweet, fried, crunchy dessert* | Kiet | *One* |
| | | Mbọk | *Please* |
| Edikaŋ ikọŋ soup | *Water-leaf soup* | Mebọkọ | *Flight/escape* |
| Ekpuk | *Family cluster* | Ndiọŋọke | *I don't know* |
| Ete | *Father (sweet terminology, akin to "papa")* | Nsido | *What is it?/What's wrong?* |
| | | Sai | *My god/See this/ An exclamatory* |
| Ete mmi | *My papa* | | |
| Etinan | *A town in Cross River State, Nigeria (now in Akwa Ibom State)* | Sọsoŋọ | *Thank you* |
| | | Stockfish | *Rock-hard dried codfish Stop* |
| Garri | *Shredded, fried, and then dried cassava root. Quite cheap.* | Tre | *Fufu* |
| | | Usuŋ | *A city in Cross River State,* |
| | | Uyo | *Nigeria (now the capital of Akwa Ibom State)* |
| Iba | *Two* | | |

## Recipe for Mma's Edikaŋ Ikọŋ Soup (from memory)

Half a large saucepot of assorted meat (beef, tripe, offal, game)

2 large pieces of stockfish (presoaked and tender)

Pieces of dry smoked fish

A handful's worth of washed and shelled snails

A handful's worth of washed and shelled periwinkles

Half a spoonful of ground crayfish

A sprinkling of ground hot red pepper

1 fresh thinly sliced scotch bonnet pepper

Fresh ikọŋ ubọŋ (pumpkin leaves), washed and shredded

Fresh mmọŋ mmọŋ ikọŋ (water-leaf), prepared and washed

Many spoonfuls of palm oil

Salt

Wash and/or clean the assorted meats thoroughly. Cut the meat into chunks and boil. Add salt, ground red pepper, and sliced scotch bonnet pepper. Add the stockfish, smoked fish, de-shelled snails, and periwinkles to the pot. Add more water if needed. Add the fresh ikọŋ ubọŋ and fresh mmọŋ mmọŋ ikọŋ to the pot. From there, add crayfish and palm oil. Cook until done.

Serve with pounded yam. Enjoy.

# Coleman '72

## CHARLIE OH

### Characters

JAMES: Korean. The father.
ANNIE: Korean. The mother.
JENN: Korean American. The oldest.
MICHELLE: Korean American. The middle child.
JOEY: Korean American. The youngest.

### Time and Place

Many places and times across America.

### Notes

( ) indicates dialogue spoken in Korean.
The play moves with pace, it should run 90–100 minutes.
Find the love.

Please note that the Korean dialogue has been romanized with the actors and not standardization in mind.

**1.**

*Somewhere neither here nor there.*

JENN  No, it was brown.

MICHELLE  Or yellow? Was it yellow?

JENN  Brown. The awning was brown. I remember.

JOEY  I could have sworn the awning was blue.

MICHELLE  Brown, blue, does it really matter?

JENN  You're right. You're right! It's fine. The awning was blue.

JOEY  I'm not saying that—

JENN  It was blue! It was blue.

JOEY  Man! It was a fun trip.

MICHELLE  It's all hitting me, coming back to me.

JOEY  It was a fun trip, right?

JENN  Yeah. Yeah for sure.

JOEY  Okay. So it was the first day of summer.

JENN  No it wasn't.

MICHELLE  Are you sure?

JENN  Sorry. But it totally wasn't. We'd been out of school for a week.

JOEY  I remember it being the first day of summer.

MICHELLE  So do I.

JENN  Mom was about to drive you to summer camp.

JOEY  It was baseball practice.

MICHELLE  I thought you'd quit by then?

JOEY  I quit in eighth grade, for track.

MICHELLE  Eighth grade, right.

JENN  We'd been out of school for a week. I remember it was a week. But it's fine. Keep going.

JOEY  But it definitely was a Coleman, right? It was a Coleman trailer.

MICHELLE  I thought it was a Puma trailer?

JENN  No, a Coleman trailer. He's right.

MICHELLE  A Coleman. Got it.

JENN  We were young.

JOEY  We were so young.

MICHELLE  I remember.

JOEY  I remember.

JENN  I remember so much.

MICHELLE  I remember he drove that trailer straight into the driveway.

JENN  The Buick could barely pull it.

MICHELLE  And Mom's face?

JOEY  Mom's face . . .

MICHELLE  Mom's face when he pulled that trailer up . . .

## 2.

*A house in Glendale, Wisconsin, outside of Milwaukee. James stands in the front driveway. Annie, Jenn, Michelle, and Joey stand at the door to the house. They're all looking at the trailer pulled into the driveway, but we don't see it.*

ANNIE  What is this?

JAMES  It's a trailer.

ANNIE  And?

JAMES  A Coleman 1972 Tent Camper trailer.

JOEY  Awesome.

ANNIE  Shh. Why do you have a trailer.

JAMES  Why does anyone get a trailer? To drive with it.

ANNIE  Where are you going?

JAMES  We're driving to California.

ANNIE  Driving?

JENN  We?

MICHELLE  Oh my god.

ANNIE  Language.

JOEY  Awesome.

JAMES  See the trailer pulls out on each side—here and here. I got it used so it's defective, apparently we have to be careful opening both sides at the same time. But it's cheaper, eh?

ANNIE  Driving to California.

JAMES  Yes.

ANNIE  For your research trip.

JAMES  Yes.

ANNIE  That the university fellowship is funding.

JAMES  Yes.

ANNIE  You were flying.

JAMES  Yes.

ANNIE  But now you're driving?

JAMES  No.

ANNIE  No?

JAMES  We are driving.

ANNIE  When?

JAMES  There're three beds.

ANNIE  I don't understand.

JAMES  So the girls will share on one side and we will share on the other. Joey in the middle.

ANNIE  I understand that. But when?

JAMES  Today. We're leaving today.

JENN  How long will we be gone?

JAMES  That's the great thing about this camper. We don't have to decide as long as I get it back by the end of the summer.

ANNIE  The end of the summer?

JENN  The end of the summer?

JAMES  I know your Marquette pre-med enrichment camp starts in August. Before August.

ANNIE  Why?

JAMES  No hotel fees! Isn't that great?

ANNIE  Why the camper?

JAMES  I just said, no hotel fees.

ANNIE  Why are we all going?

JAMES  It's a chance to see America! A Coleman camper, a Buick, and the open plains. We're like old western cowboys.

JOEY  What about my baseball camp?

JAMES  We can practice together.

MICHELLE  And band camp?

JAMES  She does so much in school already.

JOEY  What about Jenn's cheer camp?

JAMES  Cheer camp?

JENN  I'm not doing cheer camp.

ANNIE  We canceled cheer camp.

JAMES  She canceled cheer camp.

JENN  For enrichment.

JAMES  Pre-med enrichment.

JOEY  Oh.

ANNIE  But what about all of those things?

JAMES  This is better. This is an adventure!

JOEY  This camper is so cool . . .

JENN  Joey.

ANNIE  (What is going on?) ('Musun-niriya?) (무슨 일이야?)

JAMES  (We need to talk.) (Uri 'yegijome.) (우리 얘기좀 해.)

MICHELLE  What is he saying? What are you saying?

JOEY  Will we get to see the Grand Canyon?!

JAMES  That's part of the plan.

JENN  Are you serious right now?

MICHELLE  What about our friends?

JOEY  I've always wanted to see the Grand Canyon.

ANNIE  Girls. Joey.

JENN  Yes?

MICHELLE  Mom?

ANNIE  James?

JAMES  Annie.

ANNIE  We're driving?

JAMES  We're driving.

ANNIE  Inside.

JENN  We're actually going?

ANNIE  Suitcases are in the basement, there might be more under my bed.
    Pull them out and start picking out clothes.

JENN  You can't be serious.

MICHELLE  What is even happening right now?

ANNIE  Girls?

JENN  Yes?

ANNIE  Now.

JENN  But—

ANNIE  Now.

JOEY  Can I look inside the—

ANNIE  Now.

        *The kids all head inside the house.*

ANNIE  (What happened to flying?) (Biheng-gi ta-giro han-gun?) (비행기
    타기로 한건.)

JAMES  (This is better.) (E-gae na-ah.) (이게 나아.)

ANNIE  (We paid for all their camps.) (Aedeul camph bido da neh-jjan-ah.)
    (애들 캠프비도 다 냈잖아.)

JAMES  (I called. We can get most of the money back. Think of the adventure
    we can give the children.) (Cjunhwa-haet-ssuh. Guh-eui da hwanbul hae

jun-dae. Aedul-e ulman-ah jo-ah halji saeng-gak hae-bwa.) (전화했어. 거의 다 환불 해준대. 애들이 얼마나 좋아 할지 생각해봐.)

JOEY   (*O.S.*) Woah there, hold up.

> *A shift.*
>
> *Annie and James stop.*
>
> *Joey, Michelle, and Jenn reenter.*

JOEY   We don't speak Korean.

JENN   But they would have. What? I'm just saying if you're going to tell a story, you better tell it right. You better tell what happened.

MICHELLE   When it comes to speaking Korean, none of us can do more than count to ten and order soju.

JENN   I can count to like, twenty at least. Alright, fine.

> *The world starts up again. Joey, Michelle, and Jenn watch Annie and James repeat the scene.*

ANNIE   What happened to flying?

JAMES   This is better.

ANNIE   We paid for all their camps.

JAMES   I called. We can get most of the money back. Think of the adventure we can give the children.

> *A pause.*

ANNIE   We'll need to pack groceries.

JAMES   Yes?

ANNIE   Groceries and snacks for the road so we are not stopping too much.

JAMES   Yes.

ANNIE   If we pack in the next hour we can make it to the grocery store before lunch.

JAMES   Tell them to pack light.

ANNIE   We can eat at the grocery store and be on the road with time before dinner.

JAMES   I bought us a guidebook from AAA. There is a campground in Madison and one in Mason City if we make good time.

ANNIE   I have kimchee and banchan in the kitchen we can pack right now.

JAMES   For sleeping make sure they bring sheets and blankets of their own.

ANNIE   Good. Good!

> *Annie heads inside to work.*

JAMES   Annie.

ANNIE  Yes?

JAMES  Annie thank you.

    *Annie can't help but grin.*

ANNIE  Does the camper have a stove? A fridge?

JAMES  I rented a Coleman stove and cooler as well.

ANNIE  I'll pack utensils and plates.

    *Annie smiles and heads inside.*

MICHELLE  What is it, Jenn?

    *A shift.*

    *Annie and James freeze before Annie gets to the door.*

JOEY  Are we gonna stop every five seconds?

JENN  It's nothing.

JOEY  Alright, let's keep moving—

JENN  But Mom didn't want to go on the trip.

JOEY  No she totally did.

MICHELLE  It was a fun trip.

JENN  Okay. Sure. Eventually. But she sent us inside so they could duke it out. They spent that whole spring fighting about what else? Money.

    *A shift. The world starts up again.*

ANNIE  There was money from the fellowship to fund this trip. What happened to the money from the fellowship?

JAMES  Do you know how expensive hotels are in Los Angeles? This spreads it out longer.

ANNIE  And their camps? We sat down and we budgeted money for their camps.

    *James hands Annie a letter. She doesn't need to read it.*

JAMES  His business failed.

ANNIE  Like his last business.

JAMES  He needed help.

ANNIE  He's always needing help.

JAMES  You've never met him.

ANNIE  And?

JAMES  It will be a good trip. We will make it up to them.

ANNIE  We can't just keep sending him money like we're some bank. We have our own lives to—

JAMES  He's my father.

ANNIE  You're *their* father.

    *A pause.*

ANNIE   We'll need to pack groceries.

JAMES   Yes?

ANNIE   Groceries and snacks for the road so we are not stopping too much.

JAMES   Yes.

*Annie heads inside.*

JAMES   Annie?

ANNIE   Yes?

JAMES   Annie thank you.

*James reaches out to hold Annie's hand. She pulls back.*

ANNIE   I'll pack utensils and plates.

*Annie steps inside.*

## 3.

*A shift.*

JENN   That's just how I remember it.

JOEY   Were you hiding in the bushes or something?

JENN   That's not what I'm saying, I just mean that—it doesn't matter. Onward! Road trip! Woo!

JOEY   So we started in Milwaukee.

JENN   Then Madison.

MICHELLE   Rushmore, I liked Rushmore.

JENN   The Badlands were . . . fine.

JOEY   But then Yellowstone!

MICHELLE   The Grand Tetons.

JOEY   And down to Los Angeles.

JENN   The Redwoods, you're forgetting the Redwoods.

MICHELLE   The Redwoods, then LA. Then through the desert.

JOEY   The Grand Canyon.

JENN   Well . . .

JOEY   Right. You're right.

JENN   Then Las Vegas.

JOEY   We didn't even get to see a show . . .

MICHELLE   And home.

**4.**

*A shift.*

*The car. Somewhere between Milwaukee and Madison. Annie reads from a AAA TripTik.*

ANNIE  It'll be your great American adventure! And it's all laid out in this book. Have you seen this, Jenn? It's more than just a route, it has facts, recommended stops, and history. Isn't that something? All in the palm of your hand, no need to open up a big map in the front seat.

JOEY  That's cool, Mom!

JENN  Brown-noser.

JOEY  Loser.

JENN  It's really cool, Mom!

JOEY  Pass the lemon drops.

JENN  In a bit.

ANNIE  Isn't this fun? This is your great American adventure.

JENN  You said that already.

ANNIE  Because it's true. Think of the sights you'll see. Think of the culture you'll experience. *(Annie waits for a response.)* Think of the candy. When's the last time that we bought you candy?

MICHELLE  As a treat or a bribe?

JENN  When we get to our first stop can I have a dime to call Abby? I need to explain to her that I'm not kidnapped or dead in a ditch somewhere.

JAMES  She's expecting to see you?

JENN  Yeah, we're friends.

JAMES  She's the one from the cheer team, isn't she?

ANNIE  Abby, such a nice girl.

JAMES  It is good that you aren't doing that cheer camp anymore—now is the time to start focusing on the rest of your life.

JENN  Camps like that teach a lot of new skills.

JAMES  So will enrichment.

JENN  The girls who do the camps get put on the A squad in the fall.

JAMES  You will be fine without them. We talked about this.

JOEY  You ate the last of the lemon drops?

JENN  There were only a couple left.

MICHELLE  I didn't get any lemon drops.

JOEY  You were supposed to share them.

JENN  We did. I just happened to have the last ones.

JAMES  Besides, you are almost too old for things like that, you can use your time in the car to focus on your studies and prepare for enrichment camp.

JENN  I get carsick when I read in the car, so . . .

JAMES  Are you ready for camp? It is vital that you make a good impression, this could be where you get your letter of recommendation for college. I pulled every string possible at Marquette to get you that opportunity, it is usually reserved only for incoming freshmen. You will demonstrate significant interest as a pre-med candidate this way.

JENN  Yes, Dad.

ANNIE  Michelle, take a second and look out of the window instead of burying your head in a book.

MICHELLE  We're still in Wisconsin, Mom.

JAMES  We won't make it to Mason City until late.

ANNIE  You said there was a stop in Madison?

JENN  We're stopping in Madison? That's two hours away—that's the equivalent of driving down the block. Why couldn't we have left tomorrow morning?

MICHELLE  We were going to get further but you took so long packing.

JENN  I did not.

MICHELLE  Mom said to pack light.

JENN  I packed light!

MICHELLE  Three pairs of shoes?

JENN  We don't all wear the same thing every day like you.

JOEY  I still want lemon drops.

JAMES  Stop.

> *Silence.*

JOEY  Can we listen to music?

> *Annie turns on the radio. Something aggressive like The Beatles' "Back in the USSR" plays.*

JAMES  No. (*James turns on the oldies station on the radio.*)

MICHELLE  But—

JAMES  It's cacophonous. It's distracting while I drive.

> *"Danny Boy" begins to play.*

JAMES  Ah! Yes! My favorite!

MICHELLE  Oh no.

JENN  Please don't.

JAMES  "Oh Danny Boy,
> The pipes, the pipes are calling."
> This is music.

"From glen to glen, and down the mountainside."

ANNIE  The road, dear.

JAMES  "The summer's gone! And all the roses falling!"

## 5.

*A shift.*

MICHELLE  It was like he had every oldies station in every county in America memorized.

JOEY  He could sing.

JENN  Or was he just loud? And didn't we only make it like, a hundred miles before he confiscated the treats because we were bickering?

JOEY  What I remember was that was the summer I really learned how to throw. Dad took all that time to get me to stop throwing—

MICHELLE  Like a girl?

JOEY  Something like that. I had a good arm.

JENN  But you quit for track.

JOEY  There are girls on the track team . . .

MICHELLE  Unbelievable.

## 6.

*A shift. A campsite near Madison, Wisconsin. James and Joey, gloves in hand, play catch. Michelle writes in a notebook.*

JAMES  You need to follow through on your throw. Don't stop your arm as soon as you release the ball.

*Joey throws. James returns.*

JAMES  Throw the ball through my glove, not to it.

JOEY  I'm trying.

JAMES  Don't try to, just do it.

*Joey throws. James returns.*

JAMES  Okay, better. You need to work on this before the season starts, you can't be the one that no one else wants to play with.

JOEY  People want to play with me.

JAMES  For now. But if you want that to stay true then you have to be useful. Remember, through my glove.

*Joey throws. James returns.*

ANNIE   Dinner's almost ready. Give Joey a break.

JAMES   Wait.

*James walks over to Joey.*

*A shift.*

JOEY   Dad knelt right down to my level, I remember this like it was yesterday. He knelt down and he told me about learning to play catch with the
American G.I.s who manned the ration lines, so this must have been '45
or '46. How one soldier would pass him extra rations if he could "pop"
the ball into his glove. Can you imagine that? He winked and he promised me extra kimbap if I could "pop" the next throw. I didn't even want
the kimbap after that, I just wanted to make him . . . I wanted to "pop"
the ball.

*A shift.*

*James places the ball in Joey's glove.*

JAMES   One more try?

*James backs up and Joey throws the ball straight into James's glove with a
pop. A pause. James removes his glove.*

JAMES   My hand stings after that one.

ANNIE   Dinner!

JAMES   I'll get water.

MICHELLE   Let me finish this paragraph and then I'll help.

ANNIE   Jenn, help me unpack dinner.

JAMES   Wait to undo the camper until I get back! It is very specific! Michelle?

MICHELLE   Coming! Coming!

*James, Joey, and Michelle walk off.*

JENN   Joey can practice baseball wherever. I can't do cartwheels in the back
of the Buick.

ANNIE   Pouting so much will lead to the development of wrinkles at an
early age.

JENN   I talked to Abby, and she confirmed that Coach Wirtz will let me do
the August session even if I miss the July session.

ANNIE   That's good.

JENN   So that's a yes? I can do the August session?

ANNIE   I already told you yes. Grab the plates from the camper.

JENN   Because the August session overlaps with pre-med enrichment. So
you'll talk to him for me?

ANNIE   I will.

JENN   Dad keeps talking about enrichment. He said he pulled the money from the camps.

ANNIE   I'll call and put the money back.

JENN   But you'll talk to him, right?

ANNIE   . . . I'll find the right moment. Did you know that over thirty million Americans go camping each year? Says so in the TripTik. Not all at the same time, thankfully. I thought I asked you to get the plates.

*Joey returns.*

JOEY   Sometime on the road can we stop at McDonald's?

ANNIE   We bought this cooler so we wouldn't have to.

*Michelle and James return.*

MICHELLE   Guess who I saw by the water?

JENN   Steve McQueen.

MICHELLE   The Kennets!

*Jenn fumbles the plates as she puts them down.*

JENN   . . . the Kennets are here?

MICHELLE   The whole family's pitching tents near the water.

JENN   Including Casey? Casey Kennet is there?

MICHELLE   He falls under the category of "the whole family," yes.

JAMES   Let's open this camper before it gets dark.

ANNIE   We're about to eat.

JAMES   I told you, the camper is defective, it is very important we do it right. I need hands.

JENN   Michelle can you, um, do it? I need to set the places.

*Jenn ducks down and pretends to work.*

JOEY   I can help.

MICHELLE   Sorry, big kids only.

*Michelle, Annie, and James walk offstage to the camper.*

JAMES   (O.S.) The left side is a little broken, so we have to be sure to pull each side out at the same time equally or else the entire thing could tip over.

JENN   Does Casey know I'm here?

JOEY   No, we didn't say hi.

MICHELLE   (O.S.) Oh my god!

*A shift.*

*Michelle steps back on stage.*

MICHELLE   You had a crush on Casey Kennet?

JOEY   She had a crush on Casey Kennet.

JENN  I did not have a crush on Casey Kennet.

JOEY  She totally had a crush on Casey Kennet.

MICHELLE  I thought you just really cared about accuracy, telling what actually happened.

JAMES  *(O.S.)* On the count of three, we pull, okay?

MICHELLE  Casey dipped his Oreos in water.

JENN  This is speculation.

JAMES  *(O.S.)* One.

JOEY  He played the oboe.

JENN  And hearsay.

JAMES  *(O.S.)* Two.

MICHELLE  . . . you had a crush on Casey Kennet, didn't you.

JENN  Okay I had a crush on Casey Kennet!

JOEY AND MICHELLE  Knew it!

JAMES  *(O.S.)* Three!

*Offstage, the sound of a camper pulled open.*

JAMES  Pull!

ANNIE  I am pulling!

JAMES  Almost there!

ANNIE  Got it! Got it!

*A shift.*

*James and Annie step back onstage. The family sits down to eat.*

ANNIE  It was heavier than I thought! I didn't have time to roll more before we got on the road, so don't take more kimbap before everyone has some, okay? Joey?

*Jenn peeks over toward the Kennets.*

JENN  Out of all the campsites in America, why do they have to be here?

MICHELLE  We're only two hours away from Milwaukee.

JENN  Unbelievable.

ANNIE  Jenn, eat your food.

JENN  I'm not very hungry.

ANNIE  You barely eat anything anymore.

JENN  I ate snacks in the car.

ANNIE  Eat some real food.

JENN  I don't want this.

JAMES  It's good.

JENN  No one else at the campsite is eating kimbap.

JAMES  And I pity them.

JENN  Aren't there extra ham and cheese sandwiches in the car? Can I eat those instead?

ANNIE  The sandwiches are in the cooler.

JAMES  What's wrong with Korean food?

ANNIE  She wants to eat a sandwich.

JAMES  Pass it here, then.

> *Jenn unwraps her sandwich and takes a bite as everyone stares at her.*
> *Silence.*

ANNIE  Our next big stop is Mount Rushmore—did you know that over ninety percent of the mountain granite was removed not with jackhammers, but with dynamite? Just how do they do that?

## 7.

> *A shift.*

JOEY  Mom drilled us with so much trivia I thought we were studying for a test.

MICHELLE  Did you know Idaho was the forty-third state in the Union?

JOEY  And Iowa is the only state in the Union that starts with two vowels?

JENN  Oregon was the first state to have one way streets.

MICHELLE  Montana has the most grizzly bears of any state in the lower forty-eight.

JOEY  And the North Dakota state bird is the western meadowlark?

JENN  I'm still great at Jeopardy.

## 8.

> *The car.*

ANNIE  Aretha Franklin.

JENN  Bob Dylan.

MICHELLE  Carole King!

JOEY  The Doors.

ANNIE  Dear? A musician starting with an "e."

JAMES  Pass.

ANNIE  Oh, Ella Fitzgerald.

JENN  Frank Sinatra.

MICHELLE  The Grass Roots!

JOEY  George *Harrison*?

MICHELLE  Counts.

ANNIE  An "i," dear?

JAMES  Pass.

ANNIE  You're right, that's a hard one. Oh! Irving Berlin! How about "j"?

JAMES  Pass.

ANNIE  James Taylor.

JENN  Kenny Rogers and the First Edition!

MICHELLE  Leonard Cohen.

JOEY  The Monkees.

MICHELLE  You would.

JOEY  What?

ANNIE  "N"?

JAMES  Pass.

ANNIE  Try.

JAMES  I'm driving.

JENN  Ne—

MICHELLE  Nei—

    *Joey sings the tune of "Sweet Caroline."*

JENN  Not silver or gold, but—

MICHELLE  He's not the one that walked on the moon he's—

ANNIE  Come on, try!

JAMES  Pass.

ANNIE  Come on!

JAMES  I can't! I can't. I don't know.

    *A pause.*

ANNIE  That's okay.

JENN  Neil Diamond.

JAMES  I see.

    *A silence.*

MICHELLE  Dad, what are you studying in Los Angeles again?


## 9.

    *A shift.*

JENN  He'd lecture us for hours.

MICHELLE  I asked.

JOEY  I thought it was interesting.

JENN  You weren't paying attention.

JOEY  It was a temple he was studying in California, right?

MICHELLE  A religious group.

JENN  The Nichiren Shoshu.

JOEY  Right.

MICHELLE  With the chant.

JOEY  We learned the chant.

JENN  Do you remember why he was studying them again?

JOEY  It had something to do with—


## 10.

*A gas station. James lectures in the front of the car.*

JAMES  Democracy on trial!

JENN  Pass the lemon drops.

MICHELLE  You just had them.

JOEY  The chips?

MICHELLE  Gone.

JOEY  What?!

JAMES  All of Asia is on trial, facing a great opportunity to embrace democracy or fall further into authoritarian rule. That is what I am studying in Los Angeles.

JENN  I thought this fellowship was you studying some monks?

JAMES  Ah! Yes! The monks are from a group called the Nichiren Shoshu. They advocate for spreading democracy in their homeland of Japan.

JOEY  They're Japanese? I thought we didn't like the Japanese.

ANNIE  We never said that—

MICHELLE  Actually . . .

JOEY  —no you said that—

ANNIE  We don't say we don't like the Japanese.

JAMES  We do not *not* like them! We do not! Japan is a model for what Korea could become.

JOEY  Why?

ANNIE  Because Japan is richer, love.

JOEY  Why?

ANNIE  Because America likes Japan more, love.

JOEY  Why?

ANNIE  You'll understand when you're older.

JAMES  My point is democracy depends on, and this is the theory of my research, democracy depends on a flourishing economy—a vibrant professional and middle class to support the democracy. Do you understand?

JOEY  Not really.

JAMES  I just went into a store and bought lemon drops, yes?

JOEY  Thank you, Dad.

> *James grabs the bag of lemon drops from Michelle. He passes lemon drops out to the family.*

JAMES  Well what would happen in society if you went into a store to buy lemon drops, but sometimes there were no lemon drops?

> *James gets to Joey, but before he hands Joey a lemon drop, he pulls the bag away.*

JAMES  Sometimes you pay your hard-earned money for lemon drops and the man behind the counter takes the money and gives no lemon drops in return? You would start to mistrust the store that sold the lemon drops, but also the police that are supposed to protect you from theft, and the mayor who hired the police, and the governor who oversees the mayor. Up and up until you begin to mistrust the very concept of exchanging your money for lemon drops at all. And if you stop believing you will be treated fairly at the store, why should you believe that you will be treated fairly in a court of law? If your money doesn't count at the counter, why do you believe your vote will count at the ballot box? Do you see the problem here? Democracy depends on a society where people believe that you get out of life what you put into it.

> *James hands the bag of lemon drops to Joey.*

ANNIE  The American promise is that you are not bound by social status, what position in life you were born into. Anyone can become president.

JAMES  But more importantly, anyone can become rich. Rich and successful. If people do not believe in that, they will believe a strongman when he comes along and tells them that the problem is not them, and it is not the system, but it is someone over *there*. It is the Blacks. It is the Muslims. It is the Hindus. It is the Koreans. The strongman tells the people, "The system will never work for you, lose all faith in that, but believe me when I say that *I* will work for you. I *alone* can provide what democratic society has failed to produce for you." And you see, this is what happened for years in Korea. This is why your mother and I had to leave.

ANNIE   And a war.

JAMES   I left when we didn't receive what we fought for. This will be an education for you, too, children. It will not be just our generation that will make this happen. It will be you. It will be the younger generation completing the path that we before you have paved. You are the future we have envisioned. A generation of doctors, lawyers. A generation that will bring democracy to Korea.

ANNIE   But not us. Because we're here.

JAMES   Yes. Your generation.

## 11.

A shift.

JENN   "A generation that will bring democracy to Korea." No pressure.

JOEY   Did we know he was thinking about—

MICHELLE   No.

JENN   Not yet.

MICHELLE   He told us in—

JOEY   Los Angeles, he told us in Los Angeles.

MICHELLE   Right.

JENN   How long was he thinking about it before?

JOEY   Not long I think.

MICHELLE   But Mom knew.

JENN   Did she?

MICHELLE   I don't know, actually.

## 12.

A campsite near Redwood National Park. James at a phone booth next to the road.

JAMES   Yes, yes I'm flying out in two days. Staying at the Santa Monica Hilton on 4th. It's where I always stay when I'm in Los Angeles. I am looking forward to meeting him, too . . . It would depend on his commitment to real change. I understand. It would be an honor, but I require certain assurances before I—yes. Yes. I am a fan of John Wayne movies, too. Large fan, can't get enough of his films, my wife and I go all the time. That's wonderful, it will be something nice outside of—yes. Something nice to talk about. I have to go, it looks like dinner is here. We always order in on Fridays. Yes, see you later, cowboy.

*James hangs up the phone.*

JAMES   Who is John Wayne?

*A shift.*

MICHELLE   Minister of Foreign Affairs.

JENN   Talk about a title bump from associate professor.

JOEY   Talk about a pay raise from associate professor.

JENN   How financially irresponsible to go into academia. Should have been a doctor . . .

## 13.

*The campsite. James enters.*

JAMES   Guess where we're going?

MICHELLE   Los Angeles?

JAMES   Tonight! We're going to a drive-in movie.

ANNIE   We are?

JOEY   What? Awesome!

JENN   Cool.

ANNIE   When? Why?

JAMES   Because we're in California! Hollywood!

ANNIE   We're in northern California.

JAMES   I called the nearest drive-in theater and their next showing starts in forty-five minutes. Gives us plenty of time to get there. Why not, right? Maybe a John Wayne movie.

MICHELLE   John Wayne? Really? He's so old-fashioned.

ANNIE   I was about to start prepping dinner.

JAMES   Don't worry, we can eat it tomorrow.

ANNIE   But what about dinner?

JAMES   We can stop at the McDonald's we passed on the way here.

JENN   What is going on?

JOEY   Don't ruin it. That sounds good to me!

JAMES   We've been driving for days, I think it makes sense to give us all a little break, a little treat. Come on, start packing things up. We'll leave the camper here.

## 14.

*A shift.*

MICHELLE  We never went to movies.

JOEY  He never went to movies.

JENN  He thought *Planet of the Apes* was a documentary about Jane Goodall.

## 15.

*James and Annie pull up to the drive-thru.*

JAMES  Hello there. Two tickets to *Butch Cassidy and the Sundance Kid*, please.

ANNIE  We've really been looking forward to it.

JAMES  I hear it's wonderful. All the rage this year.

ANNIE  Last year.

JAMES  Last year!

ANNIE  But we never got around to it.

JAMES  Can't wait to see John Wayne—

ANNIE  —Paul Newman.

JAMES  Paul Newman in this new role.

ANNIE  Thank you. We can park wherever?

JAMES  Have a lovely night.

ANNIE  Bye bye now.

    *A beat.*

ANNIE  Alright, come out.

    *The kids crawl out from under the seats, pushing blankets off of themselves.*

JENN  I'll get up then you get up.

MICHELLE  Careful!

JENN  Ow!

JOEY  I want to sit in the front between Mom and Dad.

JENN  Joey you spilled your fries.

JAMES  Stay down until we're parked past the check-in gate!

    *A shift. The children talk as time speeds through the movie.*

JENN  Michelle had such a crush on Robert Redford.

MICHELLE  Quiet! The movie's starting.

JOEY  Dad talked the whole movie.

JAMES  There is no way someone could shoot a belt off like that, believe me!

ANNIE  Shh!

MICHELLE  Well he had a lot of questions.

JAMES  Now is that one John Wayne?

MICHELLE  John Wayne isn't in this movie, Dad. That's Paul Newman. He plays Butch. He's one of the leads.

JAMES  Ahhh. From the first scene.

JENN  I think he really liked it.

MICHELLE  See Dad, this is a movie that comments on all of the other cowboy movies that came before it, right?

JAMES  I don't understand.

MICHELLE  You keep asking about John Wayne? Well that's the old world. The world is changing too fast for Butch and Sundance. The old ways just don't work for them anymore. So it's more than just horses and guns, it's about what happens when horses and guns can't help you anymore.

    *James shouts at the screen:*

JAMES  Why would you escape to Bolivia? How is that going to help you?

ANNIE  Shh! I'm trying to focus!

MICHELLE  He liked it. I remember.

JAMES  She's dating Butch? I thought she was with Sundance.

JOEY  She is, she and Butch are just friends.

JAMES  I see.

MICHELLE  When's the last time you think he'd seen a movie on a big screen?

JOEY  I don't remember them going out much, I think.

JENN  Not ever.

JAMES  I have a bad feeling about this.

JENN  Remember at the very end.

JOEY  I could see his face.

MICHELLE  I think I was in the back.

JENN  But I think . . .

MICHELLE  When Butch and Sundance are surrounded, no way out.

JOEY  And they run out to face their fate, guns blazing

JENN  I think I saw him cry.

JOEY  I saw tears in his eye.

MICHELLE  From Butch fucking Cassidy.

## 16.

*The movie over, the family drives back to the campsite.*

JOEY  I don't think that there is any way that the posse would have been really able to track them across the country like that, right? I mean I don't believe that for a second. I get that it's a movie but I don't believe that at all, I'm sorry.

MICHELLE  You're just upset because you didn't want Butch and Sundance to die.

JOEY  I mean, yeah. But still. I thought it was just a bummer.

JAMES  No matter how far they ran . . .

*They sit in silence. Then, James turns the radio on. Something from 1972 plays, something lush, beautiful, but decidedly "hip" that would usually get turned off. Something like "Mama Told Me Not to Come" by Three Dog Night or "Share The Land" by The Guess Who.*

*The car takes it in. They listen.*

JAMES  You like this?

MICHELLE  Yeah, I like them.

JAMES  It's interesting.

*No one wants to break the spell, whatever it is.*

## 17.

*A shift.*

JOEY  There were good parts to the trip, there really were.

MICHELLE  I should go back and find my old albums . . .

JENN  But you remember what else happened that night? I mean you do remember, right?

## 18.

*Back at the campsite. Jenn, Michelle, and Joey watch their parents walk offstage to the camper.*

JAMES  (O.S.) Let's re-open the camper, I need hands!

ANNIE  (O.S.) I have the left side.

JAMES  (O.S.) You need someone else on that side—Joey, come help! Alright, on the count of three! One!

JOEY   I was too young. I wasn't strong enough.

JAMES   *(O.S.)* Two!

JOEY   I wanted to be grown up. I wanted to be helpful.

JENN   . . . it wasn't your fault.

JAMES   *(O.S.)* Three!

> *The sounds of James, Annie, and Joey pulling the camper.*

JAMES   *(O.S.)* Halfway there.

> *The screech of metal on metal.*

JAMES   Joey! Pull!

ANNIE   It's tipping!

JAMES   *(O.S.)* Don't stop! Keep going! Keep going!

ANNIE   Heavy! It's heavy!

> *More screeching.*

JAMES   *(O.S.)* I said pull!

ANNIE   *(O.S.)* Michelle! Jenn! Come help!

> *A large crunching sound.*

JAMES   The awning! It's broken!

ANNIE   It's secure! We can let go! Let go!

> *A shift. Annie and James reenter the campsite.*

ANNIE   Is everyone okay?

JAMES   What the was that?

ANNIE   The camper is broken.

JAMES   That's why we coordinate it! Together! What happened?

JOEY   I—

JAMES   Do you know what could have happened there? I could have broken my back! The camper could have completely broken and the trip would have been ruined! You could have hurt your mother!

JENN   My ankle.

ANNIE   What's wrong?

JENN   When I came to help lift, I tripped over a branch. I can't feel my ankle.

ANNIE   Jenn!

JAMES   This is great! Just great! I said that the way to open this is very specific!

ANNIE   Can you move it?

JENN   I think I need ice.

JAMES   I'll get ice.

JOEY   I'm sorry.

> *James leaves.*

ANNIE  How is it feeling?

JENN  I'm fine. I'm not actually hurt.

ANNIE  Oh.

JENN  I just wanted him to stop yelling.

ANNIE  Right.

    *Annie and Jenn stand up.*

ANNIE  For a second there I thought you'd broken it. Camp would have been out of the question.

JENN  Are you kidding? You'd have to amputate my leg to keep me from camp.

JAMES  What camp?

    *James stands next to the camper.*

ANNIE  James. We can talk about this—

JAMES  What camp, Jenn?

JENN  Mom—

ANNIE  Go get the ice and let's talk about this.

JAMES  What did you mean when you said that?

JENN  I don't . . . Mom?

ANNIE  Walk with me.

JAMES  Is this your cheer camp, Jenn?

JENN  I . . . I . . .

JAMES  Say something!

JENN  I don't want to.

JAMES  Why?

JENN  Because you're going to yell at me.

JAMES  Cheer camp?

ANNIE  I allowed it, James.

JAMES  Why?

ANNIE  Because they wouldn't let her on the team next year without this camp, James.

JAMES  Who cares?

ANNIE  She cares! I care!

JAMES  It's cheerleading!

ANNIE  It's her friends!

JAMES  Do you know the strings I pulled to get you this opportunity? Do you know how important this is?

JENN  I'm sorry.

JAMES  You're doing the god damn enrichment!

ANNIE  Not now, James.

JAMES  Don't tell me how to parent my children! Look at me. You have no idea what the real world is like outside of the life that we build for you. You have absolutely no idea, and you are throwing away your life, and it is an insult to all of us. You are so unbelievably spoiled, it is disgusting. Do you think that things are just going to come to you on a silver platter?

JENN  No.

JAMES  Do you think I can look out for you for forever? Just give you what you want?

JENN  No.

JAMES  So then what was this?

JENN  I don't . . .

JAMES  What is it?

JENN  I just. This is what makes me happy.

JAMES  Happy. Happy is not the question. Happy is not something that you have the luxury, the privilege of thinking about right now. You can think about happiness when you can put a roof over your head and food on your table. Do you think you can do that yet?

JENN  No.

JAMES  Do you want to start to try? Go ahead, try! Go do it now.

JENN  I don't—

JAMES  What?

JENN  I don't—

JAMES  Look at me when I'm talking to you!

JENN  I don't want to.

JAMES  You don't want to what?

JENN  I don't want to do it on my own.

JAMES  You don't want to?

JENN  I can't.

JAMES  You can't. You can't. You can't do it on your own and until you can and you are under my roof and are eating my food and are spending my money you do not get a say. You do not get a say in anything: you do not get to say what you eat for breakfast, you do not get a say in what music I play in my car, you do not get a say in one GODDAMN THING!

ANNIE  (You stop it right now! Stop it!) (Dessunikka 'kumane! 'Dangjang!') (됐으니까 그만해! 당장.)

JAMES  Not! Now!

ANNIE  (You scream at my child one more time I will leave you right now.

We will talk. We will.) (Nae ddal hantae hanbun-man deh sori jil-lehbwa, ae-deul e-rang ddeh nan-da. Yaegi-hae, narang yaegi-hae.) (내 딸한테 한 번만 더 소리 질러봐, 애들이랑 떠난다. 얘기해. 나랑 얘기해.)

JAMES  (Get in the car.) (Cha-e 'gaisso.) (차에 가 있어.)

> *Annie and James walk to the car and drive off.*
>
> *The kids don't move for a long time.*
>
> *Jenn gets up and takes a hamper of laundry out of the camper. She starts folding. Michelle joins her.*
>
> *Joey sits with them and starts folding laundry.*

JENN  We've got it.

JOEY  I want to help.

JENN  You don't know how to fold laundry.

JOEY  Oh.

JENN  Here let me show you.

> *She moves over to him.*

JENN  You need to make sure that you press the wrinkles out of it as you fold or else it's going to stay wrinkled and get even worse in the bag, right?

JOEY  Okay.

JENN  And you crease here, here, and here.

JOEY  Got it.

> *They fold.*

JENN  Mom told Dad that she would leave.

MICHELLE  When?

JENN  That's what she yelled in Korean. I think.

JOEY  How do you know that?

JENN  I remember a little from before you were born.

JOEY  I never knew that.

JENN  They spoke it around the house with me until my first parent teacher conference. The teacher said that I was doing great in class: I was a bright kid, I played well with others, I was good at sharing, I listened in class. I was just a little behind on my language skills. All of that good stuff and they obsessed over the one thing I was doing wrong—they never spoke Korean to me again.

MICHELLE  Why did you never tell me?

JENN  I don't know.

MICHELLE  You're getting it.

JOEY  Thanks.

MICHELLE  When I grow up, I am going to let my kids do whatever they want. You want to design popsicle shapes? Go for it. You want to study chimpanzees in Africa? Don't let me stop you.

JENN  He might love you studying chimpanzees.

MICHELLE  Yeah?

JENN  You'd have to get a terminal degree in primatology. Respectable.

MICHELLE  True.

JOEY  That's really nice, but my kid is going to eat all of the McDonald's they want.

*Jenn throws a sock at him.*

JOEY  Breakfast, lunch, and dinner. You do whatever you want when you want it.

*Jenn bows her head.*

MICHELLE  What?

JENN  'snothing.

*They fold.*

JENN  I am going to make sure that I tell my kids I love them. Every day. I am really going to say it. I am going to smother them with love, bombard them with it. I am going to repeat it to them over and over like it's mom doing her rosary at night. "I love you. I love you. I love you. I love you."

JOEY  Am I not tough enough? Is he right?

MICHELLE  He doesn't think you're not tough enough. Well.

JENN  He's trying to prepare us for the world, I guess.

JOEY  It feels like he's preparing us for a warzone.

JENN  It does.

JOEY  I'm trying. We're trying.

MICHELLE  We know.

*They fold.*

MICHELLE  I think he is, too.


## 19.


*A shift.*

JOEY  You know, I remember him apologizing. It was when we finally got to the Pacific Ocean, about to head south on the PCH.

MICHELLE  We stopped at that amazing cliff, remember?

JOEY  And we all got out of the car and watched the sun set before we found the campground for the night.

## 20.

*The PCH. The family looks out on the sunset.*

JOEY   I think I see a dolphin.

MICHELLE   I don't see it.

JOEY   No, right there!

MICHELLE   That's just a wave.

ANNIE   It's beautiful, isn't it.

JAMES   Yes.

MICHELLE   Maybe that's a fin?

ANNIE   The sun's going down. It's getting cold. Let's find camp.

JAMES   Wait.

*They stop.*

JAMES   I grew up in a little fishing village in the south, right on the water. As a child, even younger than you, I would wake up with my father before dawn and help push him onto the water as the sun rose. I was supposed to turn around and head right to school, but my father would allow me to stay and watch the sun finish rising. I'd sit there as he pushed off, but he never knew that I wasn't looking at the sun on the horizon. I was looking far past that, to the other side of the world. I was planning, I guess—planning a life here. I don't think I ever took my eyes off of the horizon, throughout the war, throughout all of it. I kept my gaze firmly forward because I knew that was what I needed to do to get here. I catch myself staring back across the horizon, back to Korea . . . but I left for a reason, and I need to remember that. That I left for a better life, for you to have a better life. I think looking out at the horizon has changed from a necessity to a habit. As I've been looking out I fail to see what is happening right next to me. I am not seeing the life that you want. Any of you.

*A shift.*

JENN   He did not say that.

## 21.

*And the Pacific Ocean disappears.*
*A massive shift.*
*The year 2010. A simple cemetery.*
*Joey, Michelle, and Jenn stand around a flat headstone.*

JOEY  Yes he did.

JENN  "Looking out at the horizon?"

JOEY  That's how I remember it.

JENN  He does not apologize, he never apologizes.

MICHELLE  Can we get to work?

JENN  But you're remembering it wrong.

MICHELLE  We can all have different opinions.

JENN  That's not how truth works.

JOEY  He could have just said it to me.

JENN  That would check out, apologizing to you about something he did to me.

MICHELLE  Jenn.

JENN  And a little fishing village? Grandpa was a failed businessman and a drunk, not a fisherman. That's why he had to keep sending money back for years.

MICHELLE  I don't know about that. What I do know is that Henry and Joan are currently outnumbered three to one by the kids, this place is still a mess, and I think it's going to rain. Can we get to work?

JOEY  Sure. For sure.

JENN  Yup. Totally.

MICHELLE  Alright good. I'll sweep the headstone.

*They all work on cleaning up the gravesite.*

JENN  Aren't we supposed to like . . . do the ancestral ceremony thingy at home? And after midnight or something? That's the tradition?

JOEY  Oh yeah we're totally failed Koreans. But this is easier.

JENN  You two are the lawyers, call it "escaping on a technicality" I guess.

MICHELLE  Thank you for letting us drag you out here right after a full day at that conference.

JENN  Thank you for inviting me. The dead have more personality than most pharmaceutical execs.

MICHELLE  It was both our ideas. I'm just glad we get this moment with just the three of us.

JENN  Yeah.

MICHELLE  Sam and Alexis are excited for dinner, to get to actually sit down and talk with you. How long has it been?

JOEY  And I don't think you've seen Declan since he was what, this high?

*Jenn snaps back.*

JENN  You know how busy things get.

JOEY  I didn't mean it like—

MICHELLE  I wasn't saying it like a—they're just excited.

    *They clean in silence for a second.*

JOEY  Maybe it was the walk in the Redwoods.

JENN  What was?

JOEY  Maybe he talked to me about that stuff when we went on a walk in the Redwoods.

JENN  We stopped in the Redwoods before we went to the movie theater.

MICHELLE  For what it's worth, I remember him apologizing.

JENN  Because mom forced him to!

    *A shift.*

      *On the PCH.*

JOEY  I think I see a dolphin.

MICHELLE  I don't see it.

JOEY  No, right there!

MICHELLE  That's just a wave.

ANNIE  It's beautiful, isn't it.

JAMES  Yes.

MICHELLE  Maybe that's a fin?

ANNIE  The sun's going down. It's getting cold.

JAMES  Let's find camp.

ANNIE  Wait.

    *They stop.*

JAMES  Sometimes people raise their voices when they shouldn't. Sorry.

    *James turns and leaves.*

      *A shift.*

JOEY  . . . well at least it was an apology.

JENN  It was like he was in a hostage video. And it was like that for the rest of the trip. Radio silence.

JOEY  He talked to us. He definitely talked to us.

JENN  Let's just get the things from the car. I just know he didn't talk to me. It was like I didn't exist. It was like I died. Maybe that's why I remember it a little more clearly.

MICHELLE  Look at it this way: if he apologized at all, it means Mom fought for you that night when they drove off together. She did.

## 22.

*Back at the trailer park. Annie and James stand outside of the car on opposite sides.*

JAMES  How could you not tell me about cheer camp?

ANNIE  You wouldn't have listened.

JAMES  Because it is a bad idea.

ANNIE  I believe it was the right thing to do. Is.

JAMES  She needs to focus on her academics.

ANNIE  She does spectacularly.

JAMES  She has to be better than spectacular. She has to be five times as good as—

ANNIE  As every other silent, obedient Asian child who sits in a medical lab? No. She will be five times as good by being liked. By having the confidence to navigate this world as a real American.

JAMES  You're saying that becoming prom queen is more important than a prestigious internship.

ANNIE  Yes! Do not scoff at that. She has the chance to be liked, to fit in. We can give that to her, she can be just like everyone else.

JAMES  Our daughter is better than everyone else. And she is more than a dancing girl, an object. She is a brilliant mind and she will be great.

ANNIE  I know my daughter.

JAMES  And you are saying that I do not?

ANNIE  I am saying that she is terrified of you! You do not really know her.

JAMES  I work every day to—

ANNIE  And so do I! She will not repeat your mistakes!

JAMES  My mistakes?

ANNIE  You would have been a dean by now if you spoke better English. We would not be sleeping five in a row in a camper trailer this summer if people looked at you and saw themselves! She will not reach the ceiling we have because she is different. She will be just like every other White girl.

JAMES  Every other White girl.

ANNIE  What I mean is that you have no right to accuse me of being senseless in all of this. I made this choice for a reason.

JAMES  What would your father think. Every other White girl.

ANNIE  Do not talk about my father.

JAMES  Every other White girl?

ANNIE  Stop.

JAMES  Every other White girl?

ANNIE  I meant—

JAMES  We are Korean! We are Korean. That is our blood. That is who we are. That means something. Our parents would be ashamed if they—

ANNIE  We are not our parents! We are not our parents.

JAMES  Back home this would have—

ANNIE  We left! We left to have a better life. For our children to have a better life! For us to be a real American family and that means we are able to leave certain things behind. That means that we are able to leave our parents behind. But how can we do that when you are sending money back to your family every week? When you are always looking back, like a ghost is chasing you? We are not in danger. We are Americans. That is what we signed up for.

JAMES  What if we don't have to anymore?


## 23.

> *A shift.*
> *The cemetery.*
> *Jenn unpacks a short foldout table.*

MICHELLE  A table! Wow!

JENN  I got it at Home Depot, it's nothing fancy.

MICHELLE  It's nice, it's really nice. Thank you.

JENN  I'm gonna start unpacking.

> *Jenn unpacks kimbap, soju, and other nice food.*

JOEY  Oh wow. You're really going for it.

JENN  Did I do something wrong? This is what you're supposed to do, right? Rice and meat on the west side of the table, fruit and fish on the east side of the table. That's what Wikipedia says.

JOEY  We don't really do anything formal like this.

JENN  You don't leave anything?

MICHELLE  No we brought stuff, too. We just kind of put it on the ground.

JOEY  Like we said, failed Koreans.

JENN  So I like, totally overdid it.

MICHELLE  No! No. It's really thoughtful of you.

JENN  Might as well unpack your stuff, too.

*Jenn reaches into Michelle's bag and pulls out a pack of cigarettes.*

JENN   Really?

JOEY   It won't kill him.

*Jenn pulls out a six pack of beer.*

JENN   We're giving him a "juicy" IPA?

JOEY   Yeah.

JENN   He literally only ever drank Coors Light. Maybe a Miller High Life it was like, an occasion.

MICHELLE   No he got really into IPAs.

JENN   Since when?

*The question hits Jenn.*

JENN   I mean, alright. IPA it is.

*Jenn pours the beer into a glass and places it on the table.*
*A shift.*


## 24.

*Back at the trailer park. Later. Annie sits deep in thought.*

ANNIE   This is what you were talking about before? "A generation that will bring democracy to Korea"?

JAMES   They could.

ANNIE   How long have you known? When were you going to tell me?

JAMES   I was looking for the right moment.

ANNIE   We would just go?

JAMES   We would.

ANNIE   But the children.

JAMES   Are smart. They would be fine.

ANNIE   They don't speak Korean.

JAMES   They would learn.

ANNIE   My work—

JAMES   You wouldn't have to work.

ANNIE   I want to work.

JAMES   We would have more money than we could ever have in America. Ever.

ANNIE   I don't want that.

JAMES   For our children.

ANNIE   I never knew you wanted to go back.

JAMES  I never did. But this wouldn't just be going back. This is a new Korea. A growing Korea. A safe Korea.

ANNIE  Safe under gunpoint.

JAMES  We would return as elites. As first-class citizens. Our family would never want for anything again.

ANNIE  He's a dictator.

JAMES  We would work within the system. We would change it. The country is democratizing. We would be part of that.

ANNIE  We would be part of the regime fighting against that.

JAMES  Better to fight it on the ground than with books from thousands of miles away.

ANNIE  The people who fight it on the ground are led into courtyards, shot in the head, and buried in the ground.

JAMES  Don't be ridiculous.

ANNIE  When were you going to tell me?

JAMES  I didn't think it was real. For a long time I didn't think it was real.

ANNIE  And you've been traipsing us across America pretending, pretending that—

JAMES  They need to know by the end of the summer.

ANNIE  Then what are you doing worrying about this research grant?

JAMES  I wanted our children to see America.

ANNIE  Before they leave it.

JAMES  They would have a future there.

ANNIE  They have a future here.

JAMES  Fine, but they would have a present there, as well. We are talking about real things there, a real house, maids, chefs, drivers. A life we could never provide for them here.

ANNIE  They are Americans.

JAMES  We are Korean. Korea is home.

ANNIE  This is their home.

JAMES  It will be a better life.

ANNIE  This is our life. I will not make them strangers in two homes. I will not.

JAMES  Do not tell me that this is for the children! If this was for the children we would have left yesterday.

ANNIE  They would grow up alone.

JAMES  They would not have to grow up poor! They would not be sleeping in the same bed in a pull-out camper in the middle of a trailer park! They will have everything.

ANNIE   Except their freedom.

JAMES   Do not talk to me about freedom. How is America so free? You are free to starve. You are free to be a slave to debt. There they would be free from want, free from hunger, free from all of these things.

ANNIE   Who are you? Who are you? This is not what you believe in. This is not what you work for. We are driving across the country to study monks on a beach who have something, just a little thing, to do with the democratization of Japan! This is your life's work and you are willing to throw it away?

JAMES   I am not throwing it away, the country is changing. I am just not being selfish.

ANNIE   Selfish?

JAMES   We do not have the luxury of living a "great American adventure!" We must act. Political theory does not put food on the table.

ANNIE   You always talk about ration lines. I waited in the same lines as you.

JAMES   In Seoul! In your fancy, beautiful neighborhood! With a nice orderly line and food every day! It was not the same. You chose to give up a good life in Korea! I never had that choice! And I will not deprive my children of that so that we can continue pretending that we are living the American dream!

ANNIE   I did not leave Korea on some flight of fancy, James. I left like we all left. It is not a democracy.

JAMES   It is changing.

ANNIE   Not fast enough!

JAMES   Don't be a child.

ANNIE   Excuse me?

JAMES   You've never had to worry like I've had to worry. You've never been hungry, you've never known cold, you've never known fear, you've never known pain.

ANNIE   I have known pain.

JAMES   No. You have not. There is a difference. You came to America. I left Korea. I ran. I had no other choice, nowhere else to go. You vacationed.


## 25.


*A shift.*
*The cemetery.*
*Jenn finishes setting up the table, a modest spread of food and drink.*

JENN  I didn't know what to do with the potato chips so I just kinda counted them as a rice.

MICHELLE  It's the thought that counts.

*Joey checks his phone.*

JOEY  Cousin Joon wants to come to dinner.

MICHELLE  Oh Jesus.

JOEY  I'll tell him you just made a small reservation for immediate family.

MICHELLE  He's gonna see right through that.

JOEY  Well it's true.

JENN  He can take my seat.

JOEY  What? No, no of course not.

JENN  No it's no big deal, I just might need to fly out tonight, is all.

MICHELLE  I thought you were staying the whole weekend.

JENN  I was checking and there's a red-eye with seats tonight. Tom can't drive Patrick to his soccer tournament tomorrow, so I might need to do it. I'll be back soon.

JOEY  . . . at least stay for dinner, right?

JENN  We'll see.

*A pause.*

JOEY  Cousin Joon. You know his kid's moving to Busan, right?

JENN  Little Ross?

JOEY  Not so little, just got his MBA.

JENN  Jesus.

JOEY  That's what the cool kids do today, move to Korea for the culture and the money. What do you think it would have been like if we actually went?

MICHELLE  We don't speak Korean.

JOEY  We would have learned.

MICHELLE  We would have been total strangers.

JOEY  We would have been rich.

JENN  And totally alone.

JOEY  I'm just saying.

JENN  You wish it happened?

JOEY  No! No. I'm just saying.

JENN  Maybe Dad was right. Maybe we would have been happier if we'd gone to Korea. Maybe we should have gone.

## 26.

*A shift.*

*Santa Monica. The beach. Joey, Michelle, and Jenn clean their campsite post-lunch.*

ANNIE  Do you feel Korean?

JOEY  I don't know, what do you mean?

MICHELLE  What does that mean?

ANNIE  I don't know what I mean, I wonder what you think. Do you feel Korean?

MICHELLE  We're obviously Korean.

ANNIE  Beyond what you look like.

MICHELLE  Sure, I guess. I mean, I don't go around thinking about it every day.

JOEY  Yeah, I'm Korean.

ANNIE  What does that mean to you?

JOEY  Good food?

MICHELLE  What about you?

ANNIE  Of course.

MICHELLE  I mean do you feel American?

ANNIE  Asian Americans have always been charged with dual loyalty.

MICHELLE  I know you are a citizen. But do you feel American?

ANNIE  I do. I always wanted to come to America, you know. To have my great American adventure. As a little girl I even mailed a long-distance application to American boarding schools without my father knowing.

MICHELLE  I'm sure that went over well.

ANNIE  He laughed, actually. My father was a very progressive man for his time. You would have liked him.

JOEY  Why did he let you go to Barnard?

ANNIE  Because I got in! There wasn't a future for me in Korea. Not one where I was educated, where I had a future for myself. So I applied again without him knowing and thought that he would be so, so angry. But I showed him the letter, he looked at me in the eye, and said who was he to deny my future?

*Annie takes a moment, but collects herself quickly.*

ANNIE  I still miss him. You know, when he said goodbye to me at the airport he slipped an American Butterfinger candy bar into my pocket. I held on to that Butterfinger in my pocket the entire journey to Idlewild airport.

And I remember before I left . . . before I left he told me that beyond the pain of saying goodbye, the worst thing to ever happen to a parent is for their children to have less opportunity than they had . . .

*Annie stops cleaning, takes in the campsite.*

ANNIE  That's why he sent me, right. Not some great American . . . For me to have a better life. For you to have a better life. You. That's right . . .

MICHELLE  Mom?

ANNIE  I'm fine, I'm fine. Don't mind me, caught up in the past.

JENN  I don't feel Korean at all.

MICHELLE  Jenn.

JENN  We eat Korean food but Kathy's family is always making spaghetti and meatballs and they are one hundred percent Irish, so I don't think that really does anything. We don't speak the language, I don't even really know that much about Korea as a place. I think that I'm American. So.

ANNIE  I see.

MICHELLE  Why, what's going on?

ANNIE  Nothing is going on, I just was wondering.

*James enters.*

ANNIE  How did it go?

JAMES  It was good.

ANNIE  Yes?

JAMES  We have to pack up.

JENN  Now? Why?

JAMES  I have to make a stop in Las Vegas.

ANNIE  Las Vegas?

JAMES  He's in Las Vegas.

JENN  Who?

JAMES  Someone for my work. From the Nichiren Shoshu.

JOEY  I thought we were going to the Grand Canyon next. Do we still get to go to the Grand Canyon?

MICHELLE  Yeah I was actually looking forward to that.

JAMES  It's work.

JENN  The Buddhists are going gambling?

JAMES  Can we be packed up in the next thirty minutes?

ANNIE  (What is it?) (Oegure?) (왜 그래.)

MICHELLE  Mom—

ANNIE  Shh.

JAMES  (They want me to meet him.) (Nabogo 'mannare.) (나보고 만나래.)

ANNIE  (Meet who?) ('Nugulmanna?') (누굴 만나.)

JAMES  (President Park.) (Paktong.) (박통.)

ANNIE  (Are you serious?) (Chongmal?) (정말.)

JAMES  (He's in Las Vegas for a conference of Korean Americans. I think
he will offer me the job.) ('Hangukkye migukin 'hakettemune chigum
lasubegase i-tte.) (한국계 미국인 학회 때문에 지금 라스베가스에 있대. 나
보고 일 하라 할것 같아)

ANNIE  Okay.

JAMES  Okay?

ANNIE  (Can we give them a better life?) (Kuromyon 'edurante do 'chongoji?)
(그럼 애들한테 더 좋은 거지.)

    *A shift.*

JENN  I didn't understand all of it, but I understood enough.

JAMES  (We can try.) (Hambon 'heboja.) (한번 해보자.)

ANNIE  (I'm doing this for them.) (Nan igo 'edulttemune 'hanun goya.) (난
이거 애들 때문에 하는 거야.)

JAMES  (I know.) (Ara.) (알아.)

ANNIE  (Not for you.) ('Dangshinttemuni 'anigo.) (당신 때문에 아니고.)

JENN  "Can we give them a better life?" A job offer? Korea?

JOEY  I mean even I could tell that *something* was going on. A secret's a secret
in any language.

ANNIE  Jenn, help me with the awning. Everyone else start packing up.


## 27.

    *A shift.*

    *The cemetery.*

    *The children do a simple toast. They drink.*

JENN  Do we say words or something?

MICHELLE  Not really. If you want to.

    *A silence.*

JENN  I dunno. Oh! You know who I ran into a few weeks ago in Palo Alto?
He said he worked at the Baker San Fran office. Maybe you know him?

MICHELLE  I don't work at Baker anymore, Jenn.

JENN  What? Since when?

MICHELLE  It's been like . . . two years.

JENN  Get out. How did I not know that?

MICHELLE  I moved into public interest law. That and I started teaching.

JENN  Wow!

MICHELLE  Yeah, yeah I really like it.

JENN  That's incredible. Wow. I'm so happy for you.

JOEY  I know, she's giving me ideas . . .

JENN  That feels so right for you.

MICHELLE  Thank you! Thank you. I'm really happy.

> *Michelle turns away, collects herself.*

JENN  Hey, what's up?

JOEY  She told you about this.

JENN  You did?

MICHELLE  I sent you a whole long email about it.

JENN  You did, right.

MICHELLE  The whole update? And the note in the Christmas card? It's fine. Things fall through the cracks.

JENN  No, right! Right I totally read it. It's coming back to me.

MICHELLE  Right. It's fine. It's fine. Let's start packing up.

JOEY  I'll tell Henry and Joan to load the kids in the car and head to the restaurant?

JENN  Let's head out, grab my bags back at your place and I can check about flights, too.

JOEY  Let's at least push dinner earlier so we can feed you before your flight.

JENN  Restaurants can take forever, you never know.

JOEY  Then screw the restaurant, we can all come to my place and we'll whip something up. I'll call Joan right now and get a pot of rice on, and we have kalbi already defrosted in the fridge. And I mean, Joan's freaking Irish and she cooks better Korean food than I do, so you can't miss that.

JENN  Let's grab my bags and then we can see about the—

JOEY  The flight. Right.


## 28.

> *A shift.*
>
> *The road to Vegas. Death Valley. Classical music plays.*

MICHELLE  Can you turn on the air conditioning?

ANNIE  It is on.

MICHELLE  Then can you open the windows?

JAMES  We're in Death Valley. That will make it worse.

MICHELLE  My god.

ANNIE  Language.

JOEY  Can we see a magic show when we're there?

JAMES  No.

JOEY  What are we supposed to do, then?

JAMES  We will only be there for a day, then we head home.

JOEY  No Grand Canyon then?

     *Silence.*

JENN  Can you at least change the station to something we actually like?

ANNIE  Jenn.

JENN  All we've done this entire trip is listen to your music. And go where you want to go. And so we're not even going to the Grand Canyon anymore, which Joey was actually really excited about, so can we listen to something that does not actively put us to sleep? Something from this century?

JAMES  Enough.

JENN  Michelle actually has really great taste in music, you've just never noticed. And maybe if you tried to listen, really listen, you would like what you hear! You know, American music. Real American things.

ANNIE  Jenn, be respectful.

JENN  When are you going to tell us? When were you going to tell us? When the bags were on the curb?

JOEY  Are Mom and Dad getting a divorce?

JENN  No! We're moving to Korea!

MICHELLE  What?

ANNIE  Jenn!

JENN  Surprise! This entire thing was a test run for ripping our lives out of the ground!

JAMES  Stop!

JENN  Why did you even care about what I did this summer if everything was changing?

MICHELLE  Really?

JOEY  What are you talking about?

JAMES  I'm driving!

ANNIE  We can talk about this later—

JENN  When? When? Does it matter if we talk about this? We don't have a say in anything that happens in this family. I don't want to go. You leave. I want to stay here.

MICHELLE  Mom, why are we leaving?

ANNIE  We're not leaving—

MICHELLE  We're not—

ANNIE  James.

JAMES  Goddamn it!

    *James slams the brakes. After a moment, the tire pops.*

JAMES  Shit!


## 29.

    *James changes the tire.*

    *Annie speaks to the kids inside the car.*

ANNIE  When your father lived in New York he would translate for Ambassador Lim at the UN. He even started to write his speeches for him, and Lim never forgot about that. In 1961, after the military coup, General Song Il Chan asked him to come back to Korea and work for him. We said no, it was too dangerous and we did not want to live in a dictatorship. We were proven right, he was arrested and tortured when he ran for President. But now, President Park has been installed, and he is talking about changes. Real changes. Democracy. And Lim is his chief of staff, and they have asked your father to serve. To serve as foreign minister.

MICHELLE  What does that mean?

ANNIE  It means a chance to make a difference. A chance to go home.

JENN  Your home.

ANNIE  It would be a different life for us. A better life. More money than either of us make now. A better house. No more camper trailers, hotels. No more cooking on gas burners, an in-home cook.

MICHELLE  I don't want that.

ANNIE  You would be able to come back to America to study for college.

JOEY  That's years away. My friends . . .

JAMES  The car's ready.

ANNIE  He is meeting President Park tonight. We're going to stay in a motel, he needs the shower. Won't that be nice?

    *Silence.*

MICHELLE  Joey, I finished my book. You said you wanted it?

JOEY  I'm okay, thanks.

MICHELLE  I thought you said you wanted to borrow it on the drive home?

JOEY  I'll just look out the window.

MICHELLE  Why not?

JOEY  It might be our last time seeing. I dunno. Seeing America.

## 30.

*A shift.*

JOEY  You know he told me about it once. What happened.

JENN  What did he tell you?

JOEY  He watched Park give a speech and then they met in a conference room in one of those big Vegas hotels.

*Joey becomes President Park.*

JAMES  President Park.

JOEY  "Professor." I remember he thought it was odd that he addressed him as Professor. "General Song has spoken very highly of you."

JAMES  It was an honor to serve under him.

JOEY  "Twice, in Korea and in New York City, is that true?"

JAMES  Yes, after my service I would assist in his administrative duties while I was a student at Columbia.

JOEY  "And by administrative duties, you mean that you wrote his speeches."

JAMES  I would assist him in—

JOEY  "I admire your tact, Professor, but you should know that I value truth over nice stories."

JAMES  Yes, I wrote his speeches.

JOEY  "General Song is many things. He is not a wordsmith. Well, I won't beat around the bush, Professor Oh. Your country needs you. Korea is entering a new age, an age of prosperity and growth, Western-style growth, and it only makes sense that we have a foreign minister who reflects that Westernization."

JAMES  I am honored by your request.

JOEY  "Don't be honored, say yes!"

JAMES  If you don't mind me asking, sir, I wanted to talk to you about the democratization efforts.

JOEY  "What do you mean, democratization? We are a democracy."

JAMES  Of course, Mr. President.

JOEY  "See, exactly."

JAMES  What I mean is that, that my research, my work concerns the relationship between economic growth and liberalization. The—

JOEY   "And that is why you are perfectly suited for this job. The language of democracy and the language of growth, married in one perfect messenger."

JAMES   Yes, the language of—

JOEY   "So it's settled then?"

JAMES   Well—

JOEY   "Professor."

JAMES   I have questions about—

JOEY   "You drive a hard bargain. Fine. Where would you like it?"

JAMES   I am not sure I understand.

JOEY   "Your residence. Where do you want it? Yeonhui-dong? Seongbuk-dong? That will be further from your work, but we will provide a driver."

JAMES   I thought that you wanted me because of my work on democratization. I thought that you were planning to liberalize now that things have stabilized.

JOEY   "The journey is not finished yet to make Korea a strong country. You understand that. Of course we are democratizing. We will."

JAMES   We will. When?

JOEY   "I thought you valued tact, Professor."

JAMES   I must know.

JOEY   "This is your country asking, Professor."

JAMES   No it isn't.

JOEY   "What do you mean?"

JAMES   This is you asking, Mr. President, and you are not Korea. My work, my life, has been dedicated to democracy, to ensuring that my people will have the thing I craved for, thirsted for as a child. And I want to believe you. I wanted to believe you. But until I know, I must decline.

   *A shift.*

JOEY   He stood him down! He fought for democracy!

MICHELLE   That's not what happened. I remember.

JOEY   No, that's what happened. He told me about it when we all flew out for your law school graduation. He told me all about that meeting.

MICHELLE   No, it was about us. He had a change of heart because of us. We talked about it when they came to visit after Alexis was born. They didn't meet in a conference room, they talked outside of the hotel, waiting for his car.

   *Michelle becomes President Park.*

MICHELLE   "And that is why you are perfectly suited for this job. The language of democracy and the language of growth, married in one perfect messenger."

JAMES   I'd be the Butch to your Sundance, is that what you're saying?

MICHELLE   "Butch?"

JAMES   Butch Cassidy. *Butch Cassidy and the Sundance Kid.*

MICHELLE   "I don't understand."

JAMES   Oh. It's a movie. I was told you like movies. Good American Westerns.

MICHELLE   "Oh! Yes yes, of course. Does this one have John Wayne? I am a fan of John Wayne."

JAMES   No, but you'd like this one, it came out recently.

MICHELLE   "Oh I do not like the newer ones. The older are better: less talking, more horses and guns!"

JAMES   My daughter says—

MICHELLE   "She says what?"

JAMES   Nothing.

MICHELLE   "So it's settled then?"

JAMES   Your offer is the most generous I have ever received. And how can one argue with a residence procured by the government? Sending my children to the best schools. Giving them the things I cannot give them here as a professor. But. In all that time waiting, looking across the sea to my home, something happened. Behind my back my children were becoming Americans. If I never go back to Korea, I will always carry that hole in my heart. But if I go, I will strip something precious from them. So either way, someone loses. And I have to choose them, I have to accept that loss for myself so that they won't have to. Maybe that means I've changed, too. Not American, but not completely Korean, either. I must decline.

# 31.

*Jenn interrupts.*

JENN   No. That's not what happened.

*The cemetery.*

JOEY   Jesus, we're playing fucking Rashomon, now.

JENN   It must be fun to believe he changed on one magic road trip: show me the version where he stood up for his kids, show me the version that he let go of the past. Do you wanna know what I remember? Do we want to revisit the parts of this story you just glossed over? Because I remember Dad screaming at you to catch a baseball.

*A shift.*

*Back at a campsite. Joey and James play catch.*
*Throw.*

JAMES  Why are you doing that?

JOEY  Doing what?

JAMES  This thing with your feet.

JOEY  I don't know what you mean.

*He replicates the jump.*

JAMES  This jump.

JOEY  I'm not jumping.

JAMES  Yes you are! Stand your ground!

ANNIE  Dinner's ready in five, everyone.

JOEY  Can I wash my hands for dinner?

JAMES  Not until you get this right. Ball.

*Return.*

ANNIE  Dinner's ready.

JAMES  We're going to get this before we wash our hands. Look where your feet are right now, okay? Don't move from that spot.

JOEY  Okay.

*Throw.*

JAMES  You did it again!

JOEY  No I didn't.

JAMES  Yes you did.

JOEY  I didn't move my feet.

JAMES  But you moved your hips. It's just a ball, it can't hurt you. Ball.

*Return.*

JOEY  I'm hungry.

*Throw.*

JAMES  You did it again! Don't move!

*Return.*

JAMES  Don't move!

*Throw.*

JOEY  I'm catching the ball.

JAMES  It's bad form. Why are you doing that?

JOEY  I don't know.

JAMES  Why are you doing that?

JOEY  I don't know.

ANNIE  Dinner.

JAMES  Why are you doing that?

JOEY  Because I don't want to get hit by the ball! It hurts! Because you're throwing the ball too hard!

*A pause. James walks toward Joey.*

JAMES  Are you going to walk into a game and tell the other team that they're throwing too hard?

JOEY  No.

JAMES  Are you going to complain to your teammate when they're trying to turn a double play, when the runner is sprinting to first, that they threw the ball at you too hard?

JOEY  No.

JAMES  You can't hide from the ball. If you don't want it to hurt you, if you don't want it to sting, you have to face it head on. Even if it hits you, you won't know where it's coming from.

JOEY  Okay.

JAMES  Okay?

JOEY  Yes.

*Joey places the ball in James's glove. James steps back to throwing distance.*

ANNIE  Dinner, dear.

JAMES  We'll eat dinner when he gets it. Look at the ball. Are you looking?

JOEY  Yes.

JAMES  So stand tall and catch the ball.

*Throw.*

JAMES  Good. Again.

*Return.*

JAMES  Catch.

*Throw.*

JAMES  Don't step back.

*Return.*

JAMES  Catch.

*Throw.*

JAMES  Good. Again.

*Return.*

JAMES  Catch.

*Throw.*

JAMES  Don't step back, come on.

*Return.*

JAMES  Catch.

*Throw.*

JAMES  Good. Step into it.

> *Return.*

JAMES  Step into the ball. It's going to come harder now. It's going to come faster.

ANNIE  You're throwing the ball really hard at him.

JAMES  It's because he needs to be ready! He can't just step away from his problems. Watch the ball. Watch the ball.

> *Throw.*

JAMES  Catch the ball, catch the ball.

> *Return.*

JAMES  Why are you afraid of the ball?

JOEY  I don't know.

ANNIE  Dinner!

JAMES  Not yet! He has to get this, he has to learn. Catch it.

> *Throw.*

JAMES  Good. Again.

> *Return.*

JAMES  Catch it.

> *Throw.*

JAMES  Good. Again.

> *Return.*

JAMES  He won't get stronger unless I throw it this hard.

> *Throw.*

JAMES  Good. Again.

> *Return.*

JAMES  You have to stand up and face the ball. Stop looking at dinner, look at me.

ANNIE  He's hungry.

JAMES  Hungry? Catch it.

> *Throw. Return.*

JAMES  I've waited in ration lines with entire villages waiting for less food than what we're about to eat, so no one talk to me about wanting ham and cheese! When you wait in a line like that you learn, you learn that if a bully tries to cut you in line, if they try to take your food, they will only come back the next day to do it again if you do not stand your ground! So do not shy away from the ball. Catch it.

> *Throw.*

JAMES  Good. Again.

*Return.*

JAMES  Catch it.

*Throw.*

JAMES  Good. Again.

*Return.*

JAMES  I am sorry that I made you soft, I don't know how it happened.

*Throw.*

JAMES  No. Do it better.

*Return.*

JAMES  I have to throw harder, you have to be ready. Catch it.

*Throw. Return.*

JAMES  Catch it!

*Throw. Return.*

JAMES  Come on!

*Throw. Return.*

JAMES  Catch the fucking ball!

ANNIE  JAMES!

*As Annie screams, James turns his head and misses a line drive Joey throws right into his chest. He buckles to the ground.*

ANNIE  James!

JAMES  I'm fine. I'm fine.

ANNIE  We're done.

JAMES  That's fine.

*A shift.*

JENN  And it was like that for sports. For piano. For school. It was relentless.

JOEY  And look at us. Really, look at us. A doctor. Two lawyers. He was tough, okay? But look how we turned out.

MICHELLE  We were better for it, I think.

JENN  You think it was magnanimous? It was never about us, it was about control.

MICHELLE  You're being dramatic.

JENN  You're doing what you always do! You underplay and smooth over and protect him!

MICHELLE  I had it easier than you, I know that.

JENN  Yeah you never saw his bad side because you always gave him exactly what he wanted! What about what you wanted? Do you even remember what that feels like to want something for yourself?

## 32.

*A shift.*

　*Santa Monica. The beach.*

　*James returns to the campsite.*

ANNIE　Oh good, go get changed so we can get there on time.

JAMES　On time for what?

ANNIE　We talked about this.

JOEY　Universal Studios!

JAMES　Where now? Universal what?

JENN　It's a movie studio.

MICHELLE　And not like I care or anything but if we want to get there on time then we should probably get going soon or something, not like I care.

ANNIE　They give tours.

JAMES　Tours?

ANNIE　I told you about this.

JOEY　This is where they shot Butch Cassidy, Dad.

MICHELLE　That was actually 20th Century Fox, but they don't give tours, but this one is still pretty cool so we should get going maybe.

JAMES　I just finished five hours of field work.

ANNIE　You can rest in the car, I'll drive.

JAMES　. . . a movie studio?

ANNIE　They show you all the behind the scene elements. It'll be exciting.

JAMES　When did we talk about this?

ANNIE　This is for the kids.

JAMES　A movie studio? Really? Is that really the best use of their time?

ANNIE　Not now. We made a plan, we're going.

JAMES　What time is it?

ANNIE　An hour past when you said you'd be back.

MICHELLE　It's okay, we have time.

JAMES　We shouldn't be spending money on something so frivolous. If we're going to go on an excursion, it should be for something substantive.

ANNIE　This is culture.

JAMES　A museum is culture.

ANNIE　Well we'll do that some other time. Today, this is what we're doing as a family. We should do this as a family.

JAMES　We pay for these tours?

*Annie throws down the laundry she was folding and starts packing up a bag.*

JAMES   What is it?

ANNIE   We're going without you, then.

JAMES   You are, are you?

ANNIE   As we've just been sitting here waiting for you, no idea when you'll come back or not—

JAMES   This is why we're here. For my work.

ANNIE   That's why *you're* here. What are we supposed to do, then?

JAMES   You know how hard I've been working to—

ANNIE   So have I—I've been working to give our children good experiences this whole summer while you—

JAMES   While I what?

MICHELLE   It's okay—

ANNIE   —so we figured something out.

JAMES   Are these tours meant for children?

ANNIE   Yes! Yes they are! What else would they be?

JAMES   A waste of money and a distraction from—

ANNIE   —it's the one thing Michelle's asked for this entire trip—

JAMES   —a distraction, no a fantasy, no a moral hazard—

ANNIE   —moral hazard—

JAMES   —yes! Filling their head with these degenerate—

MICHELLE   —I don't want to go!

        *A pause.*

ANNIE   What's that?

MICHELLE   I don't want to go. I don't want to go on the tour. We can just stay here.

ANNIE   You've been asking me about this since we crossed the California state line.

MICHELLE   I changed my mind. It sounds dumb.

JAMES   I'm going to change.

ANNIE   We can go. If you want to go, we can—

MICHELLE   I don't want to go, so can you two stop? It's stupid. It doesn't matter. It's kid stuff.

        *A shift.*

JENN   Sorry, what was that? Couldn't hear you.

        *A shift. Michelle repeats herself.*

MICHELLE   It's stupid. It doesn't matter. It's kid's stuff.

        *A shift.*

JENN  You know I never saw you pick up a notebook again. I never saw you sign up for drama club, I never saw you practice your violin. You just gave up. Everything after that was serious, everything was to make Dad happy. Make Dad happy. Because everything that ever made you happy was:

*A shift. Michelle repeats herself again.*

MICHELLE  —stupid. It doesn't matter. It's kid's stuff.

*A shift.*

JENN  So how about we don't pretend that—

JOEY  Okay stop! Stop! Stop!


## 33.


*The cemetery.*

JOEY  Back the fuck off of her, okay? You've made your point, Jenn. Jesus. Your powers of argument really are wasted in the field of medicine.

JENN  Like you haven't been selling me a narrative about Dad this whole time!

JOEY  What are you trying to prove, Jenn?

JENN  I—

JOEY  Really, what do you want? What are you trying to convince us of?

JENN  Just how it actually—

JOEY  What are you trying to take from us?

JENN  I. I don't know.

JOEY  Was he a product of his time? Sure. Of course. But what did he do? Did he hit us? Cause I've heard those stories from other families and they would make your skin crawl. What did he do, Jenn? Other than prepare us for the world. Other than work himself into the ground.

MICHELLE  Joey!

JOEY  For who? For himself? The guy who wouldn't buy an IPA for himself because it was too expensive, I had to do it for him? You know, maybe he was a tyrant, but looking back at this trip maybe you were just a spoiled brat. Maybe we all were.

MICHELLE  Stop!

JOEY  No! She doesn't get to come in here after she's been nowhere, after she's done nothing, and walk all over you. Walk all over him! Us! I mean, where have you been? Where the hell have you been? And now you're just going to say nothing? Tell me I'm wrong, tell me to shut up. Just say something! Say something!

MICHELLE  You're acting like him!

> *A silence.*

MICHELLE  Listen. You sound just like him.

> *A silence.*

MICHELLE  . . . I'll drive you to the airport, let's go.

JOEY  Wait what? No.

MICHELLE  She needs to get going, Joey.

JOEY  She hasn't even bought her ticket yet. I mean, we haven't even like, said any words yet.

MICHELLE  We spent a whole day saying words.

JOEY  Dinner. We still have time to do dinner. Let's do dinner. You'll see the kids real quick.

MICHELLE  You never know with traffic to the airport.

JENN  I'll be back soon.

MICHELLE  You won't. It's fine.

JENN  Woah.

JOEY  Michelle.

MICHELLE  I mean, this is your first time here since when? Definitely since before the funeral which you missed. We're lucky to see you once every five years, let's just call it like we see it. You did your duty. You showed up. You're absolved. Check it off the list, right?

JENN  That's not why I'm here.

MICHELLE  No?

JENN  I mean, isn't that why anyone does this? To help them move on?

MICHELLE  Move on from who, Jenn? Him? All of us?

JOEY  No. We're not done. It doesn't get to end like this.

MICHELLE  How are we going forward from this? We should just cut our losses. For all of our sakes.

JOEY  We can't end it like this. Are we just going to avoid this like we avoid everything?

JENN  Oh because it's so fun to go down memory lane

JOEY  It isn't with you!

JENN  What do you want from me? Why are you doing this?

JOEY  Because I thought it would be a good thing! Because I thought you'd remember that there was good that happened in this family, too! Because maybe you would stay!

*A pause.*

JENN  You're seeing it through rose-colored glasses, I'm just telling you how it actually was.

JOEY  Cause you're some arbiter of truth.

JENN  And you're not going to score any brownie points by sticking up for Dad.

*The children talk over each other.*

MICHELLE  Stop it!

JOEY  I am not sticking up for him!

JENN  Then what are you doing?

MICHELLE  I cannot play referee anymore.

JOEY  Maybe I'm just trying to show some respect.

JENN  Which needs to be earned.

MICHELLE  It is exhausting. Joey, stop.

JENN  Let's just leave. Can we please leave.

*They overlap, repeat themselves, repeat each other. A cacophony.*

JOEY  Not yet!

MICHELLE  Why?

JOEY  We need to fix this! We need to fix this!

MICHELLE  Stop! Please stop!

JENN  Looking back isn't going to fix what happened! Nothing can fix what happened!

*And everything stops.*


## 34.


*The children are sucked back into memory.*

*1990.*

*A back room of a church.*

*Maybe there is organ music playing in the background, maybe just the hum of a buoyant crowd chatting outside.*

*But this room is quiet.*

*Jenn agonizes over her hair in a mirror, Michelle next to her.*

*Joey peeks out of the door.*

JENN  Stop opening the door.

MICHELLE  If Tom sees her before the ceremony it's bad luck, doofus.

JOEY  Sorry, just checking—

JENN  He's not coming.

JOEY  I wasn't looking for—

JENN  You were. It's fine. But he's a man of his word, he's not coming. It's
fine. I'm fine. I'm fine other than these freaking bangs. Why did I ever
think it was a good idea to get bangs?

MICHELLE  They look great.

JENN  They look awful. Ah well, they're only memories that will last a lifetime.

MICHELLE  I'm sorry, Jenn.

JENN  It's seriously fine! Jesus! Tom and I already actually did the thing at the
courthouse so this is just for like . . . everyone else. Do you have scissors?

MICHELLE  Take a breath, Jenn.

JENN  It's just that this dress is too tight. I feel like I'm Marie Antoinette. I'm
not upset, okay? Like, I've been prepared for this, it's not like a shock. It's
not like he sprung it on me that he hates Tom's guts, ya know? So I'm not
upset about him not being here. Like, honestly, good, you know?

> *The sound of a heavy door opening and closing outside of the room. Joey*
> *peeks out of the room.*

JENN  Who is it?

> *Jenn rushes to the door and looks out.*
> *A pause.*

JENN  Cousin fucking Joon.

> *Jenn allows herself one moment of absolute and utter soul-wrenching grief.*
> *And then Jenn pulls herself together.*

JENN  Joey, you're going to have to do it. It'll be fun. You're going to have to
walk me down the aisle.

JOEY  There's still time.

JENN  He's not coming! He's not coming. No. No, I'm done. We're done.

> *A shift.*

## 35.

> *The cemetery.*

JENN  So show me this fun memory and that fun memory. But it's all make-
believe. How about you show me the version where he was a part of
my life for the last twenty plus years? Where he came to my wedding
instead of cutting me off. Where he was the one walking me down the
aisle instead of Joey playing the role of my father. Show me the version

where he was there when Tom and I had Patrick. You can't, can you? Because it doesn't exist. Show me that version and maybe it will be more fun strolling down memory lane. I'm going to remember him. I'm going to remember the real him. Maybe I wish he'd left America without us! Maybe I wish he'd left!

ANNIE  We were never going to leave.

>*A much older Annie speaks to the children.*

ANNIE  We thought about it, it was a courtesy, but we were never going to leave.

JENN  Mom—

JOEY  Jenn, I didn't know she was—

MICHELLE  I told her. I told her Jenn was in town.

JOEY  Why?

MICHELLE  Because we've waited long enough. Because it's time.

JENN  It's alright, Joey. It's alright. Hi, Mom.

ANNIE  Hello, love.

JENN  Did you drive here yourself?

ANNIE  I do every month.

JENN  You're not supposed to be driving.

ANNIE  I'm still a better driver than you, Jenn. And you're right to be angry, love. But we were never going to leave.

JENN  It sure seemed like you were going to leave.

ANNIE  Park was just as bad as anyone who came before! We had our work! I had my own career, we weren't just going to leave that behind. And he wouldn't have done that to you children. You were Americans. We all were.

JOEY  It felt real.

JENN  I think you're remembering it how you want to remember it, Mom.

ANNIE  And you are not?

JOEY  He did change, Jenn. He changed when he got—

JENN  —older? I know. That's all you've said. But it doesn't matter, I never got to see it. He was a bully.

ANNIE  He was a father.

JENN  He never respected me.

ANNIE  He worshiped you.

JENN  He didn't see me.

ANNIE  He saw the best in you.

JENN  Maybe I don't need to be my best all the time. Maybe I never wanted to be in that Coleman trailer, dragged across the country on some vanity trip to prove to himself that he could have been someone, that he could have been someone who matters.

ANNIE  A Coleman? No.

JENN  Yes.

MICHELLE  Yes. I remember.

ANNIE  It was an Apache Tent Trailer.

JOEY  I remember it too, Mom.

JENN  We all do.

ANNIE  The Coleman didn't have awnings. We had the awning.

JENN  I swear I—

ANNIE  You are remembering the bad, I am remembering it all. You were teenagers! So dramatic! I was there, too, you know.

MICHELLE  We know, Mom.

JOEY  I just Googled it . . . no awnings on the Coleman.
        *Huh.*

ANNIE  I was there, too. I was there, too. You're choosing to remember all of the bad. You're forgetting so much. So much good.


## 36.

        *And we move quickly through:*
            *A road in the Colorado mountains.*

JAMES  Look at how tall those mountains are!

ANNIE  James keep your eyes on the road!

MICHELLE  Dad!!!

JAMES  But look at how incredible they are! You don't see that in Wisconsin, do you?

JOEY  We're going to die!!

JENN  Open your eyes and look!

JAMES  Wow.

JENN  Wow.

        *Utah. A campsite. Jenn and James run in.*

ANNIE  You're soaking wet!

JAMES  Necessity breeding ingenuity, love!

JENN  The melons taste so much better chilled but we ran out of ice—

JAMES  So we stacked rocks in the river—

JENN  And are stream-chilling the fruit as we speak.

JAMES   Now give me a big hug.

    *He runs to hug her.*

ANNIE   Wet!! Wet!

    *A campsite in California.*

MICHELLE   Can we open our eyes yet?

JAMES   Not yet, not yet.

JOEY   Now?

JAMES   Now.

JENN   Woah.

JAMES   Happy Fourth of July!

MICHELLE   It looks like a mini-State Fair!

JOEY   McDonald's!

ANNIE   Where did you get all of this? These streamers? Everything?

JAMES   Happy Fourth, everyone.

    *A desert road. The radio plays "Danny Boy."*

JAMES   This is my favorite song! A classic!

MICHELLE   Yeah, we know!

JAMES   "Oh, Danny boy, the pipes, the pipes are calling
From glen to glen, and down the mountain side."

MICHELLE   We're completely alone and I'm embarrassed for you.

    *James sings even louder.*

JAMES   "The summer's gone, and all the roses falling,
It's you, it's you must go and I must bide."

    *A gas station in Wisconsin.*

JAMES   All filled up and ready to go!

ANNIE   Did you know that there are four million, seventy-one thousand miles of road in the continental United States?

JAMES   And here.

    *He hands the kids a bag of lemon drops.*

JOEY   Lemon drops!

JAMES   Just remember to share!

JENN, MICHELLE, AND JOEY   Thanks, Dad.

## 37.

    *Jenn finds herself outside of the motel pool in Las Vegas. James sits on a pool chair with a drink in one hand and a cigarette in the other.*

JAMES  What are you doing?

JENN  What do you mean?

JAMES  I mean what are you doing up so late?

JENN  Oh. I, um. I think I got up because I couldn't sleep. It was hot and I couldn't sleep.

JAMES  No one talked to me today.

JENN  You didn't say anything.

JAMES  I'd walk into a room and people would stop talking.

JENN  I think. I think they might be afraid of you, Dad.

JAMES  Huh.

JENN  I dunno.

JAMES  That's okay. That's okay. It is so easy to be soft, it is so easy to forget. But I can't forget. I won't let myself. Because what happens if I forget and we aren't ready? What if you're not ready, and you get hurt? Maybe the ends justify those means. Maybe what you need is you need to be more afraid of me than you are of the ball, right? Maybe you'll hate me—

JENN  We don't—

JAMES  But maybe that is okay. Do you see this lighter?

JENN  Yes.

JAMES  This lighter belonged to Ko Yun-ju. We grew up together in Damyang. He was always the talker, I was the listener. He could talk us into extra meals in a ration line, he could talk us into a dance hall that was already full. The Butch to my Sundance, eh? We even went up to Seoul at the same time to study for university.

JENN  Did he die in the war?

JAMES  You're getting ahead of my story.

JENN  Sorry.

JAMES  We were only in university for three months before the war started. You know how I said that we did everything together? That includes accelerated officer training. Top of our class there, too.

JENN  What happened to him?

JAMES  They split us up. They recognized my propensity for language and I became an officer who oversaw the press corp. I had my own jeep, would drive American and French press to briefings and their lodgings. That is how I met Mr. Casserly who sponsored my coming to America.

JENN  What happened to Yun-ju?

JAMES  He became a captain on the front lines.

JENN  Oh.

JAMES  What was different between the two of us?

JENN  You spoke English better.

JAMES  Yun-ju was fluent.

JENN  You worked harder.

JAMES  No.

JENN  You were smarter.

JAMES  No.

JENN  What was it?

JAMES  Nothing. There was nothing different about us. We worked just as hard, our grades were just as good. He might have even spoken French better than me, at the end of the day. They just chose me. They just chose me. And I stayed out of the front lines and he died. I was lucky, that's it. And that's what haunts me at night, that's what I lie awake thinking about. Not the things that went wrong but the things that went right . . . and how when I replay them back in my head they could have gone wrong in so many ways. That is why you need to be a doctor. Because when societal disruption comes, you need to be the person that they value. You need to be the person who does not get sent to the front. You need to protect yourself. You have to be more than lucky.

JENN  Dad, it's a different time. We don't have to worry about those things anymore.

JAMES  There will always be disruption. There will always be.

*James takes a drag from his cigarette.*

JAMES  I want things to be easy for you. I want things to be easier for you. But if they're too easy, then you won't be ready, do you understand?

JENN  Ready for what, Dad?

JAMES  Never mind.

JENN  Dad?

JAMES  Yes?

JENN  What happened at the meeting?

JAMES  It was a dinner.

JENN  Okay.

JAMES  A large council of Korean Americans, expats, the like. President Park gave a speech. I sat next to him at dinner after.

JENN  What was that like?

JAMES  He was perfectly nice. Said all the right things. But there was a moment, a moment where he looked me straight in the eyes, and I saw that this man was a killer. I felt a chill run down my spine, one that I hadn't felt since . . . I hadn't felt that afraid in a long time.

>*A silence. James takes a long drag from his cigarette. Then, with great effort:*

JAMES   I . . . love you.

>*A silence.*

JAMES   Do you know I love you?

JENN   Yes.

>*A silence.*

JAMES   Good.

>*A long silence.*

JENN   Dad?

JAMES   Yes?

JENN   Can I go to bed now?

JAMES   Oh. Yes. Go.

JENN   I'm sorry.

JAMES   Don't be. Go to bed.


## 38.

>*The children and Annie talk.*

MICHELLE   I never knew that about his friend.

JOEY   He never talked about the war.

JENN   He was scared. He was really scared. That's why we didn't go.

ANNIE   Seven years later, President Park was assassinated by his own intelligence service. He should have been scared.

JENN   He was younger than me. On that road trip. He was younger than I am now. I just realized that.

ANNIE   It's time to go.

JOEY   I can drive you.

ANNIE   Wait.

>*She faces the grave. She bows.*

ANNIE   Thank you. You did it,

JENN   That's okay, Mom.

>*She puts an arm on Annie's shoulder.*

JENN   Let's go home, okay?

>*They start to head out.*

JENN   I didn't say it back.

ANNIE   What was that?

JENN   Nothing.

> *Everyone leaves except for Jenn.*
> > *A shift.*

## 39.

MICHELLE   Jenn! Jenn! We still have bags in the trunk! Did you already go inside?

> *Milwaukee. The driveway.*
> > *Joey, Michelle, and James unload the car.*
> > *Jenn watches from the side.*

JOEY   Home sweet home!

> *Michelle yells inside the house.*

MICHELLE   Jenn! You better help us finish unloading the car before you take a shower!

JOEY   I call the shower second!

MICHELLE   Finish unloading the back of the car first.

JOEY   Can you grab my backpack from the back seat since I grabbed your suitcase?

> *Joey runs to the camper.*

MICHELLE   What do we do with the cooler and stove?

JAMES   I will return them with the camper, you can leave them.

> *Joey returns from the camper.*

JOEY   Dad, Mom wants to know if you want to eat something, or if you're going to return the camper now.

JAMES   Tell her I'll do it now.

JOEY   Mom! He says he's going to do it now!

MICHELLE   Go tell her, don't just yell.

JOEY   Right, right.

> *Joey runs to the camper.*

JOEY   Mom! Dad says he's going to do it now!

MICHELLE   Unbelievable. I look forward to my bed. I really missed my bed.

> *Annie enters, Joey follows behind.*

ANNIE   Don't drag dirt around the house, leave the bags at the door and we can unpack later.

JAMES   I think that's everything.

JOEY  Can I go shower now?

ANNIE  Hey.

MICHELLE  Oh yeah thank you for the trip, Dad.

JOEY  Yeah thank you, Dad. It was really fun.

>   *The kids head inside.*

ANNIE  Thank you for driving, dear.

JAMES  You're welcome.

ANNIE  Are you okay?

JAMES  Just tired.

ANNIE  I know.

JAMES  Have to go to work tomorrow.

ANNIE  I know. Come in, eat and shower, then drop it off.

JAMES  I just want to get it done now.

ANNIE  Alright.

>   *Annie turns to the house.*

JAMES  We're home.

ANNIE  We are.

JAMES  I'm scared.

ANNIE  I know.

>   *Annie heads inside. James sits in the car.*
>
>   *Then, Jenn walks back to the grave.*

JENN  Hi, Dad. I was about to take the rental back to the airport and I just, I came back here. I don't know why. I'd say better late than never, but I'm not sure where this lands on the spectrum. Um. I'm giving up trying to understand you. Don't think it's really possible. So I just thought I'd say some things that, you know, you missed. Tom's great. He got a real job and cut his hair, so maybe you'd like him now. I'm kidding. That's a joke. I don't know why I'm apologizing. And I know that you've seen pictures from Michelle or Joey forwarding them to you and stuff but the kids are, they're good. They're old, now. Like pretty much how old I was when you dragged us across America. And I think they like me. How do you know at this age, right?

I spent a lot of growing up trying to be what you wanted me to be and I spent the other half rebelling against that, either way I am who I am because of you. The kids don't know why I'm out here this weekend. They think it's a business trip or something. I don't really talk about it. Talk about you. And hey. I guess I'm just like you then, right?

I don't think I'm going to fly out today. I think I'm going to stay for the weekend. I think that will be . . . good.

Maybe I'm done talking. Yeah. Maybe we can just sit.

*Jenn sits down next to James.*

*James turns on the car. The radio plays classical music.*

JENN   I brought something. Stopped at a gas station on the way here and they were just sitting there so.

*James turns the dial, and he hears something new, something his children would listen to. He doesn't turn the radio off.*

*Jenn pulls out a little bag of lemon drops.*

JENN   We can share.

*Blackout.*

*End of play.*

     ·       ·       ·

# পাব্লিক অবসেনিটিস
# **Public Obscenities**

## SHAYOK MISHA CHOWDHURY

*Pradip Kumar Chakraborty*
*1945–2023*

*for Mama*
*and his dreams*

*for Mami*
*and my whole P544 family*

*and for Kameron*

*with immeasurable gratitude to*
*Ma and Baba*

## *Characters*

| | |
|---|---|
| CHOTON: | A Bengali American PhD student, approaching thirty, born in Kolkata, raised in the US. He speaks fluent Bangla and American English. |
| RAHEEM: | Choton's boyfriend, Black American, mid-twenties. A cinematographer. |
| PISHIMONI: | Choton's aunt, his father's sister. Born and raised in Kolkata, Bangla is her primary language. Speaking English exhausts her. |
| PISHE: | Pishimoni's husband, Choton's uncle, also born and raised in Kolkata. |
| SHOU: | Early to mid-twenties, identifies as kothi, a gender category native to the Indian subcontinent. |
| THAMMI: | Choton's paternal grandmother, eighties, bedridden, with dementia. |
| JITESH: | Caretaker to Thammi and the household help. Doesn't speak English. |
| BABA: | Choton's father, appears briefly on FaceTime. His English is Americanized. |
| SEBANTI: | A friend of Shou's, an elder. Identifies as hijra. |

### Setting

A deteriorating two-story house in South Kolkata. Flickering tube lights. Cracked plaster. Ceiling fans. A stairwell. Black-and-white portraits stare down from the walls, covered in a skin of dust.

### Language and Punctuation

This is a bilingual play. The Bangla is deliberately written in Roman script and visually undifferentiated from the English. Sometimes it is translated. Sometimes it isn't. The play relies on the specificity of each character's fluency and dialect. Casting should attend to these specificities. In the script, a slash indicates where the following line begins, overlapping. An em-dash indicates an interruption, either by the next line or by a pivot in the speaker's own train of thought. An ellipsis indicates searching for a thought or a word.

Please note that the Bengali dialogue has been romanized with the actors and not standardization in mind.

# 1. FILM STUDIES

*Choton, Raheem, and Pishimoni, at the dinner table. Choton eats with a fork. Raheem eats with his hands. Pishimoni observes him with delight.*

PISHIMONI  Bhalo chhele. Haat diye kheye nay, kono shawmoshya nei.
*She pinches Raheem's cheek.*

PISHIMONI  Good boy!

CHOTON  As opposed to me eating with a fork.

RAHEEM  What can I say, I'm a good boy.

PISHIMONI  Uncle has cooked this one. Not very spicy. Little spicy, little oil. Bland aar ki.

RAHEEM  It's delicious—

CHOTON  Aare *bland* na, she doesn't mean like it's light, it's not / too rich.

PISHIMONI  Hyan, light. Simple.

RAHEEM  *(mouth full)* Tastes like something my mom would make.

PISHIMONI  *(misunderstanding)* You like it?

CHOTON  Bollo "it's something his mom would make."

PISHIMONI  Ki?

CHOTON  Bolchhe or Ma o erokom ranna kawre.

PISHIMONI  Shedin dekhchhilam TV te, Vietnam e naki ora kumro phool diye / ekta—

CHOTON  English.

PISHIMONI  I am telling: on TV I saw. In Vietnam they are making—ei kumro'r ingriji ki re?

CHOTON  Mm . . . pumpkin?

PISHIMONI  Pumpkin, yes. In Vietnam I saw they are making the stuffed pumpkin flower. Bengalis we also make this pumpkin flower. We call it kumro / phool.

CHOTON  Or more like squash actually, squash / blossoms.

PISHIMONI  It is not available this time. Next time, you come in October November, I will make it. But not stuffed, we make it fried. In Vietnam I saw, they put prawn, pork. I love to watch this things, in which country which food they are eating.
*She watches Raheem eat.*

PISHIMONI  Which food you are eating there in California?

CHOTON  Aabar ei proshno?

PISHIMONI   Aare I want to know what is the cuisine. Aamar khub interesting lage. Bibhinno deshe, what type of food is available. Okhane you have
pasta na? Choton, he cook pasta for us.

CHOTON   Awnek Bangali ranna o korchhi aajkal. Raheem likes that um . . .
oi je Thammi ekta tomato ola rui-maachh korto na. I've been making that
with cod.

PISHIMONI   *(to Raheem)* You like fish?

RAHEEM   I do.

PISHIMONI   *(impressed, to Choton)* Ba ba Bangali chhele toh puro.

CHOTON   She's saying / you're—

PISHIMONI   Which food you like best, chicken or fish?

RAHEEM   Oh I like both.

CHOTON   Pishimoni, oi deshe toh—ekdin we might have pasta, next day we
might have—I don't know, Ethiopian food, Vietnamese / food—

PISHIMONI   In America you are having people from all countries. Tai na?
*(to Raheem)* Basically you are from which country?

> Choton and Raheem exchange a smirk.

CHOTON   *(to Pishimoni)* He's American, Pishimoni.

PISHIMONI   But parents are from?

> Raheem finishes a mouthful of food.

RAHEEM   I grew up in Chicago, but my parents are from South Carolina
originally—

PISHIMONI   Ei Carolina tei na Khuki Pishi thhake?

CHOTON   *(to Pishimoni)* Ota *North* Carolina.

PISHIMONI   *(to Raheem)* My father's cousin-sister, she is also there in
Carolina. Very intelligent / lady.

CHOTON   You met her at Rinku's wedding, she was the like, short one with
/ the—

> Pishimoni pops a slice of raw onion in her mouth.

PISHIMONI   *(to Raheem)* So your mother speaks which language?

CHOTON   Pishimoni—

RAHEEM   She speaks / English.

CHOTON   —or Ma toh o deshei bawro hoychhe.

PISHIMONI   *(to Raheem)* Mother tongue is English?

RAHEEM   I mean . . . that's— But yeah, yes—

CHOTON   *(to Raheem, conspiratorial)* I should give her my copy of *Lose Your
Mother*.

PISHIMONI   Ki bolchhish?

CHOTON  Kichhu na.

PISHIMONI  O ke Bangla shekha, aar eto ingriji parchhina.

CHOTON  *(to Raheem)* She's saying—

PISHIMONI  *(patting Raheem's hand)* You learn Bengali. Bengali is a very old. *Beautiful* language.

CHOTON  Hey Raheem knows shushshuri!

PISHIMONI  Shushshuri you know? Shushshuri is very important. *(extending her arm to Choton)* De to ektu.

> *Choton caresses her arm gently with his fingertips. Raheem looks slightly crestfallen. Choton notices this. Pishe emerges from the computer room.*

PISHE  Chicken ta kheyechhish?

CHOTON  Ei je khacchhi.

PISHE  *(to Raheem)* You have tasted?

RAHEEM  Yeah it's delicious, thank you.

PISHE  This one is simple preparation. No oil. Only black pepper, salt—

PISHIMONI  *(offering more)* Little bit?

RAHEEM  Oh no, I'm good thanks.

PISHIMONI  Good?

RAHEEM  I had way too much already.

PISHIMONI  *(to Choton)* O toh tao khay.

PISHE  *(to Pishimoni, outstretching his palm)* Kothhay ekta mishti dao dekhi?

CHOTON  *(to Raheem)* You ok?

RAHEEM  Mm hm.

CHOTON  Sure?

> *Pishimoni stands with great difficulty and waddles toward the fridge.*

PISHIMONI  Choton, you know. He used to take only boiled egg, boiled rice, boiled potato.

CHOTON  This is twenty years ago.

PISHE  So Rohim. How you are finding India?

RAHEEM  Oh it's— I mean so far I've basically only seen this house but it's—

PISHIMONI  *(peering into the fridge)* Dekhchhina toh . . .

PISHE  Ki?

PISHIMONI  Shondesh.

PISHE  Aare okhanei achhe.

CHOTON  We're actually planning on going up to Tikiapara to see where this—

PISHIMONI  Ki para?

CHOTON  Aare oi Howrah Station er kachhe oi slums gulo achhe na.

PISHIMONI   O ke Victoria Memorial e niye ja.

CHOTON   English!

PISHIMONI   You have seen Victoria Memorial?

RAHEEM   I've seen pictures.

PISHIMONI   Beautiful na?

*She kneels heavily in front of the open fridge and peers into its depths.*

CHOTON   Raheem's a big Mrinal Sen fan so we wanted to go see where this scene in *Calcutta 71* was—

PISHE   *(surprised)* Mrinal Sen?

RAHEEM   Yup. Yeah / my—

PISHE   They know Mrinal Sen in US?

RAHEEM   Mm . . . not really, but—

PISHE   Ray they know, but Sen—

RAHEEM   Yeah, people don't really know him, but my dad saw *Khandhar* at the Chicago Film Festival way back and it's his like . . . all-time favorite film, so I / basically—

PISHE   Bojho.

CHOTON   Yeah Raheem's dad is a *huge* movie buff.

PISHIMONI   What is his profession? / Your father—

RAHEEM   My dad? I mean he's retired now, but he did all kinds of things, he worked for the postal service for—

CHOTON   Ask him about any foreign film though, who was in it, what year it came out—

PISHIMONI   *(to Choton)* Tui Rohim ke Dadu'r Rolleicord ta dekhiyechhish?

*She plops back down in her chair, empty-handed.*

PISHE   *(re: the mishti)* Ki holo?

RAHEEM   Did—

PISHIMONI   Bolchhi nei.

RAHEEM   —you say Rolleicord?

PISHIMONI   My father's old Rolleicord is there. You like to see?

RAHEEM   I would love that.

PISHIMONI   Jitesh!

RAHEEM   Oh—there's no rush—

CHOTON   Raheem loves old stuff. If it isn't fully disintegrating, he won't even look at it.

RAHEEM   Which is how *you* caught my eye.

PISHIMONI   Ei Jitesh!

JITESH   *(offstage)* Jaiiiii.

CHOTON   O kintu aamar che maatro ek bawchhorer chhoto.

PISHIMONI   O tor che chhoto?

CHOTON   *(to Raheem, victorious)* Ha!

RAHEEM   What?

CHOTON   She thinks *you* look older than *me.*

PISHIMONI   Not older. Maane "manly" aar ki.

CHOTON   Ki??

RAHEEM   *(loving this)* She just call me "manly"?

CHOTON   Ki bolchho?

PISHE   So Rohim, photography is your subject?

CHOTON   Photography na, film, film.

PISHE   Tui je bolechhili photography.

CHOTON   *Director* of Photography.

RAHEEM   I mean photography's my subject, that's a true statement.

PISHIMONI   Many cinemas are there also very nearby. Old cinema hall.
   Priya cinema is there, Bijoli, Menoka.

RAHEEM   *(to Choton)* Oh yeah you holdin' out on me?

CHOTON   *(mouth full of food)* They're all in Hindi, no subtitles.

PISHIMONI   O ke INOX e niye ja, English films are there—

RAHEEM   Oh I want the Hindi films.

CHOTON   I don't.

PISHIMONI   Hindi is there, Bengali is there. English is also there—
      *Jitesh enters.*

PISHIMONI   *(to Jitesh)* Ei shon, Baba'r camera ta niye ay to.
      *Jitesh grabs a ring of keys from a hook on the wall.*

THAMMI   *(from offstage)* Jitesh?

PISHIMONI   Oi dyakh. Jitesh dhuklei ter pay.
      *Pishimoni goes to the door and speaks to Thammi.*

PISHIMONI   Ki Ma? Ki holo?

THAMMI   Ke?

PISHIMONI   Choton eschhe toh. Ei dyakho ke eschhe.
      *Choton goes to the door.*

CHOTON   Ki go Thammi.

THAMMI   Hm?

PISHIMONI   Choton eschhe. Ei je ektu aagey kawthha bolle.

THAMMI   Jawl.

PISHIMONI   *(to Jitesh)* De tu ektu jawl Ma ke.

PISHE *(to Raheem)* Sen is not so artistic I think. Tai na? Not like Ray.

RAHEEM  Mm . . . I—                    *(Jitesh grabs a Kinley bottle from the table.)*

PISHE  Tasteful I mean.          PISHIMONI  Ei ota na, ota Choton der jawl.

CHOTON  "Tasteful" maane?

PISHE  Dyakh Pathher Panchali, Aparajito it is . . . maane this is *art* actually. Isn't it? Even camerawork is . . . ki bolbo? . . . like a painting.

RAHEEM  Huh. That's—

CHOTON  Pishe—

RAHEEM  No that's interesting, I don't know . . . I don't know, I guess I kind of feel like Sen's films are more . . . painterly than—

PISHE  Sen?

RAHEEM  I mean don't get me wrong, Ray is a genius obviously, I just . . . I guess like . . . when I watch his stuff, I kind of feel like—like he wants us to forget there's a camera, right?

PISHIMONI  *(to Choton)* O Bangla cinema niye eto / shikhlo ki kore?

PISHE  See for Ray this is reality toh. He is showing the reality of the life in Bengal.

RAHEEM  *Totally*, that kind of like . . . slice of life, super naturalistic—

CHOTON  Sen was a realist too though.

RAHEEM  Sure . . .

CHOTON  I mean he was definitely pushing against the like . . . low-brow, song-and-dancey vibes of like mainstream Bollywood / cinema.

PISHE  See, Bengali cinema is not like Hindi cinema / actually.

CHOTON  Ei je—

PISHE  Bengalis we are interested in culture, politics / this kind of—

CHOTON  This is exactly what I was talking about, Bengalis see themselves as the arbiters of "serious" art right? Ei je bolle "tasteful," "bhawdro" . . . these were *"bhawdro*lok" . . .

RAHEEM  What's that?

CHOTON  Bhawdro's like . . . mm . . .

PISHE  Gentle.

CHOTON  Mm . . . not / exactly.

PISHE  This is "gentleman." Bhawdrolok.

CHOTON  . . . gent*eel* maybe.

RAHEEM  I mean I guess there is something kind of campy about Sen's stuff / which—

PISHIMONI  Acchha aamake ektu bawl toh, ki project niye eschhish. Aamar khub icchha kawre jante, tor kirokom kaaj—

CHOTON  Ei ta toh ekta . . . documentary thik na, kintu orokomi project /
bolte paro—

PISHIMONI  Tor na English chhilo subject?

CHOTON  Hyan maane . . . English toh . . . at the PhD level, English maane . . .
shudhu literature toh na. Anthropology, performance studies, film studies
shob kichhu miliye . . . maane interdisciplinary ja ke bawle. Kintu aami
toh asholey English thheke Gender and Women's Studies department e
transfer kore giyechhi karon—

PISHIMONI  *Women's* Studies?

CHOTON  Hyan aamar advisor jini . . . uni toh Black and Third World
Feminisms niye kaaj kawren, duto department ei joint appointment. Aar
jehetu aamar research is looking at . . . India te . . . specifically Kolkata
tei . . . ki dhawroner indigenous vocabulary roychhe around gender,
sex . . . maane ei concept gulo ki bhabe nirmito hoy in a postcolonial /
context—

PISHIMONI  *(to Pishe)* Ba ba—

CHOTON  *(uncertain)* Ki holo?

PISHIMONI  —"ki bhabe *nirmito* hoy"—
  *Pishe smiles.*

CHOTON  Doesn't "nirmito" mean—

PISHE  Tui PhD kore kawto ta pekechhish dekhchhi—

CHOTON  Aare shawrol kawthha i bebohar korlam toh.
  *This cracks Pishe and Pishimoni up.*

PISHIMONI  Maa go maa. Aabar "shawrol kawthha" . . .
  *She tries to get a hold of her giggles. Choton is deflated.*

PISHIMONI  Aare rege jash na. Ki holo?

CHOTON  Kichhu na.
  *Pishimoni clucks her tongue.*

PISHIMONI  Raag korish na Babu. Tui je kawto bawro bawro kaaj / korchhish.

CHOTON  I haven't even finished my PhD yet, Pishimoni.

PISHIMONI  *(to Raheem)* You know my father, he also was English professor.

CHOTON  Anyways long story short, it's a kind of queer archiving project,
and I roped Raheem into coming and filming—

PISHE  Acchha Chicago is near to Minnesota, tai na?

CHOTON  What?

PISHE  Na I am having one friend there in Minnesota. O bollo okhane na
ki sub-zero zone. Is it so?

CHOTON  I mean . . . it is definitely very / cold.

PISHE  *Whole* year sub-zero?

RAHEEM  It gets pretty hot in the summer. But not like—I mean what y'all have goin' on here is next level.

PISHE  *(enjoying this)* Next level na? Your Pishimoni, she says to me, why can you not put pant-shirt like a civilized fellow, but I am saying, it is a question of climate. Each one should make adjustment, tai na? This one it is tropical zone. Bengal.

PISHIMONI  Janish TV te shedin dekhlam—

CHOTON  English.

PISHIMONI  —even tropical there are different type. Ekhane naki savannah?

PISHE  Dhat.

PISHIMONI  *(insistent)* Shotti. Aami bhebechhilam shudhu—I thought only in Africa they are having savannah.

PISHE  Your Pishimoni is a great believer in TV. TV te *jai bawle / sheta.*

PISHIMONI  Aare baba eta ashol, dekho ekbar tomar Google e.

*Jitesh enters with the Rolleicord.*

PISHIMONI  Eiii je. Dekhi.

PISHE  *(to Jitesh)* Dyakh to, freeze e shondesh er baksho ta pash kina.

PISHIMONI  *(offering Raheem the camera)* You like to see?

RAHEEM  Hold on, lemme just wash my—

*He stands.*

CHOTON  *(pointing)* There.

*Choton points to the sink. Raheem walks over to it, bumping into Jitesh.*

RAHEEM  *(to Jitesh)* Oop. Sorry.

*Jitesh squeezes past him and heads to the fridge.*

PISHIMONI  My father you know. Always this camera was around his neck. He called it: another "poite."

PISHE  Ki?

PISHIMONI  Baba bolten na? Ei dyakh aamar onno poite ta porlam. *(calling over to Raheem)* You know what is poite?

RAHEEM  *(trying to pronounce it)* Pwee-teh?

PISHIMONI  Poite it is sacred thread. Worn by Bramhon.

CHOTON  *(uncomfortable with the direction this is going)* O . . . kay.

*Raheem returns to the table.*

RAHEEM  *(re: the camera)* Can I?

*Pishimoni hands Raheem the camera. He takes it, reverently.*

PISHE  Ei je. This is "poite."

*He pulls his poite out the collar of his shirt and shows it to Raheem.*

PISHIMONI  All Brahmin men they wear it. Boys they receive it twelve thirteen years. Choton still has not received / actually—

CHOTON  And will not be receiving.

PISHIMONI  Keno re? Eta toh aamader ekta auspicious occasion.

CHOTON  Cause I'm not tryna be initiated into the cult of Brahminical patriarchy.

PISHIMONI  *(to Raheem)* You know Bramhon, this is priest actually.

CHOTON  That's just . . . a totally inaccurate—

PISHIMONI  Aare now it is learned class. Tai toh? Baba jemon . . . you know here we have one Scottish Church College. Very old college. My father actually, he was first Indian principal of that college. My brother . . . Choton's father . . . he is also professor. But my grandfather see . . . he was walking village to village, performing pujas, marriage, this things. Very poor actually.

CHOTON  *(to Raheem)* This is the origin story.

PISHIMONI  But then *my* father . . . he *studied*, by candlelight, in the village electricity was not there, then it was British India. Then it was not higher secondary. Eastern India Examination bodh hoy bolto tokhon—

*Jitesh deposits the box of sweets on the table.*

PISHE  *(to Jitesh)* Kothhay peli?

JITESH  *(pointing to the fridge)* Oi je.

PISHIMONI  *(ignoring the interruption)* In that examination, my father he received top marks. Kintu khub i gorib chhilen toh aamar thakur da. He could not afford to send my father to Kolkata for studies. That time he was in East Bengal—

*Pishe pops a sweet into his mouth whole. He offers Raheem the box.*

PISHE  *(mouth full)* This is Bengali speciality. Nolen gurer shondesh.

RAHEEM  Nice, I'll try one in a bit, thanks.

PISHIMONI  But that time one Reverend Macaulay. That time he was principal of Scottish Church College. He came to know. Village boy. Erokom. Had received top marks. So that Reverend Macaulay, he offered my father *full* accommodation to complete his studies.

RAHEEM  That's amazing.

CHOTON  But for the record, all of this is *because* Dadu had caste privilege. Right?

*Raheem turns the camera over, examining it.*

PISHIMONI  *(re: the camera)* You are interested in this?

RAHEEM  Yeah I've never actually seen one, but I've always wanted to—

PISHE  *(to Raheem)* Are you trying to open it?

RAHEEM  I'm just tryna see what kind of film it takes, yeah.

CHOTON  Can you even get film for a camera like this still?

PISHE  Aare photo shop is there. Lake Market e oi Bombay Photo achhe na? Okhane niye gelei peye jabi.

RAHEEM  Do you know how old it is?

PISHIMONI  Mm... Baba must have purchased Rolleicord... I think '62 '63 must have been? That time we used to take summer holiday. Whole family, Ma, Baba, myself, Dadamoni. Choton's father, I call him Dadamoni. So many shots are there. Two of us, on the train compartment to Musoori, trekking in Dehradun—

PISHE  He preferred action shot. None of this giving pose, style mara. But zero photos are there of Baba himself actually.

PISHIMONI  Ki bolchho?

PISHE  Aare—

PISHIMONI  *(to Raheem)* My father is there in that photo.

    *She points to a framed portrait of Dadu hanging on the wall.*

PISHE  Bolchhi with this camera, Baba refused anyone else to take photo.

PISHIMONI  What do you know? Baba'r shommonde?

PISHE  Eta bhalo dile.

PISHIMONI  Shara din computer e shudhu pitir pitir. *(to Raheem)* All day he is on the computer, six, seven hours. Playing billiard, Sudoku.

PISHE  *(to Raheem)* You have played billiard? Come tomorrow I will show you.

CHOTON  Pishe, we actually have a *lot* of work to do while we're here.

PISHIMONI  Seven, eight hours he is sitting there—

PISHE  Tumi ki kawro shara din shuni.

PISHIMONI  Aami to kichhui korina.

    *Raheem manages to take the camera out of its leather case.*

PISHE  Ki kawro?

PISHIMONI  Bollam toh. Kichhui na. Chuuuup hoye boshe thhaki. Ekdom lokkhi meye.

    *She actively performs silence.*

PISHE  Good. Some peace and quiet.

RAHEEM  *(understanding the camera mechanism)* Oh wait.

PISHIMONI  Ranna banna, ghawr dor porishkar, e gulo shawb nijei hoy tai na? Magic.

    *The film magazine snaps open. Raheem looks inside.*

RAHEEM  There's a roll of film in here.

*Pishe looks.*

CHOTON  What?

PISHE  Arebbas . . .

PISHIMONI  Ki?

PISHE  Camera'r bhetor ki roychhe dyakho.

CHOTON  That's . . .

PISHIMONI  Ki? Bujhte parchhina.

PISHE  Kobekaar ekta film. Pore roychhe—
   *Pishe takes the film.*

PISHE  This is ancient, you know?

PISHIMONI  Dekhi?

PISHE  Ki kawthha ta bawle? Fossil fossil. Rohim has discovered—

PISHIMONI  Ki? Baba'r tola chhobi?
   *Pishimoni takes the roll of film in her hand.*

PISHE  Jitesh?

PISHIMONI  She ki go?
   *Jitesh emerges from the kitchen.*

PISHE  Ei dyakh. Odbhut jinish dekhbi ekta.
   *Pishe points to the roll of film.*

PISHE  Janish ki eta?
   *Jitesh stares at it.*

JITESH  Ki?

PISHE  Baba'r tola chhobi.

RAHEEM  We should put it in something, get it out of the light.

CHOTON  There's no way we could still get it developed, right?

RAHEEM  How old is it?

CHOTON  At least . . . what thirty years?

RAHEEM  Yeah, I mean, especially in this heat, film definitely / deteriorates
 but—

JITESH  Film?

PISHE  *(affirmative)* Hm.

RAHEEM  —it's worth giving it a try.

JITESH  Kothhay chhilo?

PISHE  Aare camera'r bhitor. Ei dyakh.
   *Pishe shows Jitesh the empty camera magazine.*

PISHIMONI  Bhaba jay na, na?

RAHEEM  Do you have a Ziploc bag?

PISHIMONI  Ki bag?

CHOTON  Does it need to be Ziploc or—

RAHEEM  Just something that has a good seal.

CHOTON  Like . . . *(he picks up the container of sweets on the table)* . . . something like this?

RAHEEM  Lemme see? Yeah this'll work.

CHOTON  Jitesh da ekta khali tiffin er kouto dibi?

JITESH  *(affirmative)* Hm.

> *He exits into the kitchen.*

PISHIMONI  Bolchho tokhon thekei pore roychhe? Tahle toh Choton er mukhebhaat er i chhobi hobe.

CHOTON  You think?

PISHIMONI  Tokhon Baba shudhu tor chhobi i tule beraten sharakkhon. Eto adorer chhili.

> *Jitesh returns with a tiffin box.*

RAHEEM  *(taking it from him)* Thank you.

CHOTON  *(to Raheem)* She's saying it's probably pictures of me Dadu took at my rice-feeding ceremony. Cause he died the day right after—

PISHIMONI  Two days after.

CHOTON  Oh tai? I thought it was the day after.

> *Raheem seals the film in the tiffin box.*

RAHEEM  Cool if I keep this in the fridge somewhere?

PISHIMONI  Freeze?

RAHEEM  Until we get it developed. It's the best place—

PISHIMONI  Ei Jitesh—

RAHEEM  *(getting up)* It's cool, I got it.

PISHIMONI  —Kouto ta freeze e rekhe ay to. *(to Raheem)* He will keep it in the freeze.

RAHEEM  Oh. Okay. Thank you.

> *Raheem hands Jitesh the tiffin box, awkwardly, and sits back down.*

JITESH  Freeze?

PISHIMONI  *(amused)* Bhab? Thanday rakha uchit naki.

> *Jitesh looks bewildered. He heads toward the fridge with the tiffin box.*

PISHE  *(calling after him)* Kheye phelish na kintu!

> *This cracks Choton up. Raheem looks confused.*

CHOTON  *(trying to explain the joke)* He just said like . . . like "don't eat it."

RAHEEM  What?

CHOTON  Nothing. Never mind, it's— *(still chuckling)* It's nothing.

> *END SCENE*

২। রিসার্চ
## 2. RESEARCH

*Later that night in the sitting room, the two divans have been pushed together to make a bed. Choton and Raheem are sprawled out, staring at Choton's phone, a bundled mosquito net near their feet.*

CHOTON   —or how bout just "Filmmaker couple from LA"?

RAHEEM   I feel like the pic should just be you.

CHOTON   Why?

RAHEEM   Cause. It's your project.

CHOTON   Yeah but they're gonna meet both of us if they end up participating.

*Choton rises, phone in hand.*

CHOTON   Plus. You're just hotter.

*He puts his phone down on top of the altar.*

RAHEEM   So you're using me as bait.

CHOTON   Exactly.

RAHEEM   That's fucked up.

CHOTON   Grab these two—

*Choton hands Raheem two corners of the mosquito net. He finds the other two corners and holds them up, demonstrating.*

CHOTON   Lift it up.

*Raheem does so.*

CHOTON   Yeah but keep the net on the mattress, we're basically creating this little mosquito-free zone in there . . .

*They lift up the corners of the mosquito net. Choton inspects it for holes.*

CHOTON   Wow these mawsharees are truly prehistoric.

RAHEEM   What's it called?

CHOTON   Mawsharee.

RAHEEM   Mawshadee.

CHOTON   Mawsharee.

*Choton, corners in hand, looks around the room.*

RAHEEM   *(re: the corners)* What am I doing with these?

*Choton hangs one corner on a hook in the wall.*

CHOTON   *(pointing)* How bout that hinge?

*Raheem looks at what Choton is pointing to.*

RAHEEM   This?

CHOTON   Yeah tie it around the . . . yeah around the hinge.

*Raheem tries.*

RAHEEM   Like this?

*An ear-splitting snore. Raheem startles.*

CHOTON   Yeah . . . Jitesh da has a pretty epic snore . . .

RAHEEM   Oh I'm just—

*Raheem peeks through the curtain into Thammi's room.*

CHOTON   I have earplugs.

RAHEEM   He just . . . sleeps on the floor like that?

CHOTON   I mean normally he sleeps in here, but when we're here, he sleeps in Thammi's room.

*Raheem watches Jitesh through the curtain for a moment, then returns to tying the mosquito net.*

RAHEEM   I don't think I'm doing this right.

CHOTON   Just pull the— Here.

*Choton walks over and adjusts the knot.*

And then just make sure to tuck in all the sides. Or actually— Get in first and then tuck. Like this, get in super fast so they don't get in . . . and then tuck.

*Choton is now inside the mosquito net.*

RAHEEM   How come I haven't seen any mosquitos?

CHOTON   Oh they're here. They're small. The small ones are the bad ones.

*Raheem grabs his phone charger.*

RAHEEM   I need that adapter thingy right?

CHOTON   Yeah in my backpack.

*Raheem unzips. He pulls out a bulky volt converter.*

RAHEEM   This?

CHOTON   No that's the converter for my shaver, there should just be a bunch of 'em in a little pouch. Can you plug in mine too?

RAHEEM   *(re: the adapters)* I don't see them.

CHOTON   Bring it over.

*Raheem picks up Choton's heavy backpack and plops it by the bed. Choton reads something in Raheem's face.*

What?

RAHEEM   What?

CHOTON   I'm just minimizing getting in and out.

*He peers through the netting.*

*(pointing)* There. Little pouch.

*Raheem removes two small adapters from the pouch.*

There really is malaria here, I'm not like making it up.

RAHEEM   Where's your charger?

CHOTON   Is it not— Oh wait I—

*He produces the charger from the pocket in the hoodie he's wearing.*

I brought it downstairs to charge but then—

*He untucks the mosquito net just enough to hand the charger to Raheem and retracts his hand all in one lightning-swift gesture.*

RAHEEM   Where's your phone?

CHOTON   It's right there on top of the—

*Raheem grabs it.*

*(pointing)* Plug it in over there, there's two plug points.

*Raheem walks over to the outlets.*

You can unplug the "Good Knight."

RAHEEM   This?

*He unplugs the vaporizer from the outlet.*

CHOTON   Careful, yeah, there's liquid in there.

RAHEEM   What is it?

CHOTON   It's a—like another anti-mosquito thing.

*Raheem plugs his phone into his charger, the charger into the adapter, and then attempts to plug the adapter into the outlet, but it sticks.*

Wiggle it a little, it'll . . . yeah.

*Raheem looks at his phone.*

RAHEEM   It's not charging.

CHOTON   Did you turn on the switch?

RAHEEM   What switch?

CHOTON   You gotta turn on the switch next to the—

*Raheem flips the switch right next to the outlet.*

Yup.

RAHEEM   Why?

CHOTON   Can you turn the fan down too? That little knob. Or actually, just turn it off, it's the top left switch.

RAHEEM   Won't it be too hot?

*Raheem tries the top left switch, plunging the room into darkness.*

CHOTON   Oop. Try the top right?

*Raheem switches the tube light back on. It flickers, one end lit. He flips the bottom left switch, and the fan slows and then stops.*

Yeah, no you're right, turn it back on. But turn the knob all the way down.

*Raheem obliges. He grabs Choton's phone and plugs it in. Jitesh snores.*

RAHEEM   Should I turn off the lights?

CHOTON  Hold on, now I have to—

*Choton untucks the mosquito net.*

CHOTON  Why do we have to pee? How is that not a thing we've solved yet?

RAHEEM  You pee more than normal people.

CHOTON  Cause I drank like four whole bottles of water.

*Choton scoots out from the net, retucks, and scampers into the bathroom.*

CHOTON  If you drank enough water, you'd have to pee too.

RAHEEM  I know, that's why I don't.

*The sound of Choton peeing.*

CHOTON  *(over the sound of his pee-stream)* What?

*He finishes. Flushes. Scampers back to find Raheem in bed, in his underwear, sitting up very straight, under the net.*

RAHEEM  *(re: the net)* I don't know if I like this.

CHOTON  Tuck!

RAHEEM  I did tuck.

*Choton makes a point of tucking Raheem's side of the net further under the mattress. He considers Raheem, newly cloistered.*

CHOTON  You look like a—

RAHEEM  Careful.

*Choton puts up his hands in a gesture of innocence.*

RAHEEM  Like a what?

CHOTON  Never mind.

RAHEEM  *(curious now)* Like a what?

CHOTON  Lights off?

RAHEEM  What were you gonna say?

*Choton flicks off the switch. Darkness. Light filters in through the window between the sitting room and bathroom, which remains lit.*

CHOTON  We leave the bathroom light on, Jitesh da has to take her like ten times a night and each time is a whole ordeal.

RAHEEM  I feel bad.

CHOTON  What?

RAHEEM  That he has to sleep on the floor.

CHOTON  I know it used to fuck with me too, but that's just . . . how he sleeps.

*Choton's cell phone lights up in the darkness.*

Oop.

*He looks at it.*

We got our first message. From . . . "Dreaming Exclamation Point." *(reading)* "Hot DP." What's DP?

RAHEEM   Um. *(indicating himself)* Duh.

CHOTON   *(googling)* What . . . is . . . DP? D . . . P . . . is "Double Penetration"?
 What?

RAHEEM   What are you looking at?

CHOTON   Maybe cause there's two of us in the pic? *(more googling)* Oh . . .
 "Display Picture"? Huh. Okay. Display Picture.

RAHEEM   Look at you learning the local Grindr / lingo.

CHOTON   I know, right? Research!

RAHEEM   It's happening.

CHOTON   *(typing into his phone)* "Thanks . . . you too . . . "

RAHEEM   Are you lying?

CHOTON   What?

RAHEEM   Do you actually think they're hot, or are you just saying that to
 get an interview?

CHOTON   No they're cute!

RAHEEM   *(beckoning)* Me see.
      *Choton brings the phone back to bed, with the requisite mosquito-net dance.*
      *He hands Raheem the phone.*
   Oh ok—

CHOTON   See?
      *Choton takes his phone back.*

RAHEEM   So you think an Indian boy is cute?
      *The sound of an incoming Grindr message.*

CHOTON   Look we're hoppin'. See? I told you. You're a hot commodity here
 in Cal.

RAHEEM   What do you mean *I'm* a hot commodity, it's the two of us.

CHOTON   *(reading, with difficulty)* "Ganja . . . khor." Weed something.

RAHEEM   Ganja?

CHOTON   . . . "ganjakhor" . . . what is "khor"?

RAHEEM   You call it ganja?

CHOTON   Excuse you, ganja is Sanskrit.

RAHEEM   Really?

CHOTON   Probably "pothead." "Ganjakhor."

RAHEEM   . . . I mean . . . I wouldn't mind some weed . . .

CHOTON   You want to message him? Be forewarned, the weed here is a
 little . . .

RAHEEM   What?

CHOTON   *(typing)* "Hi . . . there . . . "

RAHEEM   Or maybe don't use your professional Grindr / for drugs.

CHOTON   *(amused)* My "professional Grindr."

RAHEEM   I mean . . . isn't that what it is?

> *Choton types.*

CHOTON   How 'bout: "We are a couple from the States working on a documentary and we're looking to have some conversations with folks who use Grindr in Kolkata." *(typing)* "Would . . . you . . . be interested?" Send?

RAHEEM   Do iiit.

> *Raheem closes his eyes.*

CHOTON   You sleepy?

RAHEEM   Kinda . . .

CHOTON   It's what, like 1 p.m. in LA?

> *The sound of Jitesh snoring.*

Maybe I need to cum.

RAHEEM   *(sleepily)* You should cum.

> *Choton closes his eyes. He tries to relax.*

CHOTON   I don't not think Indians are attractive, it's just . . . like doesn't it feel like incestuous or something? Like I just know too much. It's like looking at myself in a mirror. Or like . . . looking at my dad. You know? Like I know there will be ear hairs.

> *His phone buzzes. For what feels like a long time, too long maybe, Choton messages on Grindr. The modulation of Jitesh's snoring. Raheem dozes.*

CHOTON   *(reading, to himself, tickled)* Purushali gondho?

> *Raheem opens his eyes.*

RAHEEM   Hm?

> *A pause.*

CHOTON   *(looking up from his phone)* Hm?

RAHEEM   You say something?

CHOTON   *(having a field day)* Oh I'm just like—this guy's profile just says "Wishlist," and he's like: 1) "Buke ghono lom," so like, thick chest hair; 2) "Bogoler lom ebong tar shathe purushali gondho" so like, armpit hair, and then I just love this *"purushali* gondho" so like . . . I guess like . . . manly musk. And then 3)—this one's my favorite: "dui shokto peshi'r majhe shashon korar ek dondo" which is *just* kind of like . . . genius actually, cause like . . . "shashon korar dondo" is like a . . . like a rod to like . . . discipline or like . . . yeah like a punishing rod. Between two . . . strong . . . what is "peshi"?

> *Choton googles. Raheem observes him, deep in thought.*

RAHEEM   Do you like . . .

    *He trails off. After a moment, Choton looks up.*

CHOTON   What?

RAHEEM   Oh nothing I was just . . .

    *Choton goes back to typing.*

  —like do you like . . . wish I spoke Bangla?

    *Choton looks up.*

CHOTON   What? You do speak Bangla.

RAHEEM   Like actually though—

CHOTON   *(teasing)* You know "begun" . . . and "khichudi"—

RAHEEM   I guess I'm just . . . like we just got here and already I'm like . . . you have this whole . . . like this whole other world . . .

CHOTON   For sure. I mean . . . yeah. Yeah like . . . this is home—

RAHEEM   Sure.

    *Choton's phone dings. Incoming Grindr message.*

CHOTON   Dreaming Exclamation Point wants to meet up.

    *Choton types.*

  Cool if I tell them to come over at noon?

RAHEEM   Come over here?

CHOTON   Yeah I think it makes most sense to have them come over here, especially at first, so it's a like . . . I don't know . . . a safe space to chat—

RAHEEM   So they want to do an interview?

CHOTON   I mean . . . I kinda wanna hang out a little before springing the question, right?

RAHEEM   So what do they think they're coming over for?

CHOTON   Not a booty call.

RAHEEM   I'm just making sure.

CHOTON   I mean I've told them we're working on a documentary—

RAHEEM   So I should set up before they come then.

CHOTON   But see that's what I don't want. I don't want them to see a camera and get all weird, I don't know how out they are, I don't want them to feel pressured.

RAHEEM   Okay . . .

CHOTON   I think . . . let's just set up if and when we ask. Right?

RAHEEM   . . . sure. I'm just saying it's gonna take a minute. To set up lights and stuff.

CHOTON   Do we need all that though? I feel like we should keep it pretty natural.

RAHEEM  I mean if you want it to look natural you're gonna want consistent light.

>   *Incoming Grindr message. Choton looks down. He types. Raheem yawns.*

We should probably set an alarm.

>   *Choton gives him a look.*

Hey, it's your work, I'm just the cameraman.

>   *Choton reluctantly picks up his phone. Screen light glows on his face.*

CHOTON  What time?

RAHEEM  Is that photo store walking distance?

CHOTON  What photo store?

RAHEEM  I was kind of hoping we could go drop off the film—

CHOTON  In the morning?

RAHEEM  I mean . . .

CHOTON  Yeah I think it's pretty close . . .

>   *Raheem yawns.*

RAHEEM  Cool.

>   *Choton continues Grindr-ing. A long silence. Just the sound of the clock ticking away and Jitesh snoring. Then, suddenly, violently, Choton smacks the side of his head. Choton looks at his hand. He illuminates his palm with his phone screen.*

CHOTON  Shit.

RAHEEM  What?

CHOTON  Fuck.

RAHEEM  Mosquito?

CHOTON  Fuuuck.

RAHEEM  You want your earplugs?

CHOTON  Yeah but then I won't hear it . . . These mawsharees are so fucking old. Fuck. I guess we can just . . . cover up . . .

>   *He inhales deeply. He pulls a thin bedsheet up around himself. Raheem closes his eyes. Choton, swaddled, looks up at the ceiling. He takes a slow, deep breath in and out. He tries closing his eyes. He regulates his breathing. In and out. In and out. A little snore from Raheem. Choton opens his eyes. He stares at the ceiling. He looks at his phone. It glows on his face. He scrolls. He types. He scrolls. He glances at Raheem. Then, making as little noise as possible, he puts his hand down his pants. He touches himself looking at his phone. He glances at the portrait of his grandfather. He considers it. He looks at Raheem. Then, quietly, he gets out of the mawsharee. He walks over to the portrait of his grandfather hanging on the wall and flips*

*it around, so that the face is hidden. He makes a sound. Raheem awakes*
*with a start.*

RAHEEM  What?

CHOTON  Nothing nothing—

RAHEEM  What happened?

CHOTON  Nothing, don't worry. I'm just—

*He gets back into bed.*

CHOTON  —don't worry about it, go back to sleep.

RAHEEM  *(amused)* Did you / just—

CHOTON  I just . . . felt like he was like . . . watching me. You know?

RAHEEM  Mm hm.

CHOTON  *(bashful)* What? Doesn't he look kind of scary?

RAHEEM  *(teasing)* I don't know, you turned him around—

CHOTON  It's the same one at my parents' place, you've seen it, it's in like
every room of the house. I guess I *always* kind of felt like he was watching
me . . . My dad actually used to—have I told you this?

RAHEEM  What?

CHOTON  When I first started masturbating? My dad— I think he noticed
how much time I was spending in the bathroom, so one night he was just
like, you've been spending a lot of time in the bathroom, what have you
been doing, and I was so embarrassed I just like, started crying, like, I've
been doing this thing, and it feels like I have to pee, and then this white
stuff comes out of my nunu, and he was like, it's okay, it happens, and I
was like . . . is it bad? And he was like: well, you know . . . it takes up time.
And you should think about how you want to spend your time because
you only have so much time, and then he pointed to Dadu's picture and
was like, you know when Dadu was your age, *he* spent his time studying,
by candlelight, in the village, you know same story—I mean maybe my
dad was right, by the time he was my age, my Dadu was the principal of
a college, so clearly he knew *something* about time management that I did
not inherit.

  You know that's the *only* picture I've ever seen of him?

  "Chhobi hoye giyechhe" . . .

RAHEEM  What's that?

CHOTON  That's what we say when somebody dies. Chhobi is picture.

RAHEEM  Chobi?

CHOTON  Yeah, chhobi. It's the aspirated "chh" sound.

RAHEEM  *(trying again)* Chhobi.

CHOTON  Like "ch" then "huh," "ch-hobi."

RAHEEM  Ch-hobi.

CHOTON  Chhobi hoye giyechhe. Has become a picture.

I mean that's literally what he is now, right? Just like . . . that *one* pic-ture . . . that after he died . . . somebody . . . probably my dad like . . . picked to get enlarged and framed and now . . . that's the picture . . . you know?

Like it's almost like by dying, he actually took up *more* space?

Like this house, right, it's like . . . I always call it my grandfather's house. Dadu'r Bari. I never call it Thammi's house . . . or Pishimoni's house . . .

I mean he and Pishimoni actually had a kind of contentious relationship cause she . . . had a love marriage . . . with a younger man . . . couldn't keep a steady job. And my Dadu . . . like the fact that this like, guy who graduated from St. Xavier's is just like . . . playing virtual pool all day, which, by the way, don't feel like you have to humor him with that, every time I come, he asks me, and it's just . . . you know, like the fact that he would walk around the house with just his boxers on drove my grandfather crazy, cause my grandfather . . . would like wake up at five a.m., go for a morning walk, take a shower, put on a starched shirt . . . I mean, this is what my dad tells me—

*Incoming Grindr message. Choton looks.*

Look this guy sent a bunch of pics.

*Choton shows Raheem his phone.*

RAHEEM  Nice.

*Raheem looks.*

He's kinda hot actually.

CHOTON  Yeah?

RAHEEM  Yeah, he has a nice dick.

*Raheem scrolls through the dick pics.*

CHOTON  I thought you were sleepy.

RAHEEM  Yeah . . .

*Choton notices Raheem's erection. He puts his hand on it.*

CHOTON  Oh hello.

RAHEEM  Yeah . . .

CHOTON  We should send him a pic.

RAHEEM  Like take one?

CHOTON  Lemme see.

*Choton reaches for his phone.*

RAHEEM  There's no light though.

*Choton frames a bird's eye view of Raheem's dick.*

Do it from below. Like put the phone—
>    *Choton has already positioned the phone between Raheem's legs.*

Is my face in it?
>    *Choton adjusts his angle.*

CHOTON   Hold your dick up? Like up straight—
>    *Raheem holds his dick up straight.*

Yeah it's covering your face now.
>    *He takes the pic, with a flash, alarmingly bright in the dark room.*

RAHEEM   Wow.

CHOTON   Sorry—

RAHEEM   I'm blind.

CHOTON   Sorry sorry—
>    *Choton looks at the picture.*

It looks okay actually.

RAHEEM   Lemme see?
>    *Choton shows Raheem the picture.*

My balls look huge. Here, lemme take it.

CHOTON   Why don't we just send this one?

RAHEEM   Cause it's a bad photo.

CHOTON   It's not about the photo, it's about the dick—

RAHEEM   Here, we should both be in it.

CHOTON   He doesn't want to see my dick.

RAHEEM   He literally said "your cocks" plural.

CHOTON   Yeah but . . . is this a cock?

RAHEEM   What are you talking about?

CHOTON   I'm just saying like taxonomically, does it even make sense to categorize my genitalia and your genitalia as the same thing, like . . .
>    *He indicates Raheem's dick.*

. . . if that's a penis then . . .
>    *He indicates his own dick.*

I mean what is this? It's a polyp.

RAHEEM   Okay.

CHOTON   It's a little nunu.

RAHEEM   I like your little nunu.

CHOTON   Yes, but *you* have unusual / taste.

THAMMI   *(offstage)* Maaaa—
>    *Choton and Raheem startle at the sound.*

JITESH   *(offstage)* Ei je. Hyan—

THAMMI *(offstage)* Maaaa!

JITESH Ei je. Uthun. O Ma.

THAMMI Hm?

JITESH Eiii je—

THAMMI *(offstage)* Ke?

RAHEEM Is she okay?

JITESH Uthun.

> *Sounds of movement from Thammi's room.*

CHOTON She has nightmares.

JITESH Aaaste, aaste.

> *We hear Thammi's voice: incomprehensible, viscous with sleep.*

Haat ta dhorun. Ekhane dhorun. Byas—

> *The bed creaks: Thammi struggling to rise, supported by Jitesh. Choton and Raheem listen to the muted sounds of their conversation. Backlit, the curtained window onto the foyer is a screen. Thammi, supported by Jitesh: a single, spectral silhouette moving slowly across it. Raheem closes his eyes. Choton runs his fingers gently along Raheem's arm, giving him shushshuri.*

CHOTON You okay?

RAHEEM Mm hm.

> *Quiet. Sounds from the bathroom.*

Did you set the alarm?

CHOTON Yeah, I set it for 9:30.

> *Choton lies on his back and stares up at the ceiling fan. Then he picks up his phone. The sound of Grindr messages. Crossfade to the computer room: Pishe, lit by the glow of his computer. He is chatting with minnesota76 while playing virtual pool. Pishe is K_gang. Their conversation appears as projected text. The sound of a virtual pool ball hitting a virtual pool ball.*

MINNESOTA76 nooooooo

K_GANG OHO BAD LUCK

MINNESOTA76 how do I always do that? :(

MINNESOTA76 that 8 ball has it out for me I swear

K_GANG NEXT TIME

MINNESOTA76 u always say that and then u always win :)

K_GANG :)

K_GANG WHAT TIME IT IS THERE NOW?

MINNESOTA76 Its 5

MINNESOTA76  in the afternoon
K_GANG  HERE IT IS THREE THIRTY
MINNESOTA76  am??
MINNESOTA76  go to sleep!
K_GANG  MY NEPHEW HAS COME ACTUALLY
K_GANG  FROM USA
MINNESOTA76  Oh nice!
K_GANG  HIS FRIEND ALSO
MINNESOTA76  That must be nice
K_GANG  FROM LOS ANGLES
MINNESOTA76  fancy :)
MINNESOTA76  I spent a summer in LA
MINNESOTA76  in high school
MINNESOTA76  my mother thought it would be a good idea to send me
  to my sister
MINNESOTA76  We never got along
MINNESOTA76  she was four years older
MINNESOTA76  always the princess if u know what I mean
MINNESOTA76  my mother thought it would be good for us
K_GANG  UR SISTER LIVES IN LOS ANGELES?
MINNESOTA76  Oh she died
MINNESOTA76  soon after
MINNESOTA76  in an accident
MINNESOTA76  car accident
MINNESOTA76  flew right out the window
K_GANG  HEARTIEST CONDOLENCE . . .
MINNESOTA76  it was a long time ago
MINNESOTA76  back then you know . . . Seatbelts and such . . .
MINNESOTA76  people were less careful
K_GANG  HERE THERE IS LAW
K_GANG  POLICE THEY WILL STOP IF YOU DON'T PUT
MINNESOTA76  yeah same here, front and back seat
K_GANG  BACK SEAT ALSO ?
MINNESOTA76  they love their laws in St. Paul
K_GANG  IS IT IN MINNESOTA ?
MINNESOTA76  St. Paul?
MINNESOTA76  It's the capital
MINNESOTA76  my daughter calls it St. Paul-itics ;)

K_GANG   YOU HAVE DAUGHTER ALSO ?

K_GANG   I THOUGHT YOU ARE UNMARRIED ?

MINNESOTA76   I am

MINNESOTA76   I mean I was

MINNESOTA76   married

MINNESOTA76   not anymore

MINNESOTA76   One more game?

K_GANG   YES !

     *END SCENE*


## ৩ । ভিউফাইন্ডার
## 3. VIEWFINDER

*Raheem sits at the table with the Rolleicord and a new roll of film. He removes the lens cap. It slips out of his hand and clatters onto the table. He claps his hand over it. He examines the camera's lenses.*

*Jitesh enters with three empty Kinley water bottles. Raheem looks up and smiles. Jitesh half-smiles. He places the bottles on the floor under the Aquaguard water filter, affixed to the wall.*

*Raheem unclips the camera from its case and gingerly removes it.*

*Jitesh places one empty bottle on the floor under the Aquaguard. He presses a button. A stream of water pours down, right into the mouth of the bottle.*

*Raheem snaps open the camera's magazine. He takes the new roll of film and unspools the very end of it. He snaps the spool into the camera. He pulls out the end of the spool and feeds it into a slot at the bottom. Jitesh watches. One bottle of water is full. He swaps it out for another without stopping the stream of water. Not a drip spills onto the floor.*

*Raheem winds the film until it is taut. He snaps the magazine shut and locks it. Jitesh watches. Raheem looks at the back of the camera. He looks for a viewfinder. He doesn't see one.*

RAHEEM   *(to himself)* Huh.

*He turns the camera over in his hands. He notices Jitesh looking at him. Jitesh looks away. Raheem considers every surface of the camera. He stares into the camera lens.*

*(to himself)* Where the heck . . .

*Jitesh watches, biting his lip. Raheem is staring into the camera lens.*

JITESH  Dekhun—

> *Raheem looks up. Jitesh taps the top of the filled water bottle he is holding.*

RAHEEM  *(confused)* Sorry?

JITESH  Opor ta khulun.

> *He holds out the water bottle and taps the top of it again.*

RAHEEM  Oh . . . I'm good thanks.

> *He puts up his hands to refuse the misconstrued offer. Jitesh approaches him. He reaches over and gently pulls open the top of the camera, revealing the viewfinder.*

Oh shit.

> *Raheem peers into the viewfinder.*

Wowza.

> *Jitesh watches him. Raheem peers through the camera, focusing the image on the bottle of water under the Aquaguard, which has just overflowed and is spilling onto the floor.*

Oops. Your—

JITESH  Hyan?

> *Raheem points. Jitesh looks.*

Ei, ei—

> *He hurriedly scoots the overfull bottle out from under the stream and replaces it. He hurries into the kitchen and grabs a rag. He lifts the filling bottle an inch and mops up the spilled water around it.*

CHOTON  *(from upstairs)* Jitesh da?

> *His voice echoes in the stairwell.*

JITESH  Jai!

> *The third bottle fills to the top, and he caps it. He picks up the three filled bottles from the floor and hurries into the stairwell.*

RAHEEM  *(calling after him)* Hey thank you . . .

> *Raheem turns the camera toward various sources of light.*

What a . . . crazy . . .

> *He hangs the camera around his neck, gets up, still looking down into the viewfinder. Pishimoni enters from the bedroom. As Raheem turns, looking down, he sees Pishimoni in the frame of the viewfinder and startles*

Jesus—

PISHIMONI  / Arebbas.

RAHEEM  You scared me.

PISHIMONI  Taking photo?

RAHEEM  I'm just getting used to looking through this viewfinder.

PISHIMONI   My father also like this. Always around his neck.

RAHEEM   It's like watching a tiny movie.

  *Raheem continues scanning the room.*

PISHIMONI   You have eaten?

RAHEEM   Thanks, yeah, we had some breakfast.

PISHIMONI   Breakfast what you like to have? Omelette toast?

RAHEEM   Jitesh made us some um . . . was it loo-chee?

PISHIMONI   Luchi you like?

RAHEEM   Super tasty, yeah.

  *Pishi notices the portrait of Dadu flipped around.*

PISHIMONI   E ki? Jitesh!

JITESH   Jai!

  *Raheem ambles around the room, peering through the viewfinder.*

PISHIMONI   Ki aschorjo.

  *Jitesh enters.*

  Baba'r chhobi ta erokom keno bawl to?

JITESH   Ki?

  *She gestures to the portrait.*

PISHIMONI   Baba'r chhobi te erokom oltano chhilo. De toh jhuliye.

  *Jitesh reaches on tiptoe to hang the portrait on the wall. Raheem notices.*

RAHEEM   Here I got it.

  *Raheem takes the picture from Jitesh.*

PISHIMONI   Or haat toh emni i pounchhe jabe.

RAHEEM   What's that?

PISHIMONI   I am saying that you are tall. You can reach it just like that.

  *Raheem hangs the portrait of Dadu back on the wall. Pishimoni walks over
  to the fridge and retrieves a steel tiffin box. Jitesh goes to exit.*

RAHEEM   *(to Jitesh, indicating the viewfinder)* Hey. Thank you.

  *Jitesh nods subtly in Raheem's direction. Then he exits into the stairwell.
  Pishimoni walks over to the window. She opens the container of rice. She
  scoops out a little bit of rice with her fingertips and forms it into a ball.
  Raheem watches her through the viewfinder.*

  What's that?

  *Pishimoni looks up.*

PISHIMONI   This? It is old rice. For the crows. Small birds also they come.

  *She places the ball gently on the outer edge of the windowsill.*

  You know my father . . . after he died . . . some days after, I was there in
his garden. You have seen it? Upstairs garden?

RAHEEM  I haven't yet, but Choton told me—

PISHIMONI  You must see it. For my father, garden it was . . . ki bolbo?

*She smiles, remembering.*

Now Jitesh, he maintains. But when my father took care garden maane . . . most beautiful garden.

*She makes another ball. She places it on the windowsill.*

Then after he had expired . . . two, three days . . . I was there on the chhat. And I saw . . . one crow was there. Sitting in the crysanthemum. So I said, hyat! Just like this I said, shoo! Go! But that crow . . . it just . . . like this. Looking. At me only. So I approached. Waving like this.

*She demonstrates.*

Ei! Pala! But coming close . . . then I could see. That crow . . . she had my father's eyes.

*She is lost in the memory for a moment. Then she scoops out another dollop.*

From then on, every day I put some rice.

*Raheem is watching her intently through the viewfinder. Pishimoni shapes the rice in her hand into a ball.*

RAHEEM  Look at me?

*Pishimoni looks up. Raheem snaps a photograph. Blackout. The photo of Pishimoni develops slowly in an upstage window.*

*END SCENE*


৪ | রুম টোন
## 4. ROOM TONE

*Shou, in low heels and a faux hawk, perches on the divan, a camera pointed in their direction. Choton sits near them on a rickety stool. Raheem is setting up a softbox light.*

SUPERTITLES

SHOU  Aapnake dekhe kintu NRI mone hoy na. Hab bhab puro i Bangali.

SHOU  You know, you don't seem like an NRI. Your vibe is totally Bengali.

CHOTON  Aare Bangali i to.

CHOTON  I *am* Bengali.

SHOU  Na maane Kolkatar chhele meye ra i Bangla bolte parena aajkaal, e dike aapni, baire thhekeo—

SHOU  I mean kids in Kolkata can't even speak Bangla these days, but "aapni" you live abroad and you—

CHOTON  Acchha aamake dekhe ki khub boyoshko mone hoy?

SHOU  Hyan? Moteo na.

CHOTON  Tahle please "tumi" bawlo, "aapni" ta / shunte—

SHOU  Asholey Grindr e dekhe bhablam nishchoi kono model-er chhobi lagiyechhe—

CHOTON  Dhat.

*Raheem points a light in Shou's direction.*

SHOU  Aamar o kintu boyfriend chhilo ekjon Nigerian.

CHOTON  *(surprised)* Tai?

SHOU  Mohammedan Sporting er striker chhilo, aar ki muscle re baba, oof!

CHOTON  Aalap holo ki kore?

SHOU  Ruby'r o dike jeo—Grindr e *besh* koekta footballer pabe.

CHOTON  *(to Raheem)* Faaascinating.

RAHEEM  What?

CHOTON  The gay Black footballers of Calcutta. Who knew?

SHOU  O kintu puro straight chhilo.

CHOTON  *(amused) Chhilo* hoyto.

SHOU  Maane?

CHOTON  Bollena boyfriend tomar?

SHOU  "Gay" er boyfriend to "straight" i howa uchit.

CHOTON  Oh *I* see.

SHOU  Kothi'r shathhe toh purushmanush i shoy, na ki?

CHOTON  *(to Raheem)* They're saying kothis sleep with—

SHOU  Kothi is "gay."

---

CHOTON  Okay do I seem elderly to you or something?

SHOU  What? Not at all—

CHOTON  Then please call me "tumi," "aapni" sounds so—

SHOU  Honestly, on Grindr I thought, that has to be some picture of a model he stole—

CHOTON  Oh please.

SHOU  You know I also had a Nigerian boyfriend.

CHOTON  Oh yeah?

SHOU  He was a striker for Mohammedan Sporting. And his muscles? Oof!

CHOTON  How'd you meet?

SHOU  Go over by Ruby Hospital, there's a whole bunch of footballers on Grindr out that way.

SHOU  Oh he was totally straight.

CHOTON  *Was* maybe.

SHOU  Meaning?

CHOTON  Didn't you say he was your boyfriend?

SHOU  Gays' boyfriends are supposed to be straight.

CHOTON  Mm . . . not / exactly—

SHOU  Tahle what is "gay"?

CHOTON  Kothi's more—

SHOU  Receiver. Who receives.

RAHEEM  So I'm the "kothi."

CHOTON  I mean there *is* that
    valence to it—

SHOU  Hyan? *You* are kothi? No . . .

RAHEEM  *("guilty as charged")* I'm
    the receiver.

CHOTON  —but it's also about /
    gender.

SHOU  You are *receiver*?

CHOTON  *(to Raheem)* Shou was
    saying they met a Nigerian soccer
    player on Grindr.

RAHEEM  *(amused)* Oh yeah?

SHOU  I find African men hot
    actually.

CHOTON  *(to Raheem)* You almost ready?

RAHEEM  Workin' on it.

*Shou makes a pouty face.*

| | |
|---|---|
| SHOU  Dhat. Aager thheke janle ektu sheje ashtam. | SHOU  If I'd known, I would have gussied up a little. |
| CHOTON  Kothhay? Shundor lagchhe to. | CHOTON  You look great! |
| SHOU  Kajol fajol kissu chhara. | SHOU  No eyeliner, no nothing. |

*Raheem adjusts the camera.*

| | |
|---|---|
| O Bangla bojhe? | Does he understand Bangla? |
| CHOTON  They're asking if you speak— | |

*He catches himself.*

| | |
|---|---|
| *(to Shou)* Ei sorry, tomar pronouns jigesh kori ni. | CHOTON  Hey sorry, I never asked you your pronouns. |
| SHOU  Hyan? | SHOU  What? |
| CHOTON  Which . . . I know is kind of—jehetu Banglay kono gendered pronoun / nei— | CHOTON  —since in Bangla there are no gendered pronouns— |

SHOU  Acchha, ektu cha paoa jabe ki?

CHOTON  Ei sorry, kichhui offer kori ni. Jitesh da?

JITESH  *(offstage)* Jaiii.

CHOTON  *(to Raheem)* You want tea?

RAHEEM  Mm . . . no I'm good, thanks.

*Raheem places a boom mic in front of Shou.*
*Shou winks at Raheem. Raheem smiles.*

SHOU  *(conspiratorial)* Barite aar keo roychhe?

CHOTON  Hyan aamar ishemoshai, Pishimoni roychhe bhetore—

SHOU  She ki, aamar okhane aaste boltam. Ma nei, flat khali pore roychhe.

    *(with a wink)* Complete privacy.

*Jitesh enters.*

CHOTON  Ei ektu cha khawabi please?

JITESH  Shobai khabe?

CHOTON  Duto korlei—

RAHEEM  Actually . . .

CHOTON  Yeah?

RAHEEM  Yeah, I'll have some.

CHOTON  Tahle teente kawr.

JITESH  Dud chini?

CHOTON  Aami to shudhu liquor. *(re: Raheem)* Aar oke *ektu khani* chini dish, beshi mishti pochhondo kawre na.

SHOU  Shunun aamar ei shob kom mishti fishti cholbena, full du chamoch deben. Thik achhe to? *(conspiratorial)* Aar Dada, du khana biscut hobe ki?

CHOTON  Oboshyoi hobe. *(to Jitesh)* Biscut er kouto ta niye aashish toh.

---

SHOU  Could we get some tea?

CHOTON  Ei sorry, I haven't offered you anything. Jitesh da?

JITESH  Coming!

SHOU  Is anybody else at home?

CHOTON  Yeah, my uncle and aunt are both here—

SHOU  You should have come to my place, my mom's away, the flat's empty.

CHOTON  Hey, could you make us some tea?

JITESH  For everyone?

CHOTON  Just two—

CHOTON  Three then.

JITESH  Milk and sugar?

CHOTON  Just black for me. And give him just a little sugar, he doesn't like it too sweet.

SHOU  Listen "not too sweet" isn't going to cut it for me, give me two full spoonfuls.
    And brother . . . could I get a couple biscuits too?

CHOTON  Of course. Bring the biscuit tin with you.

JITESH  Thiiik achhe.

JITESH  Sure.

*He exits.*

SHOU  Aami puro biscut ta dubiye khete bhalobashi. Cha te gole jate puro—

SHOU  I like to dip the whole biscuit in. So it melts in the tea and just—

CHOTON  Aare aamio tai kortam!

CHOTON  That's what I used to do!

SHOU  Aami *ekhon* o kori, kochi baccha'r moton.

SHOU  I still do it. Like a little baby.

CHOTON  They're saying they like dissolving their biscuits in—

SHOU  I make biscuit soup actually.

RAHEEM  Oh yeah?

SHOU  Like a baby.

*Shou makes a baby face.*

RAHEEM  *(to Choton)* Do me a favor? Look on the monitor and let me know when the mic's out of frame?

*Choton steps over to the monitor. Raheem holds the mic in frame.*

CHOTON  Yup, it's in frame.

*Raheem lowers the mic very slowly.*

In.

In.

In.

In . . .

Okay out.

SHOU  Acchha o deshe ki etai aapnader kaaj? Maane rojgar ki ei bhabei kawren?

SHOU  So in the US is this your job? Like is this how you make money?

CHOTON  *(chuckling)* Rojgar bishesh korina, aami ekhono PhD niye lore jacchhi, aar Raheem toh freelance director of / photography—

CHOTON  We don't really make money, I'm still slogging through my PhD, and Raheem is a freelance director of photography.

SHOU  *(impressed)* Director? Oishala.

SHOU  Director? Wowza.

CHOTON  Maane lighting, camerawork ei shob / aar ki.

CHOTON  Meaning lighting, camerawork, things like that.

SHOU   *Avengers: Endgame* dekhechho?

CHOTON   Hyan?

SHOU   Dyakhoni? Phata phati cinema. Dekho, INOX e cholchhe.

CHOTON   *(to Raheem)* Wanna go see *Avengers: Endgame?*
     *Raheem glowers at him.*

CHOTON   I thought you wanted an authentic Kolkata cinema experience. There'll be an intermission, all the sexy scenes will be cut—

SHOU   I also want to dance in films actually. Kintu okhane jemon dance niyei pawra shona kawra jay, ekhane toh sherokom na. Ekhane toh dance it is— especially hip hop, Bollywood, this things— It is seen as . . . maane apasanskriti aar ki.

CHOTON   *(to Raheem)* "Apasanskriti" is like—

SHOU   "Perverted culture."

CHOTON   *(to Raheem)* Yeah it sort of encompasses like a . . . a sense of the culture being corrupted by like . . . immoral foreign influences.

SHOU   Shedin jemon Lake-er dhaare boshe selfie tulchhilam. Hotath gobhir gawlay ekjon pulish ki shob bolte laglo, public jaygay naki awshleel bebohaar nishiddho, erokom apasanskriti'r chotei naki desh er ei awbosthha, aare / bhai—

CHOTON   Ki dekhe bollo?

SHOU   Have you seen *Avengers: Endgame?*

CHOTON   What?

SHOU   You haven't seen it? It's a killer movie. Go see it, it's playing at INOX.

SHOU   But over there, how you can just study dance, here it isn't like that. Here, dance it is—

SHOU   The other day I was taking selfies by the Lake. Suddenly I hear this deep voice, and this cop starts saying all kinds of stuff, "Obscene behavior in public places is illegal, this kind of degenerate culture is just a foreign influence, no wonder our country's going down the drain," I mean—

CHOTON   What did he see that made him—

SHOU  Ei je. Erokom. Heel ola choti, orna pore chhobi tulchhilam. Tarpor aamar bag tene dekhte laglo. Oi Shurokkhha Foundation achhe na? Majhe majhe giye condom tule aani, free te paoa jay bole. Du charte pamphlet o chhilo, she gulo dekhe Mama bollen naki distribution of pornographic material, aare bhai ka ke distribute, shob to nijer jonnyei tulechhilam!

CHOTON  Kisher pamphlet?

SHOU  Oi je AIDS awareness pamphlet hoy na?

CHOTON  And he called them pornographic?

SHOU  Yes! He sayed na ki Section ki ekta'r under e—

CHOTON  292 hyan, distribution of obscene materials.

SHOU  Hyan, oi obscene material i.

CHOTON  That's . . . I mean that's crazy that these . . . like even these educational brochures. Like there's still a fear of them being . . . ki bolbo. Arousing?

SHOU  Aare aami toh shei karone tulechhilam, chhobi gulo ja hot na.

CHOTON  (to Raheem, behind the camera) You're getting this right?

RAHEEM  Not yet.

CHOTON  What? Wait—

SHOU  Pulish er o pochhondo hoychhilo mone hoy. Pant er bhitor banra ta spawshto bojha jacchhilo.

SHOU  You know, I was wearing heels and a scarf like this. Then he started looking through my bag. You know the Shurokkhha Foundation? Sometimes I get free condoms from there and I had a couple pamphlets too, and Mr. Cop was like, "distribution of pornographic material." I mean, distributing to who sir? I got them all for myself!

CHOTON  What kind of pamphlet?

SHOU  You know those AIDS awareness pamphlets?

SHOU  That's why I got them, cause the pictures are so hot!

SHOU  I think the cop liked them too. I could see the outline of his dick right through his pants.

CHOTON  Ek second pause korte
　　pari? I just want to make sure we
　　get this on camera.

CHOTON  Could we
　　pause for a second?

RAHEEM  *(to Shou)* Sorry ... is it Shou?

SHOU  *(mimicking his cadence)* It is
　　Shou.

RAHEEM  Is it cool if I put a little
　　powder on your nose?

SHOU  *(to Choton)* Ba ba, ki service.

SHOU  Oh wow, what service!

RAHEEM  There's just a little shine
　　I wanna get rid of.

SHOU  Come come.

　　　Raheem daubs the tip of Shou's nose with a make-up sponge.
　　Hollywood level.

　　　　　　　*Raheem smiles.*

CHOTON  Ki kawthha ta bolle
　　ekkhuni?

CHOTON  What's the
　　word you just used?

SHOU  Ki?

SHOU  What?

CHOTON  Bolle pulish er ki ta /
　　dyakha—

CHOTON  You said you
　　could see the cop's—

SHOU  Banra ta toh besh—

SHOU  His "banra" was pretty—

CHOTON  Banra?

CHOTON  "Banra"?

SHOU  Hm besh bhalo size er—

SHOU  Yeah, it was pretty big.

RAHEEM  And—sorry. Can you
　　just run your hand through your
　　hair once?

SHOU  *(confirming)* Hair?

RAHEEM  Yeah there's a flyaway
　　that's catching the light.

SHOU  Like this?

RAHEEM  That's great thanks.

CHOTON  We good?

RAHEEM  Yup. Let's just get thirty
　　seconds of room tone.

CHOTON  Can we do it after?

RAHEEM  ... sure.

CHOTON  Or fine, let's just do it
　　now. Sorry shuru kawrar aagey we

just need thirty seconds of silence
to capture the sound of the room.

SHOU  My hair it's okay?

RAHEEM  Looks great.
   (to Choton) Wanna take a look
at the shot real quick?

                        *Choton looks.*

CHOTON  Bollam shundor lagchhe.        CHOTON  Told you you look great.

SHOU  Dekhi?                           SHOU  Let me see?

*Choton turns the monitor to show Shou. Shou fixes their hair, using the monitor as a mirror.*

CHOTON  Thik achhe?                    CHOTON  You good?

   *Shou takes a flower from a little vase and puts it behind their ear.*

SHOU  Hnu. Ebar thik.                  SHOU  Yeah, now I'm good.

                 *Choton turns the monitor back.*

CHOTON  Start korlam tahle?
   Thirty seconds silence?
   Starting . . . now.

*They sit in silence. The silence is anything but silence: car horns and street sounds filter in through the open window. Then, 15 seconds in, Jitesh's voice perforates. In the kitchen, he is singing as he waits for the tea to steep.*

JITESH  (singing) Ki ba gurguraya
   diya daake gawgon hoilo kala . . .

CHOTON  Are you serious?
   (loudly) Jitesh da?

       *The singing continues.*

RAHEEM  Don't worry / about it.

CHOTON  (louder) O Jitesh da!

JITESH  Jaii.

RAHEEM  —I think we got / enough.

CHOTON  Well either way we need
   quiet while / we—

RAHEEM  I mean—

       *A dog barks, echoing through the stairwell. Jitesh enters.*

Hyan re, aamra khanikkhon          RAHEEM  Hey we're actually
ekta interview record korchhi, tai    recording an interview for
/ jodi—                               just a little bit, so if—

JITESH  E ma.

*Jitesh sticks out his tongue and bites it, in embarrassment.*

CHOTON  Na kono awshubidha nei just / ektu—

CHOTON  No, no problem just—

SHOU  Ei aapnar gawla ta kintu phata-phati Dada.

SHOU  You've got a killer singing voice, brother.

JITESH  Hyan?

JITESH  What?

SHOU  First-class. Ma Kali'r dibbi bolchhi.

SHOU  First-class. I'm serious.

CHOTON  Ei just awaaj ta jodi *ektu* / kom—

CHOTON  If we could keep the noise down a *little*—

JITESH  Hyan hyan, thik achhe.

JITESH  Sure sure, of course.

CHOTON  Just ektukkhoner jonno.

CHOTON  Just for a little bit.

SHOU  Eshe ekta gaan shonaben kintu.

SHOU  And then I want to hear you sing.

*Jitesh smiles abashedly as he exits.*

Yarki na!

I'm not kidding!

CHOTON  *(to Raheem)* Are we still rolling?

RAHEEM  Yup.

CHOTON  Okay, so . . . tumi je bolchhile, Lake e tomar ei je ghawtona ta. Prothhom thheke ektu bawlo toh, ki hoychhilo?

CHOTON  Okay, so you were saying, this thing that happened to you by the Lake. Can you tell me about it from the beginning?

SHOU  So interview it has started?

CHOTON  I mean don't think of it so much as an interview, just think of it as a conversation—

SHOU  It should be English toh?

CHOTON  Bangla, English, whichever.

SHOU  English is no problem.

CHOTON  Sure sure, I'm just saying feel free to move between . . . maane, aamaro hoyto mone hawbe, oh, ei jinish ta Bangla tei bolte shubidha / tai—

CHOTON  I mean, I might also feel like, oh it's easier to talk about this thing in Bangla, so—

SHOU  But Bangla how they will understand?

CHOTON  Who?

SHOU  Maane eta to ekta American film i hawbe na ki?

SHOU  I mean this will be an American film, right?

CHOTON  Aare subtitles toh achhe, don't worry—

CHOTON  There are subtitles, don't worry.

SHOU  Okay, okay. So some subject is there or . . . ?

CHOTON  Well I'm interested in this question you're bringing up, 'cause it seems to me like, just tomar presence ta i . . . just the way you looked that day was enough to be seen as obscene. Right? The way you were dressed, je / bhabe—

*Jitesh enters with tea.*

SHOU  Eiii je, chomotkar.

SHOU  Here we go, perfect . . .

*Jitesh places the tray on a low table in front of Shou. There's a small plate of biscuits as well as a small plate with two sweets on it.*

JITESH  Biscut.

CHOTON  *(to Raheem)* Is that in the shot?

RAHEEM  I think it's fine if it's in there.

SHOU  O re baba, duto mishti o?

SHOU  Oh wow, two sweets too?

JITESH  Bhai er jonno ekhane rakhlam?

JITESH  I'll keep this one for brother here?

*Jitesh places Raheem's tea and sweets on the shelf next to him.*

RAHEEM  Oh thank you.

*Jitesh places Choton's tea and sweets next to him.*

CHOTON  Aami kintu ekkhuni mishti khabona.

CHOTON  I don't want sweets right now actually.

JITESH  Thik achhe.

JITESH  Okay.

*Jitesh goes to exit, plate in hand.*

SHOU  Kothhay chollen Dada? Gaan ta jate miss na hoy.

SHOU  Where are you going? What happened to my song?

*Jitesh looks to Choton.*

Oi je polli-geeti gaichhilen ekta?

That folk song you were singing?

JITESH  ... aapnara to byasto—       JITESH  ... you all are busy—

SHOU  Kothhay byasto?                SHOU  Busy with what?
  Cha khete khete to aar shooting       We're not filming while
  hobe na—                              we have tea—

CHOTON  Raheem bolchhilo—            CHOTON  Raheem was saying—
  (to Raheem) We're cool to record with the tea, yeah?

RAHEEM  Whatever y'all want.

SHOU  Cha ta kintu Dada hebbi        SHOU  The tea is killer
  hoychhe.                              by the way.

                    *Jitesh looks again to Choton.*

CHOTON  Tor ranna hoychhe?           CHOTON  Have you cooked yet?

JITESH  Bhaat chaapiyechhi.          JITESH  I just put the rice on.

SHOU  Aare du line ontoto geye       SHOU  Sing us a couple
  jaan.                                 lines at least.

            *Jitesh stands awkwardly, plate of sweets still in hand.*

JITESH  Jeta gaichhilam?             JITESH  The one I was singing?

SHOU  Hnu, shuni.                    SHOU  Let's hear it.

                    *Jitesh clears his throat. He hesitates.*

JITESH  Ektu khani i gaichhi.        JITESH  I'll sing just a little bit.

*He begins singing. A folk song. It's tentative at first, but as he sings, he gains
conviction, and a certain quiet falls over the room. Raheem turns the camera
toward him. When the verse is finished, he stops abruptly.*

SHOU  (thoroughly impressed) Oof!
  Phata phati.                       SHOU  Wow! Amazing.
  (to Raheem) You should shoot
  this, na? Local talent.

        *Raheem gives Shou a thumbs up from behind the camera.*
                    *Choton shoots him a look.*

JITESH  (noticing the camera) E ram.

SHOU  Boddo mishti kintu aapnar      SHOU  Your voice is so sweet.
  gawla.

                        *Pishimoni enters.*

PISHIMONI  Baba biraat              PISHIMONI  Wow there's
  production cholchhe to.             a serious production
                                      going on here!

CHOTON  (under his breath) Are you
  serious right now?

PISHIMONI  (waving to the camera) Hello.

SHOU  Nomoshkar Pishima.

PISHIMONI  Mishti
peyechho?

SHOU  Peyechhi, Dada'r gaan o
shunchhi—

PISHIMONI  Joy Maa.

*She collapses into the easy chair.*

Aare janabi toh bondhu eschhe
toder—

CHOTON  —Pishimoni—

PISHIMONI  —ghugni baniye
rakhtam.

CHOTON  —bollam na, aamra ektu
ei ghawre—

PISHIMONI  Ei ei sorry. Disturb
korlam? Mone holo gaan taan
hocchhe.

SHOU  Dada'r gaan er recording
cholchhe, Sa Re Ga Ma e pathano
hobe.

PISHIMONI  Tai naki?

CHOTON  Pishimoni—

PISHIMONI  Sugandha ke
dekhechho?

SHOU  *(affirmative)* Hm.

PISHIMONI  Awshadaron na?
Rong ta ektu moila kintu
ki gawla maane . . . bhaba jay na.

SHOU  Puro Lata Mangeshkar.

PISHIMONI  Ei tomar naam ta i to
jigesh korlam na—

SHOU  Aamar naam Shou.

PISHIMONI  Shou?

SHOU  Shoubhik ta boddo i purush
purush lagey—

PISHIMONI  *(to Jitesh)* Acchha
tui haat e mishti niye danriye

SHOU  Greetings Auntie.

PISHIMONI  Did you
get the sweets?

SHOU  We got the sweets, we're
listening to some singing—

PISHIMONI  You should have
said your friend was coming—

PISHIMONI  I would have
made some ghugni.

CHOTON  I told you, we
were going to be working
a little in this room—

PISHIMONI  Am I disturbing?
I thought I heard singing,
so I thought I'd peek in.

SHOU  We're recording
brother's singing so we can
send it to Sa Re Ga Ma.

PISHIMONI  Really?

PISHIMONI  Have you
seen Sugandha?

PISHIMONI  Isn't she amazing.
She's a little dark, but her
voice . . . I mean . . . unbelievable.

SHOU  Total Lata Mangeshkar.

PISHIMONI  I didn't even
ask your name—

SHOU  My name's Shou

SHOU  Shoubhik sounds
way too manly for me—

PISHIMONI  How come
you're standing there like

achhish keno orokom, statue'r moton? De ekta shondesh. Khaoa uchit na jodiyo.

a statue with sweets in your hand? Give me one. Though I really shouldn't.

*Jitesh hands her the plate of sweets. She puts one in her mouth.*

Janish, diabetes naki paa diye dhoke, krimi'r moton?

Did you know diabetes comes in through the feet, like tapeworms?

SHOU  Aapnar ki sugar? Aamar Ma'r o sugar niye awnek jhamela.

SHOU  You have blood sugar problems? My mother also has problems with her—

PISHIMONI  Aar bolish na. Kawto ki je control e rakhte hoy.

PISHIMONI  Don't even get me started. I have to control everything.

*Choton whispers something in Raheem's ear.*

RAHEEM  (to Choton)—I got it, don't worry—

SHOU  (to Jitesh) Dada, oi gaan ta janen ki? Menoka mathhay dilo ghomta?

SHOU  Brother, do you know that song? "Menoka Mathhay Dilo Ghomta"—

JITESH  (in the affirmative) Hnuu.

JITESH  Sure.

SHOU  Khub favorite gaan aamar. Sheje nechechhilam o ekbar, pujo'r function e.

SHOU  It's one of my favorite songs. I even dressed up and danced to it once during Puja—

*Shou rises and begins to recall a dance.*

SHOU  Dekhi Menoka'r rup ta mone pawre kina.

SHOU  Let me see if I can remember the moves.

PISHIMONI  Aamar gawlay toh shur i nei, tai chirokaal Jitesh er bhawjon ei bari'r pujo tujo shob chawle. Baba bolten oishworik gawla.

PISHIMONI  I can't even hold a tune, so it's always Jitesh who sings at our family pujas. My father used to say his voice is "heavenly."

CHOTON  (to Shou) Ei naach ta kawbe korechhile?

CHOTON  When did you do this dance?

SHOU  Oi class eight nagad. Ma bechari prai oggyan hoye giyechhilo dekhe, chokhe kajol, tawk tawke laal lipistick, kintu aami bhai shortcut er moddhye nei, korle, thik moton i kawra uchit. Tai na?

SHOU  Around class eight? I had on black eyeliner, bright red lipstick, my poor mother almost fainted. But I don't take shortcuts, if I'm going to do it, then I should do it full on, right?

*Choton resumes his interviewer's position, looking at*
*Raheem to make sure he is filming Shou, which he is.*

CHOTON  Aar ei naach ta ki kono—

SHOU  Dhat. Mudra ta monei aschhe na. O dada, gaiben naki ekbar?

(*singing*) . . . jamai chirokalo nyangta lo nyangta, Menoka / mathhay dilo ghomta . . .

*Jitesh joins in.*

JITESH  Menoka mathhay de lo ghomta

SHOU  Aha.

JITESH  Bechhe bechhe korli jamai
Bechhe bechhe korli jamai
Chirokali nyangta lo nyangta
Menoka mathhay de lo ghomta

SHOU  O!

*As Jitesh's singing picks up it is punctuated by Shou's rhythmic footfall*
*and occasional vocal exclamations. Every so often, Pishimoni sings*
*a line or two with him, off-beat, off-key. Raheem, in his element,*
*follows the action with his camera. Choton watches, impotent,*
*as the interview devolves into a full jam session.*

JITESH  Koti'r tawte bagham bawra
Nikommata ganjay day dawm
Koti'r tawte bagham bawra
Nikommata ganjay day dawm
Aabar haate tishul mathhay jawta
Haate tishul mathhay jawta
Thik bhikari'r dhong ta lo dhong ta—

SHOU  O ho!

JITESH  Menoka mathhay de lo ghomta

*Raheem leaves his video camera focused on Jitesh and takes the opportunity*
*to take a few photos with the Rolleicord, which is still hanging around*

CHOTON  And did this dance have any—

SHOU  I can't even remember the gesture. Brother, will you sing it once for me?

*his neck. As soon as the viewfinder opens, we see what Raheem is seeing,*
*projected on the window. He snaps a shot of Jitesh. Choton notices.*
*Peeved, he tries to get Raheem's attention.*

JITESH  Menoka mathhay de lo
   ghomta
   Menoka mathhay de lo—
*Raheem snaps a shot of Shou. Blackout. The photo develops slowly in the window.*
*END SCENE*

৫ । এক্সপ্রেশান

## 5. EXPRESSION

*Pishe as K_gang, chatting with minnesota76, playing pool, smoking a*
*cigarette. Their conversation appears as projected text.*

K_GANG  IS IT COLD THERE NOW ?

MINNESOTA76  not too bad

MINNESOTA76  past the worst of it I would say

K_GANG  HERE IN CALCUTTA APRIL IT IS VERY HOT

K_GANG  TODAY ALMOST 40 DEGREE

K_GANG  CENTIGRADE

MINNESOTA76  40 celcius?

MINNESOTA76  I was gonna say 40s not so bad it was 40 something here
   today

K_GANG  40 IS WHAT DEGREE CENTIGRAFE ?

K_GANG  CENTIGRADE

MINNESOTA76  lemme look it up

MINNESOTA76  says its 4.444 :)

K_GANG  4 DEGREE ?

K_GANG  THAT WE NEVER SEE

K_GANG  HERE BELOW 20 WE PUT MUFFLER CAP

MINNESOTA76  Whats a muffler cap?

K_GANG  MUFFLER IT IS "SCARF"

MINNESOTA76  Aaah got it

MINNESOTA76  here a muffler is something for your car

MINNESOTA76  makes it quiet

K_GANG   AGAIN EXCELLENT !

K_GANG  THIS IS BANK SHOT

MINNESOTA76  :)

K_GANG  U KNOW THIS IT REQUIRES KNOWLEDE OF GEOMETRY

K_GANG  TRIGONOMETRY

K_GANG  SO YOU ARE MATHEMATCIAN ?

MINNESOTA76  HA!

MINNESOTA76  Definitely NOT

K_GANG  THEN HOW YOU ARE ACHIEVING THIS ?

MINNESOTA76  playing with you!

MINNESOTA76  Getting plenty of practice :)

K_GANG  MY WIFE

K_GANG  SHE SAYS THIS IT IS ADDICTION

K_GANG  I AM SAYING HOW IT IS DIFFERENT ?

K_GANG  ALL DAY YOU ARE WATCHING TV

K_GANG  I AM LIVING IN-LAWS HOUSE

K_GANG  THIS IS THE TROUBLE

K_GANG  WIFE SHOULD BE LIVING IN HUSBANDS HOME

K_GANG  ISNIT IT ?

MINNESOTA76  Isnt that a little "old-fashioned" ;)

K_GANG  I COULD NOT EARN

K_GANG  THAT ONLY

K_GANG  EARNINGS WERE NOT ADEQUATE

K_GANG  WE CALL IT ' GHARJAMAI '

K_GANG  THAT HUSBAND IS UNSUCCESSFUL

MINNESOTA76  I dont know . . .

MINNESOTA76  I dont think money is everything

K_GANG  YOU ARE YOUNG . . .

K_GANG  SO WHY YOU ARE CHATTING WITH 'OLD' MAN :)

MINNESOTA76  I think . . .

MINNESOTA76  a nice man is worth something

MINNESOTA76  Plus . . .

MINNESOTA76  I find you very good looking . . .

> Choton's voice calls from the stairwell:

CHOTON  Pishe?

MINNESOTA76  Is that okay to say?

> Choton enters the apartment, an envelope and a set of small, square photos
> in his hand. Raheem enters behind him, the Rolleicord around his neck.

CHOTON  O Pishe—

PISHE  (startled) Hm?

CHOTON  Ashbo?                          CHOTON  Can I come?

PISHE  Danra, ek minit.                 PISHE  Hold on, one minute.

CHOTON  Actually—

PISHE  Khelbi na ki billiard?           PISHE  Want to play billiards?

CHOTON  E dike esho.                    CHOTON  Come over here.

*Choton walks over to the dining table, looking at the photos.*

PISHE  Ki hoychhe?                      PISHE  What is it?

CHOTON  Aare esho na. Chhobi            CHOTON  Come look, we
  gulo eschhe.                            picked up the photos.

PISHE  Danra.                           PISHE  Hold on.

*Pishe types.*

K_GANG  YOU ALSO ARE
  LOOKING

K_GANG  LOVELY

PISHE  Choshma ta niye aschhi.          PISHE  Let me get my glasses.

*Pishe logs off. He enters the sitting room, glasses and cigarette in hand.*

CHOTON  Ei dyakho.                      CHOTON  Look at these.

*Pishe sits at the table. Choton coughs feebly from the cigarette smoke. Pishe puts*
*out his cigarette in the ashtray. He peers eagerly over the bridge of his glasses at*
*the pile of small, square, black-and-white photographs. He looks closer. His brow*
*furrows. He looks at the next photo. Then the next.*

PISHE  Tullo ke e gulo?                 PISHE  Who took these?

CHOTON  Aamra to bhablam tumi           CHOTON  We thought
  janbe.                                  you would know.

  *(to Raheem)* He's asking who took
  them. And that scar is from / his—

PISHE  Surgery, hyan.                   PISHE  His surgery, yes.

CHOTON  I mean it looks like he's
  trying to—

*Choton tries looking at his back.*

  Yeah I can't even . . .

*He looks back at the photos.*

  Is that mustache drawn on?

PISHE  Baba to goph rakhten na.         PISHE  He didn't keep a mustache.

CHOTON  It's totally drawn on . . .

  I mean these must have been
  taken like . . . *right* before he
  died right?

PISHIMONI *(offstage)* Kawta bajlo go?

> *Pishimoni has appeared in the doorway, sleepy-eyed.*

Ki holo?

Shobai erom kawt mawt kore takiye achhe keno aamar dike?

. . .

CHOTON  Pishimoni—

PISHE  *(handing her the photos)* Ei dyakho.

PISHIMONI  *(eagerly)* Hoychhe develop? Dekhi.

> *She sits. She looks at the photos. The others watch her nervously.*

PISHIMONI  Na bujhte parchhina.

CHOTON  Aamrao bojhar i / cheshta korchhi.

PISHIMONI  Ke eta?

> *Choton looks to Pishe, worried.*

CHOTON  Pishimoni—

PISHE  Choshma ta niye esho.

PISHIMONI  *(to Choton)* De to choshma ta. Khat er opor roychhe.

> *Choton exits into the bedroom. Pishimoni squints at the photos.*
> *Choton returns with the glasses. Pishimoni puts them on.*
> *She looks at the photos, one at a time. Her face is expressionless.*

CHOTON  *(warily)* Pishimoni . . . eta toh Dadu.

> *Pishimoni looks through the photos again silently.*

*(to Raheem)* I mean is there any way he could have taken them himself?

> *Raheem peers at the photos.*

RAHEEM  Mm . . . I mean . . . *maybe* if he had a self-timer but like . . .

> *He looks closer at one photo.*

PISHIMONI  What time is it?

What's going on?

Why is everyone staring at me like that?

PISHE  Look.

PISHIMONI  Did they develop? Let me see.

PISHIMONI  No I don't understand.

CHOTON  We're also trying to understand.

PISHIMONI  Who is this?

CHOTON  Pishimoni—

PISHE  Go get your glasses.

PISHIMONI  Will you get me my glasses? They're on the bed.

CHOTON  Pishimoni . . . this is Dadu.

—no 'cause look, see that
shadow?
>*Choton looks.*
CHOTON  Oh you're right . . .
RAHEEM  Plus you can tell he's
looking at someone cause he's
looking up above the lens . . .
>*Everyone considers the photos.*
I mean they're kind of
beautiful.
>*Pishimoni quietly puts down the photos and walks out of the room.*
CHOTON  Pishimoni—
RAHEEM  Shit / I'm—
CHOTON  (*getting up*) Pishimoni—
PISHE  Aare chhere de.               PISHE  Let it go.
>*Choton follows her.*
RAHEEM  —sorry, I / didn't—
PISHE  What sorry? Nothing to be / sorry.
RAHEEM  I just meant like . . . as photographs they're—shit, I'm so / sorry—
PISHE  One must accept reality. Isn't it? She is not accepting. Thirty plus
years father is gone, still she is telling, "how can it be, how can it be,"
aare!
>*Pishe a cigarette in his mouth.*
She is my wife, still what she is thinking that I don't know, what I am
thinking, that she don't know. So? This is reality.
>*He fetches his lighter.*
(*re: the cigarette*) Is it a problem?
RAHEEM  No no, not at all.
>*Pishe tries lighting his lighter.*
PISHE  For Choton it is a disturbance.
RAHEEM  Oh I'm aware.
>*Pishe tries the lighter again.*
PISHE  Constitution it was always little bit weak actually.
>*Pishe tries the lighter a third time. It still doesn't light.*
Dhat.
RAHEEM  Here, I got mine.
>*He pulls his lighter out of his pocket and hands it to Pishe.*
PISHE  Ei excellent.

*Pishe lights his cigarette with Raheem's lighter. He hands the lighter back to him. He offers a cigarette.*

You like to have?

RAHEEM  No I'm good thanks. Thank you though.

*Pishe inhales deeply, his eyes returning to the photographs. He exhales a cloud of smoke.*

PISHE  You know my father-in-law. I knew him since I was 23 years— I never saw this . . . ki kawthha to bole? Expression.

*He looks again at the photographs.*

How he is looking here. At the camera, it is . . .

*He takes another puff of his cigarette.*

You have seen *Jalsaghar*?

RAHEEM  Is this . . . like a film or—

PISHE  Yes yes, this is Satyajit Ray, aare what is the—*(he clucks his tongue)*—in English I believe it is called "Concert Room"—

RAHEEM  Oh! That's um— I think it's *The Music Room* / in—

PISHE  Ki *expression*. Isn't it?

RAHEEM  Oh for sure.

PISHE  Maane with facial expression alone—

RAHEEM  I mean that scene when he looks in the mirror is iconic.

PISHE  Simple expression. Without dialogue.

*Another long drag from his cigarette.*

I had one dream like this actually, some years back. Vivid dream. I am in a cinema hall . . . and on the screen, I am seeing one young executive . . . holding a portfolio . . . leather portfolio . . . entering a hotel room. And from that hotel room, through the window, can be seen a swimming pool. Okay? And in the swimming pool, he saw a beautiful-looking girl. And this executive, he very much has a want to meet this girl. Then the shot changes. That girl is now sitting inside the room, wearing a green sari. And the girl says to him, I have a story to tell: when I was twelve thirteen years, I was walking by the river . . . suddenly, from high up, how a flood comes . . . like that a strong flood has come, and with my hands in the air like this saying save me, save me . . . Then the picture faded. Then next scene is showing one elderly gentleman . . . looks like the father of the girl, wearing a dhuti. And until now actually shots were in color, okay? This one it became black and white. Elderly gentleman he is going, basket on his head . . . as he is going, absentmindedly like this, as if he is catching a fly and putting in the basket. Catching. Putting. And seeing this I turned to my friend and sayed—all this time there was no friend there, suddenly my friend was next to me—and I sayed to him: this is trash! This cinema has no meaning. And just as I sayed this, my sleep broke. And finding Pishimoni next to me, I sayed to her . . . what a strange and beautiful cinema I have seen. Just like this I sayed. "What a strange and beautiful cinema."

RAHEEM  (*genuinely taken aback*) Whoa.

PISHE  Just like this I sayed.

RAHEEM  That's—

PISHE  Byas. This only.

 *Raheem considers something.*

RAHEEM  This might be weird but . . . would you mind telling it to me again?

PISHE  Again?

RAHEEM  So I can record you? If the details change, that's okay, I'd just love to—

PISHE  Detail meaning?

RAHEEM  I just mean—

PISHE  Here there is no detail to change, executive he was in white dress.

RAHEEM  Wait, hold on, lemme just—

 *He pulls out his phone.*

 Do you mind?

PISHE  No, no problem.

 *Raheem presses record.*

RAHEEM  And actually—can I take a picture of you? Just like you are right now, don't—

 *The Rolleicord is still around Raheem's neck. He picks it up, opens the viewfinder. Pishe takes a drag of his cigarette.*

 That's great, just like that. Look at me.

 *Pishe looks at the camera, smoke curling out of his mouth. Raheem snaps a photo.*

 Sorry you were saying . . . the executive . . .

PISHE  Executive was in white dress. Not in any suit boot, smart white dress. Okay? Portfolio was tan color. Leather portfolio. Not any suitcase briefcase. If he is coming to the hotel first time or he has come before, that I do not know. I am telling only what I am seeing in the cinema.

RAHEEM  And this guy is *in* the film?

PISHE  *In* the film, yes.

RAHEEM  So in the film, you're watching this guy enter this—

PISHE  Room on the second floor. Erokom, like this. He opens the door, window is there to his left, and through the curtain, he sees a swimming pool. And there, he sees a woman, climbing, holding the . . . aare in the swimming pool how there / is—

RAHEEM  —sure, there's the little ladder.

PISHE  Okay? This girl is beautiful to see. And so he has a want to see her. This only. It appeared so. Then it is showing he is leaving, and when he is coming back . . . that gap I don't know, that time is not shown in the cinema.

RAHEEM  Got it.

PISHE  But when he returns, woman is there . . . wearing a sari . . . bottle-green sari—

RAHEEM  In the same room?

PISHE  Inside that same room. In a chair. Where the fellow he is meant to be sitting, in that place. And just as he enters, she says to him, "You have an interest in me, and I have got a story to tell." And then she says this is what happened to me. That I was walking by the bank of the river. When I was twelve thirteen years. Suddenly there was . . . rush of water. And I was being carried away. With my hands up like this, "save me, save me." This much only.

RAHEEM  And when the woman is telling this story, you're seeing the story in the film?

PISHE  Yes, seeing the story. There are no words mind you.

RAHEEM  After she says "I have a story to tell you"—

PISHE  She did not tell to the man either, "I have something to say." Only her expression was that. That "I have got a story to tell."

RAHEEM  Oh so the woman didn't say anything.

PISHE  No didn't say. Only in her expression.

RAHEEM  *Got it.*

PISHE  Gentleman, lady, neither says anything. No words are there. Okay? He only picturized the thing. The picture came to him . . . that she is walking by the river and then the water came. She is being carried away. Byas. After this, black and white.

 Village man is walking, basket on his head. And he is catching something. With his hand, catching, putting. As if he has become insane

RAHEEM  Oh I see, so he's not actually catching flies.

PISHE  Actually nothing is there. Just catching, putting.

RAHEEM  I kinda like the image of him catching flies.

PISHE  It could be flies, it could be some . . . ki bawle? He is harvesting something, I don't know. I don't know anything more. Just that only. Then

suddenly I sayed to my friend—suddenly my friend is next to me, I sayed
to him: "What a terrible cinema." And then I woke up, Pishimoni is there,
I sayed to her, "What a wonderful cinema I saw. Wonderful dream." This
will be a short film. Maximum one minute. No more than that.

> *A pause.*

If it's possible. How it is done that I don't know. That it is your subject.
> *Raheem smiles.*

Hyan? You are director.

RAHEEM  Ha!

PISHE  You make it.

RAHEEM  I'm not a director.

PISHE  You are / director.

RAHEEM  Director of Photography / means—

PISHE  Yes.

RAHEEM  I mean I support the director, but it's not like I make my *own*
films—

PISHE  Why not?

RAHEEM  Like I'm responsible for the camerawork—

PISHE  (*understanding*) Acchha, I see.

RAHEEM  I mean I'm not saying— I don't know . . . like if everyone's just
"having a vision" then . . . I mean somebody has to actually make the
thing, right?

PISHE  Because—

RAHEEM  Which isn't to say— (*he laughs*) I feel like I'm doing the thing
where I'm making it seem like DPs aren't actual artists, we are, we're / just—

PISHE  Because in my dream . . . there I am seeing what the camera is seeing.
Isn't it? Only this. Vision is the camera. Byas.

> *Raheem considers this.*

RAHEEM  And it's like a ghost story? Am I getting this right? Cause if the
woman drowned when she was—

> *Choton re-enters, on FaceTime with his father, Baba.*

CHOTON  Ei je dekhacchhi.          CHOTON  Hold on, let
Danrao.                                                me show you.

> *Seeing him, Raheem stops recording. Choton coughs from the cigarette smoke.*

PISHE  Danra.                              PISHE  Hold on.

> *Pishe puts out his cigarette.*

CHOTON  My dad's on FaceTime.

> *Choton turns the phone to show Raheem. Raheem waves.*

RAHEEM  Hello.

BABA  Ei, how are you Raheem?

*Baba's English is Americanized.*

RAHEEM  I'm doin' well, how are
you all doin'?

BABA  Doin' well, doin' well.

*Choton coughs.*

CHOTON  *(to Pishe)* Ashtray ta ektu          CHOTON  Can you put the
onno ghawre rekhe ashbe?                       ashtray in the other room?

BABA  Everything is okay there?

RAHEEM  Yeah, everything's going
great—

*Pishe takes his ashtray into the computer room. The next line is hard to
understand because the connection is shoddy.*

BABA  Experiencing life in Calcutta?

RAHEEM  Sorry?

BABA  *(more audible)* I said, you are
experiencing life in Calcutta?

RAHEEM  I am!

BABA  Good, that's good.

CHOTON  Bolchhe poor
connection.

BABA  Hyan?

PISHE  *(re-entering, to Baba on
FaceTime)* Hello Dadamoni.

BABA  Hmm, ki awbosthha?          BABA  Yeah, what's the situation?

CHOTON  Ei je.                    CHOTON  Here.

*Choton holds up one of the photographs to the phone.*

Dekhte pacchho?                   Can you see it?

BABA  Dekhi.                      BABA  Let me see.

*Choton tries to center the photo.*

Kichhui to dekhte pacchhina.      I can't see anything.

CHOTON  Danrao.                   CHOTON  Hold on

*Choton picks up the phone and arranges the photos on the table.*

Ghabre jeo na kintu.              Don't freak out.

*He positions the camera over one of the photos.*

Ebar dekhte pacchho?              Can you see them now?

*There's a momentary pause.*

BABA  Aar ektu kachhe kor
    phone ta.

BABA  Bring your phone
    a little closer.

*Another pause.*

Kothhar thheke ashlo e gulo?

Where did these come from?

CHOTON  They were inside Dadu's
    camera.

PISHE  Bolechhilam Bombay Photo
    tei—

PISHE  I told them go to
    Bombay Photo—

CHOTON  We just picked them up.

*Choton moves the camera to the next photo.*

BABA  So the film was inside the
    camera?

CHOTON  Yup.

*Another pause.*

BABA  Tullo ta ke?

BABA  Who took them?

CHOTON  I mean it must have been
    Thammi, right?

BABA  *(unsure)* Thammi?

CHOTON  I mean who else would
    he have felt comfortable—

PISHE  Ma ke kintu kono din
    camera dhorte dekhini—

PISHE  I've never seen
    Ma use a camera—

CHOTON  We could ask.

BABA  Aare ekhon ki "ask," ekhon
    toh mental awbosthha khub i weak.

BABA  Ask what? Now her
    mental state is very weak.

CHOTON  Onno gulo dekhachhi
    danrao.

CHOTON  Let me show
    you the other ones.

PISHIMONI  Jitesh!

BABA  De toh ek second Pishimoni
    ke—

BABA  Give it to Pishimoni
    for a second—

PISHIMONI  Ei Jitesh!

JITESH  *(offstage)* Jaiii—

JITESH  Coming!

PISHIMONI  Kothhay je
    shob . . .

PISHIMONI  I don't
    know where he—

PISHE  Ki korchho?

PISHE  What are you doing?

*Pishimoni begins removing items from the fridge and placing them on the floor.*

Aare pagol er moton ki korte
shuru korle?

Are you crazy? What are
you doing all of a sudden?

*Jitesh enters.*

PISHIMONI  Bhaat ta kothhay gelo?

PISHIMONI  Where's the rice?

JITESH  Bhaat? Toh . . . korchhi.

JITESH  I'm . . . making rice now.

PISHIMONI  Aare na re baba, gawtokaaler bhaat ta fridge e je chhilo. Sheta koi?

PISHIMONI  No I mean yesterday's rice that was in the fridge, where is that?

JITESH  Sheta toh . . .

JITESH  That . . .

PISHIMONI  Ki?

PISHIMONI  What?

*Jitesh looks at Pishe.*

JITESH  Dupure . . . Jamai Babu khelen je.

JITESH  Didn't . . . Jamai Babu have it for lunch?

PISHIMONI  Bah.

PISHIMONI  Great.

PISHE  Ekhon bhaat khabe / tumi?

PISHE  You want rice now?

JITESH  Bhaat hoye / giyechhe.

JITESH  Rice is almost finished.

PISHIMONI  Aare dhatteriki.

PISHIMONI  Oh come on!

BABA  Ki bolchhe Pishimoni?

BABA  What's Pishimoni saying?

*Jitesh exits into the kitchen.*

CHOTON  Danrao. Pishimoni—

CHOTON  Hold on. Pishimoni—

*Pishimoni begins putting the items she'd removed from the fridge back into it, with loud clangs and bangs.*

(to Baba) Tomake ektu pawre phone korchhi.

Let me call you back in a little bit.

BABA  Shon, chhobi gulo'r photo tule amake text kore de.

BABA  Listen, text me pictures of the photos.

CHOTON  Mm . . . I don't know if that's such a good / idea.

BABA  Oh I see.

CHOTON  Or actually . . . let me— Danrao call back korchhi ektu pawre.

CHOTON  Hold on, I'll call you back in a bit.

BABA  Acchha okay okay.

*Choton hangs up. Using his phone's camera, he takes snaps of each of the photos of Dadu, one by one. Jitesh re-enters.*

JITESH  Bhaat.

JITESH  Rice.

PISHIMONI  Pakhi ki aar notun bhaat khabe?

PISHIMONI  I'm supposed to feed new rice to the birds?

*Jitesh is unsure what to do.*

De. Ekhane de.                    Here. Give it here.

*Jitesh places the container of freshly cooked rice next to Pishimoni. She scoops up*
*a bit of rice with her fingertips, and then immediately releases it with a yelp.*

Unun thheke tulei dili            Did you literally just
na ki?                            take it off the stove?

*She tries again, more cautiously. She blows on the rice in her hand, and then*
*forms it into a ball. She places it gently on the windowsill. She makes another ball:*
*scoop; blow; shape. The others watch silently. Choton looks at Pishe. Pishe gives*
*Choton a tired look.*

PISHE  Ki bolbo bawl?             PISHE  What am I
                                  supposed to say?

PISHIMONI  Tomar bawlar toh       PISHIMONI  You have no
kono jayga i nei.                 place to say anything.

*Pishe rises. He walks toward the computer room.*

Shara jibon shudhu computer       Whole life, just tap-tapping
e pitir pitir . . .               away on your computer . . .
Ka'r bari te tumi eta? Hyan?      Whose house are
                                  you in? Huh?

*Pishe doesn't respond. He sits silently at his computer.*

Shawrgo thhekeo manush            Even from heaven, the
ta tomar bhawron poshon kore      man is still paying your
jacchhe. Baba'r pension chhara    bills. Without my father's
shongshar cholto ki? Mashe        pension, how would we live?
mashe Dadamoni taka na            If my brother didn't send
pathale—                          money every month—

CHOTON  Pishimoni—

PISHIMONI  Na, he should hear,
na?

Kono din nijer pa e danrate       PISHIMONI  Never stood on
parlo na. Chirodin shudhu         your own two feet. Always
onnyer khabar i kheye gelo . . .  eating someone else's food . . .

*Pishe types. Pishimoni makes balls of rice and places them*
*in a line on the windowsill. Choton, Raheem, and Jitesh watch.*
*The sound of car horns and crows cawing outside.*

*END ACT ONE*

## ৬ । হ্যান্ডসাম
## 6. HANDSOME

*This scene appears as video: we see what the camera sees.*
*We see the inside of Thammi's room. She is lying in bed: skeletal, frail.*
*Choton sits on a low stool at her bedside, the envelope of photos in his*
*hand. Jitesh is barely visible at the edges of the frame. We don't see his face,*
*but we hear his voice. The Rolleicord refocuses.*

JITESH  Ma?
 Ke eschhe?

JITESH  Ma?
 Who's here?

THAMMI  Hm?

JITESH  Oi dyakho ke eschhe.

JITESH  Look who's here.

THAMMI  Ke?

THAMMI  Who?

JITESH  Naati.
 Aapnar naati.

JITESH  Grandson.
 Your grandson.

CHOTON  Ki go.

JITESH  Bhalo nei aajke.

JITESH  She's not well today.

*Choton sits next to her.*

CHOTON  Ki go Thammi.
 Ghumocchhile?

CHOTON  Were you
 sleeping Thammi?

THAMMI  Hm?

CHOTON  Ghumocchhile?

CHOTON  Were you sleeping?

*She doesn't respond.*

Dekhi, choshma koi
tomar?

Let's see, where
are your glasses?

*Jitesh grabs her glasses from the nightstand and gently puts them on her face. It's*
*clear she doesn't like it.*

Ei dyakho.

Look at this.

*Choton takes the photos out of the envelope. He brings one close.*

Dekhte pacchho?

Can you see?

*Thammi looks directly at the camera.*

Ei chhobi gulo ki tumi
tulechhile?

Did you take these
pictures?

*She continues staring at the camera.*

O Thammi, ektu e
dike takao.

O Thammi, look
over here for a sec.

*Choton puts the photo in her line of sight.*
*She continues to look past it toward the camera.*

Ke eta?                                    Who is this?
Chinte parchho?                            Do you recognize him?
Dadu naki?                                 Is it Dadu?
Eta Partho.                                It's Partho.

THAMMI  Hm?

CHOTON  Partho. Tomar bor.          CHOTON  Partho. Your husband.

*She lets out a little snort.*

THAMMI  Aamar biyei                 THAMMI  I'm not even
hoyni.                                  married yet.

CHOTON  *(amused)* Tai na ki?       CHOTON  Oh is that right?
Kawto boyosh tomar?                     How old are you?
Tomar chhele meye achhe?              Do you have children?
Naam ki tomar chhele                    What are your
meye'r?                                 children's names?
*(feeding it to her)* Kamal . . .      Kamal . . .

THAMMI  Kamal, Ketaki.              THAMMI  Kamal, Ketaki.

CHOTON  Hnu, thik.                  CHOTON  That's right!
Ketaki phool. Kamal phool.              Ketaki flower. Kamal
Thik ki na?                             flower. Isn't that right?

THAMMI  *(inaudibly)* . . . kawmolo
mukulo dolo . . .

CHOTON  Ki bolle?                   CHOTON  What'd you say?

THAMMI  *(a little louder)* . . .   THAMMI  . . . the Kamal
kawmolo mukulo dolo . . .               flowers blossoming . . .

CHOTON  *(to Jitesh)* Ki bolchhe?   CHOTON  What's she saying?

JITESH  Ki Ma? Pochhonder gaan      JITESH  What do you think
na ki?                                  Ma? You like that song?

*Jitesh sings.*

Aaji kawmolo mukulo dolo khulilo
Aaji kawmolo mukulo dolo khulilo
Dulilo re, dulilo
Manoshoshawroshe
rawshopulawke

*Thammi closes her eyes and listens intently.*

Pawloke pawloke dheu—

CHOTON  Danra ghumiye porchhe.      CHOTON  Wait, she's falling asleep.
O Thammi.                               Hey Thammi.

*Thammi opens her eyes, irritated. She notices Raheem.*

THAMMI  Ota ke?

THAMMI  Who's that?

*Thammi gestures toward the camera.*

CHOTON  Eta Raheem, mone achhe? She din aalap kawralam?

CHOTON  This is Raheem, remember? I introduced you the other day?

*Thammi stares at the camera.*

THAMMI  Shundor dekhte.

*This tickles Choton.*

CHOTON  Tai?
(to the camera) She says you're "shundor."

*We hear Raheem's voice from behind the camera.*

RAHEEM  What's that?

CHOTON  She thinks you're pretty.

THAMMI  (inaudibly, her voice catching) Handsome.

CHOTON  Ki bolle?

CHOTON  What'd you say?

THAMMI  (feebly) Handsome.

CHOTON  Handsome? Hyan, handsome.

*He points to the photograph.*

Tomar bor o handsome chhilo. Tai na?

CHOTON  Your husband was handsome too, wasn't he?

THAMMI  Hm?

CHOTON  Ei dyakho. Tumi ki tulechhile e gulo?

CHOTON  Look at this. Did you take these?

*Thammi looks at the photos for the first time.*

Ei dyakho. Partho. Chinte parchho?

Look. It's Partho. Do you recognize him?

*Thammi stares keenly at the photographs. Something flickers across her face. She looks closer, her eyes searching. She looks as if she's about to say something— Then she looks away.*

CHOTON  Ke tulechhilo jano ki?

CHOTON  Do you know who took them?

*Thammi notices Raheem again, as if for the first time.*

THAMMI  Ki shundor.

CHOTON  Looks like Thammi's got a little crush on you.

RAHEEM   Tell her I think she's . . .
   what is it? Shu—
CHOTON   Shundor.
RAHEEM   Shundo. Tell her I think
   she's shundo too.

CHOTON   Bolchhe tumi o khub          CHOTON   He's saying
   shundor.                                        you're "shundor" too.

*Thammi's face cracks into a broad smile.*
*END SCENE*


৭ । টু সেনসিটিভ
## 7. TOO SENSITIVE

CHOTON   —and he *refused* to go to the doctor 'cause he was terrified of like,
   finding out it was actually malignant. So he didn't do anything about it,
   and it kept growing, and eventually it was like . . . I mean my dad says
   it was like the size of a tennis ball just like protruding from his butt, so
   he couldn't even sit down, and it was a whole thing, and so my dad and
   Pishimoni basically were like . . . you *have* to do something about this. So
   they took him to the doctor, and it turns out it was *totally* benign, and he
   got it removed, and everybody was super relieved. And then a week later
   he just . . . died.
RAHEEM   How?
CHOTON   Like the scar got infected and he went into . . . septic / shock.
RAHEEM   Wowww—
CHOTON   *Yeah.* And I think there's a lot of—like I think my dad and
   Pishimoni both blame themselves cause if they / hadn't—
RAHEEM   Sure.
CHOTON   —like that was actually a huge part of why my parents moved to
   the States, right? Cause they like, blamed the healthcare system here, even
   though like, people die of sepsis in the US all the time too, but anyway . . .
   for Pishimoni . . . I don't know, it turned into this weird like . . . denial . . .
   Which is why I was worried about showing these to her 'cause . . . I mean
   that's *literally* the thing that killed him, right? That scar.
RAHEEM   That . . . makes so much / sense now . . .
CHOTON   Even though . . . I mean when he took these he had no idea, right?
   That he would be dead in a few days. Like in hindsight I'm looking and

I'm like . . . that's a pretty gnarly looking scar, but like . . . would I have thought that if I didn't know? Like it looks like a scar.

RAHEEM  Totally.

CHOTON  Like this is actually kinda like . . . a *celebratory* photoshoot, right? Like I had this thing on my body and now it's gone, let me see what my body looks like now.

RAHEEM  Yeah—

CHOTON  You know? Like he just looks so like . . . what's the word . . .

RAHEEM  I mean in this one, it's clearly like—like whoever took them must've cracked a joke or like—

CHOTON  Totally.

> Yeah.
>
> I guess I'm realizing . . .
>
> Huh.
>
> That's crazy.

RAHEEM  What?

CHOTON  No I've just . . . I've never seen his smile, right? Like I'm like . . . *(he points to the portrait on the wall) that's* the photo you picked? To represent him for eternity? Like mm, we only care about him from the neck up anyway, let's just crop out his body and turn him into an unsmiling like, disembodied head—

RAHEEM  I mean that's what I love about *these* cause they're just so like . . . mid-motion . . . like every shot is like, the moment just before he looks, or just after, so there's something kind of off-balance about them. I mean it's really kind of . . .

CHOTON  Like he just looks so like . . . un-self-conscious, you know? Just like . . . *in* his body.

RAHEEM  Well part of it's like . . . because you're looking down into the viewfinder, you're shooting from below, so it makes him look really tall.

CHOTON  You think he like . . . hired somebody? Like a professional?

> *They look at the photograph together.*

RAHEEM  See even these hairs on his / back—

CHOTON  Right?

RAHEEM  Like you would really have to anchor yourself like against a wall or something to get that kind of crisp focus with such a shallow depth of field . . .

> *He fiddles with the camera. Choton picks up a photo and walks to the middle of the room.*

Where even is the f-stop on this?

CHOTON  So he was standing like . . . right here, right?

RAHEEM  Isn't that that / mirror?

CHOTON  Yeah—

RAHEEM  Plus the reason you're seeing the photographer's shadow is cause there must have been pretty direct sunlight coming through this window and hitting them from behind. Just in this first one though, then they move so / the shadow's out of frame.

CHOTON  But then I'm like—why didn't he just look in the mirror? You know?

*Choton tries to look at his back in the mirror.*

I guess it's pretty hard to see down there actually.

RAHEEM  Look at me for a sec.

*Choton looks.*

Right into the lens.

*Choton tries.*

Like . . . imagine there's a little human in the center of this lens here.

*Choton peers into the lens, brow furrowed.*

But relax your forehead, he's just in there, you're not like searching for him. Actually, close your eyes.

*Choton closes his eyes.*

And when I tell you, open them, and look right at that person inside the lens.

CHOTON  Okay . . .

*Raheem focuses the camera.*

RAHEEM  Okay . . . open.

*Choton opens his eyes very wide and looks straight into the camera. Raheem snaps a shot.*

Yeah since the window's frosted, you're basically getting this like . . . diffuse glow, which is . . . I mean it's kind of amazing actually.

CHOTON  And what's crazy, right . . . is he never saw these. Like by the time the photos were developed . . .

*Raheem looks at the photos.*

RAHEEM  I love the way the photographer captures him *just* as he's pulling his boxers / down—

CHOTON  Yeah it really does kinda look like a striptease huh? I guess I kind of get why Pishimoni freaked out 'cause . . . like I've never seen this much of *my* dad. You know? Like you've seen your dad naked, right?

RAHEEM  . . . I mean . . . probably—?

CHOTON  Like there was this period in like elementary school when my dad decided I needed swimming lessons cause his colleague or something had drowned in a . . . like freak accident, swimming at the beach . . . anyway so he would take me to the pool at Stanford and—and like *he* was taking them too 'cause *he* couldn't swim. So he would pick me up after school and we would go and like . . . you know, this locker room was full of students and faculty and there were so many penises . . . Like I think I even asked if we could go to the women's room 'cause this was still when I would go to the bathroom with my mom when I was with her and . . . anyway my dad would do this like . . . elaborate choreography . . . like he would wrap his towel around his pants, and then he would take off his pants and his underwear with the towel wrapped around him, and then he would pull his bathing suit on *under* / the towel—

RAHEEM  Yeah I know this trick—

CHOTON  But then he had this *shirt* . . . like this like blue spandex shirt he would wear and like . . . here are all these athletes with these like perfect bodies just walking around with their clothes off and *we* were just like . . . covering ourselves up as much as humanly possible. Like no wonder I'm such a disaster area.

RAHEEM  What do you mean?

CHOTON  Like there's a reason I was basically a virgin, right? Like before we met, I literally never pictured myself having sex. Like even in my own head, I didn't want to *be* in the fantasy, 'cause having *my* body in there ruined it.

RAHEEM  But you do now.

CHOTON  Do what?

RAHEEM  We have sex.

CHOTON  Yeah but I'm talking about like . . . this idea that I *must* be grateful my parents moved to America and like . . . saved me from a terrible life cause India's supposedly so homophobic, but I'm like . . . maybe I would have been better off here, right? With people that actually look like me like . . . talk like me . . . might actually be *attracted* to me . . .

    *Something flickers across Raheem's face, almost imperceptibly.*

    But because we moved, I never like—like the other day with Shou, right? When they were talking about the policeman's "banra," that / was—

RAHEEM  What's "banra"?

CHOTON  "Banra" is dick. But I didn't know / that.

RAHEEM  I thought "nunu" / was—

CHOTON  Exactly. That is *exactly* what I mean, "nunu" is like . . . wee-wee. Like my anatomy vocabulary is basically baby talk cause we left when I was a toddler. But if I'd grown up here, I would have been like, talking about blowjobs and boners and like . . . I don't know . . . You know?

    Man. We didn't end up getting that on tape, did we?

RAHEEM  What?

CHOTON  When Shou was talking about the cop?

RAHEEM  I don't know.

CHOTON  Can we see if we have it actually?

RAHEEM  Right now?

CHOTON  Where's your hard drive, I can look.

RAHEEM  I mean the footage is still in RAW.

CHOTON  What does that mean?

RAHEEM  Like it's raw image data, I haven't delayered it yet.

CHOTON  . . . so—

RAHEEM  But we can look.

    *Raheem gets up abruptly and walks over to his backpack. He grabs his laptop. He sits next to Choton. He opens his laptop. Plugs in his hard drive.*

CHOTON  There's no way for me to look at it myself?

RAHEEM  Do you have Premiere?

CHOTON  I mean . . . sorry I'm not tryna—I guess I'm just getting used to the workflow.

    *Choton looks over Raheem's shoulder.*

RAHEEM  What day was that?

CHOTON  I mean . . . it was the day after we got here so . . .

RAHEEM  Here, I found it.

    *Raheem pulls up the file.*

CHOTON  Can you make it bigger?

    *Raheem does so.*

RAHEEM  Just start at the top?

CHOTON  Yeah let's just see—

    *Through the laptop, we hear the start of the interview with Shou:*

RAHEEM  *"Let's just get thirty seconds of room tone."*

CHOTON  *"Can we do it at the end?"*

RAHEEM  *"Sure."*

CHOTON  *"Or fine, let's just do it now. Sorry shuru kawrar aagey—"*

    Yeah I'm pretty sure we missed the part I'm talking about. When they were talking about the cop getting a boner—

RAHEEM  When was that?

CHOTON  Scrub forward?

> Raheem scrubs ahead.

I mean we were talking in Bangla so you probably didn't clock it.

> Raheem starts playback. The sound of Jitesh singing comes through the laptop speakers. They watch and listen.

I'm just like . . . even the fact that I never saw another uncircumcised penis, right? Or talked to anyone who / was—

RAHEEM  Your dad never talked to you about it?

CHOTON  Are you kidding? Have you *met* my parents?

RAHEEM  I'm just asking.

CHOTON  Have you ever seen them touch?

RAHEEM  Your parents?

CHOTON  I'm just saying—

RAHEEM  I feel like they're pretty affectionate with each / other.

CHOTON  Okay.

RAHEEM  Right?

CHOTON  I feel like you're like deliberately playing devil's advocate / or something—

RAHEEM  No I'm just trying to understand. 'Cause like . . . didn't your parents—

CHOTON  I mean they had a love marriage, sure, but that doesn't—like I don't think *physical* attraction was part of their calculus, right? And maybe I'm not being clear, 'cause like . . . it *is* such a culturally specific thing like . . . like I can be gay as long as I get a PhD in gay, right?

RAHEEM  I mean . . .

CHOTON  Does that make sense?

RAHEEM  . . . I'm just like . . . like my parents had no clue *what* to say to me about college. Or any of it, it was just like . . . not a thing they knew about.

CHOTON  Sure . . . / but—

RAHEEM  I mean they were super supportive, but it wasn't like they could give me advice or anything. It was just a totally foreign world to them. And I guess I just . . . like sometimes it sounds to me like you're saying your family's whole focus on education is like a bad thing / and I—

CHOTON  Wait what? When / did I—

RAHEEM  Or maybe . . . I don't know. I know I don't always have all the like vocab—

CHOTON  / that's not—

RAHEEM  —but I'm like . . . you had a great education. Your family loves you. Your family loves *me* which / is—

CHOTON  But how is that what I'm talking about?

RAHEEM  Maybe I don't get what you're talking about.

CHOTON  I'm talking about like . . . I literally can't pull my foreskin back, right?

RAHEEM  Sure . . .

CHOTON  And that is a literal physical consequence of like—I mean genuinely like, when the head is exposed, I can't even touch it, it's just way too sensitive—

RAHEEM  Isn't it—

CHOTON  —like I've pulled it back a couple times in the shower, but even the water hitting it is / like—

RAHEEM  But it's supposed to be sensitive though, right?

CHOTON  Yeah but this isn't—like I don't think it's supposed to be painful to pull the foreskin back from the head of your penis.

RAHEEM  Can I see?

CHOTON  See what?

*Raheem walks over to him. He kneels down.*

What are you doing?

RAHEEM  Just . . . lemme just . . . try, okay?

*He undoes the drawstring of Choton's pajama so it falls to his ankles. Raheem takes hold of Choton's penis gently.*

CHOTON  I mean I'm not making this up, I genuinely—

*Raheem gently pulls Choton's foreskin back.*

Okay careful, ow—

RAHEEM  Too much?

CHOTON  It's just super sensitive. Like even just the air on / it—

*Raheem blows gently on the exposed head of Choton's penis.*

Okay okay—

*He blows a little harder.*

—okay, hold on one—

*Choton takes a slow deep breath in and out.*

RAHEEM  It's so pink.

*Raheem gently inspects the head.*

CHOTON  . . . see those little bumps?

RAHEEM  Mm hm.

CHOTON  That's—like since I never cleaned the head—

RAHEEM  Have you tried getting hard like this? With it pulled back?

CHOTON  I mean my foreskin is too tight. See that's what I mean. Like no one ever showed me how to pull it back, so it never got stretched / out—

*Raheem takes Choton's penis in his mouth, very gently. Choton inhales sharply, eyes shut tight.*

Fuck.

*Raheem releases.*

RAHEEM  Okay?

CHOTON  Yeah it's just . . . intense.

RAHEEM  Let me know if it's / too much . . .

CHOTON  No no it's . . . I mean I think it feels good, it's just . . . a lot.

RAHEEM  Yeah . . .

*Choton glances at the portrait of his grandfather.*

You smell good.

*Raheem gives Choton's head a lick. Choton winces.*

CHOTON  I haven't showered in a couple days.

RAHEEM  Mm hm . . .

*He takes Choton's penis in his mouth again.*

CHOTON  Fuck.

*Raheem gently sucks. Choton shuts his eyes. Just then, Jitesh walks in. He sees them. It takes a moment to register what he's seeing. Choton opens his eyes and sees Jitesh standing there.*

CHOTON  Ei—

*Raheem turns to see Jitesh hurrying into the kitchen, avoiding eye contact. Choton pulls his pajama up swiftly; it brushes against his exposed penis.*

Ow. / Fuck.

RAHEEM  Shit.

*Raheem looks at Choton, mortified.*

/ Fuck.

CHOTON  Wow.

Is there like no fucking privacy in this—

RAHEEM  Shh!

CHOTON  What?

*Raheem indicates Jitesh in the kitchen.*

RAHEEM  He's *right* / there—

CHOTON  Ow—

*Choton, with his hand down his pajama, is trying to pull his foreskin back up.*

Can you like—help me? I can't get it to—ow.

*(re: his pajama)* Can you hold this open?

*Raheem obliges, his attention still focused toward where Jitesh exited.*

See this is why I—it just like, gets stuck.

RAHEEM  Can we like, do this in the bathroom or / something?

CHOTON  It's just painful when it like brushes against the pajama.

*Choton manages.*

I think I—okay.

Well.

*He re-ties his pajama.*

That was interesting.

RAHEEM  I feel like we should apologize.

CHOTON  To Jitesh da?

Yeah . . . I bet that's the first time he's walked in on something like that though, huh?

*(gently)* Hey. It's okay.

Seriously.

It's just Jitesh da.

*He goes to plant a kiss Raheem's head, but Raheem avoids it.*

CHOTON  What is happening?

RAHEEM  I'm just—

I think I just need a minute.

CHOTON  Okay . . .

*A long, tense pause.*

. . .

You okay?

. . .

Hey . . .

What's up?

. . .

. . .

If you don't tell me, I'm just gonna keep thinking about it.

. . .

Okay fine—

*Choton walks toward the kitchen.*

RAHEEM  What are you—

CHOTON  Jitesh da?

Ay ek second.

*Jitesh enters.*

Tui thik / achhish toh?

RAHEEM  *(to Jitesh)* Hey I wanted to—

> *He realizes he's started talking without knowing what to say.*

Sorry, I—

> *Raheem looks to Choton.*

Can you tell him "sorry"?

CHOTON  *(to Jitesh)* Bolchhe sorry . . .

> *Jitesh is profoundly embarrassed.*

Kono awshubidha hoy ni toh?

JITESH  Na na.

CHOTON  He's fine.

RAHEEM  *(to Jitesh)* Sorry.

CHOTON  Ei, ekta jinish dekhbi? Ei dekh. Ei dike ay.

> *Jitesh comes over to the table, tentatively. Choton reaches across Raheem*
> *and starts playback on the laptop. Jitesh watches himself. He sticks his*
> *tongue out and bites it.*

Bhalo na?

JITESH  *(pleased, and embarrassed)* Hei Ram.

CHOTON  *(to Raheem)* He's probably never seen himself recorded.

> *Raheem doesn't respond. They watch the video.*

PISHIMONI  *(offstage)* Jitesh?

JITESH  Jaii.

> *Jitesh hurries off.*

CHOTON  Yeah . . .

Looks like we got a bunch of him singing but none of that Shou stuff
unfortunately.

. . .

RAHEEM  Well . . .

. . .

CHOTON  No I'm not / blaming—

RAHEEM  I said it would take time to set up the shot—

CHOTON  No I know, I'm just—

. . .

Like I'm just saying this isn't a "shot" we're "setting up" right? We're just
archiving speech acts, so it's more important to just capture the content
period / than it is—

RAHEEM  Then why does it matter if I do it?

CHOTON  Whoa.

RAHEEM   You could just set up a camera.

CHOTON   I thought . . . I mean, obviously documenting is a whole skill set—

RAHEEM   But it doesn't really sound like you need a DP.

CHOTON   I thought we—I mean I thought . . . you know, part of this was like . . . we've been wanting to come, and this is a way we could get you here using my grant—

> *Raheem is silent. Eventually he gets up. He goes over to his bag and grabs his hat. He returns to the laptop. Saves. Closes his laptop.*

Where are you going?

> *Raheem grabs his shoes.*

RAHEEM   Gonna go for a walk.

CHOTON   Wait can we just—

—can we talk about what / just—

RAHEEM   I need a minute. I'm gonna go for a walk.

> *Raheem puts on his shoes. He ties his laces. He walks to the gate.*

CHOTON   Hold on, I need to open it.

> *He grabs a key from the wall. He unlocks the padlock on the gate. Raheem steps into the stairwell, and then remembers something. He walks back into the room. He grabs the Rolleicord from the table. He exits down the stairwell. Choton locks the gate, returns the key to its hook. He sits back down at the table, very still. He stares directly ahead: a practiced, deliberate stillness. He pulls out his phone. He stares at it. The sound of Grindr messages being sent. His jaw muscle twitches.*
>
> *END SCENE*

৮ । প্লেশার
## 8. PLEASURE

> *Pishe at his computer, playing billiards with minnesota76.*

K_GANG   OBSERVE THIS ONE . .

K_GANG   IT WILL STRIKE 6

K_GANG   RIGHT SIDE

K_GANG   JUST SOFTLY

> *Pishe assumes a posture of deep focus. Then he clicks the mouse.*

PISHE   Dhat!

MINNESOTA76   Oooh almost!

K_GANG   WITH COMPUTER ACTUALLY

K_GANG  SENSITIVITY IT IS NOT THERE

K_GANG  NOT POSSIBLE ACTUALLY

MINNESOTA76  Yeah its not the real thing

MINNESOTA76  Than again I could never play the real thing so this is
  better for me ;)

K_GANG  TRY 10

MINNESOTA76  U think?

K_GANG  MAY BE POSSIBLE

K_GANG  A LONG THIS SIDE

MINNESOTA76  I'll try . . .

K_GANG  GENTLY . .

> *A pause.*

K_GANG  AHA!

MINNESOTA76  Im surprised that went in!

K_GANG  WHAT SURPRISED?

K_GANG  THIS IS STRATEGY :)

MINNESOTA76  Ur pretty good at strategy huh ;)

K_GANG  WHOLE LIFE IS A STRATEGY

K_GANG  GAME OF STRATEGY

MINNESOTA76  I guess that's right!

> *A pause.*

K_GANG  UR DAUGHTER SHE IS WHAT AGE?

> *A pause.*

K_GANG  U KNOW YOU DONT LOOK

K_GANG  LIKE MOTHER ACTUALLY

K_GANG  MOTHER IS HOMELY

K_GANG  ISNT IT?

K_GANG  IN THE FACE SOME AGING IT SHOULD BE THERE

> *A pause.*

K_GANG  BUT HOW YOU ARE MAINTAINING GIRLISH FIGURE?

> *A longish pause.*

K_GANG  PLZ DONT TAKE ANY OFFENCE . . .

> *A pause.*

K_GANG  I MEAN IT IS APPEALING ;)

> *A pause.*

MINNESOTA76  What do u find appealing . . .

MINNESOTA76  :)

> *A pause.*

K_GANG   U R LOOKING FIT . . .

K_GANG   MEANING HEALTHY

K_GANG   SHAPELY I MEAN

MINNESOTA76   You look like u have strong arms . . .

K_GANG   ONE POINT OF TIME I BOWELED ACUTALLY

K_GANG   IN CRICKET CLUB OF DHAKURIA

K_GANG   BOWLED !

MINNESOTA76   I would love to see that

MINNESOTA76   I love bowling :)

K_GANG   MANY YEARS BACK

K_GANG   NOW I AM AGED

MINNESOTA76   I like how you look;)

MINNESOTA76   I think youre very sexy . . .

> *Pishe stands furtively and closes the shutters to the computer room. He is invisible to us now. But the conversation continues as projected text.*

K_GANG   YOU ALSO ARE

K_GANG   SEXY . . .

MINNESOTA76   I wish we were together . . .

MINNESOTA76   In the same place

> *A pause.*

K_GANG   I ALSO WANT THIS

> *A longish pause.*

K_GANG   PARDON BUT YOU MENTION . . .

K_GANG   YOU ARE DIVORCEE OR ?

> *A long pause.*

MINNESOTA76   Im divorced yes

K_GANG   U LEFT U R HUSBAND ?

> *A pause.*

MINNESOTA76   He left actually

K_GANG   WHY HUSBAND WOULD LEAVE THAT I DONT KNOW

K_GANG   I WOULD NOT LEAVE SUCH A LADY

K_GANG   :)

MINNESOTA76   I dont know about that

> *Jitesh enters the flat with some food items and disappears into the kitchen. He can't see Pishe through the shuttered window.*

MINNESOTA76   Dont mind me lets talk about if you

MINNESOTA76   If we were together right now :)

MINNESOTA76   What would we do

MINNESOTA76  ;)

MINNESOTA76  Would you let me pleasure you . . .

MINNESOTA76  ?

MINNESOTA76  Sorry . . . I didn't mean to make u uncomfortable

MINNESOTA76  Hello ?

> *From the kitchen, we hear the clang and clatter of Jitesh doing dishes.*
> *END SCENE*

৯ । ডাইনোসরস
## 9. DINOSAURS

> *It is late afternoon. Jitesh sits at the table. The photos of Dadu are laid out, just as Choton left them. Jitesh looks at them. He picks one up. He peers at it. The doorbell rings, a tinny ringtone-y "Memory" from Cats. It startles Jitesh. He walks over to the gate and sees Raheem coming up the stairs.*

RAHEEM  Hey. Sorry, I don't have a key.

> *Jitesh takes a key from a hook on the wall. He unlocks the gate. Raheem comes in.*

Thank you. Sorry—

> *Raheem notices all the lights are off.*

JITESH  *(a whisper)* Ghumocchhe shob.

RAHEEM  *(mimicking his whisper)* Ah. Okay. Sorry.

> *Raheem unties his shoes. Jitesh hangs the key back on the wall.*

JITESH  Cha khaben?

> *Raheem looks up, uncomprehending.*

RAHEEM  Hm?

> *Jitesh mimes sipping a cup of tea.*

JITESH  Cha?

RAHEEM  Oh! No. Thank you. I'm good. Thank you though.

> *Raheem clasps his palms in a gesture of thanks. He immediately feels weird about it. The grandfather clock strikes four. Jitesh opens Thammi's medicine box. He pops a pill out of its packaging. Raheem enters the sitting room. He smiles at Jitesh. He sits on the divan. He allows himself to collapse, back first. He stares up at the ceiling fan. Jitesh takes a carton of juice out of the fridge. He pours a glass. Still supine, Raheem fingers the camera around his neck. He pops up suddenly. He goes over to his backpack. He pulls out a little pack of rolling papers. He reaches into his pocket. He pulls out what*

*looks like a bit of crumpled newspaper. Jitesh looks up from his pill-counting. Raheem notices.*

RAHEEM  You want some?

*Jitesh looks at it, uncomprehending. Raheem unfolds the newspaper to reveal some green nuggets.*

Ganja?

*Jitesh smiles in embarrassment.*

JITESH  *(refusing it)* Na na—

RAHEEM  You sure?

*Raheem puts his finger to his lips.*

I won't tell.

*Jitesh smiles.*

Mind if I—

*Raheem indicates the weed again. Jitesh reads it as another offer. He shakes his head. Raheem takes out a rolling paper. He takes a nugget of weed and begins breaking it apart with his fingers. Jitesh watches. He goes into the kitchen to grab a mortar and pestle. He takes two pills and places them in the mortar. He crushes them with the pestle. Raheem watches.*

RAHEEM  *(pointing)* What's that?

JITESH  Hm?

RAHEEM  That um—

*Raheem thinks. He points again at the mortar and pestle.*

Bangla?

JITESH  Ei ta?

RAHEEM  Yes.

JITESH  Ei ta toh haman dista.

RAHEEM  Itatoha man-dee-sta?

*Jitesh smiles, amused.*

Itatoha man-dee-sta.

*Raheem begins packing his joint.*

JITESH  English?

RAHEEM  Hm? Oh. Yeah . . . motor and . . . I actually don't even—

*Raheem meticulously rolls his joint. Jitesh's eyes come to rest on the Rolleicord around Raheem's neck. Raheem notices.*

This?

*Raheem indicates the camera. Jitesh averts his gaze.*

Bangla?

JITESH  Camera?

RAHEEM   But in Bangla?
*Jitesh looks confused.*
JITESH   Hm. Camera.
RAHEEM   Oh it's— Ha. I'm dumb. Okay.
*Raheem finishes rolling his joint. He pulls out his lighter.*
Sure you don't want some?
*Jitesh shakes his head. Raheem walks over to the window. He takes a hit.*
I like that the windows are just open here.
*Jitesh pours the powdered medicine into the glass of juice and stirs with a
spoon. Raheem takes a hit. He notices Jitesh looking at the photos of Dadu.*
RAHEEM   They're pretty amazing right?
*Jitesh looks up at him.*
JITESH   Hm?
RAHEEM   The um—
*He considers how to proceed.*
Oh wait—
Chobi?
*Jitesh stares at him.*
Is that—
*Raheem walks over to the table. He holds up one of the photos of Dadu.*
Isn't it . . . chobi?
*They two of them look at the photograph.*
I love the um—
*Raheem touches his own face with his hands, mimicking the photo.*
—hands?
I love how crisp they are. With everything else out of focus.
It's beautiful.
*He looks at Jitesh. Jitesh avoids his eyes.*
It's um—
Oh!
No wait.
Shu—
. . . shundo?
*Jitesh looks at him.*
Yes?
This—
*Raheem points at the photo.*
—is shundo?

Shundo chobi?

It's a beautiful picture.

*Something changes in Jitesh's face. He looks at the photo. For a long moment,
they look at the photos together without saying anything. And then: a crow
flies in through the window and lands on the table.*

Jesus!

*Raheem jumps out of his seat, knocking over his chair.*

Christ, holy—

JITESH  Oi!

*Jitesh waves his hand in the crow's direction.*

Pala!

*The crow doesn't budge. It cocks its head. Jitesh takes a step closer.*

RAHEEM  Careful. Fuck.

*Jitesh moves toward the window. He makes a little noise with his mouth. The
crow looks at him. Jitesh makes the sound again. The crow preens.*

JITESH  Oi pagla—

*Raheem notices the camera on the table. He takes a tentative step forward.
He reaches toward it, but just then: the crow caws. Raheem stumbles back.*

RAHEEM  Nope. No thank you.

*Jitesh walks to the fridge. He grabs a container of leftover rice. He opens
it. He tiptoes toward the crow.*

RAHEEM  Careful! It might—

*The bird snaps its beak.*

—bite. Fuck.

*Jitesh walks toward the window with the rice.*

RAHEEM  Wow. Birds really are just dinosaurs.

*Jitesh has an idea. He exits into the internal rooms of the apartment.*

RAHEEM  (to the crow) I see you.

*The bird stretches its wings. Raheem imitates the gesture with his arms.*

Caw!

*The bird looks right at him. Raheem steps boldly forward.*

That's right, bitch. I speak your language.

*From offstage, right behind the shut window where Pishe's computer is:*

JITESH  Jamai Babu?

*Raheem grabs the camera. He points it at the crow. He cocks the shutter.
Again, Jitesh from behind the window, more urgently now:*

Jamai Babu? O Jamai Babu—

(calling to Pishimoni, a wire of fear in his voice) Didi!

*And just as the crow launches into flight, Raheem snaps a photo.*
*Blackout.*
*END SCENE*

## ১০ | ফিল্ড ওয়ার্ক
## 10. FIELD WORK

*Choton and Shou on a bench by the Lake, looking at the photos of Dadu on Choton's phone.*

SHOU  Gonph ta toh puro Raj Kapoor—

CHOTON  Tai na?

SHOU  Hmm . . . besh sexy lagchhe.

CHOTON  Ei ota aamar Dadu kintu.

*Shou clucks their tongue.*

SHOU  Shetai toh bolchhi. Puro zaddy vibes.

CHOTON  Ha!

SHOU  *Shotti.* Dekhun ki bhabe cheye achhe camera'r dike.

CHOTON  Shetai toh Raheem ke bojhanor cheshta korchhi. Amake chirokaal bawla hoychhe Dadu na ki ekdom lok dekhano pochhondo korto na—

SHOU  Dekhe toh mone hocchhe besh pochhondo. Aamar Ma o sharakkhon bawle, why you are putting such gaudy dress. Lok er nawjor na tene ektu pawra shona kawr.

CHOTON  Ei je. Aamar Baba o exactly erokom—

SHOU  Aare aami to chai loke aamar dike nawjor dik. I want to stand out toh? Stand out

SHOU  The mustache is totally Raj Kapoor—

CHOTON  Right?

SHOU  Yeah, it's sexy.

CHOTON  Hey that's my Dadu you're talking about.

SHOU  That's what I'm saying. Total zaddy vibes.

SHOU  Seriously. Look how he's gazing into the camera.

CHOTON  That's what I was trying to explain to Raheem. Everyone always told me Dadu didn't like any kind of showing off—

SHOU  It looks like he likes it. My mother always says to me, why you are putting such gaudy dress. Instead of calling attention to yourself, why don't you focus on your studies.

CHOTON  My dad is exactly the same way—

SHOU  But I want the attention. I want to stand out right? If you don't stand out, who will na korle, ke pochhondo korbo tomake? Shudhu gay na, gay straight, everyone they are wanting something special. Shou is that something special. Tai na? Chhoto belar thhekei chhele ra aamar pechhon chutchhe, chumu dicchhe. I like this feeling actually. Ma to aar sheta bujhbe na.

CHOTON  Aami *etai* Raheem ke bolchhilam—

SHOU  Shei karonei toh aami school jibon thheke Lake e aschhi. Tokhon toh Grindr, Romeo ei shob kichhu chhilo na, didi ra shob Lake ei ghora phera korto. Ki shundor lagto aamar shobaike. Puro mayur er moton. Aami shudhu boshe boshe dekhtam.

CHOTON  Ekhane?

*Shou points.*

SHOU  Oi je Lake Mosjid achhe na?

CHOTON  Kon ta?

SHOU  Oi je Lake er majh khane mosjid ta? Class kete, o dike giye boshtam. Ekdin dekhi ekjon purush aamar dike dyab dyab kore takiye achhe. Tokhon toh kichhui jantam na, ekdom i shishu chhilam. Lok ta haath tene jigesh korlo, "Kawto?" Aami shashosh kore bollam, "Amake dekhe ki mone hoy magi?" O bollo "Dusho debo." Aami bollam "Teensho." Byas. Jhop

like you? Not only gay, gay straight, everyone they are wanting something special. Shou is that something special. Isn't it? From a very young age boys have been chasing after me, kissing me. I like this feeling actually. Of course my mother can't understand that.

CHOTON  This is what I was saying to Raheem—

SHOU  That's why I've been coming to the Lake since my school days. There was no Grindr, no Romeo back then, all the sisters would just cruise by the Lake. I used to think they were all so beautiful. Just like peacocks. I would just sit and watch.

CHOTON  Here?

SHOU  You know the Lake Mosque?

CHOTON  Where?

SHOU  See that mosque in the middle of the lake? I would cut class and go sit over there. One day I saw this guy staring right at me. I honestly didn't know anything then, I was just a kid. Then he pulled my hand and asked "How much?" I gathered myself and said, "Do I look like a whore to you?" He said, "I'll give you two hundred." I said "Three hundred." That

jharer moddhyei shob khule phello.

CHOTON  Tar por?

SHOU  Tar aar por ki? Lok ta khub i hot chhilo, kintu prothhombar toh? Ki byathha, maa go maa, bujhi morlam. Tar por aste aste gajor thutu diye aamar chipti ta ke ready korte laglam. Ekhon toh aar kono i shawmoshya nei. Byanka shoja shob shocchhonde dhuke jay.

was that. He took everything off, right there in the bushes.

CHOTON  And then?

SHOU  What then? The guy was super hot, but it was my first time, right? It was so painful, god, I literally thought I was going to die. After that I started preparing my "chipti" slowly, using a carrot and spit. Now of course I have no problems. Straight, curved, anything slides in easily.

*Shou winks. Choton smiles. He jots something down in his notebook.*

Ki likhchho?

What are you writing?

CHOTON  Na just—aami toh kono din Banglay erokom alochona korini, tai—

CHOTON  No it's just—I've never talked about these things in Bangla, so—

*Choton writes. Shou looks at the photos of Dadu on Choton's phone.*

SHOU  Shotti i ki handu chhilen tomar Dadu.

SHOU  Your Dadu really was so handsome.

*Shou swipes left.*

CHOTON  Ki kawthha ta bolle? "Chipti"?

CHOTON  What's the word you used? "Chipti"?

SHOU  Oh my gawd . . .

*Shou looks mischievously at Choton.*

CHOTON  Ki?

CHOTON  What?

SHOU  Eta tomar boyfriend?

SHOU  This is your boyfriend?

CHOTON  Ei ei—

CHOTON  Hey, hey—

*Choton reaches for the phone, but Shou keeps it away from him.*

SHOU  Danrao dekhi ektu mal ta.

SHOU  Hold on, let me see what we're working with.

CHOTON  Ei, please—

CHOTON  Hey, please, that's—

SHOU  Tar erokom size?

SHOU  He's this big?

*Choton clucks his tongue.*

CHOTON  Please dao.

CHOTON  Please give it to me.

*He tries again to grab the phone.*

Aare!

SHOU  *Eibar* bujhlam.

CHOTON  Dao na—

SHOU  Jamai jutiyechho bhaloi.

SHOU  *Now* I get it.

CHOTON  Give it!

SHOU  You've found yourself
a good husband huh?

*Choton grabs Shou by the wrist and manages to wrestle
the phone from their grasp.*

Kotdin dhore cholchhe
prem?

CHOTON  Ei . . . prai teen
bawchhor hote chollo—

SHOU  O baba, tahle toh puro puri
i dompoti.

CHOTON  Dompoti maane?

SHOU  Dompoti? Dompoti
maane . . . maane bibahito /
aar ki—

CHOTON  Na na aamra biye tiye
kichhu / bhabchhina—

SHOU  Korbe na biye?

CHOTON  Aare aamra dujonei biye
byapar / ta bishesh pochhondo—

SHOU  Aha kawro na, aami
ashbo.

CHOTON  Tumi ashbe? *Tahle* toh
kortei hobe.

SHOU  Hyan kawro kawro, shobai
miley hoichoi korbo. I *love* biyebari.

CHOTON  Aaj shokale aamar
Thammi ke Dadu'r ei chhobi
gulo dekhacchhilam. Bollam,
ei dyakho tomar bor. Thammi
dekhe bollo: "aamar ekhono biyei
hoyni."

SHOU  Aha re ki sweet. Aamar
khub i sweet lage buro manush
der ei kawthha gulo shunte. Shesh
awbosthhay aamar Thakurda ekdom
baccha'r moto hoye giyechhilo.

How long have you
been together?

CHOTON  It's almost
been three years.

SHOU  Oh wow, so you
really are a "dompoti."

CHOTON  What's "dompoti"?

SHOU  Dompoti? Dompoti
means like . . . like married—

CHOTON  Oh no no, we're not
doing the whole marriage—

SHOU  You're not going
to get married?

CHOTON  Neither of us are
really into marriage—

SHOU  Oh come on, do
it, I want to come.

CHOTON  Well if *you're*
coming, we have to.

SHOU  Yes, do it, do it, it'll be
a big party. I *love* weddings.

CHOTON  This morning I
was showing my Thammi
these pictures of Dadu. I told
her, look it's your husband.
And Thammi said, "I'm
not even married yet."

SHOU  How sweet! I love
it when old people start
talking like that. My
grandfather, at the end, he
was just like a little baby.

CHOTON  Thammi'r o *exactly* tai. Aaj dekhe mone hocchhilo . . . *aamar* buro boyoshe . . . dhawro aami deathbed e . . . aar Raheem i roychhe shathhe, amake comfort kawrar cheshta korchhe . . . boley jacchhe, it's ok, it's ok, kintu aami bujhte parchhi . . . maane morey jacchhi je . . . aar aami bolchhi "Bhoy korchhe. Aamar bhishon bhoy korchhe" . . . kintu o toh bujhte parchhena . . . karon ami Banglay bolchhi . . . aar aami bujhte parchhi je o bujhte parchhena . . . aar or o bhoy korchhe karon . . . he can see . . . that I'm dying . . . and he doesn't know what I'm saying . . .

CHOTON  My Thammi is exactly the same . . . today I was looking at her and I was like . . . in *my* old age . . . like imagine I'm on my deathbed . . . and Raheem is the only one there, and he's trying to comfort me . . . he keeps saying, it's okay, it's okay, but I can tell . . . that I'm dying . . . and I'm saying to him . . . "I'm scared. I'm so scared" . . . but he doesn't understand me, cause I'm speaking in Bangla . . . and I can tell that he doesn't understand me . . . and he's scared too cause . . . he can see . . . that I'm dying . . . and he doesn't know what I'm saying . . .

*A long moment. Just the sound of dogs barking.*

SHOU  Esho.

SHOU  Come.

*Choton looks at Shou.*

SHOU  Ekhane esho.

Come here.

*Choton, recognizing the familiar maternal gesture, lays his head in Shou's lap.*
*Shou gently massages Choton's head.*

Ma ke bollam. Hollywood thheke eschhe. Aumurto da.

I told Ma. This guy has come from Hollywood. Aumurto da.

*Choton smiles to himself.*

Ki holo?

What?

CHOTON  Na just—amake keo i Aumurto bole dake na / tai—

CHOTON  No it's just— no one calls me "Aumurto," so hearing it is—

SHOU  Maane?

SHOU  What do you mean?

CHOTON  Bhalo naam dhore toh keo i dake na.

CHOTON  No one calls me by my good name.

SHOU  Ki bole dake tahle?

SHOU  What do they call you then?

CHOTON  Choton bolei dakey.

CHOTON  They call me Choton.

SHOU  Choton?

CHOTON  Aare oi deshe toh keo janena je amake "Choton" bole beracchhe, oder kachhe toh *otai* aamar naam.

SHOU  Kaajer jiboneo?

CHOTON  Shob jaygay.

SHOU  *(trying it out)* Choton Da. Dhat. Parlam na. Eto shundor ekta naam, Aumurto.

CHOTON  Dadu i diyechhilo naam ta.

SHOU  Dekhi aar ekbaar, chhobi gulo?
Ekdom tomar moton dekhte kintu.

CHOTON  Ki bolchho?

SHOU  Puro twins. Mukh bawshano.

CHOTON  Dhat.

*Shou is lost in thought. A long moment. Just the sound of dogs barking.*

SHOU  Acchha, o deshe, tomar ki green card?

*Choton is surprised by the question.*

CHOTON  Aamar toh . . . US citizenship.

*Shou clucks their tongue.*

SHOU  Ki kopal go tomar. Aamar kawto din dhore icchha, America jaoar. Kintu shobai bawle na ki visa pete bohut jhamela.

CHOTON  I don't know . . . sometimes I feel like I would have been better off if I'd just stayed here . . .

SHOU  Aapni toh Hollywood er lok.

---

SHOU  Choton?

CHOTON  I mean in America they don't know that they're calling me "little one," to them that's just my name.

SHOU  Even at work?

CHOTON  Everywhere.

SHOU  Choton Da. I can't do it. Aumurto's such a beautiful name.

CHOTON  Dadu's the one who called me that.

SHOU  Let me see the pictures again?
You know he looks just like you.

CHOTON  What?

SHOU  Total twins. Same exact face.

SHOU  So, over there, do you have a green card?

CHOTON  Me? I . . . have US citizenship.

SHOU  You're so lucky. I've been wanting to go to America for so long, but everyone says getting a visa is such a problem.

SHOU  But "aapni" you're a Hollywood man.

CHOTON  Aabar "aapni"?

SHOU  Acchha acchha tumi. Thik achhe? Tumi tumi tumi—

*Shou plays with Choton's hair.*

Aar ei kaaj je ta korchhi ek shonge—tar jonno visa paoa jabe na?

*Choton looks up at Shou.*

CHOTON  Tar maane?

SHOU  Aami toh asholey tomader moton i korte chai. Cinema, acting e gulo i. Maane this is my dream actually. Creative / work—

CHOTON  Danrao, eta kintu . . . cinema noy, eta ekta—

SHOU  Jani aami—

CHOTON  —ekdomi onno / byapar—

SHOU  Aare byapar ta bujhechhi, aami ekjon documentary subject. Thik ki na?

CHOTON  Orokom documentary o na / thik—

SHOU  Maane it will show India te, kirokom gay, transgender e der otyachar—

CHOTON  Na na—

SHOU  Thik dhorechhi ki / na?

CHOTON  —ekdomi na—

SHOU  Tahle?

CHOTON  —it's not about "showing" anyone anything, it's not that kind of—

*Sebanti enters. She notices Shou and Choton. Her eyes light up.*

Maane aami toh ekjon Bangali . . . nijer community / niye—

CHOTON  Again "aapni"?

SHOU  Okay fine, "tumi." Better? You, you, you—

And this work that we're doing together—couldn't I get a visa to do that?

CHOTON  What do you mean?

SHOU  Cause I want to do what you're doing actually. Cinema, acting, these things. Like this is my dream actually. Creative work.

CHOTON  Wait, this isn't a movie though, this—

SHOU  I know—

CHOTON  —is something totally different—

SHOU  Don't worry, I understand, I'm a documentary subject. Right?

CHOTON  Not even . . . a documentary exactly—

SHOU  Meaning it will show, in India, how gays, transgenders, what kind of oppression—

CHOTON  No no—

SHOU  That's what it is, right?

CHOTON  —not at all—

SHOU  Then?

CHOTON  First of all I'm a Bengali . . . looking at my own community—

SEBANTI  Kothhay peli? Hyan?

SHOU  Oi je bollam na, eschhe bidesh thheke, Aumurto / da—

SEBANTI  Olebaba dekhi. Ki shundor lagchhe dujonke. Agal bagal. Ekdam bar-bahu.

*Shou rests their head on Choton's shoulder. Choton is visibly uncomfortable.*

Ba ba, ki lawjja!

SHOU  Sebanti di kintu aamader shobaike bhalo bashe. Aador kawre, jawtno kawre—

*Sebanti focuses on a lady who is walking past.*

SEBANTI  Ki dekhchhen Didi?

*Shou looks in the direction Sebanti is looking.*

Dekhun, bhalo kore dekhun.

SHOU  Jolchhe puro hingshay.

SEBANTI  *(to Choton)*
Dekhish. Haate bajare gelei bhawdromohila ra phish phish kore bawle: eto shundor blouse kothhar thheke baniyechho, tomader moto bawro golar blouse porte aamader khub bhal lage, kintu janoi to aamader shaami achhe, baccha kaccha achhe, oder shamne toh pawra jay na. Jara pawre to aamader dekhei pawre. Emon ki cinema'r heroine rai toh aamader shundorjo dekhe copy kawre.

SHOU  Aumurto da kintu bikkhato director.

CHOTON  Aare—

SEBANTI  Tai naki?

---

SEBANTI  Where'd you find this one? Huh?

SHOU  Remember I told you, Aumurto da, he's come from America—

SEBANTI  Oh my goodness, let me see. Looking so pretty the two of you. Side by side. Bride and groom.

Look at you blush!

SHOU  Sebanti di loves all of us. She dotes on us, takes care of us—

SEBANTI  What are you looking at, sister?

Look. Take a good look.

SHOU  She's burning with jealousy.

SEBANTI  You'll see. When I go to the market, the ladies they say: where did you get such a beautiful blouse made, we love wearing the kind of low-cut blouses you wear, but you know, we have husbands, we have kids, we can't dress like this in front of them. And the ladies who do wear them are modeling themselves after us. Right? Even movie actresses try to copy our beauty.

SHOU  Aumurto da is a famous director.

CHOTON  What?

SEBTANTI  Is that so?

CHOTON —bhul dhorechho byapar ta—

SEBANTI Nibi shona aamake?

SHOU Aare orokom noy, eta documentary cinema.

SEBANTI *(to Shou)* Janish serial e aamake ekbaar nite cheyechhilo? Director aamake *khub* pochhondo korechhilo.

*Shou giggles at this.*

CHOTON Acchha aapni ki aamar shathhe ekta interview korte chaiben?

SEBANTI Interview maane?

CHOTON Emni, informal. Ei aamader moto queer manush e der icchha, itihash ei / shob—

SEBANTI Thak baba, aami oto kichhu janina, queer feer / aami—

CHOTON "Queer" / bolte—

SEBANTI —shadharon manush, ashirbad korlam.

*She touches the top of Choton's head.*
Ei ei, aamar paa chhuite nei, Bramhon manush. Aamake pronaam kawre na babu, aamake challa day.

*She claps resonantly and extends her hands to Choton.*

CHOTON Challa maane?

SEBANTI Shono tumi toh cinema kore rojgar kawro. Sebanti Di'r rojgar toh etai. Eta ke challa bawle, aamader bhashay. Mouli Mata ka challa.

*Choton jots in his notebook.*

CHOTON You're getting this all wrong.

SEBANTI Will you take me sweetie?

SHOU It's not that kind of film, documentary film—

SEBANTI You know they wanted to give me a part in a TV series? The director *really* took a liking to me.

CHOTON Actually . . . would you be interested in doing an interview with me?

SEBANTI Interview meaning?

CHOTON You know, queer folks like us, our desires, experiences, stories, things like—

SEBANTI Look, I don't know much about any of this "queer" business, I'm—

CHOTON "Queer" meaning—

SEBANTI —a simple person, bless you.

*Choton reaches down to touch her feet.*
Hey hey, you don't touch my feet. You're a Brahmin. You don't pay your respects to me, dear, you give me "challa."

*Choton looks to Shou uncertainly.*

CHOTON What's "challa"?

SEBANTI Listen you earn by making movies. Sebanti earns like this. We call that "challa" in our language. "Challa" for Goddess Mouli.

CHOTON  Ki Mata?

CHOTON  Goddess who?

SEBANTI  *(to Shou)* Proshno'r awbhab nei.

SEBANTI  He's got a lot of questions huh?

CHOTON  Sorry, sorry—

> *He fishes in his pocket for his wallet.*

Aami toh asholey erokom subject niyei project korchhi tai—

CHOTON  This is actually what my project is focused on so—

> *He pulls a 2000 rupee bill out his wallet and hands it to Sebanti.*

SEBANTI  Ba ba. Bikkhato bole bikkhato.

SEBANTI  You weren't kidding about famous.

> *She and Shou exchange a smirk as she stuffs the bill into her blouse.*

*(to Choton)* Bhalo thhakish baba, shusthho thhakish.

Take care dear, be healthy, be well.

> *She taps Choton's forehead and exits singing a Bollywood song,*
> *an inside joke with Shou. Shou cackles. Choton's phone rings.*

CHOTON  *(into the phone)* Hey.

I'm just—

. . .

What?

Are you—

I'm coming.

No, I'm coming right now.

I'm on my way.

> *END SCENE*

## A DREAM

> *A glow from the door to the computer room.*
> *Pishe wanders out into the sitting room, in a smart white dress, with a brown leather portfolio.*
> *He sees Pishimoni sitting there, in a bottle-green sari.*
> *They look at each other.*
> *There are no words.*
> *A crescendo of Bollywood strings.*
> *Pishe swoops Pishimoni into his arms.*
> *They dance.*
> *Pishe walks across the threshold of the stage and out the door of the theater. Pishimoni watches him go.*

## ১১। বিকামিং এ পিকচার
## 11. BECOMING A PICTURE

*Raheem on the divan with a photo album. Choton standing at the table with another one. The AC is on.*

CHOTON   I'm just like how does a city with twenty million people have like *no* emergency medical services. You know? Like why were *you* the one trying to carry him down the / stairs?

RAHEEM   I mean Jitesh was trying to get him out of the chair himself, I just helped carry him out here cause Pishimoni was still trying to—like by the time *you* got here things had calmed down a little, but at first it was just like . . . chaos / 'cause—

CHOTON   I'm sure.

RAHEEM   —I couldn't really understand what they were saying, and Pishimoni was like, trying to wake him up, but— I mean . . . he'd clearly been there for a while—

CHOTON   Like I'm like . . . have you seen either of them leave the house even one time, this whole week we've been here?

*He returns to the divan with the little photo album.*

Jitesh is literally the only person that leaves this house, everyone else is just like sitting around and eating sweets all day. Like Pishimoni has diabetes. Who's monitoring that?

And what are these homeopathic pills Thammi's been on for the last twenty years? You know? Like there's no fucking *logic* to it—

RAHEEM   *(re: a photo in the album)* What about this one?

*He goes over to look at it.*

CHOTON   I mean . . .

RAHEEM   I could try and maybe get rid of the crease in Photoshop . . .

CHOTON   There's a better one, I swear, I just don't know which album it's in.

*He looks up at the AC.*

Why is the AC on?

*Raheem looks up.*

RAHEEM   I think Jitesh turned it on 'cause they were worried about his like . . . body in the heat . . .

CHOTON   Like what fucking century are we living in—

RAHEEM   Hold up.

*Raheem points to a picture in the album.*

Is that you?

*Choton looks.*

CHOTON  Oh yeah that's from when Thammi was visiting us in the US and she came to my third grade class to talk about Pujo—

RAHEEM  Choton!

CHOTON  What?

RAHEEM  Look at you!

CHOTON  I know, right? Then what happened.

RAHEEM  I'm serious.

CHOTON  And I was so excited 'cause I got to wear my little panjabi to school that day and bring mishti for the class—

RAHEEM  I would have had such a crush on you.

CHOTON  *(amused)* Oh yeah?

RAHEEM  Yeah you're such a little stud.

CHOTON  *(pointing to a picture of Pishe)* This is the one I was talking about.
　　　*They look at it.*

RAHEEM  Yeah that one's okay—

CHOTON  It's like impossible to find pictures of *just* Pishe. You know?

　　　. . .

RAHEEM  You know he told me about this dream he had?

CHOTON  What? When?

RAHEEM  Was that yesterday? It was when we got the photos back—

CHOTON  What did he say?

RAHEEM  I don't know, he had this dream. And it was crazy, 'cause in the dream he was watching a movie, in a movie theater. And he basically like . . . described the whole movie to me.

　　　Like you know how sometimes . . . like I'll wake up with a song stuck in my head, but it's not a song that exists, it's a song that was just like there in my dream, but then when I try to remember it, like if I try to record myself singing it or anything it's just like . . . gone?

　　　But he like . . . remembered this whole movie, shot for shot. And then he told me to go make it . . .

CHOTON  What do you mean?

RAHEEM  Like he was like . . . you're a director. Go make this movie.

CHOTON  *(amused)* What?

RAHEEM  And I was like—

CHOTON  What was the movie?

RAHEEM  It was this like . . . *(he pictures it . . . a man in white . . . a woman in a green sari . . . )*

I don't know . . .
I don't know, it's kind of hard to describe . . .
. . .

CHOTON   Maybe we should make it.
. . .

RAHEEM   (*uncertain*) Yeah . . .
. . .

Yeah . . .
I don't know . . .
I don't know, I guess I've been thinking.
. . .

CHOTON   About . . . ?
RAHEEM   Oh no just about like . . .
I don't know . . .
Like I used to think I didn't *want* to be the ideas guy. You know?
But I don't know . . .
I don't know, being here . . .
. . .
Like I think maybe that was a little bit of a cop-out.
For me at least . . .
. . .

CHOTON   I mean there *is* this grant I was looking at. Through FWB. Basically
for collaborations between scholars and practitioners.
I mean not that this is—
RAHEEM   Yeah—
CHOTON   But I don't know, it could be kind of—
Dream as Archive. I don't know—
RAHEEM   Yeah . . .
. . .
I don't know . . .
. . .

*Pishimoni enters, carrying a copper tray with two neem leaves.*

PISHIMONI   Jitesh phirechhe?

CHOTON   Na ekhono na.

PISHIMONI   Paula phone kore
bollo ekhoni aaschhe. Bari te
kichhui nei.
Tora snaan korechhish?

PISHIMONI   Has Jitesh returned?

CHOTON   No not yet.

PISHIMONI   Paula called and
said she's coming over right
now. There's nothing at home.
Have you both showered?

CHOTON  Ei geyser ta chalalam—

PISHIMONI  She ki ekkhuni ja, smashan thheke phire i snaan korte hoy.

CHOTON  Jacchhi. Pishe'r chhobi ta dekhe nicchhilam—

PISHIMONI  Ei ne.

*She hands him a neem leaf.*

CHOTON  Ki eta?

PISHIMONI  Neem pata.

CHOTON  Pishimoni . . . aar koek din i roychhi, er moddhye pet kharap / hole—

PISHIMONI  Aare toder mineral water diye i dhuyechhi. Ne. Cheba bhalo kore.

*Choton puts the neem leaf in his mouth, uncertainly.*

Rohim? Take this.

RAHEEM  What's this?

PISHIMONI  This is neem leaf. For purification.

CHOTON  Baba re ki teto.

*Choton's face is twisted from the bitter taste. Raheem observes him.*

PISHIMONI  (to Raheem) This is little bit bitter.

CHOTON  You don't have to.

*Raheem puts the neem leaf in his mouth. Pishimoni notices the album on the table.*

PISHIMONI  Peyechhish chhobi?

CHOTON  Ekta peyechhi, beshi bhalo na jodiyo.

*For a long moment, Pishimoni looks at the photo of Pishe.*

PISHIMONI  Shobai chhobi hoye gelo . . .

---

CHOTON  I just turned on the hot water—

PISHIMONI  What? Go now, you have to shower right when you get back from the crematorium.

CHOTON  I'm going, I was just figuring out Pishe's picture—

PISHIMONI  Here.

CHOTON  What's this?

PISHIMONI  A neem leaf.

CHOTON  Pishimoni, we're only here for a few more days, if we get a stomach bug—

PISHIMONI  I washed it with your mineral water, don't worry. Here. Chew it well.

CHOTON  Wow. So bitter.

PISHIMONI  Did you find a picture?

CHOTON  We found one.

PISHIMONI  Everyone's a picture now . . .

*Choton puts his arm around her. She closes her eyes. She inhales deeply. She recites something, quietly, under her breath, in Sanskrit. Then she opens her eyes.*

Tora snaan korte ja. Jitesh toh
ekhono chhute beracchhe.

You two go and shower.
Jitesh is still running around.

*Pishimoni walks into Pishe's computer room and
begins looking through his desk drawers.*

RAHEEM  Oh you know what? I
took a picture of him yesterday.

CHOTON  Oh yeah?

RAHEEM  Yeah when he was
telling me the dream.

CHOTON  With the Rolleicord?

RAHEEM  We could probably
get the film back in a day or /
two—

CHOTON  That's fine his "kaaj" isn't
for eleven days / so—

RAHEEM  And that way they can
blow it up—

PISHIMONI  Eta toh na.

PISHIMONI  Not this one.

CHOTON  Ki korchho?

CHOTON  What are you doing?

PISHIMONI  Pishe'r Aadhar Card
ta khunjchhi.

PISHIMONI  Looking for
Pishe's Aadhar Card.

CHOTON  "Aadhar Card"
maane?

CHOTON  What's an
"Aadhar Card"?

PISHIMONI  Ei re. "Aadhar Card"
ki kore bojhabo jani na.

PISHIMONI  Yeah . . .
I have no idea how to
explain "Aadhar Card."

*She pulls open another drawer.*

Dhat. Eto i jotno kore rakhto
shob . . .

He kept things so carefully,
it's impossible to find—

*Pishimoni exits into the inner rooms. From offstage:*

Ei Rohim.

RAHEEM  Yup?

PISHIMONI  Come. You can reach
this—

CHOTON  Ki?

RAHEEM  *(exiting)* I / got it.

PISHIMONI  *(offstage)* Tui ja snaan
korte!

PISHIMONI  You go shower!

*Left alone onstage, Choton looks at the photos of Dadu. He notices his own reflection in the mirror. He takes the photo and sticks it to the mirror with a bindi. He looks at his own reflection. He imitates Dadu's pose.*
*END SCENE*

## ১২। ফ্যামিলি ফোটো
## 12. FAMILY PHOTO

*Pishimoni, Choton, and Raheem in the sitting room. Packed suitcases, camera gear, backpacks. An altar has been set up with a large photo of Pishe, a bulky flower garland hung around the frame. It's the photo Raheem took: Pishe, looking piercingly at the camera, smoke curling out of his mouth.*

CHOTON   You grab your phone charger?

RAHEEM   Yup.

CHOTON   Passport?

*Raheem pats his pocket.*

PISHIMONI   Aar ektu kichhu kheye ja.

PISHIMONI   Have something to eat before you go.

CHOTON   Na beshi khele aabar awsshosthhi lagbe.

CHOTON   If I eat too much I'll feel nauseous.

PISHIMONI   Kichhu pack kore di tahle.

PISHIMONI   Then let me pack you something.

CHOTON   Aare dorkar nei, awnek granola bar achhe.

CHOTON   It's okay, we have lots of granola bars.

PISHIMONI   Rohim?

RAHEEM   Hm?

CHOTON   You hungry?

RAHEEM   Oh no I'm good thank you.

PISHIMONI   Dekhi gari ta eshe pounchholo ki na.

PISHIMONI   Let me see if the car has come.

*Pishimoni looks out the window.*

CHOTON   You got all your gear and everything?

RAHEEM   Pretty sure.

CHOTON   I should do one more sweep.

PISHIMONI  Dekhchhina toh.
  Dhat. Aamar mobile ta koi?
CHOTON  Ei je.

PISHIMONI  I don't see it.
  Dhat. Where's my mobile?
CHOTON  Here.

*Choton sees Pishimoni's phone on the divan. He hands it to her.*

PISHIMONI  Kawtobaar kore
  bollam—

PISHIMONI  How many
  times did I tell him—

*Pishimoni dials.*

Hello, Mr. Mitra? Gari
kothhay? Barota'r shomoy ashar
kawthha chhilo.

Hello, Mr. Mitra? Where
is the car? It was supposed
to arrive at noon.

*She listens.*

"On the way" maane? Aamar
bhaipo eschhe America'r
thheke, return flight panchtar
shomoy—

What do you mean on
the way? My nephew has
come from America, return
flight is at five o'clock—

*She listens.*

Bollei holo? International
flight er tin ghonta aagey
reporting.
  Hm.
  Acchha, gari ta— *(to Choton)* ei
Dadamoni kawtay pounchocchhe
re?

Excuse me? International
flights must report three
hours beforehand.
  Yes.
  And the car— *(to
Choton)* ei what time is
Dadamoni arriving?

CHOTON  Dekhchhi danrao.

CHOTON  Let me see.

*He searches on his phone.*

PISHIMONI  Gari ta kintu bhor-
  raat porjonto lagbe, mone achhe
  to?
  Hm.
  Next du shoptaho lagbe puro.
Mr. Ganguly has expired.

PISHIMONI  You remember
  we will need the car
  overnight, yes?
  Yes.
  We will need it for a full two
weeks. Mr. Ganguly has expired.

*She listens.*

Aapnar ki mone achhe, ki
mone nei, aami ki jani?
  Hm.
CHOTON  Yeah, he's arriving at—
PISHIMONI  *(into the phone)* Thik
  achhe. Rakhlam.

How do I know what
you remember, what
you don't remember?

PISHIMONI  Okay. Bye.

*She hangs up.*

CHOTON   2:20 a.m. Emirates er flight.

PISHIMONI   Tahle airport e neme aabar pathiye dish gari ta. Ratre aabar pathiye debo Dadamoni ke tulte.

PISHIMONI   Then when you get to the airport, send the car back. Then I'll send it back tonight to pick up Dadamoni.

CHOTON   I wish we could stay.

PISHIMONI   Tui to ashol shomoy ta te chhili.

PISHIMONI   You were here for the important part.

CHOTON   I know, but still. Kaaj er jonno thhakle bhalo hoto.

CHOTON   It would have been nice to be here for the service.

PISHIMONI   Tor to phire awnek kaaj.

PISHIMONI   You have lots of work to get back to.

*Choton sighs.*

CHOTON   Ki je kaaj.

CHOTON   What work?

PISHIMONI   Aare kaaj thhaka toh bhalo.

PISHIMONI   Having work is a good thing.

*Pishimoni looks at the photo of Pishe. Her gaze lingers on him.*

PISHIMONI   Besh hero-hero lagchhe na?
(*to Raheem*) He would have liked this photo.

PISHIMONI   Doesn't he look like a movie hero?

*A car honks outside.*

RAHEEM   I actually—

PISHIMONI   Oi je gari eshe gechhe.

PISHIMONI   There, the car has arrived.

RAHEEM   —wanted to say thank you.

PISHIMONI   Hyan?

PISHIMONI   What?

RAHEEM   I just wanted to thank you. For—

PISHIMONI   O baba, aabar "thank you"? Kisher "thank you" babu?

PISHIMONI   Oh goodness, "thank you"? Thank you for what babu?

RAHEEM   No really, you did so much, feeding us, taking care of us. And for letting me use the camera.

*Pishimoni points to the Rolleicord, which is sitting on the table.*

PISHIMONI  Some photo you took?

RAHEEM  I did, I took a bunch.

PISHIMONI  You take it with you.

RAHEEM  No, no, I—

PISHIMONI  Please.

RAHEEM  It should stay here.

PISHIMONI  Here it is only
gathering dust.

RAHEEM  I'll just have to come
back and use it then.

PISHIMONI  Yes please come
again. This is your home.

| | |
|---|---|
| *(to Choton)* Khub pochhondo hoychhe aamar. Simple chhele, kono shawmoshya nei. | *(to Choton)* I have really taken a liking to him. Simple boy, no trouble at all. |

*Choton chuckles.*

| | |
|---|---|
| Homely ja ke bole. | What we call "homely." |

CHOTON  Who you calling
homely?

PISHIMONI  Yes, homely.

*She reaches up and holds Raheem's face affectionately.*

| | |
|---|---|
| Ekdom bari'r chhele'r moton. | PISHIMONI  Just like a member of our home. |

CHOTON  Oh shit did you grab the
toothpaste from the bathroom? I
left it out—

RAHEEM  Yeah, I got it.

| | |
|---|---|
| PISHIMONI  Itinerary ki re toder, ekhan thheke? | PISHIMONI  What's your itinerary from here? |

CHOTON  Kolkata to Delhi. Delhi to
Newark. Newark to Los Angeles.

| | |
|---|---|
| PISHIMONI  Baba re. Aamar ekhan thheke Delhi jetei ja awbosthha— | PISHIMONI  Goodness. I can barely manage flying from here to Delhi. |

CHOTON  Last time I came the
in-flight video was broken on the
way back. Sixteen hours—

PISHIMONI  *Sixteen?*

CHOTON  —zero movies.

PISHIMONI  Ei chanachur ta bhule  PISHIMONI  Ei don't forgot
jash na kintu.  to take the chanachur.

  *Pishimoni hands Choton an enormous packet of bhujia.*

CHOTON  Pishimoni—kothhay  CHOTON  Pishimoni—where
dhokabo eta?  am I gonna put this?

RAHEEM  Here, I have space in my
backpack.

CHOTON  You sure?

  *Raheem takes it from Choton.*

PISHIMONI  Aabar ashbi  PISHIMONI  When will
kobe?  you come again?

CHOTON  Ashbo shiggiri.  CHOTON  I'll come soon.

  *Pishimoni reaches up and holds Choton's face.*

 *Tumi* kobe ashbe bawlo?  When are *you* coming?

PISHIMONI  Kothhay?  PISHIMONI  Where?

CHOTON  America?  CHOTON  America?

PISHIMONI  Thhak baba.  PISHIMONI  No thank you.

CHOTON  Keno?  CHOTON  Why?

PISHIMONI  Ei aamar shathhe  PISHIMONI  Hey don't
ekta chhobi tulbi na, jaoar  you want to take a photo
aagey?  with me before you go?

CHOTON  *(to Raheem)* Hey can you
take a picture of us?

RAHEEM  Sure.

  *Pishimoni squeezes Choton's face.*

PISHIMONI  Shona chhele aamar.  PISHIMONI  My sweet boy.
He is like my son, you know?

  *Raheem picks up the Rolleicord.*

CHOTON  Oh you're gonna take it
with that?

RAHEEM  Don't worry I'm gonna
take one with my phone / too.

CHOTON  No, do it, I like that.
There's film in there?

RAHEEM  Here, let's do it this
way—

*Raheem turns so that his back is to the light.*

PISHIMONI  Ei Rohim, come in
the photo. Ei Jitesh!

RAHEEM  I got it—

CHOTON  He *wants* to take it,
Pishimoni.

*Jitesh enters.*

PISHIMONI  Ei amader ekta
chhobi tule dibi?

PISHIMONI  Can you
take a picture of us?

*Jitesh looks uncertainly at Raheem.*

RAHEEM  You—

*Raheem offers Jitesh the Rolleicord. Jitesh takes it. Pishimoni beckons to Raheem.*
Come. Family photo.

*Raheem squeezes between Pishimoni and Choton. Pishimoni puts her arm around Raheem. Jitesh hangs the camera around his neck. He opens the viewfinder. He looks down into it. He adjusts the camera settings, like someone who knows them intimately. He takes his time. Focus. Aperture. Shutter speed. The others hold their pose, smiling stiffly. Jitesh cocks the shutter. Winds the film—*

PISHIMONI  O jane?
Ki bhabe—

PISHIMONI  Does he
know? How to—

*The camera clicks. Blackout. For a split second, the still contour of Jitesh and the camera glows in the darkness. A cacophony of crow calls.*

·     ·     ·

# Sanctuary City

## MARTYNA MAJOK

### People

G, female, ages 17–21
B, male, ages 17–21
HENRY, male, older

G and B were born in other countries and brought to America young. Henry is a second-generation immigrant. Born in America to immigrant parents. All have American mouths. All were raised working class.

### Place

Newark, New Jersey, and thereabouts. 2001–2006.
A bare stage. And then, perhaps, a surprise.

### Dialogistics

Slashes / indicate overlap.
Ellipses . . . are active silences.
[Words in brackets] are intended but unspoken.
(Non-italicized phrases) within dialogue are meant to be spoken.

*   *   *

*Knock knock knock on a window. Late night. Winter 2001.*

G  Can you let me in

B  You climbed up the fire escape?

G  Can I come in

B  What time is— You know I have a test / tomorrow—

G  Open the window

B  *(Continuing)*—first period—

G  Quick before someone calls the cops

B  No one's gonna— No one ever calls the / cops

G  Or just come downstairs and / let me in

B  Hold on

G  It's freezing

B  Hold on

G  It's freezing

B  HOLD—

     *Window's open.*

G  I didn't wanna wake yer mom, buzz the—

B  It's freezing

G  *(Continuing)* —so I climbed up the—

B  Where's yer coat?

G  I know it's late

B  Where's yer coat? It's freezing. Fuck it's freezing.

G  I know.

     *He sees her.*
        *He knows.*
        *A gust of wind.*

B  What happened.

     . . .

G  Can you close the window.

*   *   *

*Knock knock knock on a window. Spring 2002.*

B  She's goin back—

G  *(Surprised to see him here)* What the fuck

B  She's goin back!

G  What? Who— Hold on, manager's lookin at me.

B  I don't know what to do.

G  Just—meet me outside.

B  I don't know what to do.

*     *     *

B  What happened.

G  Can't wait to get away from—

B  Yer neck.

G  —one day I'll—

B  Did you see yer neck?

G  It's at home.

B  What?

G  My coat.

   Didn't have a chance to grab it.

   Can you close the window? My arm's [hurt]—I [can't]—

B  Yeah.

G  I never wanted to hurt someone so fuckin bad.

   For him to hurt so fuckin

   First opportunity I get, man, I'm outta there.

B  Is your mom okay?

   . . .

   . . .

G  Can I get under yer blanket real quick?

B  Yeah.

G  It's cold.

B  Better?

G  Yeah.

B  Good.

G  Can I crash with you tonight?

*     *     *

G  What happened.

B  She's goin back.

G  Who?

B  Back home, my mom.

G  / Back—?

B  (Coded shorthand of being in public; finality) She's goin back.

She's afraid of stayin in the country. There's some shit at work, she said. Boss keeps takin money from her tips cuz, y'know, he can. What's she gonna do? Report it? To who? And she's afraid what happened to Jorge's gonna happen to her and so she's goin back.

    And cuz of September.

    Cuz of the towers.

G  Keep yer voice down they think I'm in the bathroom.

B  *(Referring to 9/11)* Like—now anything can happen. Now anything can happen here too now.

    She didn't say that but

    So she's goin back.

G  What about you?

B  She said I can decide.

G  Decide what.

B  If I wanna stay. / Or go back.

G  WHAT.

B  Yeah.

G  Did she give you a day—?

B  Like now Like she'd love to know right now. Soon. Real soon.

    I'm seventeen, she says. Almost grown, she says. So she says I can decide what I wanna do.

G  She didn't wanna wait 'til you finish school?

B  No.

G  But it's just one more year!

B  / No—

G  Yer senior year!

B  No she doesn't wanna wait.

    I've been here ten years, man Ten years, we've been— That's half my life More than half my— I got everything here. Yeah, like, my family's there. But everything from over half my life? That's all here.

G  Why would she just go—

B  I don't know what to do.

G  —without you?

B  . . .

G  She came here fer you. So why would she be goin back? Without you?

    . . .

    . . .

    Did something happen?

   . . .
   . . .
B  I don't know what to do.

           \*    \*    \*

    *Late night. Quiet. In bed.*
    . . .
    . . .
    . . .
G  I got blood on yer sheets.
B  Oh—!
G  From my arm.
    I'm sorry.
B  It's okay.
G  I'm sorry.
B  It's okay.
    It's fine.
    . . .
    I'll say it's mine.

           \*    \*    \*

G  But then what're you gonna do about next year? Can you graduate?
B  If I stay.
G  What about college?
B  I can't go.
G  Why?!?
B  Unless I pay for it myself.
    Which
    I can't go.

           \*    \*    \*

B  What are you gonna say at school tomorrow?
    About yer arm, yer neck—
G  I'm not goin.
B  Yeah.
    Yeah prob'ly you should maybe don't.

           \*    \*    \*

What are you gonna say at school? About yer face—

G I'm not goin.

B Yeah.

Yeah prob'ly you should maybe don't.

\*     \*     \*

B What are you gonna say at school? About yer eye—

G I'm not goin.

B Yeah.

\*     \*     \*

B What are you gonna say at school? About—

G I'm not goin.

B Yeah.

Yeah prob'ly you should maybe / don't.

G Last time this shit happened, (remember? my eye?), Miss Romano saw, sent me to the nurse, nurse called my mom, Mom said I fell, then she freaked the fuck out on me when I came home. She said to say I fuckin fell, whatever. Said to say I always fall, I fell.

Which I think they'll buy once.

B I can bring you the homework.

G Say I'm sick.

B The flu?

\*     \*     \*

B I can bring you the homework.

G Say I'm sick.

B The flu.

G Used flu last time.

B A cold?

G Yeah just say a cold.

\*     \*     \*

. . .

. . .

B I'll bring you the homework.

. . .

G *(Not looking at him)* Say I'm sick.

B   A cold?

G   Something longer.

B   Right.

G   *(Continuing)* Need a few days this time.

   . . .

B   Chicken pox?

   . . .

G   Yeah

   say chicken pox.

*   *   *

B   I can bring you the homework.

G   Say I'm sick.

B   Chicken / pox.

G   Used that already.

B   Right. Measles?

G   *("No")* Mm.

B   Mumps.

G   The fuck's mumps?

B   Stomach bug.

G   No.

B   Why.

G   Cuz no that's nasty no.

B   Lice.

G   NO.

B   Crabs.

    *She is not amused.*

      *He is.*

   A cold.

G   Yeah I think it's fine to use a cold again.

B   A cold.

G   A bad one.

B   A really bad / cold.

G   DON'T SAY LICE.

*   *   *

B   I can bring you the homework.

G   Say I'm sick. The flu.

. . .

B  Are you sure you don't just wanna tell / somebody—?

G  *(Finality)* No.

   She's scared they'll send us back if they find out what's goin on at home.

B  Who?

G  *(Continuing)* Or just her.

   She's scared they'd separate us.

B  Who would send you back?

G  America. If they wanted to investigate. If they like—checked. She worked with a fake social security for years. He's threatened to report her before. Everyone's more, y'know— *[Careful, nervous]*

B  Yeah.

G  —cuz of September. Cuz of the towers.

   Or maybe they'd put me in some kind of—some place for kids—separate us. I don't know if she even knows specifically what to be afraid of but she is. She's scared. There's that place on Fish Kill Road. In South Kearny. The place Rogelio's dad got sent to.

B  That's just for guys, that place, / I think.

G  I don't wanna get separated. Or for her to go to Fish Kill Road.

B  It's just for guys.

G  So where do they send women? They gotta have somewhere to put the women. Where's the women go?

B  I don't know.

   Farther away.

   I guess.

   . . .

G  I don't wanna get separated.

   I don't want anything like

   Like Fish Kill

   I know there's people— Even if it's just for guys

   I know there's people there on Fish Kill Road.

   Behind wire.

   I see them. We drive by and I see.

   There's barbed wire and people and I don't wanna go.

B  You wouldn't hafta go—

G  That place is real.

   It's just better not to talk about anything that happens at home.

Better I say I fell.

Or have the flu.

B   Maybe it would be good to be separated.

G   Not from my mom.

B   No but—

G   (*Firm finality*) She's never gonna leave him. You think I haven't asked?
    I asked.

    . . .

    You want me to hide under yer bed? From yer mom—

B   It's okay.

G   (*Continuing*) Or I can just jet right now. Before she wakes up. If you need
    me out.

B   It's okay, my mom won't care.

G   (*Continuing*) I'll just walk around the neighborhood. Go to Tops. Hang out
    there. Eat some eggs. I didn't finish the math anyway.

B   You can just stay here.

G   I've been comin by a lot.

B   So stay. Eat breakfast with us.

G   You eat breakfast?

B   Not usually but. I could.

    . . .

G   Yeah?

B   We could. Together, yeah. I got eggs.
    Stay.

                    *    *    *

G   Don't go.

B   Then I'd end up just like her. If I stay in the country, I'd be just like my
    mom, doin whatever job—shitty job—whatever shitty job would take her
    just to fuck her over down the line.

G   But you went to school—

B   (*Continuing*) Always scared.

G   You did like, all of school here.

B   Doesn't matter. My mom brought me over. And she kept me over.

G   So?

B   So when she overstayed her visa, so did I.

G   But you were a kid.

B   We were supposed to go back nine years ago.

G  And you were supposed to know that? You were supposed to buy a plane ticket? At fuckin, eight?—

B  Doesn't matter.

G  You were a kid.

B  It doesn't matter. If they find out how long we've been here, we won't even be allowed back for another ten fuckin years.

G  Don't go.

*  *  *

*The urban version of crickets.*

. . .

. . .

G  Yer mom's gonna think we're sleepin together.

B  We are sleepin together.

G  I mean like, together.

B  I don't think so.

. . .

G  WHY THE FUCK NOT.

*  *  *

B  Which

    I can't go.

G  But why?

B  Cuz I can't pay for that! For college? By myself?

G  Neither can I but—aid.

B  I can't apply for aid.

G  Why.

B  CUZ I'M NOT SUPPOSED TO BE HERE.

    . . .

    . . .

G  Okay wow cuz I never scream at you when you ask me / questions.

B  We came here legal but we didn't stay here legal. We overstayed. So I'm a fuckin criminal, according to Here. I could pay for school. If I could pay for school. They'd like, take my money—if I *had*—like, happily Listen I could do a lotta things if I had money.

    *(Finality)* I can't get aid. Can't apply for federal financial aid. Can't go.

G  Yer mom can't help?

B  *(Firm finality)* My mom is leaving.

. . .

. . .

G   What about community college?—
B   No.
G   But you could / still—
B   No fuck that you know how fuckin hard I worked since comin here fuck
     that.
         I get better grades than fuckin, everyone in there.
         I work harder than
         Fuck that.

*   *   *

G   G'night.
B   G'night.
G   Hey.
B   Yeah?
G   Thank you.
B   No problem.
G   For real though. Thank you for lettin me stay.
B   It's okay.
         G'night.

*   *   *

G   Hey.
B   Yeah?
G   Thanks.
B   All good.
         G'night.

*   *   *

G   Hey—
B   (Impatient) Yeah?

     . .

G   (Quietly, feeling like a burden) Thank you.

     . . .

B   (Truly) Any time.
         Good night.

*   *   *

G  We'll find a way for you to stay.
B  There isn't one.
G  We'll make one.
B  I don't know if I can even Like how would I even My mother's workin a
   full-time job for this roof AND she has to borrow money from me some-
   times. Comin home like, half-a-person, after work, exhausted. How'm I
   gonna do all that AND school? How'm I gonna do that?
G  You can live with me! At mine's!
B  You don't even wanna live at yours.

                         *     *     *

B  Good / night.
G  Hey.
B  Yeah?
G  Thanks.
B  (It is) It's okay.

                         *     *     *

G  Thank you.
B  (It is) It's okay.

                         *     *     *

G  Thank you.
B  (It is) It's okay.
G  I owe you.
       Thank you.
       . . .
          Nighttime.
       . . .
       . . .
B  (In G's first language) Good night.
       . . .
G  (In B's first language) Good night.
       . . .
B & G  Good night.

                         *     *     *

G  I can help you pay rent!

B   What?

G   On this apartment. I'm over here all the time. We sort of kind of already live together here, sleep to—I sleep here sometimes. So I should help. I can pay.

B   Fer a year and then yer gone.

G   . . .

B   "First opportunity you get, man."

G   Just—finish school at least.

B   And then what?

     Keep workin at the restaurant? Moppin floors? Washin dishes? Go to war?

     See if *they're* checkin papers.

     Ship out with all the seniors still failin algebra.

     Be like a fuckin, high school reunion—in Afghanistan.

     . . .

G   We'll find a way for you to stay.

*    *    *

     *Knock knock knock on a door. Lost. Autumn 2002.*

B   *(Heartbroken)* She left.

G   What?

B   She's gone.

*    *    *

     *Knock knock knock on a window. Found. Autumn 2002.*

G   *(Elated)* We're leaving!

B   What?

G   She's gonna leave him! We're leaving!

*    *    *

B   And how're you gonna help me pay rent?

G   With my *job*.

B   And how much you make? Hundred a week?

G   Varies.

B   Can't bank on varies.

G   It varies but I'm there almost every day after school except Thursdays.

     Shit I've come away with a HUNDRED sometimes just on Fridays cuz of tip-out.

B   Really?

G  Almost once yeah almost.

      If things keep goin how they're goin at home, I'll be at yer place a lot.

B  *(Concern, not inconvenience)* Really?

G  Unless you don't want me to.

B  No yer good.

G  Doesn't look like anything's gonna change. So I'll prob'ly be here a lot.

      If you'll like, have me.

      . . .

B  I'll make you a key.

G  So I'll contribute.

      That way, you won't hafta do this completely alone.

      And you can finish school.

      . . .

B  You sure?

G  Make me a key.

      . . .

      . . .

B  Yeah.

      Yeah okay.

      Yeah maybe I can do this— Yeah.

G  And you can rent out the extra room!

B  What room?

G  For extra money. You can rent out the extra room in this apartment!

B  . . .

G  When she. Eventually.

B  . . .

G  Sorry.

*   *   *

B  Yer leaving?

G  My mom 'n' I!

B  Where?

G  Schuyler Ave! Like right on the border! Close!

B  How did she—?

G  She got naturalized!

B  What?

G  She's a citizen now! She was takin all the tests, secret! She got a naturalization certificate, a restraining order, and a fuckin moving company, all secret! We're gonna, when he leaves for work, we're gonna pack up all our shit and GO.

B　When?

G　Tomorrow morning. Today! In a few hours! TODAY! Movin guys are comin soon as he's gone, then we gotta pack up everything we can and haul that shit out fast. We gotta be outta there by four, when he's back from work.

　　Back to an empty fuckin apartment!

　　She had this shit planned for months. *(Proud)* Fuckin, months!

　　I can't believe it. We're finally leaving! And I don't even hafta switch schools!

B　*(Something off)* That's great.

G　I know!

B　Congratulations.

　　To yer mom.

G　We're both moving!

B　On becoming a citizen.

G　Oh and I'm one too!

B　What?

G　She snuck me in right under the deadline.

B　What do you—?

G　Right under the wire. Cuz if yer under eighteen, if the kid's under eighteen when the parent gets it, then it gets transferred to the kid. Automatic.

B　So you didn't hafta pay none of those fees?

G　Guess not!

B　Or hafta take the test?

G　Nope!

　　. . .

　　. . .

　　. . .

　　I'm sorry—

B　You gonna need help?

　　With packing?

G　We got the guys—

B　I know but do you need more help?

　　You gotta pack up an entire apartment in how long?

G　Yeah but it's during school.

B　So how are you gonna—

G My mom's gonna call 'n' say I'm sick. She planned that shit too!

B So I'll say I'm sick.

G No but you'd hafta miss school.

. . .

B *(He did)* I didn't do the math anyway.

. . .

G Okay.

Okay! Tomorrow, then.

B You wanna crash here? Tonight?

One last time?

G Why one last time?

. . .

*And she realizes.*

B *("Right," an end)* I'll make eggs.

\*   \*   \*

G And you can rent out the extra room!

B What room?

G For extra money. You can rent out the extra room in this apartment!

B . . .

G When she. Eventually.

B . . .

G Sorry.

B It's okay.

\*   \*   \*

G When?

B *(Heartbroken)* This morning.

. . .

. . .

G *(Doesn't know what to say)* . . . Did she say goodbye to you?

B *(Not an answer to her question)* I rode the train with her to the airport.

Helped carry her stuff.

They don't let you wait anymore. Did you know that?

They don't let you wait with yer person that's gonna board the plane.

Cuz of September.

So if yer not gettin on a plane, they don't let you past security.

I watched it out the window.

Watched for hours.
Imagined her in one of em.
Knew she was in one of em.
Flyin away.

. . .

. . .

. . .

Fuckin, of course we said goodbye.

G Sorry.

B We've been sayin goodbye since she bought the fuckin ticket. You wanna crash?

G Tonight?

B With me? At mine's?

. . .

I don't wanna go back there.
By myself—

G Yeah. / I can.

B I know you got yer new place now.

G I'd love to crash.

B She left a glass of water on the table.
She drank out of it this morning and left it on the table.
It'll still be there.
There's gonna be parts of her all over the apartment.
Things she left. Clothes she wants me to donate.
I don't think I can . . .

G It's okay.

B Thanks.

G It's okay.

* * *

B There's so much to pack.

G *(Thrilled)* There is
so much
to pack!

B I mean you could just leave him a mess right? If there's shit you don't want.

G True.

B *(Continuing)* Shit you don't wanna clean.

G Yeah.

B  Yer never comin back so leave that fuck a mess.
G  I thought about pissin in his bed.
B  Why don't you.

      . . .

G  [Actually . . .]
B  [Just sayin . . .]

      . . .

G  We'll see how we're doin on time.

                    *     *     *

B  (Heartbroken) Would you want any of em?
G  What.
B  Her clothes?

                    *     *     *

G  Let's start with the clothes.
B  (On a mission) Clothes.
G  I can do that if you wanna box the books.
B  (On a mission) Books.
G  I dunno how I coulda done this shit alone. Even with the guys.
B  [Gimme the] tape.
      Yeah I dunno how you coulda either, those guys're garbage, get yer
   money back.
G  I'm gonna miss this place.

      . . .

B  How could you miss this place?
G  Twelve years.
B  Yeah but.
G  Longer livin here than anywhere else.
      Than
      Longer than I known you even.
B  Still.
G  It's a place I was.
      I'm *from* here.
      Even though I was born in
      I'm from *here*.
      Wherever I end up endin up,
      I'll have gotten there from this place. Here.

. . .

And it's closer to you than my new place is gonna be.

*     *     *

G   (*Pissed*) There's another one.

B   Another / what.

G   We JUST moved and there's already another guy. Like a weed.
     Like a fuckin— At least he doesn't knock her unconscious—
     YET—that I KNOW OF—YET—just—
     I dunno, man. I can't seem to keep a dick outta that woman.
     . . .

B   That woman gave you life.

G   Yeah well so did yers and here we are.
     Can I crash.

*     *     *

G   You still can't sleep?

B   . . .

G   Don't you have a test tomorrow? It's late.

B   (*Quietly; lost*) There's so much stuff. She left a life of stuff.

G   You don't hafta do this all right now. Come to bed.

B   Would you want any of em?

G   What?

B   Her clothes?
     . . .

     . . .

     You don't have to / if—

G   No—just—you sure you don't wanna keep this?

B   If you like it, take it.

G   You sure?

B   Take it.
     . . .

G   Thank you.

B   But don't throw it out okay. If you take it, don't just throw it out.

G   Okay.

B   Wear it.
     Like, sometimes.
     . . .

G  Come to bed.

                    *    *    *

G  Good / night.
B  Hey.
G  Yeah?
B  Thanks.
G  *(It is)* It's okay.

                    *    *    *

B  Thank you.
G  *(It is)* It's okay.

                    *    *    *

B  Thank you.
      I owe you.

      . . .
G  *(It is)* It's okay.

                    *    *    *

G  No fuckin way.
B  Cmon.
G  It's racist!
B  Not if I'm tellin you it's okay.
G  This is so fucked up.
B  So you'll do it?
G  No.
B  Cmon!
G  Why can't you just write a note? I could forge a note.
B  Just be glad they don't want her to come in.
      I'm calling.
G  No!
B  It's ringing
G  I'm not ready!
B  You've heard her talk enough / times—
G  This is so racist
B  *(Continuing)* —you've had like, nine years of research
G  This is so racist

B  It's ringing

G  This is so Hello!
      (*In B's mother's accent*) Yes—hello! Good morning also to you.

B  (*Quiet*) Yes!
         *G is mortified.*

G  Yes Hello Yes, Um, So, My—son—

B  (*Quiet; finds this hilarious*) Oh my god.

G  —is sick.
      The flu.
         *B stifles laughter.*
            *G sees this.*
      No sorry.
      Lice.
      He is disgusting yes and cannot be in school Tell everyone
      Thank you Bye.

*   *   *

B  What'd they feed you tonight?

G  Chicken Milanese.

B  Nice.

G  I brought some.

B  WHAT.

*   *   *

B  What'd they feed you tonight?

G  Penne vodka sauce.

B  YES.

*   *   *

B  What'd they feed you?

G  Penne vodka sauce.

B  YES.

G  With chicken.

B  YES FUCK YES.

*   *   *

B  What'd you get tonight?

G  Spaghetti.

B Oh.
   Okay.

                  \*     \*     \*

B What'd you get tonight?
G Chicken—
B YES.

                  \*     \*     \*

B What'd they give you? What'd you get tonight?
G Actually so they want us to eat family meal at work now actually.
B Oh.
G Cuz people Yeah Cuz people take too much.
B Sure.
G Bring it home.
   For their actual families.
B Right.
G You eat?

   . . .

B Yeah.

                  \*     \*     \*

B What's that?
G Chicken / Milanese.
B WHAT!

                  \*     \*     \*

B What'd they give you tonight?
G Oh I'm so sorry. I forgot to grab food.
B You didn't eat?
G I forgot.
B Oh.
   Okay.
   You hungry?
G There might be somethin in the fridge.
B Not much. Want me to run / to the store—
G Why don't you check?
B ShopRite's / open still—

G  Why don't you just check the fridge.

>    . . .

>    *B suspects something.*

>    . . .

>    Check the fridge.

>    . . .

>    *He looks at her, suspiciously . . .*
>    *. . . and moves to an unseen fridge.*
>    *He looks inside.*

>    . . .

>    *His face changes.*

>    . . .

>    *She lights a lighter.*
>    *This is the only time we see a physical object in this entire section.*
>    *It glows between them.*
>    (*Singing*) Happy Birthday to you, Happy Birthday to you, Happy—
>    *She sees his face.*
>    (*Serious, grave*) I'm sorry.
>    I meant it as a nice thing.

B  (*Resisting tears—of loneliness*) I know.

>    . . .

G  (*"For your loss," that she can't be here*) I'm sorry.

*   *   *

G  Where've you been?
>    It's three in the—

B  (*As he enters, passes her by, exits to bed*) Out.
>    *A door shuts.*

>    . . .

G  (*Alone, sass*) Okay.

*   *   *

G  Where've you been—?
B  Good night Out Good night.

*   *   *

B  Where've you been?
G  Where've *you* been?

B  [*Oh okay. You want a secret too.*]

G  [*Yeah, I want a secret too.*]

B  (*Sass*) Okay.

G  (*Sass*) Okay.

         *   *   *

B  Where've you been?

G  ("*Nowhere good*") Can I get under yer blanket real quick.

B  Yeah.

G  It's cold.

    . . .

B  Better?

G  Yeah.

    . . .

    . . .

    *The feeling of home.*

    Yeah.

B  Good.

         *   *   *

    *Knock knock knock on a window. Spring 2003.*

B  (*Jumps, annoyed*) Jesus Christ.

    *Knock knock knock on a window.*

G  (*Knocking*) Can you open the / window?

B  The fuck—

G  (*Knocking*) Hello!

B  (*To himself*) Are you fuckin kidding me right now.

G  (*Still knocking on window*) What? I can't hear you!

B  I'm comin.

G  (*Can't hear, still knocking*) You gonna open the / window?

B  I'M COMIN AND I'M OPENIN IT NOW.

    . . .

    . . .

    . . .

G  You mad?

B  I'm exhausted. These fuckin essays, fuckin, homework I'm just not—
I'm not doin this fuckin math homework. Fuck math. Fuck all of math.
They called me into work tonight and what could I say. Now it's two

a.m. I'm so tired I don't even WHY DON'T YOU JUST TAKE THE FUCKIN STAIRS.

G   Tradition.

B   You have the key.

G   I left it.

    Can I crash?

B   I'm not doin well, you know.

G   Yer sick?

B   No. I'm / not—

G   What's wrong?

B   I'm tellin you. I'm not doin well. In school. I'm not doin well with any of it. Work. I can't keep up. I'm so tired. I'm so Like It's like I'm runnin in my sleep. Everywhere. All the time. Runnin. Use the key. Please. Next time.

G   I got into school.

    . . .

B   What.

G   I got / in—

B   Where.

G   . . . Boston.

    . . .

    . . .

B   Scholarship?

    . . .

    . . .

    . . .

    *(Referring to what's in her bag)* What's that?

G   A bottle.

    The rest of a bottle.

    To celebrate.

B   . . .

    *G feels the absence of his joy for her. And she turns away from him.*

G   You can copy my math.

*   *   *

B   Check the fridge.

G   Why.

B   Why don't you just check the / fridge.

G  It's not my birthday / Why're you stealin my idea.
B  Just—
   Check the fridge.

   . . .

     *She does, suspiciously.*
       *Her face changes.*
   There isn't a song for it but
   Congratulations.

   . . .

   Oh no.
G  *(Through tears—of appreciation)* We clearly can't put shit in fridges!
B  No.
G  Thank you.
B  Congratulations.

   . . .

G  *("You have no idea how much")* Thank you.

*   *   *

B  So you wanna go with me?
G  To the fuckin—?
B  Cmon!
G  *("Lame")* That shit's so—
B  What.
G  You like that shit?
B  You don't wanna dress up?
G  Isn't it like, seventy dollars? Don't they want like, seventy a head?
B  Yeah but.
G  And then I gotta buy a dress?
B  It doesn't hafta be expensive though.
G  A limo—
B  The bus, man, I dunno who you think I am.
G  And I gotta hang with these clowns all night? For seventy dollars?
B  There'll be food!
G  For seventy dollars!?!
   *("No way")* I dunno, man.
   I dunno.

*   *   *

B  You look so good.

G  You look so good.

B  No you look so / good.

G  Shut the fuck up.

B  You do You look so good.

G  I'll punch you in the face.

B  I'd punch you in the face you'd still look good.

    . . .

G  Where do I put this expensive-ass flower shit?

B  *(Moved)* You got me a—?

G  It's fuckin tradition.

    You wanna do it yerself?

B  No you.

G  Okay how do I—?

B  I think you— Here, there's a—

G  Yeah

B  Just yeah pin it on my FUCK OW / FUCK

G  FUCK

B  TAKE IT OUT

G  FUCK

*　　*　　*

G  When did you meet?

B  Third grade.

G  What school?

B  Franklin.

G  Where was it located?

B  Hundred Davis.

G  In?

B  Kearny.

G  You went to a public school in Kearny but listed in your application your address during that time as being in Newark?

B  I lied. Gave a friend's address in Kearny. So I could go to the better school.

    . . .

G  I don't know if you wanna tell em that.

B  You asked!

G  We'll hafta figure that one out.

    Okay. Who was the teacher?

B  Which? When?

G  Third grade, when we—

B  Miss Ramirez.

G  What color was her hair?

B  Gray.

G  What's the best pizza in town?

B  It asks that?

G  No but—

B  Can we skip to the harder ones?

G  We should start with the basics.

B  But we know this shit.

G  We should start with the basics.

\*    \*    \*

B  I got you some flower shit too.

G  Aw.

B  Fer yer wrist.

G  Aw.

B  But now there's blood on the petals.
    You wanna put it—?

G  No you. You put it. You Can Put It On My Wrist, Sir.
    No wait!

B  What.

G  *(Sly)* Do it on the bus.

\*    \*    \*

B  Just skip to the harder questions—

G  They could trick us.

B  How? All this shit is true. There's nothin to memorize. No new information.

G  What if you forget?

B  I'm not gonna forget where I went to school. Or where we met.

\*    \*    \*

*The recognizable beginnings of a corny song that was popular in 2003. Something like The Backstreet Boys' "I Want It That Way."*
    *B and G enter prom.*
    *G instantly sprouts a look of judgment and regret. She is above this. B is not.*

*He's kinda into it, in fact.*
*Then he sees G's face. Full of opinions and blame.*
*. . .*
*They stare out at prom.*
*. . .*
*Then B moves ever so slowly . . .*
*. . . 'til he's dancing.*
*G is mortified. Wants none of it. Nope. No thanks.*

*   *   *

G  *(Annoyed, challenging)* Fine. What did the two of you have in common? Where did you go for dates? When did your relationship turn romantic? Wanna start there? When did your relationship turn romantic? Wanna start there?

*   *   *

*A fun LOUD song that was popular in 2003. Something like OutKast's "HeyYa!"*
   *They're having a great time.*
G  THIS IS THE WORST.
B  YEAH.
G  I HATE THIS.
B  I KNOW YOU DO.
G  I HATE THIS SO MUCH.
   *She's having the greatest time.*
   SPIN ME!

*   *   *

G  *(Continued, still annoyed, challenging)* Did your parents approve of the match? Why or why not? Have you ever had an argument that resulted in one of you sleepin in another room? Who, and which room?—
B  *("Stop")* Okay.
G  *(Still annoyed)* No where you wanna start Where do you wanna start You don't like how I started so where do you wanna start?

*   *   *

*Distant popular music from 2003. Near the end of the night.*
*They are somewhere more secluded, apart from the rest of prom.*

*A slowness. They smoke. Smoke around them.*
*They stare forward.*
*They're connected enough to not need to look at each other.*

. . .

. . .

. . .

G  He knew I was watchin.

. . .

    *They stare ahead.*

. . .

. . .

There was this dog on my street.
My old street.
Neighbor's dog.
Big.
Ugly big.
Head like a fist.
A big gray fist.
In summers, they'd keep it chained out in front, to the fence, while they were inside makin dinner—

B  How you know they were makin dinner?

G  You could hear the pots and pans from the street.
    And everything else you could hear that too.
    Which I guess meant people could hear everything that was goin on in our place.
    They could hear it from the street.
    Which I guess meant nothing at all to people, I guess.

B  You want any of this?

G  *("No")* I'm good.
    They kept the dog tied up outside cuz I guess it got in the way when they were makin dinner.
    My stepfather would be comin back from work or from wherever, the bar, someone's stoop, and . . .
    I think he knew I was watchin.
    That from the window, I would watch him.
    I think he knew cuz, on his way home, he'd stop at that dog.
    He'd kneel down next to that dog.
    And he would pet its big ugly head with the softest hands I ever seen.

He knew I was watchin.

He knew I was watchin him care for something.

That he had the capacity to be good to something.

That he was able to do that.

If that was what he wanted—

I started a lot of the fights—

B  *(Fact, not pandering/comforting)* No you didn't.

G  Didn't stop em.

Didn't ignore him.

If I'd just kept my mouth shut and more often.

Prob'ly wasn't always worth The Last Word when the guy's got a hammer in his hand. Kitchen knife.

B  I got another bottle if you, in my jacket, / the pocket—

G  Nah.

Wait what kind.

B  Vodka.

G  Nah yeah I thought you might have something else.

Still got the vodka I Duck-Taped to my leg.

B  That's gonna hurt later.

G  I shaved.

B  There are easier ways to do things.

. . .

*They stare out.*

. . .

. . .

. . .

G  It was worth it. I guess.

The seventy dollars.

*They stare out.*

B  That chicken parm.

G  Yeah that was bomb-ass chicken fuckin parm.

*They stare out.*

*Smoke.*

B  That cheese—

G  Hey.

B  Yeah.

G  Thank you.

B  It's okay.

G  Do you miss her?

> . . .

> . . .

B  I'll send her the pictures of us.
> You in yer dress.
G  She prob'ly thinks we're sleepin together.
B  I don't think so.

> . . .

G  What're you gonna do about next year?
B  Keep workin.
G  At the—
B  Yup. Pays. Close to home.
> And they feed me after shifts.
G  Did you hear back? From any of the / schools—
B  *(End of conversation)* Can't afford it. Cmon let's go inside—
G  I wanna help you.
B  You can help me go inside.
G  I'm serious.
> I wanna help you.
> How can I help.
> *(A proposal)* I'm a citizen now so.
>> *B realizes. Knows exactly what she means.*
B  . . .
G  How can I help.

*     *     *

G  *(Still annoyed)* Have you met each other's parents? How often do you see each other's parents? Where do they live? When was the last time you saw them? Where? For how long? What color are their kitchen curtains?—
B  Let's skip back.
G  Back to the—? / Uh-huh thought so.
B  The more basic ones, yeah.
G  Okay.
> When did you meet?
B  Third grade.
G  What school?
B  Franklin.
G  Where was it located?

B  Hundred Davis.
G  In?

*     *     *

G  I'm serious.
      I wanna help you.
      How can I help.

*     *     *

   *Alone. Private. Quiet.*
B  What time does your spouse arrive home from work
      who takes care of payin the bills
      do you have a joint bank account
      where

*     *     *

G  *(A proposal)* I'm a citizen now so.
      *B realizes. Knows exactly what she means.*
B  . . .
G  How can I help.

*     *     *

   *Alone. Private. Quiet.*
B  What did the two of you have in common
      who proposed to
      did your parents approve of the
      why or
      when did your relationship turn romantic

*     *     *

   *The last song at prom. Something like K-Ci and JoJo's "All My Life."*
      . . .
      *They dance.*
   . . .
   . . .
B  Hey.
G  I step on yer feet?
B  Hey.

G  Yeah.

B  *(The biggest gift in the world)* Thank you.

   . . .

G  It's okay.

\*   \*   \*

*The late-night public transit bus ride home from prom. Enthusiastically drunk.*

G  Oh shit are we on the Express?

B  "How many people attended the wedding?"

G  *(Drunk-happy)* Every people!

B  "Where was it held?"

G  Could we elope? / You wanna elope?

B  Oh shit could we elope?

G  I'd elope.

B  Then we wouldn't hafta feed people!
   "Did you go on a honeymoon? / Where?"

G  Yeah, man, where we goin!

B  Are we really doin this?

G  I'm really doin this are you really doin this?

B  Cuz I'd really do this.

G  THEN LET'S REALLY DO / THIS.

B  *("Not so loud")* Okay. / It's late.

G  WE'RE REALLY GONNA DO THIS.

B  That man's starin at you.

G  I'M GETTING MARRIED STARE ALL YOU WANT.

B  He looks mad.

G  I CAN TAKE HIM.

\*   \*   \*

*G is over these questions. She knows this.*

B  What size is your bed? Twin, / queen, or—?

G  Twin. But eventually queen.

B  Do you have a mattress, futon, or waterbed?

G  Waterbed, who wrote these? Yeah we have a twin / waterbed.

B  Who sleeps on each side of the—?

G  *(Points to self)* Left.
   *(Points to B)* Right.

B  What form of contraception (birth control) / do you use?

G  I know what contraception / means.

B  I'm just reading what's there what's written there!

*    *    *

    *The quiet of task-doing.*

B  Yer not gonna fold that?

G  I did fold that.

B  You just sorta rolled it.

G  That's folding.

B  You'll need warmer clothes than that.

G  They give you sweatshirts there.

B  You gotta buy those.

G  No everyone wears one they give you them.

   . . .

   . . .

   *(As if to self, not happy)* There's so much to pack.

B  Can I keep this?

G  What.

   No I'm takin that with me.

B  Can you bring it? When you come back? At break?

   We're gonna need pictures. Proof. Of years together.

G  We can take more before I go. And at break.

B  You'll need to leave me some of your things.

G  What things?

B  For my room. In case of a home visit.

   They surprise you sometimes, drop by where you live.

G  Home visit?

B  Yeah.

G  . . .

B  Just—leave me some like, personal things.

   Things you'd leave at a—y'know. Makeup. Underwear. An earring.

G  . . .

B  Just leave me something of yourself.

*    *    *

G  When was your wife's Oh Jesus when was your wife's last menstrual period?

B  Yer gonna hafta make me a chart.

G  Have you ever had an argument that resulted in one of you sleeping in another room?
B  . . .
G  Who, and which room?
B  . . .
G  Why?

*     *     *

B  Just leave me something of yourself.

*     *     *

G  Who, and which room?
B  . . .
G  Why?
    What do you disagree about?

*     *     *

B  Just leave me something of yourself.
    Before you go.

*     *     *

G  What do you disagree about?

*     *     *

B  Hey.
G  Yeah?

*     *     *

B  What do you disagree about?

*     *     *

G  Hey.
B  Yeah?

*     *     *

*The bus stop. G keeps looking after the bus in nervous anticipation.*
G  These bags, it's like I'm movin my whole life away.
B  Boston's not far.

G  Feels far, Boston.

B  You'll be back soon.

G  I'll be back in December.

B  Not Thanksgiving?

G  Depends.

B  Really?

G  Depends who she's got in that apartment with her, yeah.

B  Just come stay with me.
    If you came down for Thanksgiving, we could just do it then.

G  I'll only have like, a day off—for—
    I'll be back in December. At the latest. For winter break.
    But we can call all the time. We'll talk all the time.
    . . .

B  Are you nervous?
    About . . . ?

G  School?                                    B  —the marriage?
    . . .

    *G looks at B.*
    . . .
    . . .

B  Don't be nervous.

G  I wish I'd flown.

B  Then we wouldn't get to say goodbye.
    You know they don't let you wait anymore with yer—

G  *(Sees bus approaching)* Oh no!

B  It's gonna be okay.

G  I can still turn back.

B  It's gonna be great.

G  I don't wanna go. I don't wanna / get on this bus.

B  You'll be back soon.

G  *(A threat, to someone offstage)* HEY MAN.

B  He's just / It's okay

G  *(A threat)* HEY.

B  *(Continuing)* He's just gonna put em under / the bus.

G  WHAT IF THEY FALL OUT.

B  They won't.

G  WHAT IF SOMEONE TAKES MY SHIT.

B  I think you made it pretty clear to everyone on that bus they shouldn't.

G  I don't like they took my bags.

B  It's okay.

G  *(Continuing)* I don't like any of this.

B  Hey.

G  *(Continuing)* I don't wanna—

B  Hey.

> *He holds out a ring.*
> *This is the only other time we see a physical object in this section.*

> . . .

> . . .

> . . .

G  . . . where did you . . .

B  My mom left it for me. In case.

> . . .

> . . .

> *Carefully and respectfully, he takes her hands.*
> *Is this the kindest way a man has ever touched her hand?*
> *He puts the ring in the palm of her hand.*
> *And she puts her hand over his.*
> *They hold all four hands.*
> *And look at each other.*

> . . .

> Good luck.

> . . .

G  Good luck.

> . . .

> . . .

B & G  I'll see you soon.

> *A light goes off.*
> *Dark.*

*         *         *

> *In dark, they part.*
> *Two people stand apart, alone, in different cities.*
> *Weeks.*
> *Months.*
> *Years.*

\*   \*   \*

*A light goes on.*

*Winter 2006. A few days away from a new year. Very late night.*

B  *(Offstage)* Hold on Can't find my / keys—

G  *(Offstage)* Oh I've got mine.

*A key in a door.*

*A string of Christmas lights has been turned on.*

*This is what we may or may not see:*

*A small apartment in the Ironbound section of Newark.*

*A top floor of a four-story building located on a residential street, just around the corner from the main drag.*

*This place belongs to people who work often and work late.*

*It is a mixture of things bought at the ABC Store on Ferry Street, the Goodwill or the Kmart over the bridge in Kearny, and inherited from roommates now long gone. And family who came over for a summer to work, now also long gone.*

*On the walls are a few things brought over in a suitcase from across an ocean many years ago, now collecting dust. Things made of straw or wicker. Art purchased at the dollar store.*

*There is nothing intentionally kitschy about this place.*

*It is someone's genuine attempt to make a home out of the things they have on hand or can afford.*

*Beyond the windows, we hear the last of the night's drinkers, a car or two pumping merengue.*

*A cat walking up a fire escape.*

*Nighttime in a small city.*

*B and G enter.*

*Winter coats. G carries a wine bottle.*

*Tension between them.*

*B is not happy to see her. G feels it.*

*(Referring to the lights)* That's nice. Where's the tree?

B  Not this year. You need water?

G  *(Referring to drinking more)* Actually I thought we could—

B  I'm getting you water.

*He goes into the kitchen.*

*She, alone in the space, taking it in.*

G  Did you take it down already? The . . . ?

    *He enters with water.*
    Did you take it down?
    . . . The Christmas tree?

B  No.
    Just didn't really bother after that first year.
    Or the second year.
    Or the third.
    *(Referring to his mother/family)* It's different without—

G  Right.

B  Yeah—family— So I didn't think, a tree, / y'know—

G  Right.

B  —that there was really any point.
    . . .
    Not you though.

G  What?

B  Different.

G  *(Pleased)* Yeah?

B  Still drink like / it's yer last meal.

G  Oh.

B  Like everything's just—yours.
    Yeah.
    Yer exactly the same.

G  Well if it's free, I'm gonna drink it. I'm not wasteful.

B  Who said that shit was free?

G  What?

B  That shit tonight was not free.

G  Wait.

B  *(Continuing)* None of that shit that you consumed tonight / was free.

G  Did you hafta pay for all those?

B  I woulda, yeah, if someone saw. So next time you decide to ambush me at work—

G  Next time you won't be workin when we made plans.

B  *(Jab)* I will always have to work.
    . . .

G  Why'd you keep refillin my glass / if—

B  Had to give you something to do.

G  I came to see you.

B  Yeah but I got called into—I said we'd reschedule.

G  (*Sore point*) We did. Couple times. Been tryin to see you since I got in but
you said they got you workin every day.

> . . .

Even Monday.
When they're closed.

B  Holiday season's different. You looked up the schedule?

G  I remember the schedule.

B  You thought I was lying / to you?

G  No.

B  Look I'm sorry—

G  It's okay.

B  (*Jab*) —I'm sorry *I* had to work.
("*Fuck you*") Here's yer water.

G  ("*Fuck you too*") Thank you.

> . . .
>
> . . .

B  (*Ending the night*) So listen I'm gonna / need to head to bed soon—

G  Oh shit did I give you this? Here. It's wine. Merry Christmas. Belated.

B  You shouldn't have—

G  Yer welcome.

B  (*Continuing*) —I work at a bar.

G  Can I crash?

> . . .

B  Bus is still runnin.

G  It's not actually. Not the 40. Last one left a half hour ago.

B  You need money for a cab then?

G  No.

B  ("*Bye*") Okay. So.

G  She's got this other guy in the apartment now.

B  So where've you been staying?

G  There. While I was waiting for you.

B  For me to what.

G  Appear. Respond. I came down to see you. Not to sleep on their couch
and get twenties jacked from my purse. You think I'm on vacation? Here?

B  Okay so if you need money—

G  No!

B  Then what.

G  I'm goin back in a few days.

B  And I've been workin all night.

G  I brought a bottle.

B  And thank you but do I hafta drink it now?

G  I didn't get a chance to talk to you at all / at the bar.

B  I was workin. On gettin you free / drinks.

G  I didn't want free drinks.

B  You seemed to.

G  I wanted to see you.

B  And you saw me. You saw the place. Like you wanted. You got everything you wanted—

G  How's yer mom—

B  You already asked me that. So I can walk you over to Penn and you can catch a cab—

>  CRACK.

>  *B turns back to see she's opened the wine.*

G  It's a twist-off.

>  *An irrevocably open bottle of wine between them.*

>  I didn't want any barriers and/or obstacles—I'll grab glasses.

>  *She exits to the kitchen. Takes off her coat.*

>  *He stands there, alone. Angry to be trapped.*

>  *G enters, with glasses, muscling an energy of Everything's Fine.*

>  *(Reentering)* It's good to be back. This place. The fire escape. I missed this place—

B  I think you need to go home.

   . . .

G  You called me down here.

B  I called you last month. And you didn't come.

G  You told me not to!

B  *("Just go")* It doesn't matter.

G  *(Continuing)* When I called you back, you told me don't come.

B  Well you had exams. So.

G  I told you I would though! I said fuck exams, soon as there's a bus, there's no bus outta Boston at two in the morning, what could I do—

B  It doesn't matter—

G  *(Continuing)* And then you said don't come—

B  And you listened. So.

G  I'm here. I'm here now.

B  Well it was nice of you to stop by on your way to a future.

G  ...

B  Nice of you to make the time. The trip. The effort. Eventually. Nice to
finally fuckin see you. You know they cost a dollar, some of these buses?
From Boston. If you book early. Here.

   *A dollar. Which she won't take. So he drops it before her. Cold.*

   Hope your next visit will be just as pleasant.

G  Wanna practice?

   ...

B  What.

G  When did you meet?

   What school?

   What did the two of you have in common?—

B  Why'd you back out.

   Wanna start there?

   How bout Why'd you back out, wanna start there?

G  ...

B  What.

   Please.

   Cuz all I got was a letter. After three years of waiting. Three and a half
years of planning. Tellin me you changed yer mind.

G  What if I changed it back?

B  Just like that.

G  I'm here.

B  So am I. I've been here. For three and a half years, I've been here. I felt
like I had the key, a key, in my hands. I never felt that before in my entire
life. I made plans. Schools. What schools I might— Doors opened up for
me, everywhere, in my mind, the things I could imagine for myself. There
were things I was finally able to really imagine for myself. I was gonna join
the world I live in. The world you got to live in for three and a half years.
And then—a letter.

G  Stories were comin out every day, what could happen, if we were caught.
Lady jailed five years, couple in Texas fined a quarter-mil—

B  I was always up-front about what you'd be risking.

G  Yeah well it didn't sink in. It didn't sink in 'til it did.

B  Three and a half / years—

G  Last month. At two in the morning.

   It didn't sink in how much I was risking
   'til you called me last month,

at two in the morning,
and were finally,
actually
Up-Front.

. . .

I ignored the stories, the news, my feelings—any feelings I coulda had—for anyone else. I never even kissed anyone. For three and a half years. I wore the ring. And then you called. And it sunk in.

. . .

Cuz no.
You were not always up-front.
About everything.
No.

. . .

You shoulda told me.

B  I didn't tell anyone.

G  Yeah but you should have told *me*.

B  You knew. You always knew.

G  Yeah but—

B  That that could happen, you knew.

G  It wasn't supposed to.

B  You never asked me not to.

G  I didn't think I needed to! If it's a quarter-mil or jail!

B  Well what did you expect?—

G  For you to be smarter.

B  No one knew.

G  And not that.

B  / What did you expect.

G  Not a call like that—

B  What did you expect.

G  Nothing!
   Congratulations.
      *She takes their ring from her pocket.*
         *Leaves it—*
   I wish you both the best.
      *—and moves to exit.*

B  You can crash on the couch.
      *She stops.*

      If you have to.

      Had to get a roommate so the other room's got—

G  Shit sorry. I've been loud.

B  No she's gone this week. Got family in Philly so she's there now.

      Through New Year's.

      I just don't wanna go in her room while she's away.

G  No problem.

B  Trust, y'know. Cuz of trust.

G  Yeah. Couch is fine.

      Or I could—

B  What.

G  No yeah couch is fine.

B  I'll get you sheets.

        *He does. She feels strange here for the first time.*

          *He returns with sheets. She tries to change the temperature, lower the tension.*

G  Surprised you had as many people at the bar tonight. Figured people'd be with family.

B  Well that's not a thing everybody has.

G  . . . I know that.

B  Oceans away, for a lotta people.

      It's actually been a pretty good week for me at work. Busy, this neighborhood.

      *(Referring to immigration status)* There's a lot of us that can't go home.

        *He tosses sheets at her.*

      You for real?

G  . . .

B  You'd do this?

        *She drops the sheets.*

          *Takes back the ring.*

          *Looks him in the eye.*

          *And puts it on her finger.*

      When.

G  Name the day.

B  June 4th.

G  *("Yer a dick")* My graduation?

      Okay.

      June 4th.

B   Bring yer mom.

> *B tests her.*

We would need one of our moms there. For photos. As a witness.

G   And you already have yours?

> Your person.
>
> To witness.

B   I thought about it. Yeah. I dunno, it might be . . .

G   Yeah.

B   Nice.                                             G   Pretty fucked up.

> . . .

G   So you feel safe? With your witness—?

B   Yeah.

G   —bein involved in all this? Cuz it's a lot. It'd be a lotta fuckin trouble.

B   I know that.

G   *(Continuing)* This would be both our lives if we're caught. So I would just need to know before June fourth if you feel safe. With your witness.

B   I do.

G   Really.

B   Yeah.

> . . .

G   Really.

B   Yeah.

> . . .
>
> *G tests him.*

G   You think we'd need to answer personal stuff in the interview?

B   Like about money?

G   Like about our bodies.

B   . . .

G   You think they'll ask about our bodies when they bring us into separate rooms?

B   Like, what our bodies are like?

G   Personal things, yeah. Things only we're supposed to know about each other.

B   Why.

G   You think they might?

B   They might, maybe.

G   So what should I know.

B   What.

G   About yer body.

B   . . .

G   I head back in a few days—

B   We don't hafta talk about this now.

G   Then when.

B   Are we really doing this?

G   When would we talk about that.

B   I don't know.
     The honeymoon.
     I guess we'd go over that on the honeymoon.

G   Always looked forward to that.

B   Me too.

G   Never went on vacation.

B   I'd always looked forward to it too.
     . . .
     . . .
     . . .

G   You think we'd have to . . .

B   What?

G   . . . on the honeymoon?
     . . .

B   I don't think so. Not like, actually.

G   Then you'll have to describe it to me.
     What it might be like.
     With you.
     . . .
     . . .
     . . .
     What do you look like.
     . . .
     . . .
     . . .

B   . . . I um— Really?
     I . . .
     I have a mole here. (Points somewhere on his chest)
     I think you saw that when we went down the shore.
     And here. (Points somewhere else on his chest)
     And . . . here. (Gestures around an intimate area)

G Where?

B There.

  Here.

G I think I have one there too.

  And here. *(Points to her collarbone)*

  And here. A few here. *(Points to the back of her neck)*

  And here. *(Points to one of her ribs)*

  And two here. *(Points to the inside of one of her thighs)*

B You got a lot.

G There might be more. I can check later on myself. For you.

B Yeah I'll check on me too.

G You have one here.

> *She touches a part of his face.*

  You missed that one.

  What are you like? When you—

B We're doin this right now?

G It's the only part we haven't covered. So if you wanted to tell me—or show me—now's the time. I'm here.

  I make noise when I'm—

B Okay.

G When I'm about to—

B I don't think they'd ask us this—

G What about scars.

  Things that might turn into scars.

  Bruises.

B . . .

G Any scars.

  Bruises—

> *Keys in a lock.*
>> *They both turn toward the sound.*
>> *A man at the door.*
>> *Henry.*
>> *Wearing an overnight backpack, carrying a paper bag.*
>> *He sees a woman in the apartment—and freezes.*

  . . .

  . . .

HENRY Sorry wrong apartment.

> *Henry exits.*

B   You don't have to—
         *("Come back")* Henry!

         . . .

              *Henry stops. Returns.*

HENRY   Did I just fuck everything / up?

B   No no no it's okay, come in.

HENRY   I tried calling—

B   I've been at work since four. / Didn't get a chance—

HENRY   Since four? You can't keep doing this to yourself.

B   I know. "Wrong apartment"?

HENRY   Well it was either that or, *(Referring to the paper bag)* "Somebody order delivery?"

   From apparently that restaurant that's got everybody's house keys.

   Chicken parm.

   Surprise.

B   Aw.

         *The two men kiss. Committed lovers.*

HENRY   I was getting nervous something happened.

B   Something did.

         *B gestures toward G.*

              *And now Henry recognizes her.*

HENRY   . . .

G   . . .

HENRY   Is this . . . ?

G   Yeah.

         . . .

         . . .

HENRY   *("Look at that")* Huh.

G   What.

HENRY   Uh-huh.

G   What.

HENRY   . . .

G   . . .

B   . . .

HENRY   *(To G)* Can you excuse us?—

G   No thank you.

B   *(To G)* Could you though?

   Fer like, a minute?

G ...

   ...

   ...

   ...

   ...

   ...

*Eventually, she moves to exit—stops, turns back to take her wine glass with her, showily mistrustful of Henry—and continues to exit.*

*B and Henry watch her disappear into the bathroom until they think she can't hear them.*

*Then turn to one another.*

HENRY  I thought we weren't doing this anymore.

B  She just showed up at the bar, then she asked to come up, I didn't think she was gonna wanna crash—

HENRY  She's spending the night?

B  I wasn't planning on it but—

HENRY  What's she doing here.

B  Visiting.

HENRY  But what's She said she didn't wanna do this.

B  She changed her mind.

   ...

HENRY  (*"We're not doing this"*) No.

B  It's a lot to ask someone to risk a quarter-mil and five years in jail.

HENRY  It's a lot to ask of you. To hold out hope for / all this time—

B  What's our other option? What other option do I have? Marry you?

HENRY  I wish you could.

B  Well I wish a lotta shit.

I can't wait for something that might never happen.

I can't watch all my days disappear into a stupid under-the-table restaurant job on Ferry Street. I panic every time I jaywalk I'll get locked up in a fuckin detention center.

HENRY  So don't jaywalk.

B  I want to start my life. My life . . . I'm losing it.

She's goin back in a few days. Tonight might be my only chance—

HENRY  Why don't we just ask one of my / friends—

B  No one knows me like she does. No one else could do this.

HENRY  We need to talk about— Just— / Hold on.

B  She'd be doin a huge thing for me. For us.

HENRY  And when she backs out? I can't watch you go through that / again—

B  I'll be fine.

HENRY  You were not fine, baby, I was there. You barely left the bed for a week. This whole month, you've / been a ghost.

B  I'll be fine.

HENRY  *(Continuing)* Every time you don't pick up your phone, I think I'll find you / in the bathtub—or the closet—

B  It's not a big deal if she crashes.

HENRY  To who it's not a big deal?

G  *(Returning)* I brought wine.

HENRY  Oh are we staying up?

B  *(To Henry)* If that's okay?

G  But you can go, Henry.

   If yer tired.

HENRY  No I'm awake.

G  We were gonna practice a little. I dunno if he told you—

HENRY  He told me, yeah, that you're reconsidering.

G  So you can go home.

   . . .

HENRY  Y'know what:

   *WINE. Henry brought a bottle too. A nice one.*

   Let's all have a glass. Get to know each other. You and I don't really, y'know, know everything there is to know about each other. We can talk about the honeymoon—

G  Oh we talked about—

HENRY  Since I'd be coming on the honeymoon.

   *G looks at B.*

   . . .

B  . . . I was gonna mention . . .

HENRY  *(A bad joke)* I mean I gotta get something out of all this!

G  You'd be getting a lot.

HENRY  So would you. Did you decide on a number?

B  Let's / start over.

G  A what?

HENRY  Your fee.

G  For what.

HENRY  Your services.

   . . .

G  I don't want money.

HENRY  I think you will once you're outta that school 'n' back in this world. It's not easy out here.

G  I know.                                        B  She knows, Henry.

HENRY  You'll be paying off that school a while.

G  I'm on scholarship.

HENRY  So was I. And then I graduated. You know it's not all scholarship, right?

G  What.

HENRY  When they say you got an award, it's not necessarily a scholarship. Sometimes those awards are loans.

G  *(Had no idea)* . . . Yeah I know.

HENRY  You might wanna look into that.
     We insist. On paying you.
     If you actually did this . . . we'd insist. Cuz it would be a lotta work. Lotta time. Some money would be helpful along the way. Like if you need a hotel.

B  *("Can you not?")* Okay.

HENRY  So no one ever loved you?

G  Wow.                                    B  Okay. / Starting over.

HENRY  *(Continuing)* You don't believe in love?

G  I do.

HENRY  You never wanted to get married?

G  I am getting married.

HENRY  I mean really.

G  We would be. Really.

HENRY  Not really, no.                    B  I mean, not really really.

G  I think we'd hafta do it pretty really.

HENRY  Cuz of your mom?

G  . . .

HENRY  Is that why you never wanted to get married—really? Never seen it go well?

G  *(To B)* What else you tell him?

HENRY  Did they love each other?

G  Who.

HENRY  Your examples. Of folks for whom it didn't go well. In marriage.

G  For whom, / wow.

HENRY  You go to school in Boston, fuck yeah for fuckin whom.

G  I think they did, yeah.

I think they really did, yeah, once.

HENRY  And what happened?

G  *(Finality)* A lot.

. . .

Maybe some people shouldn't marry for love.

For what they say is love. At first.

Some people maybe it's better they marry for other things.

HENRY  *(As if Boston were G's name)* Like what, Boston.

G  Kindness.

Respect.

Some "love" can maybe blind yer respect.

HENRY  It shouldn't.

G  No.

It shouldn't.

Should it.

HENRY  Yeah maybe you shouldn't marry really. If that's how you think of love. Maybe a situation like this would be the best option for you actually.

G  A situation like what.

HENRY  *(Referring to B's desire)* Something that would never . . . y'know.

Me, I always wished I could.

Marry.

For love.

*B draws to Henry. Affection.*

*G watches, feeling outside of it.*

G  Yeah well it's too bad you can't.

So listen you got me here the rest of the night, *(Referring to B)* yer workin all the time and I'm in class or studyin or work-studyin all the time—

HENRY  So busy.

G  *(Continuing)* So if you really wanna do this—

HENRY  Why the sudden change of mind.

G  What.

HENRY  Why are you here.

. . .

G  *(To B)* To help someone.

. . .

B  *(To both)* You wanna practice?

HENRY   *(To B)* Can I talk to you in private?

G   Nope.

HENRY   My face was not speaking to your face.

G   Nothing can be private between us.

HENRY   Among us, Boston.

G   If we're really doing this, then nothing can be private. There's people whose only job it is to smell out deception in exactly what we'd be doing. So nothing can be private—anymore—among us.

HENRY   *(To B)* I don't like this.

G   Then what would you like, Henry?
    How would you like to help the man you wish you could marry for love?

HENRY   By marrying him.

G   Well that's a solid plan.

HENRY   It passed in Massachusetts.

G   States don't / count. Not for citizenship.

HENRY   I know that.

G   *(Continuing)* Not even for a green card.

HENRY   I know that. Obviously I know. Still, just the fact of Massachusetts—

G   One state.

HENRY   Is a huge deal.

G   One state and nothing since. You need the whole country to agree—all fifty / states—first to even let you marry and then for that to count—

HENRY   —to recognize, correct, on the national level and then for that to count for citizenship, I know.

G   Yeah? What do you know about it?

B   Henry goes to law school.

    . . .

G   No he doesn't.

HENRY   Yeah I really do though.

    . . .

G   Where.

    *Henry's pleased she asked.*
        *He presents his ID.*
        *She walks up to it.*
        *Sees the school is impressive and she hates that.*

    . . .

    . . .

    I heard the buildings are ugly.

B   Henry actually knows a lot about this. He coached his parents for the citizenship test—in high school—

G   Oh yeah that's nice so what's his solution for you? Just wait it out for Alabama, Arkansas, and the other forty-seven to agree? For that DREAM Act, any news?

    I can offer you something actual. Something concrete and now, not just some hope for Someday Maybe.

HENRY   And all for free.

G   I never wanted money.

HENRY   And you'd close up shop? For the entire two-year waiting period— after a wedding—and the entire three-year period—after the interview— you'd close up shop? For five-plus years?

G   Been doin it these past three.

HENRY   Have you?

G   And a half, yeah.

    *(To B)* No one's gotten any calls about *me* at two in the morning.

HENRY   So what's in it for you?

G   I made a promise.

HENRY   Three and a half years ago.

G   That's right.

HENRY   But you're here now.

    Why didn't you do it earlier? I'm just curious. Before you left. Or after your first semester. Your first year. Second. Third. Why didn't you do it as soon as you could?—

G   Cuz we're doin it now.

HENRY   Uh-huh.

    I'm not going anywhere.

G   Okay.

HENRY   I'm part of this.

G   We'll see but okay.

B   He is.

    I'd like him to be.

HENRY   *(To B)* I am.

G   Fine. Then I guess you'll both have to agree. You have to agree—both of you—that I'm the only person who could do this. Well enough to not get caught. Decent enough not to just take your money and run. Or extort you. Good enough to let you be a part of this, Henry. To do any of this at all.

HENRY  *If* you / do it.

G  *(Continuing)* You'd both need to agree if three and a half years has been a long enough test of all that.

HENRY  Til you found out about me, / it seems, and called it off.

G  Right.

   . . .

Til I found out. About you. After you'd been together—apparently—for years. Two—that I know of. Makin decisions about me, for me, while I knew nothing. And had no one. And all while you've been at law school, Henry—harboring a criminal. Technically. Aiding and abetting THIS. *(Referring to herself and B)* A felony.

   . . .

I mean, from the outside, it might even look like I was purposefully misled. Doesn't it? From the outside, I mean. To a court of law.

HENRY  . . .

G  I guess you'd both need to agree I'm the best option he has. To start his life.

   . . .

That is, if that's something you would like. If that's something you would like, Henry, for the man you say you wish you could marry for love.

   . . .

   . . .

HENRY  Okay y'know what. There's some fuckin cheese in the fridge. I'm gonna put it on a fuckin plate 'n' we're gonna eat it—

B  . . . That brie I brought from work?

HENRY  Did you eat it.

   . . .

Here then Here's some chicken fuckin parm Do you know he loves chicken / parm—

G  I do.

HENRY  Please excuse me while I plate this shit Wine?

G  Please.

HENRY  Yer welcome.

B  *("I'm sorry")* Henry—

HENRY  I want what's best for you.

   I want you happy.

   But you need to be sure this is how.

     *Henry exits to the kitchen.*

*B and G alone. A strange air between them.*

*G is pleased to have won the moment—then feels B pull away.*

*B is aware how much this is costing Henry. He's angry to be in this situation. And so, ices G out.*

   . . .

   . . .

G   *(Trying to connect)* When did we meet?

   . . .

B   . . .

   . . .

G   What school?

B   . . .

   . . .

G   Where was it located?

B   Hundred Davis.

G   In?

B   . . .

   . . .

G   What's the best pizza in town?

   What did the two of you have in common?—

B   Not much anymore.

   *Henry enters, behind them. Watches.*

G   What's your favorite aspect of your partner? You remember our old answer?

B   Her kindness.

G   What did the / two of you—

B   *(Continuing)* Was our old answer.

HENRY   You met in Miss Ramirez's class. ESL. Third grade. You forgot your lunch. She shared hers. You brought extra the next day to pay her back. Your idea. You were the only two students to move up to English-speaking classes that next year. Both your favorite color's blue. Cobalt. Teal. And the best pizza in town was Joe's.

   Is.

   Joe's.

   . . .

   What else should I know?

   As your witness?

B   *(Quiet love)* Thank you.

HENRY  First "date"?

G  Well we've known each other forever so. It's hard to really pinpoint / exactly—

HENRY  *(To B)* Is that how she's gonna respond? *(To G)* Is that how you're gonna respond?

    First date.

G  The movies. Two-for-one Tuesday.

HENRY  Which was when.

G  '98. Let's say—

HENRY  When exactly.

G  Summer. Junior high.

HENRY  What's each other's shoe size.

B  Both of us? Fuck—eight?      G  Like, current shoe—nine?
    Six?                                                     Ten!

HENRY  *(To G, a brag)* He's a twelve.

    Brand of shampoo, both of you, go.

B  Um . . .                                   G  I can . . . check.

HENRY  Deodorant.

B  Really?                                 G  Old Spice?

HENRY  Brand of toothpaste.

B  Wouldn't we use the            G  We can just make a list of
    same one?                                this stuff.

HENRY  Yes, Love, ideally, that's what you'd both answer.

    What's your favorite aspect of your partner.

G  His kindness.                            B  Her— . . . yeah.

HENRY  When did you decide to get married?

G  High school.         B  Right after high school. Not long after.

HENRY  Who proposed to *whom*.

B  I did.

G  He did. My last day in town.

HENRY  Where. How.

B  At the bus stop.

G  He waited with me at the bus.

B  Her last day in town.

G  I didn't wanna go.

B  My mom left a ring.

    I carried it around for days cuz I knew she was leavin for school.

G  You did?

B   In my pocket. I safety-pinned it inside my pocket so it wouldn't fall out.
    I carried it for days.

G   He proposed at the bus.

B   Her last day in town.

G   I didn't wanna go.

B   My mom left a ring.

G   *(Genuine)* I didn't wanna go.

B   I carried it around for days cuz I knew she was leaving.

G   He was always there when I needed him.

B   She was—

    . . .

    She was always there.

    When I needed her.

G   *(Genuine)* . . . What did you do while she was away?

B   I worked.

    Saved.

G   Wasn't much money to visit. But we talked all the time.

B   A lot of the time, yeah. We'd talk.

G   I sent postcards.

B   She sent postcards.

G   And books.

B   Thank you.

G   From my classes. Yer welcome.

    She'd call. At night.

    Every night.

    Before she went to bed, she'd call.

B   I took the bus up to Boston once. To see her.

G   . . . He took the bus up to—

B   But she didn't see me.

    . . .

    . . .

    I took a bus.

    The T.

    And I walked to her campus to find her.

    . . .

    I snuck into a class. I smelled the books. I sat on leather. I watched the
people. I felt the life. Someone let me in a door. Thought I was a student.
Just forgot my ID. They let me in. Didn't think twice, they let me in. I

listened to lectures. I raised my hand. I answered a question. About a book I'd read. Coincidence, I'd read that book. I got it right. The question. Very right. Made people wonder who was, who's this guy, people wondered who I was. I found the dining hall. Someone swiped me in. Forgot my ID, I said, so they let me in. Didn't think twice. I ate the food. I went for seconds. I ate dessert. I touched the stone. I walked the grass. I passed by windows. I heard the laughs. I watched the night. And I went home.

> . . .
> . . .

G  Did you see her?

B  I did.

G  But she didn't see you?

B  No.

G  What if she did.

> What would you have done.
>
> . . .
> . . .

B  I would have walked away.

> Let her pretend she didn't see me.
> I'd never take that away.
> The trees. The books.
> As much as I . . .
> I couldn't.
>
> . . .
> . . .
> . . . Why'd you stay away?

G  . . .

B  (Not unkindly) . . . All this time.

> Why'd you stay away.

G  Money.

> Time. And money.
>> B is disappointed and further saddened by her answer.
> Guilt.
> About the trees and the books.
> Guilt about not loving it up there.
> When that's all you ever wanted.
> And guilt about loving it.
> Sometimes.

> . . .
>
> . . .

I'm sorry.

> . . .
>
> . . .

B   *(Heartbroken)* It's . . .
>       *He can't say "okay."*

> . . .

HENRY   When did your relationship turn romantic.

> . . .

>       *B looks back at Henry,*
>           *who has been witnessing a genuine relationship . . .*
>           *and is becoming concerned.*

> . . .

B   She used to climb up my fire escape at night. And I'd sneak her into my bedroom.

HENRY   They'll want more details than that.

B   I don't think they will.

HENRY   I think they very likely might, My Love, if that's how you're gonna answer.

B   This didn't actually happen.

HENRY   Well don't tell them that.
>       When did your relationship turn romantic.

B   She used to climb up my fire escape at night and I'd sneak her into my bedroom and one night . . .

HENRY   Yeah?

B   —it turned romantic.

G   I used to climb up his fire escape at night and he'd sneak me into his bedroom and one night, as we're layin there, close cuz his bed's a twin, one night as we're layin there, I feel his breath on my neck.

> . . .

>       And it feels like he's peelin back my skin.
>       Just from his breath on my neck.
>       He says my name.
>       He knows I'm awake but he says my name.
>       And then we

B   Yeah.
>       And then we.

G  Yeah.

   . . .

   . . .

HENRY  You've really created a little . . . Yeah . . . world. For yourselves.
   I'm nowhere in your story.

   . . .

B  . . . Well . . . no . . .
   Really?

HENRY  I'm gonna be nowhere in your . . .

B  I'm not doin this for fun.

HENRY  I know.
   It's just a thing I'm fully realizing.
   That's all.

G  How long have you known each other.

HENRY  Two years. And a half. / Almost.

G  No, me and him.
   How long have you known each other.

   . . .

HENRY  Since third grade.                   B  Thirteen years.

G  Two-thirds of our lives.
   First kiss?

B  *(Concerned about Henry)* I don't remember when we said.

G  May 22nd.
   What's your favorite aspect of your partner.

B  His kindness.

HENRY  . . .

B  *(Moving to him)* His ambition. His intellect. His body. His mouth. His
   kindness.
   First kiss: First day. June. In the city. I missed my train. Last one of the
   night. On purpose.
   How many lies have you had to tell for me. How much have I asked of
   you—

HENRY  It's okay.

B  How late would I call and how quick would you pick up—
   *Henry kisses B. "It's okay."*

G  What's yer favorite part of her body.

B  No we're done.

G  What's yer favorite part of / her body.

B  We're done.

G  His mouth. What's yer favorite part of / her body.

B  Her hands.                    HENRY  *(To B)* You don't have to do this.

G  I'm not convinced. Did your parents approve of the match Why or why not Why or why not Did your mother fuckin wish we were sleepin together?

   . . .

B  *(Wounded)* That's not why she left.

HENRY  *(To B)* We don't have to / do this. Not like this.

G  I'm not convinced.

B  She left cuz it was harder here for her—

HENRY  It would be years of this.                    G  I'm not convinced.

B  —and cuz of September—

HENRY  Baby, do you want *years* / of this?

B  I never wanted any of this. I never wanted to have to do any of this. For this to be my only option—

G  Tell me about his body, Henry. / In case they ask.

B  No.

G  *(Continuing)* Anything distinct I should know? Any scars, / bruises—

B  No, we're done for the night.

G  *(Continuing)* Anything like that? Scars? Bruises? You know he called me that night—

HENRY  Okay.

G  *(Continuing)* Middle of the night, cold as hell he said— He called me from a pay phone and said someone had kicked him out / without his shoes.

HENRY  I didn't kick him out—

G  *(Continuing)* He was walkin around Newark at night in the cold without his shoes—

HENRY  We had a fight.                    B  I left.

G  And you kick him out without his shoes? It's his apartment.

B  He didn't— / I just—

G  *(Continuing)* You called me! He / called me!

B  I called you Yeah I called but you weren't here. You stayed in Boston.

G  I told you to go to my mom's.

B  I wasn't gonna go to yer mom's in the middle of the night.

G  You coulda come to Boston.

B  I had no shoes!

G  What did you do that night?

B  I went to a diner and waited 'til the Kmart opened, bought some shoes, and went to work. I just—I needed to talk that night. To someone. To you. We had a fight—

HENRY  We had a fight and now we're fine people fight. But do you know what he did when you backed out? I couldn't get him to eat. Shower. He wouldn't leave the bed for a fuckin week.

G  I got nervous.

HENRY  No you became aware of what this really is. This isn't some game, some fuckin fantasy. This shit is for real.

G  Then why the fuck did I not even know about you 'til a fuckin month ago?—

HENRY  Prob'ly cuz he knew it'd go THIS well.

G  First time I ever heard your damn name was over sobbing on a pay phone! I got nervous cuz who the fuck was fuckin Henry—

HENRY  I am.

G  —and would he risk a quarter-mil and five years in jail?

HENRY  I *am*.

G  Not like I am. You could deny. You could say you didn't know. You could step away.

HENRY  I haven't.

G  You don't have to risk a quarter-mil / and five years in jail—

HENRY  I would if I could.

G  (*Continuing*) —just to help somebody.

HENRY  You'd be getting paid.

G  Would you risk all that just to help someone?

HENRY  Yes.

G  Okay so you go marry someone.

HENRY  I don't— What—                                    B  What?!

G  If it's so easy then you go marry / someone and help her—

HENRY  What are you even— This isn't a trade.

G  Then you can't know how scary this is. You can't tell me shit about this.

B  He's not marrying anybody.

HENRY  Unless it's you.

G  WHICH YOU NEVER WILL. YOU WILL NEVER DO THAT YOU WILL NEVER BE ABLE TO EVER LEGALLY DO THAT IN THIS COUNTRY. IT'S 2000 FUCKIN 6 ALMOST 7 IN A FEW FUCKIN DAYS SO IF IT HASN'T HAPPENED NOW IT NEVER FUCKIN WILL. YOU WON'T EVER, EVER MARRY HIM.

. . .

   . . .

   . . .

HENRY  Well.

    Neither will you.

G  I'm helping.

HENRY  You seem to want love so fuckin bad, you'd settle for it fake.

G  . . .

HENRY  The only reason someone takes someone's fuckin shoes is so they stay.

    I didn't want him goin out in the middle of the night in fuckin November. You think I wanted that? I went out to look for him. All night. While you stayed in Boston. I knew. I suspected. But he said no. She's not like that. I knew but he kept saying She's not like that. And so we had a fight. We had a fight that night—about you. And then you backed out. And you proved me right. I wish you coulda seen what that did to him, your backing out, cuz then you'd never put him through that again. You wanna help? You're here to help? Yeah? Up to what point?

G  . . .

HENRY  *(To B)* Do we have to do this? Is all this worth it?

B  *(Lost)* I've been hiding and lying for the past thirteen years of my For every For just basic human Because I didn't get some Some paper means I cannot be a full person here. I have had to hide who I am at every fuckin turn of my life—

HENRY  I know that.

B  —I've been lying so long I'm not even sure what's real.

HENRY  Then maybe you should question a couple things in your life.

G  Yeah maybe you should question a really major thing in yer life. If you don't know what's real.

B  . . .

G  I got nervous and I'm sorry but I'm here. I'm ready to risk a quarter-mil, jail, whatever future I might have—for you. So you can be a full person here.

HENRY  And what's that gonna cost him.

G  You.

   . . .

    *(To B)* I don't trust him.

B  You don't know him.

G  That's not my fault.

B  If you'da come down any time in the last year you would've met him.

G  Not even his name. That he existed. I didn't even know a Henry existed.

B  (*Referring to his sexuality*) But you always knew—

G  Not that a Henry was currently existing. Currently stealing your shoes and / doin who-knows-what-else to you—

B  We had a fight—once—

G  Didn't seem like just a fight when you called. I never heard those kinda sounds outta you—

B  And you didn't come.

G  I'm here now.

B  You never heard those sounds and still you didn't / come.

G  You wanted me to take a bus in the middle of the night from Boston?

B  YES.

How can I trust you?

G  (*Lunges for him*) Take off yer shirt.

B  What. / No.

G  Take yer clothes off. Lemme see what "once" looks like.

/ Lemme take a look at Henry's "once."

B  That's not what this is.

G  (*Continuing*) My mother denied it too / 'til she got naturalized—

HENRY  I'm not like your house.

G  (*Continuing*) Kept thinkin he'd follow her, blackmail her, fuckin, disappear her, who'd know? Who'd care about her fuckin—unregistered body somewhere?

B  Henry was here when you weren't.

G  I was always here.

B  You weren't!

. . .

I promised myself I wouldn't take anything else. Told myself, She'd be doin this huge thing for you—for the rest of your life—so don't ask a thing more of hers. Don't ask to come up. Or for her to come down. But three and a half years . . . I thought you'd at least have wanted to.

. . .

But you had something to lose.

You found something more than just me . . . to lose.

. . .

It's a beautiful world up there. Boston. If I were you, I might not have come back either. But it's ending. It's ending soon.

. . .

Where you gonna crash when life breaks for you next. Or has it already?

. . .

G  You better be sure Henry's worth ten-hour shifts on yer feet. Not seein yer mother for years. The crushing fuckin panic every time you see a cop. You better be sure he's worth me walkin out. I hope your secret fuckin boyfriend of two and a half years would be worth every second of Fish Kill fuckin Road.

. . .

What's it gonna be.

. . .

. . .

. . .

*B becomes nervous.*

. . .

B  Why won't you say anything.

HENRY  I can't choose for you.

B  . . .

HENRY  If all your days disappear into an under-the-table restaurant job on Ferry Street, you'll resent me.

B  No—

HENRY  As much as I'd like to, I can't be the one to choose this.

B  Why do I have to?

HENRY  I didn't make the terms.

. . .

*B looks at Henry. At G.*
*At Henry.*
*At G.*

B  You would go ahead with a wedding? With all the tests, questions? With livin with me, livin in Newark, with all the hiding, the lying, the risks, for two more years—at least—and who knows how much longer after that, you'd do that?

G  Yeah.

B  You'd do all that?
    If I throw Henry out of my life?

G  Yeah.

B  Then no.

G  . . .

B  No.

. . .

*G understands this means an end.*

G   Third grade

Franklin

Hundred Davis

Kearny

He waited with me at the bus

Carried it around for days in his pocket

My last day in town

His kindness

> *She removes the ring.*
>> *And returns it to B's hands,*
>> *as he had once placed it into hers.*

Good luck.

> *G moves to gather her things. Moves to exit.*

HENRY   *(To B)* I'm sorry.

B   It's. . .

> *He can't say "okay."*

HENRY   We could ask one of my friends—

B   No.

I don't want to do this again.

Maybe we can just . . . live our life somewhere else.

If it's this or Fish Kill Road.

Maybe I can finally see my mom.

. . .

Would you come with me?

If I had to move back?

> *G stops at the door, turns back.*
>> *Henry clocks he's being watched by G. And B.*

Would you / come?

HENRY   Let's get ready for bed.

. . .

. . .

To live?

B   Yeah.

HENRY   Really?

. . .

We never talked about this.

B   We're talking about it now.

HENRY   What would we do there?

B   We'd live our lives, a version of our lives, like we've been living here.

HENRY   There is no version of my—

    Let's talk in the / morning.

B   Henry.

HENRY   I'm going to school here. Studying the laws of here. What would I do there?

B   You could go to school there, study there—

HENRY   Baby. I know like, all of two words of—

B   I didn't speak English when I first came. You'd learn.

HENRY   My family's all here.

B   You can visit your family. They can visit you.

HENRY   Wouldn't it just be more hiding?

    Another version of hiding. There. For you and me. I've done so much of that. For so much of my life.

    I lost too much of my life already to that. Even before this. I'm done with that.

B   I know but— Maybe—

HENRY   We never talked about this.

B   Why would you want to stay in a country that doesn't want me in it?

    *Henry realizes something. And it breaks his heart.*

HENRY   This isn't gonna stop.

    No matter what you choose, this isn't gonna stop.

    You never talked about going back before. You never wanted to.

    And if you did, you'd blame me—

B   No.

HENRY   You would. And if you don't go through with this—with her—then every night you came home and nothing's changed, it'd be my fault.

B   No. Just—

HENRY   *(Continuing)* It'd be my fault you stayed.

B   Let's just go to bed.

HENRY   *(Continuing)* And if you left, that would be my fault.

B   Just forget I even—

HENRY   We wouldn't make it.

    Here or there.

    And if you leave, you won't be allowed back.

    And all of that would be my fault.

    I'm sorry.

B  No— Listen— Just— We'll keep living how we've been living—
HENRY  She should stay.
B  Henry—please.

    *B clings to Henry, trying to hold him here in some way.*

HENRY  This was never for me. So you could stay with me.
    You were never doin this for you and me.

    *Henry softly pulls away from B.*

      . . .

    *B feels abandoned—again.*
    *And he throws Henry away.*
    *Henry looks at B. At his back.*

    (*A gift*) It was never for me.
    *Henry turns to exit. Sees G there.*
    (*A curse*) But it was definitely never for you.
    *And Henry exits.*
      *B stands there, an island of grief.*
      *And then he sees G.*

  . . .
  . . .
  . . .

B  . . . You gonna need another blanket?
    Or is that enough,
    what I set out?

    . . .

G  I can just catch a cab.
B  Yer not gonna stay?
G  I don't think I should be doin this.

    . . .

B  "This"?
G  . . . Stayin over.
B  Is that what you meant when you said "this" the first time? Stayin over?
    You shouldn't be stayin over?
G  . . .
B  Please.
G  Maybe you should think about things a little / more—
B  No. Please.
G  Why don't we talk in April / when—
B  No.

G During break. If I'm back. Maybe we could . . . talk again then.
  . . . What are you doin for New Year's?

B Workin. Just stay the night—

G It'll be light out soon. I could also just walk.

B You could stay here.

G I know.
  I know.
  *(Referring to ending up here)* I could.
  I'll call you in April?

B Only if you—

  . . .

G *(An end)* Okay.

  . . .

  I really liked practicing.

B I know.

G I really liked . . . our time.

B Please don't call.

G Okay.
  . . . Happy—

  . . .

B You can say it.

G Happy New Year.

B Thank you.

G *(Genuine)* Happy New Year.
  And
  Good luck.
   *G exits.*
    *B is alone.*
    *The sounds of an empty apartment and a small city, beyond the windows.*
    *B holds the ring.*
    *B goes to the window.*
    *The sounds of the small city outside fill the apartment.*
    *The light of approaching day.*

B When did you
  decide
  what do you have in
  when did your
  relationship

did your parents
why or
have you ever had
have you ever
. . .
what are you gonna
   *The sounds and lights of another day,*
     *another night,*
     *another week,*
     *another year,*
     *years.*
     *Years passing by a young man in a small city.*
     *But still,*
     *he continues.*
what are you gonna
   *Lights.*

·     ·     ·

# Wolf Play

## HANSOL JUNG

### Characters

| | |
|---|---|
| ASH | AFAB, Late 20s. Southpaw Boxer. |
| ROBIN | Female, 30s. Ash's wife. |
| RYAN | Male, Late 20s. Robin's brother. |
| PETER | Male, Late 30s. A father. |
| WOLF | A mix of the familiar with the terribly unexpected. |

\* Cast should be racially diverse.
\* Wolf should be of East Asian descent.

### Notes

—     A cutoff either by self or other.
/     A point where another character might cut in.

Different spaces/realities are denoted with margin indentation and line alignment.

## [WHERE WE ARE]

*Hello Wolf.*

WOLF  What if I said I am not what you think you see.

I am not an actor human, this floor is forest earth, and to the left of that glaring exit light, a river flows, the width and length and velocity of the Egyptian Nile.

You are not what you feel you are, you are a spider the size of your eyelash. Or an eagle flying two thousand feet above our heads. Or the mother of the newest freshest pinecone dangling over that aisle. We are riding on the back of a giant turtle, hurtling through the cosmos, in a four point five four billion year race against the tiniest of the tiniest white Easter rabbits.

What if I said, you are the single most important breath in my space. You are the first gear that turns the clock of my world. You are the final drop of dew that breaks down the universal dam of miscommunication. I need you with every blood cell and cranial nerve I possess.

And you believed me?

Does that change anything?

What if I said Oops, actually no, we are sitting in a rented space on top of concrete ground, laid upon a planet fast losing her steam. You are barely a breath in the time space continuum, you're here, you're gone, we'd all move on without a care. You do not make an impact, you do not give or take anything of import in your ridiculous little life on this plastic earth.

I am exactly what you think you see. I am indeed an actor human, paid in cash or credit or So Much Love and cookies to say these lines that a writer human wrote so that I might speak them in my actor human resonant voice. You are indeed the idiot that decided to pay to be squeezed in that little seat in the dark, for the next some hours of your life that you shall never retrieve, you may not take pictures or recordings, you must silence all cell phones beepers candy wrappers alarm clocks and all alarmedness in general, or we will tweet about you and your ignorance to the entire world during our greenroom smoke break, and you are exactly what you feel you are.

That is the truth. Is that the truth?

You may think about this while the people who haven't turned their things off already turn their things off already. Go on.

*People turn noisy things off.*

The truth is a wobbly thing, we shall wobble through our own set of truths like jello on a freight train, and tonight I add a bump to that journey and put to you my truth:

I am not what you think you see.

I am the wolf.

Aow.

Yes, I am the wolf.

Aooow.

And then again because three translates to God in the Bible, infinity in Asia, and funny in theater:

I am the wolf.

*Real wolf howl. Terrifying and beautiful.*

Wolves get a bad rap for being evil, they will eat your lambs, limbs, and grannies, and sometimes blow your house down without giving two shits about your chinny chin chin. But you gotta understand these evil wolves are abandoned wolves. Solo wolves, not necessarily out on the prowl to steal your red riding hoods. But stories need conflict, and fighters are sexy and boy, do wolves know how to fight.

*Lights: Ash in the boxing ring.*

However, an abandoned wolf will rarely actually fight. He will slink in the shadows, trying his best to stay unseen and unheard and unsmelled, basically invisible.

See, wolves suck at being alone. Wolves need family.

*Lights: Robin and Ryan on a couch with a blue balloon.*

We sleep in packs. Hunt in packs. Travel in packs.

*Lights: Peter in the car.*

The world is actually a very dangerous place for an orphaned, lone wolf.

*An Asian boy doll appears.*

But I am the wolf. So I admit to some bias.

There is a Korean saying that goes "Naturally, the arm folds inwards."

It means, you will tend to fight for your family, back your pack, defend your bloodline, over mostly anything and anyone else.

It makes more sense in Korean.

But we're not here to talk about Koreans.

*Wolf sets the boy doll in the car next to Peter.*

We're here to talk about Americans. These two Peters are both Americans. These two Peters live in the desert lands of Arizona. Early one morning, the two American Peters opened the desert gate, and went out into the narrow desert road.

   *Sound: VRROOOM.*

   Far down the road they traveled, over the hills and valleys low.

   Until finally they came upon the great big jungle of shadows and concrete walls, the watery airs of San Francisco.

   And in this jungle was a house, filled to the edges with blue balloons . . .


## [MEET THE PARENTS]

   *Ryan and Robin blow balloons.*
       *Robin's balloon is very large.*
       *It gets larger. And larger. And just before it looks like it'll pop, it gets larger.*
       *Robin takes in her village of blue balloons.*

ROBIN   Is it too much?

RYAN   I mean—nooo.

ROBIN   It's too much. It's trying too hard. I'm trying too hard.

RYAN   What's wrong with trying too hard?

ROBIN   What's wrong with trying too hard? There's nothing wrong with trying too hard, I want him to know how hard I am trying and loving and wanting, to make him feel—

   What am I trying to make him feel?

RYAN   Like a person who is surrounded by very very many blue balloons.

ROBIN   I should've gotten more yellow.

RYAN   Yellow balloons look like boobs. You don't wanna throw a three-year-old boy into a room full of boobs.

ROBIN   Boobs?

RYAN   You want the boy to feel like it's okay to be a boy.

ROBIN   —

RYAN   What? I'd know better than you, don't you think? How a boy feels like it's okay to be a boy?

ROBIN   Ryan, I love you, I thank you for being here with all the brotherly love and support and information on how boys feel like they are boys but I really really need you to turn the dick off for today, okay?

RYAN   Can't. Not how dicks work.

   *Ryan does a joyous penis dance.*

I man! I bring food for fire! I flaunt my big dick that hath no off-switch and put it in everything to make many more boy babies! Oomf oomf, uh oomf oo— (*off Robin's look*) And we are turning it off.

Where's Ash?

ROBIN   No idea.

RYAN   Woah.

ROBIN   Yep.

RYAN   —

I mean,

ROBIN   What.

RYAN   Can't blame them?

ROBIN   Can't blame them?

RYAN   We're about to go pro, they've got a lot on their plate. You're dumping a kid on a person who's got no time / to sit around picking out balloon colors,

ROBIN   I am not dumping a kid on— You know what. I don't need you I don't need Ash I don't need any of you idiots, I am a goddamn adult I can goddamn get a child if I want.

RYAN   Okay.

   *They blow balloons.*

But if you really want my opinion on / this whole thing,

ROBIN   Oh my God.

RYAN   it's a little shady.

ROBIN   It's very legal.

RYAN   Oh come on, Robs, I can barely trust the internet to get a pair of jeans that fit, you just got yourself a kid, it's a little shady.

ROBIN   Jeans and children are very different things—

RYAN   You've never met the kid, or these people who put the kid up on a website, hello internet I hate this boy, yours for a couple of bucks if you'll sign this paper, we'll even throw in the basket of toys. Who does that?

ROBIN   Lots of people are doing it.

RYAN   Yeah you and the six people at clubs dot yahoo dot com—

ROBIN   There are over a thousand members, Ryan.

RYAN   On clubs dot yahoo dot com, Robin—a thousand, ten thousand, whatever, it's still fucked up?

ROBIN   Why? Why is it so fucked up? Because we're bypassing some kind of institutional governmental system? Sure, cuz they're so good at dealing with international orphans, so good that Russia, huh, has banned the US from adopting their children—

RYAN Well no. That's because we do gay and they don't.

ROBIN —

His room is done. We have balloons. My child is coming. So fuck you fuck Russia I do not have to convince either of you.

*Ryan makes a balloon fart.*

ROBIN Sometimes I really wish you were a sister.

RYAN Yeah, but can a sister do this?

*Ryan does the joyous penis dance.*

*Knock knock.*

ROBIN He's here. Oh shit. Oh shit O Shit. Oshitoshitoshitoshito.

*Robin does a last-minute-getting-things-perfect.*

RYAN Hey. Breathe.

You got this. Okay?

ROBIN Okay. I do. I do got this.

*(to Ryan)* Don't be dumb.

RYAN —

*She opens the door.*

*Peter stands at the door with a large suitcase.*

*Next to him stands the Asian boy doll. Puppeteer is Wolf.*

*Maybe Wolf and Doll look like Calvin and Hobbes in reverse.*

ROBIN Hi!

PETER Hi I'm Peter.

ROBIN Peter. Come in. Wonderful to meet you, I'm Robin.

PETER Hi Robin. Excellent. And you must be Ash.

*Ryan looks to Robin.*

This is Pete Junior.

WOLF I am a wolf.

ROBIN Hey there Pete.

WOLF Wolves are not friendly in general. Especially the lone wolf.

ROBIN I'm Robin. I am so glad to finally meet you.

PETER Junior wanna say hi to Robin and Ash?

WOLF The wolf knows that he is alone, that all he has is his paws and his cunning to survive in the ever-changing environment.

PETER He's tired. It's a tough drive.

ROBIN Oh, yes. Of course.

WOLF  Wolves are never tired. We just like
to lay low. And watch.

PETER  Here, this is his / suitcase, it's mostly—

ROBIN  Would you like anything to drink or, we have some snacks, Reese's
Pieces—unless you have a peanut allergy—or dinner?

WOLF  Wolves are able to survive up to two
weeks without food if need be.

Wolves are cautious, the masters of
survival.

RYAN  We were going to order in some pizza—

ROBIN  Or there's a great Korean place around the corner—

*Wolf attacks a balloon. POP—*

WOLF  We know that every living being,
even the tiniest and weak-looking-est
has the potential of poison.

ROBIN  We were trying to decorate, festive, we got so excited, over-ballooned.

PETER  No it's great, looks great. Junior likes blue.

ROBIN  Really? Oh wow, I didn't even know, it's like we connected on a
subconscious level or something. I mean, not that a color of a balloon
would indicate that we are Super Soulmates or something, not that we
should be, because we are not, we are, I am just really very happy to have
you. Here.

Would you like some snacks, or Reese's, or something to drink? No?

PETER  He's shy. Takes a while to open up. But he will.

WOLF  We lay low. Observe. Calculate.

RYAN  He's kinda big for—how old you say he was?

ROBIN  Really quite big, you didn't look so grown-up in your pictures! Do
you play any sports? Basketball? Volleyball?

PETER  Sadly no he doesn't, I keep putting him on a team, any team, but
the team spits him out, like a Canadian quarter.

*Peter sets up a home-made tent.*

Do you mind if I—? It's his little fort. We made it together and he's a
bit attached to it still.

ROBIN  Of course, please.

PETER  It's not him, just that he is so shy and kids take a while to warm up
sometimes.

WOLF  It's highly unlikely that a wolf will
bond with non-wolves.

PETER  It's a pity, he's very athletic, I mean especially for being Asian, I mean. It's a special quality. I mean, where we are from. I mean it in a good way. It could be different here, the city kids are open to a lot more, diversity and all that, so.

RYAN  Maybe we could try for a more individual sport, if team spirit is not his thing.

ROBIN  Yeh! He's a / trainer.

RYAN  I'm a trainer.

PETER  Trainer?

RYAN  Is that okay?

PETER  No no, yes, no sorry, Katie said, that you were, made games.

ROBIN  Oh no it's me, that's me, I make video games. Or, work at a place, they make the games. I'm, I do stuff.

PETER  Yeah? Yeah yeah, that makes so much more sense, I mean, I was thinking, you have that build, like you do something with it,

RYAN  Have a club in the city, here.

> *Ryan gives Peter his card.*

PETER  Oh. Aren't you—

RYAN  Huh?

PETER  I thought your name was Ash.

RYAN  Oh. No. It's not.

PETER  Boxing?

RYAN  Mostly. We do some other stuff too, basic kickboxing, cardio for the ladies—

PETER  That's actually pretty perfect. That would take the aggression out a bit.

RYAN  Oh.

ROBIN  Oh?

PETER  Oh. Oh! Nothing, nothing unusual, just boys will be boys, kind of deal. He's really a good kid. Beautiful, when he wants to be. I mean, Katie and I, we had such a great time together, as a family.

> WOLF  Sometimes wolves will ally with another species for co-existence.
>
> Wolves are not above making friends if it means survival.

PETER  You must think I'm an animal, what kind of human being does this, but it's really—

It's been hard with the baby, we have a newborn, we never thought we could, but anyway, he's um, a lot to take care of. The baby, not—

WOLF  It's always about survival for the lone wolf.

PETER  Junior's been having trouble with our split focus, and we love him so much, we love you so much, but he was just so unhappy. Katie was trying so hard.

WOLF  But wolves hate Katie.

PETER  I'm between jobs, which I thought would help, but it turns out not.

WOLF  Katies hate Wolf.

PETER  And you have to know, when you're just not a good fit. It just wasn't a good fit anymore, and,

WOLF  But Katies live with Peters.

PETER  and we didn't know what to do.

WOLF  So even though Peters are very often allies, Peters are not a hundred percent for the wolf.

PETER  This is his stuff, mostly clothes, some toys and uh—

Katie and I wrote up a little thing, a booklet, we kept an observation log for the first few months.

I typed it up. It's in the folder with the papers—

WOLF  Peters are a hundred percent for papers. It is his fortress of survival.

ROBIN  Could I—

PETER  Yes yes of course.

ROBIN  Oh great. So it's been signed / and notarized.

PETER  Absolutely. I keep a copy and you also—

ROBIN  That's it? We don't need to go to court or—

PETER  Yeah no that's it. I mean, technically this uh Power of Attorney contract is all it is, that's how people do it on the website. If we go to court he might slip into the cracks of the system, so it's just simpler, this way, it seems? And uh, affordable, a lot more.

WOLF  Peters love to talk about the cost of things.

ROBIN  Of course. I mean, that helps. Both of us.

PETER  Yeah children, you know. Cost.

WOLF  It seems to give him tremendous comfort to do so.

ROBIN  This is—

PETER  Yes, thanks.

   We also included some of his photos, when he was younger—

RYAN  Hey that's the one on the website.

PETER  Is it? Katie posted and kept up with all that stuff. I'm not—

ROBIN  He is six? Years old?

PETER  Yup.

ROBIN  Oh I thought—

PETER  Uh huh?

ROBIN  No, I was under the impression that he was younger, I thought I saw that on the post—

PETER  I'm pretty sure Katie wouldn't lie about—

WOLF  That is a lie. Katies lie all the time. She lies about her age, her weight, and what she ate for dessert.

PETER  Actually. There's one more thing we need to—
   *Another document.*

RYAN  What's that?

ROBIN  *(reads)* Affidavit of waiver of interest in child. Wow.

PETER  Since the POA doesn't transfer custody, technically, so Katie thought, just in case. You know?

ROBIN  Oh no I get it. Final sale, no returns?

PETER  We thought it would be best if—he would adjust better if we weren't around. At all.

WOLF  What?

PETER  We're really not terrible people. We really want what's best for him. We love him. So much. We do.

   It was wonderful to meet you.
   *Peter heads toward the door; the doll is attached to him.*
   Junior, Junior let go of daddy this is your new home now, okay?

WOLF  Wolves are an extremely adaptable species / the wolf is one of the few that survived the last ice age.

ROBIN  Junior, come on, wanna see your new room? We got a blue spaceship bed, and whole new page of glow-in-the-dark / planet stickers. We could help you stick them on your ceiling—

WOLF  Pluck from the desert and throw into a sea a wolf will never drown a wolf will survive

But it takes TIME

It takes / TIME.

RYAN   Hey hey, come on big boy, let's come to Uncle Ryan.

*Doll is unattached from Peter,*

*Ryan holds the doll.*

*Wolf howls.*

PETER   Um wait wait, you can't do that to him, it'll just aggravate the tantrum.

ROBIN   Tantrum? I think it's a little more than a tantrum.

PETER   Junior. Junior. Hey son, it's alright, huh, it's alright, it's—

Be a big boy for daddy? Huh? Everything's gonna be alright, okay? Everything's gonna be just fine.

You gotta be a big boy right now, okay? I love you, so much, you know that right? You know—

*Door slam. Ash is home.*

*Wolf stops howling.*

Oh! Hi I, I'm Peter.

*Peter holds out his hand.*

*It hangs there in the air.*

*It's awkward.*

ASH   You're the dad.

PETER   Um, yes. Well, I was. Legally at this / point I might not—

ASH   I hope you go to hell.

PETER   Woah.

ASH   Get the fuck out of my house.

PETER   I don't think that kind of language is necessary—

ASH   Get your ass the fuck out of my house or I'll throw you out the window like your mother should've done.

RYAN   Hey, come on, let's let the man go, okay?

ASH   Did I say anything but? I said get out. Get out. Get the fuck out of my house.

PETER   How about you back off, alright? I didn't drive all the way out here to be disrespected by some,

ASH   By some?

PETER   I don't know who you are but you have absolutely no right to talk to me that way.

ASH   Yeah?

PETER   You just watch your mouth, alright? The kid is just six.

ASH  We can import him from Asia, we can put him up for auction the minute something doesn't Feel Right, but hey now be careful of the f-word cuz that will really fuck him up.

ROBIN  Ash. That's enough.

PETER  Ash? You are Ash.

ASH  ?

PETER  You're— You are the— *(to Ryan)* You know about this? Did you know this, that—

RYAN  Hey look man—

PETER  *(to Robin)* Does Katie know? Did you lie about—

ROBIN  I'm sorry, did I lie about what?

PETER  She would never just—

RYAN  Peter I think you better leave now.

PETER  He won't have a father? You're depriving my boy of a father?

ROBIN  Wow okay I'm sorry but if anyone's depriving / him of anything it's—

RYAN  Ash no don't—
    *Ash slaps him.*

PETER  AAAAAAAAAAARRRRGH / ARGH!

RYAN  Ash. Calm it, okay, just not worth it.

PETER  Crazy fucking bitch!

RYAN  Careful what you say now.

PETER  She punched me!

RYAN  Do you need some ice for that?

PETER  What? No I don't need—

RYAN  Then close the door on your way out.
    *Peter leaves.*
  The fuck was that?

ASH  Go home Ryan.

RYAN  Where the hell were you? You can't just disappear and appear and smack a guy in the face like that, they have a place for people who do that—it's called prison.
    *Ash looks to the puppet.*

ASH  What's your name?

ROBIN  Peter. His name's Peter.

ASH  Hey kid what's your name?

ROBIN  Ash.
    *The wolf growls.*

RYAN  Ash, lay off, you're scaring him.

*Ash crouches down to meet the puppet's eyes.*
*The wolf growls.*

ASH  You okay over there?

*The wolf growls, lunges at Ash.*
*Ash catches his arms. Gentle but firm, like a coach guiding a punch.*
*But the boy's fist is odd.*
*His arms are weird too. And his chest, legs . . . face.*
*Behind the puppet, Ash is surprised to find Wolf's eyes.*

. . .

*Wolf's growls come to an abrupt, equally surprised stop.*
*Ash removes the puppet from between them,*
*and stands up to meet Wolf.*
*A mix of the familiar with the terribly unexpected.*

Huh.

*Ash looks to the puppet, to the wolf, to the puppet—*
*Wolf snatches the puppet back.*

. . .

*HOOOOOOOOOOWWWWWWWWL!*

. . .

*Wolf recovers.*

WOLF  Contrary to popular belief, wolves do not howl at the full moon any more often than at other shapes of the moon. They do, however, howl more during the sunset and sunrise—during the change of light.

*Light changes.*


## [NIGHT]


ROBIN  Done. Took two hours, five stories, three repeats, but the kid is finally asleep. None of it helped, I don't think. He just exhausted himself, crying. But hey, it's done, we finally have a sleeping child in our child-sleeping bed. Wanna come see? I keep having this urge to go peek at him sleeping. Is that super predatory or super parental? Ash. Ash? Hey, you awake?

ASH  It's late.

ROBIN  No it's not. Come let's go look at him, kids are great when they're conked out.

You know you want to . . .

ASH  I don't.

ROBIN  Okay I know you're still, not on board with this, but he's here now. He'll know if you're not on board, he'll know if you don't like him. Please like him. Or just pretend-like him. Pretend will become present, present will become past, and it'll be like you've known and loved him all your life.

Ash, come on. Talk to me.

ASH  I don't want to talk right now.

ROBIN  Then when? When do you wanna talk about it, when he goes to college? Cuz that's gonna come around real—

ASH  Oh My God Robin will you Let Me Sleep.

ROBIN  I just think we should talk. While he is asleep.

ASH  It didn't cross your mind to "talk" before you went and bought a kid off Facebook?

ROBIN  Yahoo. And we did talk—

ASH  And I said no.

ROBIN  You said you would think about it.

ASH  Robs, I really don't want to deal with this right now.

ROBIN  When do you ever want to deal with anything?

I'm so happy about this, Ash. I really am.

I'm sorry I couldn't wait for you to be done thinking about it,

for someone's unaffordable sperm to catch my sad shriveled eggs

but right now there's a child, in our house, can we please just be grown-ups about this?

ASH  This is grown-up? Getting a child from Yahoo? You're pissed cuz I won't deal with you wanting to get a child from Yahoo?

ROBIN  I know it wasn't the / best way to go about it but—

ASH  Like a pet, like some kind of second-hand toy.

I have my pro debut in a couple months, I'm stressed the fuck out, and then this—

So I won't sacrifice my whole life and body to your needs, I'm the asshole.

ROBIN  I never asked you / to sacrifice—

ASH  No. You didn't ask. You just went and did and reported.

ROBIN  Okay I fucked up.

He was there.

And nobody wanted him.

You were thinking, for so long,

and I kept—I was lingering at the toy aisles,

watched back-to-back episodes of *Power Rangers*,

shy Korean boy with beautiful smile eager to please loves *Power Rangers*, the posting said,

   I couldn't stop reading his post. I've memorized that post.

   And I just had to, if nothing else, I had to get him off the internet.

   I called them to see, just to see if he was still there,

   but he was still there and they were so, quick, everything happened so fast and—

   I fucked up. I'm sorry. Be mad at me, not at him.

ASH   I'm not mad at him I don't know him Robin I can't feel stuff for a stranger overnight.

ROBIN   I know.

ASH   I can't develop an attachment to someone just cuz he lives in my house now.

   I've barely developed an attachment to myself.

ROBIN   Not asking you to feel anything overnight. I'm asking you to come look at a sleeping child with me. That is all I ask.

ASH   Fine.

ROBIN   Yes? Yes! Okay but you have to be real quiet, you have no idea how hard it was to—

   *(off Ash's look)* We go.

> WOLF   Wolves use different locations for rest.

ASH   This is the weirdest stupidest—

ROBIN   Shhh...

> WOLF   Dens are usually constructed for pups,
>    to protect them from natural dangers of the wild.

ASH   I'm not gonna fall in love with him over a—

ROBIN   Ash shut up you're gonna wake him. Isn't he great?

ASH   Yeah.

> WOLF   Wolves are very territorial.

   *Wolf squeezes a bottle of water on the puppet.*

ROBIN   Wait what is this smell?

ASH   What smell?

ROBIN   It's like—

> WOLF   And so the wolf uses scent to mark territory.

ASH  Oh wow.

ROBIN  I've never seen it actually happen before. I mean, in real time, happening before me.

> WOLF  However, captive wolves have even been known to urinate in strange places, such as ponds and streams—to confuse potential enemies.

ROBIN  Should we wake him up? I mean we can't let him sleep like this? Do people just let their kids sleep in pee?

ASH  I don't think most people know cuz most people don't spy on their kids while they are sleeping.

ROBIN  Well I did, and now I know, and now I'm gonna be the mom who knew and left her kid to roll around in his own pee.

ASH  Have fun Mom. I'm going to bed.

> *Ash leaves.*

## [DAILY LIFE]

WOLF  The habitats of wolves can be found in areas that you may not ever imagine them surviving. In the arctic, in the swamps, deserts, caves . . . kitchens.

> *A familiar kitchen/dining area.*
>
> *Ash runs in from their morning run, gulps some water.*

Give them a place to eat, a place to play, and a place to rest and any wolf pack will be okay.

> *Ryan enters with his earphones in. Same space, different place.*
>
> *Ash leaves to take a shower.*
>
> *Ryan gets bacon and eggs from fridge, gets his morning routine going.*
>
> *Phone rings. Ryan clicks earphones.*

RYAN  Mom! Hold up.

> *Robin enters, carrying her purse.*

ROBIN  Ash? Ash, are you back?

> *Ryan spits to basin, runs water, wipes mouth.*

RYAN  Good morning, how you doing?

ROBIN  I'm getting some things for breakfast. Wait to eat, okay?

> *Robin gets Post-it, writes a message for Ash.*

RYAN  Yeah I saw him. Was there almost all night.

I don't know, he looks like what Asian kids look like, like
an Asian kid.

Nah, way older. Six.

*Peter enters.*

*Same space, different place.*

*Gets a saucepan, fills it with water, puts it on stovetop. Opens fridge, looks.*

PETER  Katie? Katie, where'd you put the milk?

RYAN  Of course it's insane. Tried what I could, but you know,
stubborn Robin.

*Robin sticks note on fridge.*

*Robin leaves.*

*Peter closes fridge, opens freezer, looks.*

PETER  No, not in the freezer either.

RYAN  Ha, no. She didn't know either. She thought he was three.
She got punked, you know, what you gonna expect from the internet.

PETER  It's alright I got it, but it's okay to mix formula
with breastfeeding? Yeh, okay.

RYAN  No, no, we didn't press it with the father.

*Peter makes the baby formula by mixing powder with cold water and sticking
bottle in the pot of water as it gets heated (it's wrong, but it's how he does it).*

PETER  Honey, do you have the email, of those people
that you found?

RYAN  There was no time to ask, the kid was crying like a siren.

PETER  I thought we should check in to see—

RYAN  Yes he was crying—

PETER  No I'm not being clingy.

RYAN  it's a new house with new people,

PETER  I just wanted to check in to—

RYAN  everything was blue and—

PETER  Because you never told me they were—

RYAN  Listen Mom why don't you talk to her yourself—

PETER  It's okay. Never mind.

RYAN  Does she even know you know that they adopted?

PETER  I said never mind.

RYAN  Jesus—

PETER  Katie it's fine it was just a question, okay?

*Peter disappears to the unseen Katie.*

RYAN  You guys have some issues to sort out. Just give her a call.

　　　　I feel like the fucking Wimbledon ball boy running back
　　　　and forth between you two.

　　*Ryan disappears with bacon and eggs and phone.*
　　　　*Wolf and puppet sit at kitchen table.*
　　　　*Ash, back in kitchen after a shower.*
　　　　*Ash gets out bowl, spoon, cereal . . .*
　　　　*catches Wolf sitting, staring at them.*
　　　　*Freeze.*
　　　　*A weird form of silent showdown.*

ASH　Robs? Robin you up?

　　*Puppet and Wolf continue to stare at Ash.*
　　　　*Ash finds Post-it, chucks it in the trash.*
　　　　*Ash pours themself some cereal, milk.*
　　　　*Puppet and Wolf continue to stare at Ash.*
　　　　*Ash stares back for a while.*
　　　　*Then they find another bowl, spoon, get two boxes of cereal.*

　　　　Want some? We got Lucky Pops and . . . Organic Multigrain
　　Squares, from Kashi.

　　*Puppet and Wolf continue to stare at Ash.*

　　　　Have a preference?

　　*Puppet and Wolf continue to stare at Ash.*
　　　　*Ash pours both kinds into the bowl.*
　　　　*Hands the breakfast to the kid.*
　　　　*Back to reading. Ash eats.*
　　　　*Wolf picks up a spoon.*

　　　　You're a lefty, huh?

　　*Wolf changes the spoon to his right hand.*

　　　　Me too.

　　*Ash holds up their spoon. In their left hand.*

　　　　It's the cooler hand. No one can see it coming.

　　*Cautiously, Wolf changes back to left hand.*
　　　　*They eat.*

WOLF　Jeenu.

ASH　Huh?

WOLF　My name.

ASH　Jeenu.

　　*Puppet nods.*
　　　　*Enter Ryan. He puts empty plate and fork into sink, rinses etc.*

RYAN  Their name is Ash, mom. They've been married to Robs for—

        I really wish you'd get over this.

  *Robin with groceries.*

ROBIN  Good morning! Who's up for some Eggs Florentine, huh?

ASH  I'm good.

ROBIN  Oh. You didn't get my note?

ASH  I did.

ROBIN  Oh.

      RYAN  Alright. I'll tell her you said so.

ROBIN  Pete?

  *Wolf and puppet stop eating cereal.*

    *Looks to Ash. Looks to Robin.*

  *Peter rushes in.*

           PETER  Oh fuck me.

      RYAN  Okay. I won't.

*Peter squirts the bottle contents on his wrist to check temperature. It's hot. Ow.*

           PETER  Ow.

ROBIN  That's okay, maybe tomorrow then.

  *Ding! Like the end of a round of boxing.*


## [PLAY-FIGHT]


WOLF  Wolf packs rarely succeed in adopting other wolves into their fold.

RYAN  Chin down, kid,

WOLF  Discovered loners are typically killed,

RYAN  you're all open.

WOLF  eviscerated.

  *Ryan taps puppet on cheek*

RYAN  See? And then you're out. Guard up. Guard up.

  *Wolf's guard is up.*

                WOLF  A new wolf will be challenged to fight to secure a place in the hierarchy,

RYAN  Uh uh, no kicking buddy, just the fists one two one two.

                WOLF  and will undoubtedly shift the order of things,

ROBIN  Easy Ryan.

RYAN  Guard up!

    *Taps puppet in the face, Wolf growls.*

ROBIN  Okay that's enough.

RYAN  He needs to be a little more assertive.

ROBIN  He needs to not be punched in the face is what he needs. Come here, you okay? Pete?

RYAN  He's fine. You really shouldn't coddle him Robin.

ROBIN  He's six.

RYAN  Robs, it's like a jungle out there for boys like him. We gotta prep little Petie, for when he's out there, gotta stand up for himself like one of Uncle Ryan's boys, right Pete?

ASH  Jeenu.

ROBIN  What's that?

ASH  Name's not Pete. It's Jeenu.

ROBIN  How'd you know?

ASH  He said his name was Jeenu.

ROBIN  He said that?

RYAN  It speaks!

ROBIN  The papers didn't say—

ASH  Yehwell, the papers are wrong.

ROBIN  Hey wait, when? What else did he say?

ASH  Nothing, I asked if he wanted cereal, he said his name was Jeenu, I said cool and we ate some cereal.

RYAN  Alright round two, ding, round's started, kid, guard up, guard up.

ROBIN  Why didn't you tell me?

ASH  Thought you knew.

ROBIN  Why? Why would I go on calling him not his name if I knew that wasn't what he—

ASH  Okay, chill, now we know.

ROBIN  United front, Ash, we agreed on united front—

ASH  I don't even know what that is, so, no, we didn't agree on—

    *Another punch to the face, the puppet growls.*

ROBIN  Ryan what is the matter with you?

    *Robin holds the puppet.*

      *Wolf growls, circles Ryan.*

RYAN  Hey you're the one who asked me for the favor.

               WOLF  lay low.

ROBIN   Okay well you suck at this.

RYAN   Some of these kids, you just gotta knock 'em down to get them out of their shells, okay? Just send him over to the club with Ash.

ROBIN   Ha, yeah that's not happening.

WOLF   Observe, calculate,

RYAN   It's not good for him to have his mom all over his face.

WOLF   we know to wait for the time to . . .

*Wolf leaps on Ryan.*

RYAN   OWW! You little shit you little fucking little shit.

*Wolf continues to beat up Ryan, in a small vicious way that animals do.*

ROBIN   Pete—Jeenu. That is not nice, you don't ambush people when they are not ready, / that is not what—

RYAN   Kid's got a little asshole behind all the pussy.

ROBIN   Ryan please. Jeenu did you hear what I said? Look at me please, if you want to throw a punch, train at the gym and follow the rules. We are not animals.

WOLF   I'm a wolf.

ROBIN   Can you apologize? Say I'm sorry? Pete—Jeenu. It's not okay to hurt people like how you just hurt Uncle Ryan.

WOLF   I'm a lone wolf.

ROBIN   Pet—fu—Sorry. Jeenu. Look at me please?

WOLF   I'm a lone wolf I have to protect myself.

ROBIN   Hello? Anyone there?

*Wolf howls. Attacks Robin.*

*Ryan holds puppet. Wolf howls and growls.*

RYAN   That's got to not ever happen again, alright?

ROBIN   Ryan! Turn it off.

RYAN   You don't lay a finger on your mom, do you understand me, I asked you a question.

ROBIN   He's six. There's a limit to the damage he can do.

RYAN   He's six. You keep saying that like it's like some safety net.

*Ryan puts him down.*

ROBIN   Safety net from what? No one is falling, Ryan.

RYAN   I'm telling you there are some seriously fucked-up six-year-old boys out there, okay?

*Ash walks up to Wolf.*

*Wolf slugs at them but they jump back.*

ASH Keep that up you'll be wrung out by round two. Right foot forward.
No, right foot, cuz you're a southpaw, lefty right? Like that.

*Ash places Wolf's right foot in front and turns his body.*

*He slugs again and Ash jumps back.*

Uh uh, not yet. Gotta lay low, lay low,
observe, calculate.

WOLF Observe, calculate!

*Somehow the puppet is gone.*

ASH Cuz you don't know how they gonna fight, do you?
Light on your feet, scouting for an in, right? Up up up.

*Ash jump-jump-jumps lightly.*

*Wolf emulates.*

Good, that's very good,
right foot forward so you got the distance to run back when you need to—
keep jumping gotta keep light,
jump jump, left hand at your ear like you're on the phone, hello?

JEENU Hello.

ASH That's right. One two, one two, good. One two, one two, good good.
Okay but if you're fighting against orthodox, right handers,
they're gonna be coming fast, cuz the distance is shorter,
see, comes at you real fast—
So what do you do? Side step, like this, one two shift, one two shift, right?
Okay one two shift, one two . . .

*Wolf watches, mesmerized.*

WOLF Pups of a pack will "play-fight" with each other, forming a hierarchy at the kids' tables.
The hierarchy will shift with the development of the pup, as he matures into a grownup wolf, as a member of the pack.

## [FINDING FOOTING]

*Phone rings. Machine click.*

RYAN Thank you for calling Ryan's Den Boxing Club the official boxing club of the cub. Our office is currently closed. Please leave a message after the beep or call back during our official business hours.

PETER  Hi, this is Peter Hunt, I don't know if you remember me, we met briefly when I dropped off Junior at your house. Or, rather, not sure if it was your, anyway—

I wanted to thank you for being there, to help out with the negotiations that night,

I think we all could have handled the situation a little better, me included, so.

I do realize that we had agreed that there would be no contact from our end but,

well that is why I didn't call to the house, or attempt to reach them.

I had some concerns, regarding—I found your card, you know that you gave me and so.

I had some questions regarding Junior's adjustments, and well, quite frankly

how he is responding to having a, two moms.

And so I thought I would call to see, to um, reach out to you, since we did meet before.

Again, Peter Hunt, you can reach me at this number. Thank you.

*During message: Ryan and Ash in the ring.*

RYAN  Alright stop. What the hell, Ash.

ASH  Fuhhhhhck.

RYAN  We're weeks away from the fight, you can't afford to shit away time like this.

ASH  Sorry. A little off. A little off today.

RYAN  It's not—

ASH  What.

RYAN  It's not just today.

ASH  Sorry. I'm distracted.

RYAN  You a smarts boxer not a power boxer, gotta keep your head in the ring. Hundred and ten percent.

ASH  Mm hmm.

RYAN  Tommy Tavarez has never been in a ring with a southpaw. He's got no clue how to fight you, Ash. He'll see that left hook and be like woah, what? Bam down. We really have a chance at winning your debut. Real prize money. Ker-ching right?

ASH  Yeh yeh.

RYAN  Ash.

ASH  Mm?

RYAN   Are you with me?

ASH   Sorry. Yes. God, I'm just all over the place.

RYAN   Do I have to worry?

    *Ash shrugs.*

    How's stuff at home.

ASH   You know. Robs is insane busy, even with the maternity leave from her work,

    there's the school stuff, the shrink stuff, and she's trying to get him into yoga.

    He's so quiet most times but then we're getting calls about broken windows, goldfish bowls, other kids' noses . . . The other day we got called in cuz he glued his eyes shut with bubble gum.

    He's something, the kid.

RYAN   Yeh, he's a bit not so ordinary.

ASH   He's a freak a bit, but smart, I think. They said he's at least two grade levels above his age group in comprehension and fine motor skills, as well as—

    *Ash laughs.*

RYAN   What?

ASH   I was just thinking, that time when you tried to teach him boxing, he beat the crap outta you?

    He's not a natural by any means, not what I'm saying, he's definitely not the build, a little demented—

    He—kinda reminds me of when I was a kid. I was kinda demented.

RYAN   Was?

ASH   Yeah shut the fuck up.

RYAN   It's a compliment. I like my fighters slightly deranged. Feral. Grr.

ASH   Yup.

RYAN   But in the ring, right? Be feral in the ring. Gotta be ferally focused, k? Grr.

ASH   You know, I was thinking.

RYAN   ?

ASH   No it's just, there's so much going on, I feel so ungrounded.

RYAN   I can see that, that's why I'm / saying you gotta—

ASH   and I'm wondering if we should, cancel.

RYAN   Cancel.

ASH   Or, postpone.

RYAN   —

ASH  I know I know I know, it was real hard to get this bout, and I appreciate everything you've done to make shit happen, but you told me to tell you if I feel like I'm not ready and you know, I feel like—

RYAN  You are.

ASH  Come on, I'm a mess, Ry.

RYAN  So you wanna cancel.

ASH  Or postpone, if we / can.

RYAN  No. Don't do this. You are not doing this to me.

ASH  To you? What am I doing to you? It's my ass getting whupped up there if I'm not ready.

RYAN  So Be Ready! Be fucking ready!

Do you understand—your career, should you choose to have it, could change the game forever—

ASH  What if I am not interested in changing—

RYAN  What if it's not all about you or what you are fucking interested in?

You wanted this. You wanted to fight a fucking dude for your pro debut that you could've killed two years ago fighting a chick—You wanted this, I said yes to you I made that happen I have been making it happen five years now. Look. I know I was never gonna top it like you are gonna top it and I am—Happy to be in your shadow, in your corner, I've been there, haven't I?

You're not gonna throw in the towel on our five years.

Ash.

ASH  Okay.

RYAN  Cancel, postpone, can't be saying shit like that.

ASH  Alright.

RYAN  We're a team. One boat. What you do is what I've done.

ASH  Yeah. Yeah okay. I get it. Sorry.

> *Back to the ring.*
> *Phone rings.*
> *Machine click.*

RYAN  Thank you for calling Ryan's Den Boxing Club the official boxing club of the cub. Our office is currently closed. Please leave a message after the beep or call back during our official business hours.

PETER  Ryan, hi this is Peter,

I just wondered if you got my message . . . s.

I don't want to hound you, if that's not what you're about

but I just wanted to make sure I'm calling the right guy,

or that I'm getting through, you might have a, unstable intern situation or.

I don't know why I said that.

Anyway, I'd really love an update of any kind. On Junior. Pete.

Thanks. Bye.

*Click.*

WOLF Peters tend to worry too much. This is because he doesn't understand.


## [DAILY LIFE 2]

*A familiar kitchen/dining area.*

WOLF . . . wolves are an extremely adaptable species. They can survive in the arctic, in the swamps, deserts, caves . . . kitchens.

*Ash runs in from morning run, gulps some water, earphones in.*

You get the picture.

*Ryan enters, brushing teeth, earphones in.*

*Ash goes to shower.*

*Ryan gets bacon and eggs from fridge, frying pan on stovetop.*

*Phone rings.*

RYAN Mom!

Good morning to you too.

Oh, um, haven't been over there for a while. Been busy.

I told you, our club's first pro bout—

ROBIN Ash? Wait to eat, okay?

*Robin leaves.*

RYAN No Mom, I did tell you, but whatever.

Alright, well I'll keep telling you till you remember,

I'm nothing if I don't keep you from going senile.

Whatever, you love me.

*Peter enters.*

*Same space, different place.*

*Peter gets a saucepan, fills it with water, puts it on stovetop*

*Opens fridge, looks.*

PETER Oh come on. Seriously?

RYAN He's fine, I guess. She's fine. They're all fine, no one's burned the house down just yet.

*Peter opens freezer, looks.*

PETER  Katie, we're out again.

*Slams both.*

RYAN  You're just waiting for something to go wrong so you can wag your finger at them.

PETER  Yes we are.

RYAN  I'm kidding!

PETER  You know honey, if you don't wanna do something, just don't start it?

RYAN  Mom it was a joke, okay?

PETER  I really don't give a shit about formula or breast milk, just pick one and commit to it you know? Can we do that? Can we fucking commit to one fucking thing, for a change?

RYAN  Geez, lighten up a little.

PETER  Yeh well it's hard for me too, for us both okay?

RYAN  They're managing fine, she got some kind of maternity leave, it's stupid if you ask me.

PETER  Seriously?

RYAN  Well because the boy is six! I don't see other moms with six-year-olds getting paid to stay home?

PETER  Don't talk to me like that. Don't fucking, yeh? Really?

RYAN  Yeah, he's still wetting his bed, apparently, kid's got issues.

PETER  Okay well I'm sorry but fucking fuck fuck fuckitty fucking fuckfuckfuck.

RYAN  I did not! You're remembering wrong, I didn't.

PETER  You want to do this? Let's do this.

RYAN  Okay that's enough, fun is over.

*Ryan disappears with bacon and eggs and phone.*

*Peter leaves.*

*Wolf and puppet sit at kitchen table.*

*Ash gets out two bowls, two spoons, milk . . .*

*And the two boxes of cereal.*

ASH  Pops? Kashi?

*Puppet and Wolf shrug.*

*Ash pours the cereal, milk, hands one bowl to Wolf.*

*Sits on the counter, opens something to read. They eat.*

*Wolf pulls out something to read too. Maybe Pinocchio.*
*He eats. Ash notices his little book. Maybe Ash finds it funny.*
*Wolf and puppet look up at them. Did he do something wrong?*
*Ash goes back to their reading.*
*Wolf continues to look at them.*

WOLF Where do you go every morning?

ASH Running.

WOLF From?

ASH What do you mean?

WOLF What are you running from?

ASH Nothing, I'm just running. Sometimes around the park, sometimes down the pier.

WOLF Why?

ASH Just, I don't know. It's a nice way to start a day. My ritual, you know?

WOLF Can I come with?

ASH Oh. Um. Well, it's kind of a solo thing, buddy.
And I run very fast. And you'll have to get up very early.

WOLF I am always awake before you are.

ASH Yeah? Having trouble sleeping?

WOLF No. And I am fast. I am faster than you.

ASH We'll see about that tomorrow morning.

*Enter Ryan. He puts empty plate and fork into sink, rinses etc.*

RYAN Jeenu. It's Korean. It's a Korean name.
I don't know Mom, no one gives a shit whether he's bilingual or not.

*Robin enters, sees cereal party.*

ROBIN Oh come on.

ASH What.

ROBIN I said I was making pancakes.

ASH I can't do pancakes right now.

PETER Fuck this.

ROBIN Jeenu? Do you want—

RYAN God can we stop talking about this kid already, I'd think he had a platinum penis the way all of you gab on about him.

*Wolf and Puppet stop eating cereal.*
*Looks to Ash. Looks to Robin.*

ROBIN   That's okay, I'll make some for me.

    RYAN   What. I can say penis to my mom I'm a grown man.
Penis penis penis pe—
Hello? Mom?

      PETER   You make the formula. I'm going for a walk.

*Ding! Like the end of a round of boxing.*


## [SOMETIMES ALLIES]


    *Ryan's gym. Peter enters.*

RYAN   We're closing down for the weekend, sorry man. Oh.

PETER   Hi.

RYAN   Okay.

PETER   Nice space. It's very, spacious.

RYAN   You're the guy.

PETER   The guy. Who sold his kid on the internet. Yes. I am him.

RYAN   What do you want?

PETER   I just thought, you gave me your card. I left, um, on your machine.
You weren't responding to my messages.

RYAN   No cuz you're the guy who sold his kid on the internet.

PETER   Right.

RYAN   So what the fuck do you want?

PETER   I wanted, well, to get more diapers. Because we were running out
and Katie's not very future-oriented at the moment. And then I missed
my exit thinking about how Katie is not very future-oriented or hasn't
been ever really and I just kept driving, thinking about things like that.
And got here. So I thought I would come by. To see if you had gotten my
messages. Which you have.

    And so. Now.

    I'll, leave. Sorry.

    *Peter turns to leave.*

RYAN   Hey. What are you doing, man.

PETER   I don't know.

RYAN   You gotta stop. Can't leave me messages, can't come around like this,
it's not right.

PETER   I miss him. I miss him a lot.

RYAN   So then why did you do it?

PETER  I don't know. I was underslept, and Katie was crying all day, the baby was crying all day, I kept thinking something had to give, something had to change, and we changed the wrong thing. I think we changed the wrong thing. But if he's doing good. I have no right to miss him. I've had my chance I've had my run and I fucked it up I get that. But I just wanted to make sure that he is okay. Then I can move on, you know? I can just focus on my life and my family. Is he? Okay?

RYAN  Yeah. Sure. I mean, there are some issues, at school and stuff, like with windows, and goldfish bowls, he's apparently super smart, they're taking him to a shrink and yoga.

PETER  Yoga? He likes yoga?

RYAN  You know what, I don't know. If you wanna check up on the kid, I'm not that guy. He's not here.

PETER  I thought of going to the house but—

RYAN  Why didn't you?

PETER  I just need to know he's okay.

RYAN  Kid's got issues, it's gonna be bumpy but he's not your problem anymore.

PETER  He was never a problem. Are they treating him as a problem? He's aggressive sometimes, but it's just boys will be boys kind of thing, they don't understand, see this is what I'm talking about.

RYAN  Okay no don't talk about my family like you know them, you don't. They aren't treating him like anything that he is not and even if they are you do not have a say in any of this, do you understand?

PETER  How is he taking to you?

RYAN  What?

PETER  Does Junior, does he take to you? Listens?

RYAN  Sure, yeah.

PETER  And you, you are around a lot at the place, right? Do you, you get along with Junior?

RYAN  Peter. You did a shitty-ass thing and it is eating at you, I get it. Good news is, you lucked the fuck out in finding my sister. Kid is surrounded by people who want him to come out on top.

PETER  But you—

RYAN  I am around a lot at the place.

PETER  Okay. That's all I wanted to know.
          Okay. Thank you.

## [WHO'S YOUR FAVORITE, MOMMY OR MOMMY?]

*Wolf shadow-boxing in his fantasy world.*
    *Puppet is chucked away somewhere else.*

WOLF  A new wolf will be challenged to fight, for his place in the order of things.

And the omega wolves of the pack (like dumbass Ryan) will feel threatened.

The omega wolves (like dumbass Ryan) will do anything to put the new wolf in his place.

    *Ash walks by, and sees.*

    *Wolf notices Ash but pretends to not notice.*

But the new wolf will put up a great fight. Because the wolf is a fighter.

> Up, up, up, he is light on his feet, scouting for an in.
>
> Super on the phone, talking on the phone.
>
> I'm like, hello? That's right, hello.

    *Robin walks in on the secret intimacy.*

ROBIN  Jeenu! In a gym, with gloves and a grown-up, okay? Come on, do you have your yoga things ready?

    *Wolf immediately turns back to Puppet.*

ASH  Why yoga?

ROBIN  Oh, hey babe, didn't see you there. He likes it.

ASH  Six-year-old boys don't do yoga, usually.

ROBIN  Well. He does, right Jeenu.

> WOLF  Wolves hate yoga.

ROBIN  I'm just waving a stick in the dark here, see if I can strike something. If nothing else, it's a nice bonding event for us, right champ?

> WOLF  Wolves hate yoga.

ROBIN  I'd ask you to come, but you're not into that sort of—

ASH  Yeh, I can't be seen with my ass in the public air.

ROBIN  We're gonna go to In-N-Out later if you wanted to come—

ASH  God no, Ryan would kill me, still have three pounds to lose before the fight next week.

ROBIN  Yeah, how is all that going?

ASH  Fine. It's fine.

ROBIN  Are you feeling—

ASH  It's fine. Anyways, I was on my way to the club so. You guys have fun.

ROBIN  See you later.

WOLF  Can I go to the club with Ash?

ROBIN  Oh. But we were gonna go to In-N-Out after, remember? You don't wanna do that?

ASH  I can take him, I don't mind. If you're coming with me, be ready in two minutes cuz I'm late.

*Wolf and Puppet run off.*

ROBIN  I mean, it's just exercise, but if you don't want to, that's fine, I guess. I'm sure I can get a refund for the rest of the sessions.

ASH  Okay.

ROBIN  Okay.

ASH  Are you? Okay?

ROBIN  I'm fine.

ASH  I can't do the passive-aggressive nodding decoding, you know that right? Shoot straight, Robs.

ROBIN  No it's fine. I'm sorry.

ASH  Cool . . . Jeenu? Tick-tock tick-tock kid let's go!

I'm gonna go start the car, bring him out when's he ready?

ROBIN  Okay actually no. I can't do this, I feel like the fucking maid, popping around doing chores while you're the one getting any kind of real Anything out of him, I barely know the sound of his voice, until you're there, and he's all like, hi my name is not the name you thought it was and you're like cool, okay, and you "forget" to tell me, just like you "forget" that I told you I wanted to make breakfast for us and you "forget" I asked you to wait till I got back and you "forget" to make it to the appointments with Dr. Schneider and so Jeenu thinks I'm the evil boring mom while you're the cool boxing mom. Meanwhile you don't do the laundry you don't do the groceries you don't pick up his tens of thousands of tiny toys you keep loading down on him every time you go for a "hangout" at IKEA, while you conveniently forget things that make you the not-cool mom.

ASH  Okay.

ROBIN  No! Not okay. It's not fair to think like this, if he's good with you, and happy, I should be happy too but I'm not. If he hates yoga and likes to punch people I have to step back and let him be him and be proud but I don't know how to not want the things I want first.

ASH  What do you want.

ROBIN  A child.

ASH  He is one.

ROBIN  Or someone who eats some meals of the week with me or I don't know, looks my way and talks to me about things they are feeling and maybe wants to go to yoga with me because my wife clearly can't be doing any of—

ASH  Don't make this about me, Robs.

ROBIN  You didn't even want him in the first place.

ASH  Okay wow that helps nothing. This is, I can't. I have to go I'm late. Take him to yoga.

ROBIN  You can't just leave you promised Jeenu you would take him to the club—

ASH  Robin Oh my god!

WOLF  Wolves do not need yoga.

ROBIN  Hey you. When d'you sneak back. You have your jacket?

*Puppet nods.*

ASH  I have to go.

ROBIN  Make sure he keeps his jacket on. He's had a little cough lately, I've noticed.

*Ash and Wolf leave.*

*Ash comes back.*

ASH  You do not get to blame this on me, sit in your sad corner and make me feel bad. You fucked me up. I'm about to go pro, Robin, I have a shot at being something real. But this thing this person is taking over my head space my life space, I have a six-year-old with me on my morning run which is now a walk and, Fuck I like it I actually love it and it is really not a great time to be loving anything else but the ring, but I could give two shits about the ring and this has never happened before and it's scary and I am not ready and it's your fault and so I hate you.

ROBIN  I didn't know you felt that way.

ASH  Me neither.

ROBIN  I deserve it. I guess.

ASH  No you don't.

ROBIN  No I don't.

ASH  I want to win.

ROBIN  You will.

ASH  At all of it. I want to win at all of it—the boxing, the mom thing, the dad thing. The becoming the world champion of everything thing. The wife thing.

ROBIN  I know.

*Robin and Ash try to think of next correct thing to say.*

*HOOOOONNNNNKKK.*

Is that our child?

ASH  I should go.

ROBIN  Yes.

*HOOOOONNNNNKKK*

Oh woah boy's serious.

ASH  Jeenu I'm coming stop honking the—

*HOOOOONNNNNKKK.*

Okay I'm gonna—

ROBIN  Go. We can talk more—

ASH  Later, when we get / back from—

ROBIN  Yeah. Okay. Bye.

*Moment of indecisive, something, do we want to, hug? Kiss?*

*What do you do when you're still kind of in a fight but almost resolved but your kid is honking a horn?*

*Sound of car starting.*

ASH  The fuck.

ROBIN  Jeenu!

*They run out.*

You left the keys with / him? What is wrong with you?

ASH  I'm gonna kill him I'm gonna fucking kill him!

*Offstage.*

Jeenu! In the passenger seat. NOW. Move over or I'm taking you to yoga.

ROBIN  Seriously? We're making yoga the punishment?

WOLF  I can't be seen with my ass in the public air.

*Reluctant scuffling.*

ASH  Hey, whatever works.

*Car door open and shut.*

*Windows roll down.*

ROBIN  Okay, well, I'll see you guys later.

ASH  Wanna come with?

ROBIN  For real? You won't be distracted?

ASH  Yeah, but he's pretty cute in his gear. We got some yoga-ey stuff in the club too if you still wanted—

ROBIN  You sure? Okay. Okay then. Let me get my stuff.

ASH  Be quick tho, I'm late!

*Robin re-enters.*

*Has a moment of quiet happiness.*
*Gathers her stuff.*
*HONK.*

ROBIN  Coming!

*Car rolling out driveway.*

PETER'S VOICEMAIL  (*voice of a six-year-old boy*) This is Peter Hunt's phone. Peter is right now unavailable to pick up. Goodbye. (*inaudible sounds of a side-coaching adult*) Oh, leave a message please. Goodbye. BEEP.

RYAN  Hey, it's Ryan. Hope you got home okay the other day.

I didn't mean to chew you out like that, I just get really protective where my family is concerned.

I wanted to let you know, the boy's started at our club, it's looking good.

Uh, and if you give me your email I could send you some pictures of him in his gear.

Took some with my phone. It's cute.

He's really taking to me, and we had some cute moments.

So, don't worry so much. Kid's gonna be fine.


## [GO PRO]

*A boxing ring.*

RING ANNOUNCER (WOLF)  Ladies and gentlemen, introducing in the red corner with black and white trunks Tommy Tavarez! And in the blue corner, gold trunks, the challenger, Ash Michaels!

RYAN  You nervous?

ASH  No.

RYAN  Don't be nervous.

ASH  I'm not.

RADIO GUY (ALSO WOLF)  Ash Michaels, five foot five, hundred and forty-seven pounds at 26 years old,

ROBIN  Woohoo!!! That's my wife!!!

RADIO GUY  facing Tommy "The Tiger" Tavarez, towering over Michaels at five foot nine—

RYAN  Don't rush it, pacing!

RING ANNOUNCER  Round Number One!

*Ding.*

ROBIN  Jeenu, can you see?

　　　　　WOLF  The wolf has a 250-degree visual range.

RYAN  Calm and steady Ash you got this.

RADIO GUY  Nice left to the body by Michaels.

RYAN  Good! Stay focused, three two three. Three two three.

ROBIN  Get him in the balls! Woot woot!

RADIO GUY  Surprising speed from the rookie.

*Ding.*

RYAN  How you doing?

ASH  Good.

ROBIN  Having fun?

　　　　　WOLF  The wolf will use their paws and cunning to eviscerate the prey. *(GROWL)*

ROBIN  No no, come here. We can go say hi after fourteen more dings.

RYAN  You're doing great. Stay focused okay?

ASH  Mmmkay.

*Ding.*

RADIO GUY  Round Two!

ROBIN  Alright baby now kick some ass kick some ass up in there!

RADIO GUY  Tavarez starts with a strong right cross—

ROBIN  WE LOVE YOU ASH MICHAELS!

　　　　　WOLF  Observe, calculate!

ROBIN  Jeenu, wanna cheer with? Come on, cheer with me so they can hear us.

RYAN  That's good, play it cool Ash!

ROBIN  On three, we love you Ash Michaels, ready?

　　　　　WOLF  The wolf is always ready.

ROBIN  One two three—

ROBIN / WOLF

We love you Ash Michaels! We love you Ash Michaels! We love—

RYAN / ROBIN / WOLF

YES!

RADIO GUY  Michaels scores a strong left!

RYAN / ROBIN / WOLF

Yes yes!

RADIO GUY   Series of blows to the body and—

> *Ding.*

                         WOLF   Wolves know how to fight!

RYAN   How you doing?

ASH   Good.

RYAN   Good? That was fucking excellent.

                         WOLF   Wolves know how to fight!

> *Ding.*

     ROBIN   No no, Jeenu. Gotta wait for six more rounds.

                         WOLF   Wolves know how to fight!

     ROBIN   Okay you know what maybe we can move up.

RYAN   Move back move back come on reset—

     ROBIN   Wanna get closer?

RYAN   Keep distance—

     ROBIN   Wanna find a seat in the front?

                         WOLF   Wolves know how to fight!

     ROBIN   Okay let's move closer. Come on.

> *Ding.*

RYAN   Don't let him lead.

     ROBIN   Jeenu!

RYAN   You're getting sucked into his pace. Don't get sucked into his pace—

     ROBIN   Hey Jeenu slow down wait for me.

> *Ding.*

                         WOLF   Wolves don't wait for you.

RADIO GUY   Power cross to the body! The Mexican tiger is bringing it, a narrow miss.

RYAN   Slow and steady, slow—

     ROBIN   Wanna cheer again?

     WOLF   Yes please.

RYAN   Breathe! Three two three—

     ROBIN   Okay on three. One two three,

     ROBIN / WOLF   We love you Ash Michaels!

RADIO GUY   Michaels backed into a corner—

     ROBIN   We love you Ash Michaels!

RYAN   Keep breathing baby—

     ROBIN   No!

RADIO GUY   The rookie takes a hook to the left.

RYAN   Geroff the ropes get the fuck—

ROBIN  Come on Ash, we're right here, we're / all here for you
    okay?

RYAN  Three two three. Three two three!

*Ding.*

RYAN  Spit spit how is it how are you doing—

ROBIN  They're okay, baby. It's just a game.

RYAN  *(to someone else)* Hey, Vaseline on the cut.

ROBIN  They're just playing.

*Ding.*

RYAN  Ash, get outta there!

ROBIN  Just a stupid little game—

RADIO GUY  Punishing combos to the body—

ROBIN  It's okay, they're gonna be just—

RADIO GUY  Tiger's giving back all / he took—

RYAN  Roll back!

ROBIN  No.

RYAN  Move!

RADIO GUY  And another blow to the head.

RYAN / ROBIN
NO!

ROBIN / RYAN / WOLF
One Two Three.

RYAN  GET UP.

ROBIN / RYAN / WOLF
Four.

WOLF  Get up.

ROBIN / RYAN / WOLF
Five Six.

ROBIN  Stay down.

ROBIN / RYAN / WOLF
Seven Eight.

RYAN  Yes!                                          ROBIN  Shit.

RADIO GUY  Michaels is up, looks like it's a go.

RYAN  Come on Ash! Shake it off, reboot.

ROBIN  It's alright baby, you got this.

RYAN  Stay up kid. Few more seconds.

WOLF  The hunt is impossible for the lone
    wolf.

> You're alone in the desert, just you
> and your prey.
> Wolves suck at being alone.

*Wolf escapes from Robin.*

   ROBIN Jeenu!

> WOLF Wolves need family.

   ROBIN Where are you going?

> WOLF There's a Korean saying, "Naturally,
> the arm folds inwards."

RYAN The fuck, time out! / Stop the clock Stop the clock Hey ref!

   ROBIN Jeenu! Jeenu, Ryan / stop him.

> WOLF Fight for your family, back your
> pack, over mostly anything and anyone
> else.

*Wolf has climbed onto the ring, Ash is distracted.*

   ROBIN Jeenu.

   ASH Wha—

*Bam. Ash falls.*

   *Ding ding ding.*

WOLF When a member of the pack is injured, they are groomed by the rest of the pack, for mental as well as physical support. But when the injured wolf has been separated, there is nothing to do but howl till they follow the sounds back home.

   *Howl.*


## [SHIFT]

*Wolf is asleep in Robin's lap with the puppet.*

*Robin speaks in an almost half whisper, words as lullaby.*

ROBIN And people are going crazy, leaping up, yelling Ash Michaels! Ash Michaels!

I go wait in the locker rooms, as usual.

Few minutes later the Newest Amateur Golden Gloves Champion struts their butt through the door, gloves still on, smelling like a dishcloth, and they're like, undo my gloves.

No kiss, not even hello, just, "undo my gloves Robs, undo my gloves".

My mind jumps, obviously, to worst possible scenario, what's wrong, what broke, on a scale of one to ten what is your level of pain—until their left hand opens up and I see, finally, the ring.

But then they are on their knee, holding up toward me the most beautiful piece of silver. And the noise melts away. The bout, the problems with my mom, and all that is left in my head is this giant neon sign that says You keep this person.

You keep this person. And so I did.

*Robin kisses Wolf on his head.*

I keep my people.

*Ryan and Ash enter.*

RYAN  C'mon Ash, that's the loss / talking, don't—

ROBIN  Guys.

ASH  Ryan, Go Home I'm tired, we can talk / some other—

ROBIN  Guys shht!!

RYAN  What.

ROBIN  He's sleeping.

RYAN  You got any beer?

ROBIN  Hushed tones, please. *(to Ash)* Honey come here, how are you?

ASH  I'm okay, what happened to you guys?

ROBIN  He wouldn't stop crying so I had to take him home. Are you okay? What did the doctors say?

ASH  I'm fine. It's fine. Four stitches.

RYAN  Exactly It Is Fine. It's just one bout nothing to freak out over.

ROBIN  Ry keep it down.

ASH  I'm not freaking out. I'm just saying, I just need space to think.

RYAN  About what?

ASH  About how I am going to subsist on the nothing I got for a fight I just KO'ed out on.

RYAN  You did not KO, they stopped the fight because that stupid kid hopped into the ring.

ROBIN  Okay time out, Ryan, take yourself home.

ASH  Come on Ry, we know I was losing that fight before what happened. If anything Jeenu probably saved me from getting my jaw shattered off my face.

RYAN  You don't know that. We could've turned it around—

ASH  I just need a break. For a few months maybe to figure stuff out.

RYAN  What like Robin's fake maternity leave?

ROBIN  Oh, go stick your dick in a trash can.

*Wolf stirs.*
*A moment of tension, will he wake up?*
*He doesn't.*

Okay so. This boy cried for two hours before he finally fell asleep, I love you both very much but if either of you wake this kid up I am going to have to kill you.

RYAN  Did you talk to him?

ROBIN  Talk to who?

RYAN  Did you get it through his head that you don't go hop into a ring when you feel like it, that you're supposed to respect other people's spaces.

ROBIN  Ryan keep your voice down.

RYAN  Robin raahhrararhaaaraahhhaararahh!

WOLF  A wolf will sleep only several minutes at a time.

ASH  Hey kid, how you doing? You okay?

WOLF  He is always alert for lurking opponents.

ROBIN  Hey sleepyhead.

RYAN  You wanna know why he keeps acting out? Wanna know why he fucked up your bout tonight Ash, and you know it was his fault you got nothing in your wallet right now, you wanna know why?

WOLF  The wolf stays quiet, but hears everything.

RYAN  It's cuz you guys are treating him like princess fucking Disney, someone's gotta show him some discipline.

ROBIN  Who? Who's gonna do that? The high school dropout second string nothing who's living off the gym his mother bought him?

RYAN  —

WOLF  A wolf never attacks without learning about his prey.

ASH  He has nothing to do with this, Ry. I want to take a break for myself, okay.

RYAN  Bullshit. You've got your head so far up his ass you can't even see right from wrong.

WOLF  But once the wolf attacks, it is not to wound or slow his target.

RYAN  At this point you are probably bad for the boy. Cuz what's he gonna learn from you, huh?

WOLF   He attacks for one purpose only—

RYAN   If it don't work out, spaz out, right?

WOLF   —to kill.

RYAN   Give up, throw in the—

*Wolf attacks Ryan.*

RYAN   ARGH!!!! ARRRRRRRRRRGH!

ASH   Jeenu!

RYAN   Okay you're done.

*Hoooooooooooowl.*

ROBIN   What the hell do you / think you are doing.

RYAN   Geroff me!

*Hoooooooooooowl.*

*Ryan takes Puppet and Wolf to the bathroom.*
*Ryan, Puppet, and Ash in the bathroom are depicted in shadows.*
*Sound of shower.*

RYAN   Cool down. Sit there and cool / down.

ASH   What the hell / are you doing?

*Something or someone is knocked down or thrown against door etc.*

RYAN   Ow! What the fuck Ash.

*Shower off.*

ASH   Out.

*No more howl.*

Hey buddy, you okay? Ryan was just playing, it's okay.

Come on let's get you to bed, yeah?

Hi-ho Hi-ho off to bed we go . . . No?

Okay. Scooch over a bit, I'm coming in.

Hey, it's so cool, you took a shower with your clothes on. Can I try?

*Sound of light shower.*

Ah . . . that's so nice. It's like being in the rain. C'mere. Come. It's okay.

*Ryan is back out onstage with Robin.*

RYAN   *(to Robin)* It worked. I'm just saying.

ROBIN   Don't you ever dare touch that child again.

RYAN   Robs. You're overreacting.

ROBIN   Ever.

RYAN   He needs discipline.

ROBIN   Not your call what he needs. No one asked you what he needs.

RYAN   I'm the only one that has the balls to be some semblance of a role
model, / the fuckturd jumped into the middle of an ongoing bout—

ROBIN   You aren't his, don't you dare call him—
    Get out of my house. Get out.

RYAN   Someone's got to be the man of this family.

ROBIN   Do whatever you need to do to get over yourself and your issues.
    But outside my house, away from my son. Pull some shit like that again
    and I promise you Ryan—

RYAN   What. What will you do? You gonna choose the eBay kid over your
    own brother?

ROBIN   Yes. Always yes.
    I choose my son. I choose my wife. Over you. Always.
    Don't make me choose.
        *Ryan leaves.*
            *Robin alone.*
            *She hears, coming from the bathroom:**

JEENU   Does it hurt?

ASH   A little. But I'll get over it.

JEENU   Are you mad at me?

ASH   No.
    I'm just glad you didn't get hurt. Cuz you could've gotten very seriously hurt.
    That would've made me really mad. And totally sad.

JEENU   —

ASH   Jeenu, can you promise me you won't do something like that again?

JEENU   But what if I said,
    I'm not what you think you see?

ASH   Hm?

JEENU   What if I said I am something else.

ASH   Like what?

JEENU   What if I said I am a wolf.

ASH   A wolf?

JEENU   Yes. And. Wolves hunt in packs. A wolf never lets their pack's asses
    be whupped.

ASH   I see.
    Whoever's in your pack must feel very safe.

JEENU   It's you.

ASH   What?! It's me? I had a whole wolf in my pack? A robin *and* a wolf? I
    gotta start myself a safari!

---

* The shadow of the puppet is now perhaps the shadow of Wolf, the actor.

JEENU   Robin is a robin too?

ASH   No. Robin is still human.

JEENU   But she is as pretty as a robin.

ASH   You think so?

JEENU   Sometimes. Don't tell her.

Do you know how to howl? Will you howl with me?

ASH   Sure.

JEENU   On three. One two three.

*They howl.*


## [DAILY LIFE 3]

*Robin enters, earphones in.*
*Same space, different place.*
*She sets table for three cereals.*

WOLF   Robins are a very delicate species. They don't like to fight.

They like to downward dog, and to tuck their tails under the sit bones.

They believe they can breathe through the tension. It's the truth, Robins love to breathe.

AUDIO MEDITATION (WOLF)   Take a cleansing breath in . . . and breathe out the tension in your body . . .

WOLF   See?

AUDIO MEDITATION   Feel relaxation beginning at the bottoms of your feet. It might feel like stepping into a warm / bathtub . . .

ROBIN   MOTHERFUCKER.

*Robin has stepped on a Power Ranger.*
*She pulls out her earphones and picks up enemy ranger.*
*(to Lego ranger)* I Hate You So Much.

*Ryan enters, brushing teeth.*
*Ryan spits, rinses his mouth. He calls a number.*

RYAN   Look, I don't know what your deal is with screening my calls, but it's not right, Ash.

We should talk. Call me back.

*Phone rings.*

ROBIN   Hello? Mom?

*Robin checks caller ID on phone. It is indeed Mom.*

*Ryan calls another number.*

How, I mean, good morning to you too.

*Peter enters, opens fridge and takes out a box of stale pizza.*

We were just about to eat, yeah.

Cereal, probably.

*Peter sprinkles some sugary cereal onto a slice of cold pizza and bites into his breakfast.*

I know, I tried, but Jeenu won't eat anything else. Oh, Jeenu is our— oh, you know, of course.

RYAN Robs. It's me again. You two have got to stop being dicks about this. Call me back.

ROBIN I'm glad Ryan's been keeping you in the loop.

I've been so swamped with all the mom stuff.

RYAN Mom. I've been trying you all morning.

ROBIN I've been thinking about you a lot too. A ton, actually. With Jeenu and—

RYAN Hope you're okay.

ROBIN Ha no. No I don't think so. Have zero idea what I'm doing.

RYAN I'm getting worried so call me back when you get this alright?

*Ryan hangs up.*

ROBIN Really? No of course I want to, I would love that. Let me um, get my calendar . . .

*Robin disappears.*

*Wolf and Puppet and Ash run in from morning run, gulp some water.*

ASH Pops or Kashi?

*Puppet and Wolf point to the Lucky Pops.*

You had that yesterday. And the day before. And the day before that.

*Puppet and Wolf point to the grown-up cereal. Reluctantly.*

That's right kid. I got your number.

*Peter dials a number.*

*Ash pours the cereal, milk, hands one bowl to Wolf.*

*They read and eat the cereal, side by side.*

*Ryan gets a call.*

RYAN Hey.

PETER Hey. What's going on.

RYAN Um.

PETER  How is he?

RYAN  Peter, what are you—

PETER  I saw what happened, on the Google. About the boxing game.

RYAN  Bout.

PETER  Huh?

RYAN  Bout. Nevermind. Yeah. It was pretty bad. Your kid is fine.

PETER  Yeah. Hey, I was wondering if, are you free? Today?

RYAN  Oh. Today?

PETER  Or, not, or later, I'm in town so.

RYAN  You are?

PETER  Yeah. I am. It's a little, aaaagh. We're separated, me and Katie—

Mind if I come over? To yours?

RYAN  Oh . . . I don't think—

PETER  I had some ideas and I wanted to run them by you.

RYAN  Um, okay. Yeah. I'll text you my addy now.

*Ryan hangs up. Sends text.*

ASH  What you reading today?

WOLF  There's a theory that our earth is being swallowed by water, bit by bit every day, and it is actually something we can't do much about. We can't pump the water outside of the earth, like we do when a boat is sinking, because gravity will just bring all the water back to the ground. We could evaporate it, but the sun and wind are already trying, but it ended up just bringing more water from the Arctic. I think the only solution is that we could all learn how to live under water. Either we could build a billion oxygen tanks, or we could develop gills. Like how when the trees grew taller, and animals got faster monkeys stood on their feet and became humans, like that, all the mammals could become half fish. Our lungs would transform into fish lungs and we'd know how to separate the water from the air.

ASH  That's what you're reading?

WOLF  No. It is what I am thinking.

ASH  Is it for school?

WOLF  No for you. Because we are very close to the water. And I can adapt, because wolves can live in the arctic, the swamps, deserts, kitchens, and they find their way okay, but you guys are just human so I was thinking of solutions.

ASH  That's very kind and forward-thinking.

WOLF  I want you to like me.

ASH  I do.

WOLF  Okay.

ASH  I like you lots.

WOLF  Then why didn't you want me to come in the first place?

ASH  Where'd you hear that?

*Wolf shrugs.*

Been sitting on that for a while, huh?

WOLF  No.

ASH  Okay. The reason I didn't want you to come in the first place. Is because.

I didn't know you were a wolf, and I know how hard it is for humans to deal with change and new places and new families, and I thought it was really unfair for you.

Cuz it's a lot to deal with.

WOLF  But I am a wolf.

ASH  Exactly. So I take it back. Cool?

WOLF  Okay. Do you know how to make oxygen tanks?

*Robin enters.*

ROBIN  No that's not far but

or I mean if you wanted to come over. Yes here.

Mom, of course you can. Any time. Any time you want.

I've missed you too. Love you too.

Bye.

ASH  Mom?

ROBIN  Uh huh.

ASH  Wow?

ROBIN  Uh huh.

ASH  You, okay?

ROBIN  Yeah. No. I don't know. She wants to see us.

ASH  Us? Like, us us? *(meaning Ash and Robin)*

ROBIN  Um, no, us. *(meaning Jeenu and Robin)*

ASH  Oh.

*Robin pours Lucky Pops into a bowl.*

ROBIN  I don't have to.

ASH  No you should. It's, you should.

> *Ash kisses Robin.*

ROBIN  Baby steps. We'll get there.

ASH  Exactly.

> *Jeenu swaps out his Kashi bowl with Robin's Lucky Pops bowl.*
>
> Jeenu.
>
> *Jeenu sadly returns Lucky Pops bowl to Robin.*
>
> > *Ding dong, someone at the door.*
> >
> > > RYAN  Coming!
>
> *Ryan opens the door. It's Peter.*
>
> > > > PETER  I got beers. Do you do day beers?
> > >
> > > RYAN  Come on in.
>
> *Ding! Like the end of a round of boxing.*

## [KNOCK KNOCK]

WOLF  Knock knock. Say who's there.

Knock knock.

> *Wolf waits till audience says "Who's there?"*

Donut.

> *Wolf waits till audience says "Donut who?"*

Donut do day beers with the guy who sold his kid on the internet, dumbass.

I can't believe you just did a knock knock joke with me. Nerds.

ROBIN  *(offstage)* Jeenu!

WOLF  Okay another one, knock knock.

> *Wolf waits till audience says "Who's there?"*

ROBIN  *(offstage)* Jeenu come here right now!

WOLF  Little Old Lady.

> *Wolf waits till audience says "Little Old Lady who?"*

Group yodel! Get it?

> *Yodels little old lady who.*

ROBIN  *(offstage)* JEEEEEEEEEEEEEEEEEEEENNNNNNNNNNNNN-OOOOOOOOOOOOOOOOOO!

## [PETER AND THE WOLF]

> *Puppet on couch. Puppet playing video games.*
> *Robin enters, with pair of small trousers.*

ROBIN   Hey mister, when I call you, you come to me not the other way around. Jeenu, look at me when I'm talking to you.

> *He does.*
> *Robin takes a deep breath of great perseverance.*
> *She turns the game screen off.*
> *Robin kneels down to face the puppet, eye level.*

ROBIN   Jeenu darling I love you you are the awesomest, can we please not put our food in our pockets.

Can we please please please never ever put spaghetti in our new, cream-colored slacks.

JEENU   Knock knock.

ROBIN   Jeenu.

JEENU   Knock knock.

ROBIN   Who's there.

JEENU   Jeenu.

ROBIN   Jeenu who.

JEENU   Jee, Nu Pants are kinda hard to keep clean.

ROBIN   Did you make that up?

> *Wolf and Puppet nod.*

That's really good. I'm very proud.

No more pasta in pants, okay?

> *Wolf and Puppet nod.*
> *Buzzzzz.*

ROBIN   Who is it?

> *Game is back on.*

Jeenu, you get five more minutes, and then piano, okay?

> *Robin opens door.*

Oh. Hi.

> *It's Ryan.*

RYAN   Hey.

ROBIN   What do you want?

RYAN   Can I come in?

> *Robin lets him in.*

We need to talk. Is Ash around?

ROBIN  No.

RYAN  Where are they?

ROBIN  Out.

RYAN  They've not been to the club for a while.

ROBIN  They want a break.

RYAN  A break from what, boxing? Cuz you can take a break from boxing and still pick up my calls.

ROBIN  Maybe they want a break from you.

RYAN  Family don't take breaks from each other.

ROBIN  Yes they do when family is being a dick.

RYAN  We need to talk.

ROBIN  What we've been doing.

RYAN  Drop the guard Robs. I was trying to help. I'm on your side.

ROBIN  Who's on the other side? There is no fight. Stop trying to help.

RYAN  Peter's in town.

ROBIN  Peter who?

RYAN  His father.

ROBIN  You're joking, right?

RYAN  He wants to take him back.

ROBIN  Ryan what did you do.

RYAN  Don't get all hysterical.

ROBIN  Jeenu go to your room.

RYAN  Let's be honest now you and I both know, this isn't working out.

ROBIN  Room. Now!

*Wolf takes Puppet to the room.*

RYAN  Robs, you have got to stay calm. Peter broke off with the crazy wife, he's on his own and now he wants the kid back. He's been talking to a lawyer, okay? We thought—

ROBIN  We?

RYAN  He thought that it would be better to just get this cleared up before the kid gets too comfortable here. Am I the only one who can see what's happening to this family since that kid came into this house? I barely see you any more. Ash is retiring out of the blue, you guys are just being sucked in, into this kid's Black Hole of Needs, he is breaking up our family! I want you to be happy. I need Ash to be happy. I know how badly you want a child and so we tried this out but Robin, it is not working. I am gonna be the bad guy and tell you the thing you are not willing to tell yourself because you are a beautiful kind stubborn-ass woman who will never give up on people.

You are unequipped to take care of this child.

ROBIN  Okay.

RYAN  You have to be rational about this, think about what's best for the
kid, okay?

ROBIN  Okay.

RYAN  Okay?

ROBIN  Okay.

RYAN  Good.

ROBIN  I'm gonna go help Jeenu with his piano practice, and then we're
going for froyo.

When we come out to go for froyo, you are not going to be here. Okay?

RYAN  Robin.

ROBIN  And you are not coming back again.

RYAN  Robin you're being—

ROBIN  Mmm.

Not coming back.

Not calling.

Not anything.

RYAN  I am your brother.

ROBIN  And I love you. And so I will forgive you. One day.

But right now, my son needs help with his piano practice.

RYAN  He's not your son.

ROBIN  So that is where I need to be.

RYAN  The law's on his side. Pete's gonna go to court in Arizona with
this if—

ROBIN  Goodbye Ryan.

WOLF  This is CV 12-1189, in the matter of Peter Hunt and Robin Shephard.
Ready to proceed?

  *A shift.*

Don't you sometimes just wanna walk out?

Or turn it off, leave the story.

You know it's not real

it's just a bunch of what-ifs

but sometimes it feels so real.

Like when the Green Ranger is under the power of the evil witch and
turns against the other Power Rangers, you're like that's okay don't be
worried that's not actually the Green Ranger he is Jason David Frank born-
again Christian actor-human

but still when Green Ranger defeats the Red Ranger and breaks the
heart of Pink Ranger

you're like noooooooooooooooooooooooooooooooooo stop itttttt!

But then next season he comes back as the White Ranger and you're
like oh phew.

Mostly, you don't walk out,

you get through the moment of noooooo because you know you'll get
to the phew,

but in some stories, you can't be sure

if there ever will be a phew.

In some stories, the what-ifs break away and all you get is the what-is.

And that shit can sit in your gut like a rock for a while.

And that rock is real and that rock fucking sucks

and so sometimes

you're like

what if I just walk out before it hits?

But also you're like,

what if there's a phew coming,

what if there's a phew coming that will blow that dumb rock to dust
Forever

and I miss it, cuz I walked out?

## [PULL]

*A boxing ring, four adults, four corners.*

JUDGE* This is CV 12-1189, in the matter of Peter Hunt and Robin Shephard.

WOLF You wanna do this? Let's do this.

Ladies and gentlemen, introducing in the right corner, the challengers
Team Hunt.

And in the left corner, the world champions of everything, Team
Shephard-Michaels!

*Everyone raises their right hand.*

Do you swear the testimony you are about to give is the whole truth and
nothing but the truth so help you God?

ALL I do.

---

* Judge's voice is a recorded voice, a new voice we have never heard before.

WOLF   Round number one!

> *Ding.*

ROBIN   Presenting the documents related to original power of attorney signed and dated.

PETER   The fact is, a power of attorney document does not transfer custody permanently.

ROBIN   The affidavit of waiver of interest in child is permanent.

PETER   We approached the defendants with desire to nullify contract, induced fraudulently.

ROBIN   Your honor, there was absolutely no direct contact with Mr. Hunt since the initial handoff.

> *Ding.*

> WOLF   Robins are a very delicate species. They don't like to fight. But sometimes a downward dog can turn into a bite because wolves fight for each other.

PETER   Petitioner would like to call to the stand, Mr. Ryan Shephard.

> WOLF   But the omega wolves like dumbass Ryan—

> *Ding.*

RYAN   Yeah I was there, he thought I was Ash. But on the other hand, we thought the kid was like two years old so—

PETER   Claim of information fraud has been corroborated.

> WOLF   Peters love papers, a fortress of papers.

ROBIN   The real question is why it's okay to put your child up on the internet.

PETER   The real question is why it's okay to lie about being a dyke.

ROBIN   Objection, argumentative.

> WOLF   We love you, Robin Shephard! We love you—

PETER   Respondent's domestic partner displayed acts of violence toward the petitioner.

> *Ding.*

> WOLF   Wolves can't let their pack's asses be whupped.

> *Ding.*

RYAN   Yeah, Ash roughed him up a bit, but honestly he was asking for it.

ASH   What does that have anything to do with—

> WOLF   Wolves know how to fight!

ROBIN   Your honor, this is irrelevant information regarding the issue at hand.

PETER   It's evidence that the child was placed in a hostile environment.

> WOLF   Peters worry too much. Wolves can adapt, to anywhere.

PETER  Ms. Ashley Michaels to the stand.

    WOLF  Right foot forward.

ASH  I was late that day, yes, when Jeenu was dropped off at our house.

    WOLF  Guard up, like Hello.

ASH  No, it was not because we were trying to hide we were fucking married.

    WOLF  We love you, Ash Michaels!

ASH  They put a child on the internet. Would You agree to get a kid from the internet?

    WOLF  Yes!

PETER  Did you or did you not want him there on that day, answer the question.

ASH  No I did not want a child I do not know being dropped off at my house, like a book I got off of Amazon.

    WOLF  What?

PETER  No further questions.

ASH  Who does that?

PETER  Thank you, Ms. Michaels.

    *Ding.*

    WOLF  Um, something about, oxygen tanks,

    *Ding.*

PETER  The documents are based / on the date of agreement.

ASH  What about the affidavit!

    *Ding.*

    WOLF  gills, under water, to separate the, um,

    *Ding.*

ROBIN  Under the federal laws, state laws forbidding joint adoption by same-sex / couples is illegal.

PETER  Temporary custody.

ROBIN / ASH  Designed to be irrevocable!

    *Ding.*

    WOLF  the trees grew taller, and animals,

    *Ding.*

       to separate the, um, monkeys from humans, no, water from the—

RYAN  Hostile / environment for the—

ROBIN  Durable Power / of Attorney contract withstands—

PETER  Temporary custody / as are the limits of—

ASH  Who does that?

    WOLF  Kitchens!

*Ding.*

PETER  The doctor mints are based on the date of a green mint.*

ASH  What about the After David!†

ROBIN  Under Fred's evil claws, the claws / for bleeding joint abortion by same-saying couplets isn't evil.‡

PETER  Temper / baby cuts the meat!§

ASH  Designed / to be a record table!¶

ROBIN  Gerbil power / of a bunny.**

PETER  For temper baby cuts the meat!††

ROBIN / ASH  Look at the After David!‡‡

    *Ding.*

RYAN / PETER  Power of a bunny is temper baby.§§

    *Ding.*

    WOLF  I'm a wolf. I am a lone wolf. I have to protect—

    *Ding.*

ROBIN  It's stunning that this prepped kiss of never riding children on the internet, does not seem to violin hate any—¶¶ Presenting After David of Razor of Interest in Child—

ASH  Who hazmat?

    *Ding.*

ROBIN  A record table after the 11th day it was motorized.

    *Ding.*

ASH  But for the child's sake—

PETER  To come to an agreement—

ROBIN  No.

ASH  To settle.

RYAN  For the child's sake.

ROBIN  Jeenu's interests are—

---

\*  The documents are based on the date of agreement.

†  Affidavit

‡  Under the federal laws, state laws forbidding joint adoption by same-sex couples is illegal.

§  Temporary Custody

¶  Designed to be irrevocable

\*\*  Durable power of attorney

††  for temporary custody

‡‡  Affidavit

§§  Power of attorney is temporary.

¶¶  It's stunning that this practice of advertising children does not seem to violate any—

PETER   What's better for the boy.

    *A breath.*

JUDGE   I understand there was a motion to interview the child in chambers. If there's no other evidence or testimony to be presented, we'll call the child forth to put on tape.

ASH   Jeenu?

PETER   Junior?

RYAN   Well, say something.

    *Everyone looks at Puppet.*

JEENU   . . .

WOLF   No. I'm done.

    *Wolf leaves the puppet, and walks out of the story.*


## [DAILY LIFE 4]

    *Same space, trying to be a different space.*

    *Puppet sits alone, sans Wolf.*

      ASH   Morning champ.

RYAN   Hi mom.

        PETER   No, I didn't get custody.

      ASH   How'd you sleep?

        PETER   They didn't get him either.

*Robin watches these people go about their performances, not sure what to do next.*

RYAN   Depends on when they set the court date, I don't know.

        PETER   I told you, the State has him. I don't know why, Katie!

      ASH   Wanna go for a run?

        PETER   Because we fucked up!

RYAN   They're fine.

        PETER   Because you put our son on / the internet, Katie.

RYAN   He's / fine.

      ASH   Let's go for a run. / Just a quick one before—

RYAN   It's just temporary! I didn't! The guy showed up / at my door, it wasn't me, okay?

        PETER   Yep, you're right about that he's not our son.

      ASH   Or, cereal?

PETER  You made sure of that.

ASH  Pops or Kashi?

*Robin disappears the stage space (lights, curtains, whatever you got).*

*It's just Robin and her son.*

*Robin holds the lifeless puppet, sets him down, touches his arms, face, little*

*legs . . . tries to connect to the wolf through the object, and then an idea:*

ROBIN  What if I said:

I am not what you think you see.

I am not human, this floor is forest earth, and to the left of that glaring exit light, a river flows.

You are not what you feel you are, you are a spider, an eagle.

Or a wolf. What if I said you are a wolf? What if I said you are the single most important breath in my space. You are the first gear that turns the clock of my world. What if I said I will fight for you with every blood cell and cranial nerve I possess.

*A tiny entrance.*

*Wolf returns, like a little childhood memory.*

*Robin addresses Wolf.*

And you believed me?

Does that change anything?

. . .

# a river, its mouths

## JESÚS I. VALLES

### Content Warning

This play depicts violence against migrants, the drowning of migrants at the US–Mexico border, depression, suicidal ideation, and suicide.

### Time

Summer of 2019; the drowning summer.

### Place

A river and the Texas town that belongs to it; the US–Mexico border.

### A Note on Casting + Staging

Please double where needed. Challenge realism where there's give. Versatile actors with voice-acting experience are excellent for this piece. Perhaps this piece is done as folklore with actors sitting at a table, perhaps it's a story told through object theater, perhaps it's played by one actor as You and two actors in every other role, perhaps it's an audio play. Like all ghost stories, its life depends on its variations. Below is a character track list for six actors (but could be done with fewer).

### Characters

YOU . . . You. He/him or they/them, Mexican-American. Late twenties, early thirties—played by a singular actor who maintains the role throughout the play. Law school dropout, prodigal child, struggling with severe depression, suicidal ideation, and longing for water. (Please change and adjust pronouns as needed.)

MOUTH ONE plays

- AN OFFICER . . . a fascist.
- MARC . . . he/him, your friend, sometimes lover; your siren.
- THE LADY ON THE LOUDSPEAKER . . . somebody's auntie with very long nails.
- STEFFANY . . . she/her, your little niece, a stream.

- THE DROWNED THING ... old, vast, terrifying, furious, full of grace, made of everything the river remembers. The "mermaid."

## MOUTH TWO plays

- THE CHILD CROSSING ... a migrant child.
- XANDRA ... she/her, your forever homie, loves a King Cobra.
- ROSARIO ... she/her, your mother, Mexican national, a healer.
- TRY IT AGAIN ... a coyote, deeply caring, deeply reckless.

## MOUTH THREE plays

- ANOTHER OFFICER ... another fascist.
- YESI ... she/her, your new friend, loves Xandra, hates ghost stories.
- DIANA ... she/her, your sister, a fury.
- AN ANCHOR ... a news anchor whose hair doesn't move.
- ANOTHER CHILD ... another migrant child.

## MOUTH FOUR plays

- THE DROWNING MAN AHEAD OF THEM ... that poor man, drowning. A migrant.
- OFFICER IN TRUCK ... a fascist.
- LA LOCA, CROSSING FOR THE FIRST TIME ... they/them, a queer migrant, terrified.
- ERASMO ... he/him, late fifties, Mexican national, American-raised, your godfather.
- FIRST TIME CROSSING ... a migrant woman crossing for the first time, a mother.

## MOUTH FIVE plays

- THE MAN CROSSING ... a migrant man escaping one country for another, a father.
- OFFICER DISPATCH ... dispatches fascists.
- DON FITO ... he/him, late sixties, knows everyone, sees everything.
- AND THE WOMAN WITH THEM ... a migrant woman crossing with La Loca, devout.
- A CORRESPONDENT ... the one person who can speak Spanish at the news station.
- GILBERTO ... he/him, early sixties, Mexican national, American-raised, Erasmo's brother.

### A Note on Language + Mouth Sounds

This is a noisy play. The people in this town are the river You left years ago. The mouth sounds throughout the piece are "the grammar of the river." I imagine this as a play that could be done with Foley and the actor's instrument if no technology was available. Thankfully, sound designers are a boon. But please, play inside the mouth sounds throughout and let go of language when it feels right. The sound of water should become increasingly heightened throughout the show. We move from scene to scene with the sounds of water—water transitions us from one scene to the next. Water running, rushing. Let water set the tempo.

### A Note on "/"

Where you see "/" feel free to jump over the next line and finish out what you need to.

### On Scenes, Stage Directions, and Photos

Feel free to project scene titles onstage or don't. Stage directions are written in the second person to invite the reader into the internal world of the protagonist. If you'd like them spoken aloud in production, go for it. All text is fair game.

### A Final Provocation

Imagine this play is a spell. Imagine all language is just skin, Spanish, English, just a thin film of sound covering all that we actually are: water. Imagine that moments of crisis allow us to detach ourselves from the sense-making of time, of language, of logic. Imagine life besides itself.

## MOUTHS MAKE NIGHT, A RIVER, A TOWN

*In darkness, every Mouth emerges.*

MOUTH ONE  *(The wind.)* Whhhhooo / whhhhooo

MOUTH TWO & FOUR  *(The water's skin.)* Sssshhhh / sssshhhh

MOUTH THREE & FIVE  *(The smallest creatures.)* Crrrr / crrrr

MOUTH ONE  Pssst Did you see?

MOUTH TWO  Pssst You hear what / happened?

MOUTH THREE  Psssst Válgame / dios. Qué horror.

MOUTH FOUR  Pssss Lo que pasó, ahí, / en el río.

MOUTH FIVE  Pssss Right in the river. / Esa pobre gente.

MOUTHS ONE, TWO, THREE  *(Like wind.)* Down here, where nothing / happens.

MOUTHS FOUR, FIVE  *(Like water.)* Aquí, tan cerca / del agua.

ALL MOUTHS  Whhhhoooooo / Sssssshhh / Crrrrrr

Sssssssshhhhhhhh *(The Mouths become cicadas, or locusts, and the water, the water, the water. The Mouths become the people, too.)*


## NIGHT, BY THE RIVER

*Nighttime. It sounds cliché because it is, because crossings are repeated things. Far away, voices over a radio.*

AN OFFICER  Kksshk

There's some rustling over by the kksshk

It looks like a group of kksshk

One of them's carrying a kidkkssshk

ANOTHER OFFICER  Kkksshk

Got it.

You're breaking up.

Headed that waykksshk

Over kksshk

AN OFFICER  Kkssh Looks like they're heading towarkksshk

The river lookkkshsshk

We'll need kksshhk

ANOTHER OFFICER  Kkkshk

We're headed over if you neeekkkshk

AN OFFICER  Kkksshh Hurry.

> They're almost on this side ofkksssshk
>
> They're getting in the waterkkksshhk

## JUST ON THE OTHER SIDE OF THE SAME RIVER, ALMOST IN IT, THEN . . .

> *A group prepares to cross the Rio into the US; the river rushes, runs.*

THE MAN CROSSING  Sssshhhh shh shh shh

> Mija mija, ya no llores.
>
> Ya por favor no llores.
>
> Shh shh ya no llores, chiquita.

THE CHILD CROSSING  *(Crying, trying not to.)* Estoy cansada, papi.

> Quiero dormirme, papi, por favor.
>
> Quiehheroohhho a mami, mi maamii.
>
> Quiero irme a mi casa, papi.

THE MAN CROSSING  Ya, ya, ya, mi cielo.

> Ya chiquita. Ven. Dame la manita.
>
> Así.
>
> Aquí te subes a mis hombros.
>
> Ándale. Así.
>
> No te me dejes ir, chiquita.
>
> No te dejes.

THE CHILD CROSSING  *(Trying to compose herself.)* Siiiihhh siiih si.

> ¿Papi, a dónde—

THE MAN CROSSING  Aquí en la agua. Mira—

> Como ese señor. Miralo.
>
> *They walk closer to the river now, the dirt beneath them snitching. The Drowning Man Ahead Of Them goes first. His body slips in the river, and just like that he becomes what he is here.*

THE DROWNING MAN AHEAD OF THEM  Shhhhhhhhhhhhhhgggggg ghhhhhh

> Sssssooccoorrrrrrgggggggh *(He struggles against the water.)*
>
> Gllllllllllggllllllggglllsshhrhrs
>
> Rrrrrrrrsssshhhhhhhhshhshhshhshshs *(Silence. He drowns.)*

THE CHILD CROSSING  No! Papi! NO NO NO!

> *They stop.*

THE MAN CROSSING  Shhhshhhh Calladita. Okay, chiquis.
>    Okay. No. (*He decides to fare the waters by himself. To his daughter.*)
>    Aquí me esperas, chiquis, porfis.
>    Aquí estás bien. Ándale.
THE CHILD CROSSING  Papi, no. No papi, yo quiero ir contigo—
>    Papi paaaaahhhhhh!!
>        *She cries. Her father goes to the water.*
THE MAN CROSSING  Quédate ahiiiiiii
>    Te digo que te quedes ahí!
>    Echenme luz por favor.
>    Echenme luzzzgghhhhlllllll (*He fights the water.*)
>    Glllgllglglgssssshshshshshshs
THE CHILD CROSSING  Paaaaaaapiiiiii
>        *The Man Crossing struggles in the water. Then a howl, a bellow—the hungry, sad cry of a vast creature.*


## AT THE SAME TIME, THE OFFICERS AGAIN, ON THIS SIDE OF THE RIVER:

>        *Over a radio.*
AN OFFICER  Kksshhk
>    They're getting in the water.
>    One of them jussskskssks
>    He's gonnaskkskshhk
>    Another man, he's going to drownsshhsskkksshk
>    What should I—
>    Kksshhk
ANOTHER OFFICER  Kkksshk Let them.
AN OFFICER  Let them? Tssshk
ANOTHER OFFICER  Drown. Tssshk
AN OFFICER  Ksshshshk—
>    . . . kksshk
>        *In the distance The Man Crossing struggles in the water. The same cry, bellow, howl from before, now through the radio. A creature. Vicious. Louder. Closer to making An Officer prey.*
AN OFFICER  Oh God OH SHHIkssskskshk
>    FUCKhhhgggggggKksshshhk

*Terrifying and vast, The Drowned Thing holds An Officer's mouth open by his tongue and claims back the water that made this man, every drop from his body, to make the river fat. It leaves behind only the radio, his skin, his bones; it leaves An Officer's corpse.*

ANOTHER OFFICER  Kkksshh

Hello? Martinez?

Hellokksshk

*The Man Crossing lands on this side of the river having almost drowned. The howl, the bellow, the cry gulps itself back into the water.*

THE MAN CROSSING  Chiquiiiiiisssss!

Ya llegué. Estoy bien, chiquis! Estoy bien!

THE CHILD CROSSING  Papi.

Paaaaaaahhhhhhhhh

Sshshhhhhhhhhhhssssssssssssssssshhh

*The Child Crossing turns into the sounds of the rushing river, until it quietly becomes your breath. Then, next to You, these same sounds, but coming from a recording on Marc's phone.*

## YOU'RE BACK IN TOWN, AT YOUR HOTEL, IN BED, WITH MARC

*There You are, in bed with Marc. The both of you breathing in the moments just after sex. He's a longtime friend You have sex with when you're home. Marc is nice and Marc loves You and you'd never date Marc because you'd never date anyone, but god, he's warm, sweet. Those hands. There You are, the glow of Marc's phone on your skin. From his phone, the sounds of the river.*

MARC  Hhhhhrrrrgghh

Shhh sh sh sh

Listen—

YOU  . . .

So, all this happened / when? Last—

MARC  A week ago. Not the first time, though.

YOU  I still don't see it. Can you turn up the / brightness, or—

MARC  Yeah, yeah. Look. Here.

*From Marc's phone, a howling, this hungry sound, old and vast, full of thirst and made of water and longing. A man screams and then, another man*

*rolls ashore. Then, faintly, distorted "Kkkssshk. Martinez? Helloksssshshk."*
*In the distance, The Man Crossing lands on this side of the river, gasping.*
*The bellow, the cry, gulps itself back into the water. The river runs.*

MARC  There. (*Marc taps the screen.*) Right there.

Wild, right?

YOU  I still can't tell . . .

This video's shit. What am I . . .

Am I looking at drowning

or swimming or . . .

MARC  A man,

trying to cross the river

he's got his daughter,

he leaves her on the other side,

he's going after someone or trying to get himself across or, or something

and you can hear his little girl crying after him.

He gets in the water and here

and you can hear it,

see (*Marc taps the screen again; the cry, howl, bellow.*) right here?

Something

something comes up from the water

shiny. Like skin, but it's not—

Not a person, / like—

YOU  It looks like it could be a person

or just the water. / It's probably—

MARC  Like, some kind of—

Like a water zombie.

YOU  That's not a thing, Marc.

MARC  But it is! Look at this fucking thing!

(*Marc's phone dies.*) Ah, shit.

You got a charger?

YOU  Not for an Android.

Why do you still have / an Android?

MARC  I woulda charged it longer

had I gotten an actual heads up about a certain asshole coming to town.

But I didn't.

So, here we are, with a dead phone. / And an asshole.

YOU  Oh my fucking god.

Here we go. It wasn't—

You know how I am.

MARC  Trash?

YOU  Utter fucking garbage.

MARC  Mostly, yeah.

YOU  I fucking hate you.

MARC  . . .

How was your flight here?

YOU  Gross. Sad.

Full of Texans.

MARC  You came to Texas.

The fuck you think the flight was gonna be full of?

You came for,

for work or?

YOU  No. Just came. Just to visit.

MARC  Oh. You gonna be at this hotel

the whole time you're—

How long are you here for?

YOU  Just three nights. But, I might

I dunno. Might stay at my mom's if I stay past that.

Might end up at Xandra's. I told her I / was—

MARC  Ah, cool cool cool. Yeah, so so

Xandra gets a call ahead of time

and dick-on-demand gets a text when you're already here.

Yeah, that— That feels right for you. Consistent. /

Consistently disappointing.

YOU  Shuuuut the fuck up.

No, I mean,

I just figured

I'd give her a heads-up

in case I'm trying to /

To stay here longer, or—

MARC  You could stay with me, y'know?

If it's just a couple of days.

It'd be nice to have you, if you want.

I can— Yeah.

I mean, just saying you could.

YOU  I could.

Yeah, thanks, it's just

I just got out of this /
This thing with this other guy / and I'm not really trying—
MARC  Hey, no, you don't have / to—
YOU  No, I know, I just wanted to let you know
      I'm not really in a place to get into / anything—
MARC  You're good. You're good.
      Just saying.
      Whatever you need, I'm around.
      . . .
      I missed you, fucker.
YOU  Me too.
MARC  You a lawyer yet?
YOU  What?
MARC  You were in law school, no?
YOU  I was, but I—yeah, I stopped doing that.
      And uh was just sorta working at this (*Here You are, flailing.*)
      Well volunteering at this— Um.
      Yeah I was, I was doing that. But then, uh I dunno.
      Ugh I got let go from that. (*Pathetic.*)
      From volunteering. Oh god. That sounds fucking stupid, right?
      But yeah uh that's what's that's uh / just been—
MARC  Oh, man. Hey, I'm sorry.
      I didn't mean to bring all this shit up.
      I just didn't know if you.
      If you were still / if you finished school or—
YOU  Stop.
      Please. Just.
      Yeah.
      What's /
      What's new with you?
MARC  Same shit as always.
      Just work.
      Taking care of my dad. He's on disability now.
      So that helps a little, but still. Yeah, just work and him, really.
      You know how it is here.
      No shit ever happens.
YOU  I mean.
      From the news, it seems like a lot happens here, / because—

MARC　Oh, cuz of the / mermaid.

YOU　—the border, the caravans, the cages at the underpass,
　　the kids at the detention / centers.

MARC　Oh, shit / right yeah, my bad, that's yeah. Yeah.

YOU　Mermaid?

MARC　That's what people are calling it.
　　The thing from the video. The Rio Grande mermaid.
　　Did you hear about it on the news up / there or—

YOU　About the detention centers here / yeah I—

MARC　No. About the mermaid / did you—

YOU　I mean that's not in the news / but I guess.

MARC　Well, Facebook or / did someone—

YOU　That's not news, Marc. You all down here are so / I don't—

MARC　Whoa, we all down here? Okay, / wow, somebody's—

YOU　No, I didn't mean. No—I'm /
　　Ughhh yeah. Yeah, I mean, I did hear something about it.
　　My sister sent me a thing. Some audio chain letter shit
　　on WhatsApp, from our cousin. He— Here— *(You get your phone. And
　from there, the howl, cry, the bellow again.)*

MARC　You hear it right? *(Marc holds you closer. He puts the phone to your ear,
　holds you tight. Marc presses play on your phone again.)* Listen.

YOU　. . . Yeah.

MARC　Like, you can hear
　　this kind of Hhhrrrgghhsssh

YOU　What?

MARC　The thing. It howls. It calls.
　　In the water. Listen.
　　Hhhhrrrrrgggggghhhhhh
　　Ssssssshhhhhhhhhh
　　　*Marc's mouth is a river that becomes the sound of a soda machine's rush.
　　　You leave your hotel.*

## XANDRA, YESI, AND YOU, AT TATA'S TACOS

　*You meet Xandra and Yesi at this shitty taco joint. Everyone loves it. You
　drink your sodas and wait for your order. The Lady on the Loudspeaker is
　what you hear.*

THE LADY ON THE LOUDSPEAKER  Kssssssh

    Frrrrssshhh

YOU  What did she say?

    Is . . . is that for us?

THE LADY ON THE LOUDSPEAKER  (*muffled*)  Forttyysixx doubledoubleswithcheessee

    Kssshshsh orden numerocuarentaysseisss

    Dobledoblesconquessossh

XANDRA  Nah, that's not for us.

YOU  How have they still not fixed the speaker?

    Is the food still as bad as the service / or—

XANDRA  Nobody comes to Tata's Tacos because the food is good.

YESI  I think the tacos are pretty good!

    Oooh! And the hot dogs on a burger bun with chorizo beans and pickles / and—

YOU  Oh shit, the King Dog with chorizo beans and pickles?!

    So fucking good!

YESI  Right?! I keep telling Xandra, "Dude, it's good!"

    but she thinks weenies are nasty,

    so she don't wanna try it.

XANDRA  I just don't think the food here is that good / I—

YOU  Why did you wanna meet here, then? / If you don't—

XANDRA  I figured you'd want Tata's—

    You haven't been home in a while. / I—

YESI  You fuckin' liar! We were at work and this bitch goes,

    "Ooh, Yesenia, you know what would be good? Tata's!

    We should go!" Like that, all excited!

YOU  Xandra's been like that. She'll talk shit about something.

    Next day, she'll be all into it. Then, she fucking hates it again.

    Lesbians, I swear.

YESI  Oh my god!

    Liiiterally! She's like that with girls, too!

    Like, you talk sooooo much shit and next thing you know /

    You're married!

XANDRA  Oh my fuckin' god. I knew this shit would happen!

    I was like, "Yesenia and this fool are gonna gang up on me."

YOU  Who's ganging up? / We're just—

YESI  You do the same shit, too! Es una bully, dude.

I swear, when I first joined Mariposas,
Xandra and all the other comadres, they knew I was all shy,
so when I started working / with them—

YOU   What's Mariposas?

YESI   Oh, it's this thing where we like,
we like, help people / who are—

XANDRA   It's a migrant aid organization I been working with for a while.

YOU   Oh, you working with like Annunciation House / or—

XANDRA   Fuck no. No, nah not like that. It's just a group of us from here.
This chick Marcia I was dating started it, but then she moved to Tucson,
so now I organize it.
We go out by the river and we set out jugs of water, food, blankets,
bags with socks and underwear, band-aids, disinfectant,
just whatever people need to come over.

YESI   I joined like two weeks ago cuz I work with this bitch *(She means Xandra.)*
at Albertson's right now. I had to get a second job aside from the bar, / so—

YOU   You still working at El Tapatio?

YESI   Yeah, but fewer days now. Anyway, I started working at Albertson's,
at the deli, and Xandra was telling me about Mariposas, / and—

XANDRA   I hate that name. Marcia named the group that shit. Butterflies
are corny / shit—

YESI   Shut up! It's cute! Anyway, she was like, "Oh, you should come out." I
love helping people, so yeah,
but now with all the mermaid shit—

YOU   Yeah, Marc showed me a / video of it—

XANDRA   Wait. You fucking Marc again?

YESI   Xandra, ¡no seas chismosa!

XANDRA   Called it. Soon as you were like, "Oh,
I'm gonna stay at a hotel for a few days,"
I was like, "Oh, you're gonna fuck Marc."

YOU   You're a fucking mess. But yeah.
He's nice. It's nice.
Anyway, my sister sent me this weird audio, too /
From the river. Was like / a—

YESI   It's creepy, huh?! I was telling Xandra
I was like, "Dude, what if the mermaid eats us?"

YOU   So you think, you think it's like /
Like a real thing?

XANDRA  People are just excited to have some shit to talk about.

It's so fuckin' boring here that I think once the video hit / it was—

YOU  Boring? Even with all the shit happening—

Didn't a little girl die at the detention center not too long ago?

And the people being gassed at the border.

I mean, you see it firsthand, I'm sure. Even with all / that—

XANDRA  It's different.

You heard about that man that drowned that night,

right before the video? He's the fifth one to die out there this summer.

More at other parts of the river.

Everything is so fucked. Poor river.

YESI  Yeah. It's real sad.

That's how my dad crossed,

through the river. Back in the day.

It's scary how it is now.

XANDRA  But this mermaid stuff—

I mean, you get it. Mexicans love this kinda shit.

YESI  I think it's exciting to think that something is down there!

XANDRA  See?! Everyone keeps saying that it's helping people cross.

Keeping some from drowning. It's just a story or whatever,

but I think if it's inspiring people to help others stay alive,

maybe we should just keep telling it, y'know?

YESI  Biiiiiitch—what if we change the name to like,

Sirenitas, instead of Mariposas, y'know?

That'd be cute, huh? We could get mermaid shirts!

XANDRA  Ha! Imagínate, dude! *(She turns to You.)*

So what are you doing back?

YOU  Just hanging out, mostly. I needed time to think,

I've been—

THE LADY ON THE LOUDSPEAKER  Ksssshfortyseven—singlewithcheess-sssseee,

singlenocheeessse, hotdogwithchorizobeanschhshhs

ORDENCUARENTAYSIETE-SENCILLOCON / QUESSSSO—

YESI  That's us. I'm coming! *(Yesi leaves to pick up the order.)*

XANDRA  Hey, what's up?

You don't look right.

YOU  Uh. *(A pebble in the throat—small.)* Fuck hahah. Uh / Everything?

I uh I dropped out of school—I couldn't really keep up. It's so expensive out there and I tried to set myself up with this job. (*Water is coming. Fight it.*)

Well, not really a job but uh. Yeah, I got let go from this.

(*It pours out of You.*) Ugh. Just feeling pretty useless.

I don't know what the fuck I'm doing, honestly.

Maybe I just stay here, maybe /

Or. Or maybe /

I keep thinking I'll—

> *You could almost say the horrible thing you want to do to yourself, but you wouldn't.*

XANDRA   Well, stop that shit. Thinking?

That shit never got nobody anywhere good.

You should come out with us,

help out with the food and the water.

It helped me a lot, after Marcia and I broke up.

Might be good for you, too,

to throw your head into something else.

Have you seen your 'ma yet?

YOU   No, not yet. Going over after this.

XANDRA   You're the fucking worst.

Does she even know you're here?

YOU   My sister does.

Wanna surprise my 'ama.

XANDRA   What do you call a surprise when it's bad?

YOU   Fuck you.

XANDRA   Fuck you, too.

For real, though. You okay? You look glgl—

> *Xandra drinks from a cup.*

YOU   What?

XANDRA   You look sunk. Like, like you're /

glglglglgl

> *Xandra drinks from a cup, loudly. The soda machine rushes in your head, louder. The rushing turns into water in a kitchen sink. You are tossed to your mother's kitchen.*

## EAT SOMETHING

> *The kitchen sink runs, the dishes get done. You're home! Your sister, Diana, at the sink. Your mom, Rosario, lulling your niece, Steffany. Steffany's been so fussy lately. Your sister's first kid with some dude nicknamed Palo. But he left her. Your mom has mostly been raising the baby while your sister tries to figure things out at work. Anyway, everybody in the house is tired. But they're glad to see You! Welcome back.*

ROSARIO  Sshh shhh

Ru ru ru ru sh sh sh

Ya. Ya casi se duerme.

Diana. Toma tu niña.

DIANA  Gracias, 'ama. *(She puts Steffany in another room nearby.)*

Ufff. Steffany didn't use to cry this much when she was little little

but she's / been so fussy lately—

ROSARIO  Todavía está little! Todavía está chiquitita, Diana!

DIANA  She's almost two, 'ama!!

ROSARIO  Oye, ¿a quién le estás gritando tú, eh?!

¡Igualada! ¡A mí no me gritas!

DIANA  I'm not yelling! I'm just saying,

she cries more now because you treat her like a baby!

You gotta talk to her like she's big.

Ugh. She's such a crybaby, dude.

And its because 'ama spoils her

so now she only cries and yells—

ROSARIO  ¡Porque tú eres mala con ella! Por eso llora.

STEFFANY  *(From another room, un berrinche in her throat.)*

Aaaaaa uuuhhhaaaaaa aaaaa

Mami!!!! Tita!!!

Huaaaaaaa—

ROSARIO  Virgen María purísima

la pobre chiquita ya /

Ya la despertaste /

Por estar gritando, Diana!

DIANA  ¡Qué no estoy gritando!

Ugh. You see how she is?

*(an accusation)* She never yells at You!

ROSARIO  Because he doesn't yell at the baby!

¿Verda'?

DIANA  Because he's never fucking here, 'ama! / So—

ROSARIO  ¡No digas "focking," Diana! Qué feo.

STEFFANY  Mami! Tita!! Aaaahh huuaaaaa!!!

ROSARIO  Ándale, ve cuida a tu niña /
    Que yo ya crie a mis niños.

DIANA  Just let her cry, 'ma!
    She needs to get used to being by herself.

ROSARIO  You see how she is?!
    She don't wanna take care of her baby.
    Venimos a este mundo a sufrir.
    Did you eat?

YOU  No, but I'm not / really—

ROSARIO  No, huh?
    You don't eat.
    Diana es igual.
    She don't eat nothing for breakfast
    Then, when she's back from work /
    Se atasca como cochinita.
    She eats everything! Big dinners every day!
    Muy apenas deja de comer para uno.

DIANA  Oh my god—
    Ya, 'ama!

ROSARIO  I'm not lying.
    Por eso estás como estás.
    You got bigger.

DIANA  I just had a baby!

ROSARIO  Two years ago!

DIANA  See?!
    (Diana goes to check on Steffany.)

ROSARIO  Si! Ya ves que si!
    She got bigger, huh?!

YOU  I mean, everyone got a little / older—

ROSARIO  I tell her, lose weight, Diana, por favor!
    Pero bueno, Panza llena, Corazón contento.
    Thank god we have food.
    If you're fat, it's cuz God bless you.
    God, must really like us.

Oye, y aver, cuéntame que haces aquí.

¿Cómo estás tú?

YOU    I'm good, 'ama.

DIANA    Liar.

What? You need money? You got jury duty?

YOU    No. No, I'm good. I just wanted to come see y'all.

Really.

ROSARIO    Mmm.

I don't know why you don't stay here.

We don't see you. Pero, pues /

Si quiere el señor andar en hotel /

Pos que gaste su dinero entonces.

Ahi dichoso usted.

No. Más les dura un pedo en la cola que'l dinero.

YOU    'ama!

ROSARIO    That's okay! You wanna waste your money, you do that.

¿Ándale, no quieres comer algo? Andas muy delgadito.

YOU    No thanks, 'ama.

I'm good, I had breakfast with Xandra and Yesi, / so—

ROSARIO    Ay, la Xandra. Cómo me cae bien. La Yesi también, pero parece perico, esa. How are they?

YOU    They're good, 'ama.

How's everything been here?

ROSARIO    Pos bien. De la casa al trabajo, del trabajo a la casa.

De vez en cuando batallando con la niña. Ya sabes, lo mismo de siempre.

But we're healthy, gracias a dios.

YOU    That's good.

. . .

'ama, you hear about the mermaid?

What / do you—

DIANA    *(coming back in the room)* Ay, no dude!

Don't even ask her—

ROSARIA    ¡CA-YATE Diana!

DIANA    'ama, I know you don't like that stuff!

You don't believe—

YOU    You don't believe / in mermaids?

ROSARIO    I didn't say I didn't believe in them!

There's lots of stuff we can't see that's real!
En mi pueblo, allá en Guerrero,
había muchas cosas así, historias así de fantasmas,
La Llorona. Pero yo pienso que la gente— Ay no sé—
¡La gente se inventa cosas!

DIANA  Y el video?

ROSARIO  Ya van a empezar con el mentado video.
Bueno, hay video de marcianos.
And you never seen an alien have you?

DIANA  'ama, it's just a lot of people seen stuff
they been seeing stuff and hearing stuff
out there by the river—

ROSARIO  ¡Yo no digo que no!
Pero mira todo lo que pasa en este mundo, ¿eh?
It's people hungry, gente sin casa, enferma de cancer.
Kids getting taken from their parents, kids they can't find.
Cops killing people, narcos matando a mundo y medio.
El gobierno más corrupto que la chingada,
y uno que apenas le alcanza pa' los biles.
And nobody does nothing!
People wanna think about mermaids. Hmphm.
No, qué bonito.

DIANA  You believe all kinds of things!
You put out water for San Judas every day!

ROSARIO  Because he's doing me a favor! Because he's a saint and saints
get thirsty, Diana!

DIANA  It's a picture 'ama! He can't drink the water!

ROSARIO  Then why's the water disappear, then?

DIANA  It evaporates 'ama!
Because it's so hot in here,
because you never turn on the AC!

ROSARIO  You don't pay the bills!

DIANA  I pay the electric!

ROSARIO  Fine!

DIANA  Okay, fine!

ROSARIO  Fine.
. . .
Aver. Turn on the AC.

Mira, tu pobre hermano.

He's sweating.

YOU  I'm good, 'ama. You don't have to turn / on the AC.

ROSARIO  *(She interrupts You and remembers her baby.)*

You used to like mermaids a lot. Cómo te gustaba *La Sirenita.*

When you were little little.

DIANA  You wanted to be Ursula.

ROSARIO  But you never learned to swim.

Igual que yo.

Mmm.

Imagínate, if we lived when God flood the world?

We woulda drown.

YOU  Noah had an ark, 'ama.

ROSARIO  But he was over there and we would be here.

Maybe we woulda turn to mermaids, verdad?

Unas Tlanchanas, cómo decía mi 'ama.

YOU  Mi abuelita Josefa, she talked about mermaids?

ROSARIO  Sí. De cuando era niña ella. Allá en su rancho.

Las Tlanchanas no eran así, like fish.

Snake ladies.

En los lagos. En los ríos.

And if you did them favors, they would do you favors.

And if you didn't. If you were mean. If you were bad.

They would eat you. If you were bad, te chupaban todo.

Leave your nails and bones and nothing else. Make you go away.

YOU  So, they were good.

ROSARIO  They were hungry.

Mmm.

. . .

You shoulda learned to swim.

We shoulda taught you.

In case God ends the world again.

*[She should have. Too late.]*

Bueno, pues pa' que te ruego más, pero si quieres comer aquí.

Mañana en la mañana viene tu padrino Erasmo.

Y su hermano, Gilberto.

You should come have breakfast.

Pa' que los saludes, que ya hace mucho que no los ves.

DIANA  Yeah, they'll be so honored. How lucky for them.

YOU  I'll be here, 'ama.

DIANA  Your funeral.

STEFFANY  (*From another room, water.*)

　　　Titaaaaaaaaa!!!

　　　Tita! Ahhuuuaaaaaaaaa

　　　Aaaaaaaaaaaaaa

DIANA  Ugh.

　　　Fuck.

　　　　　*She goes to Steffany.*

ROSARIO  ¡Ya voy, mija! . . .

　　　　　*She goes, too.*

STEFFANY  Aaaaaaaaaaaa Tita.

　　　Titaaaa!!!

YOU  (*A pebble in your throat. God, why won't the baby shut the fuck up?*) 'ama?

ROSARIO  Rrrruu / rrrruu rruuu

YOU  (*You, trying to reach your mother in another room. Your head. Your throat.*)

　　　. . . 'ama.

　　　I haven't . . .

　　　(*God, You want to say the ugly thing You want most right now.*)

　　　I think / I'm . . .

　　　(*Shut the fuck up, Steffany. The water is coming. Oh god.*)

DIANA  Shhhh / shhhh shhh

YOU  . . . tired, maybe

ROSARIO  What?

YOU  I just haven't been . . . (*The water is coming for You. God.*)

　　　Gl— 'ama h— (*No, they can't hear You. They should have taught You to swim.*)

　　　I think I'm /

　　　I'm going / to get a drink at Yesi's bar.

　　　I'll / see you—

DIANA  Ssshhh shhh shh

ROSARIO  Shhhh shhhh shh

　　　　　*The women lulling the baby streams into the rush of water from a spout at*
　　　　　*a bar. The tap. Sshhhh.*

## "YOU SANK ME!"

*The tap runs. Then, the pour from a bottle into a shot glass. You're at a dive, El Tapatio, to drink. To hang out with Yesi. There's Don Fito, a regular, very drunk, very handsy. He's working on two more shots.*

DON FITO  Glglglgl

Uno para mí.

Y otro para mí.

Glglglgl

Gracias, Yesenia!

YESI  You're welcome, Don Fito. Pero esta vez no se ponga tan pedo.

You want anything, dude?

YOU  Vodka soda? Tito's. Please!

*You try to pay. Yesi declines your card.*

YESI  Bitch, don't be dumb. It's on me. Welcome home, girl!

It's really good to see you!

You look like shit, but still.

Give me like fifteen, we can head out. *(She brings your drink.)*

It'll be a slow night, anyway.

YOU  Yeah, that sounds good. No rush.

Just happy to see / you—

DON FITO  Ey, mi Yesi!

¡Un buen mezcal

pa' que descanse el animal!

YESI  ¿Otro, Don Fito?!

DON FITO  Ahuevo!

YESI  A sus ordenes, mi capitán.

DON FITO  Oye, chavo. *(He leans in, hungry, shit-faced.)*

'tas chulo, cabrón.

¿Quieres un trago? Te lo compro, papacito.

*Don Fito puts his hand on the small of your back. He presses gently.*

YOU  Uh, no. This is good. Thank you.

DON FITO  Okay, pos cómo tu quieras, chiquitito. *(He removes his hand.)*

Oye, si viste lo que pasó, ¿verdad?

They found another Border Patrol dead by the river.

Found a man's body, too. In the water. Un migrante.

It's crazy, huh?

Bueno, solo dios sabe lo que nos manda.

¿Tú que opinas, mi rey?

YOU  It's terrible. Having to leave your home, your family behind,
     having to risk your life in the river / just to—

DON FITO  No sea mamon, mijo. Eso, eso ya se sabe.
     Eso ya lo vimos. You think it's a monster out there?
     That kill that Border Patrol?

YOU  It's just a story, right?

DON FITO  Pues sí, pero no. Mira, chulo, I'm gonna tell you something.
     Back in the day, I remember growing up,
     and that's the thing you have to remember,
     you have to remember all the things
     from growing up,
     there was all kinds of stories, mijo / my titi.
        *Don Fito puts his arm around You.*

YOU  Oiga, oiga, no soy / su m'—

DON FITO  Mi titi Adela, que dios la tenga en su gloria,
     she said que según esto, este, she heard this story
     de una sirena, y un día la sirena, she appeared in front of this man
     and she asks this man to take her to a church
     cuz if he took her to a church, she would have a curse lifted!
     She would be cured of a curse. She said,
     "Ey vato, if you take me to a church, I will give you riches!"
     She was beautiful, and this man was very poor and very sad about it,
     so the man said "No, pos 'ta bien. I'll take you."
     And she said, "We have three days to get there.
     And you gotta carry me on your back."
     Imagine you gotta carry a mermaid on your back?
     Ha! He was the first wetback jajajaja
     You get it? /

YOU  / No. /

DON FITO  Yeah, well he asks her—No—
     Wait, she asks him, yes SHE asks HIM
     To carry HER—a chingados—
     I'm getting lost! The mermaid asks this man
     to carry her on his back to a church, and she says,
     "No matter what happens, no matter what you hear,
     Don't look back at me!" But she's beautiful, so she's gotta remind him,
     "I'm serious, man, don't look at me! Que ni se te ocurra, cabrón."

So he's carrying her on a sheet on his back for almost two days.
Taking her to this church. She's heavy as shit.

YESI Like Juan Diego.

DON FITO Juan Diego met a mermaid?

YESI Juan Diego saw the Virgen
and she told him to take her to a church.

DON FITO No, this is about a mermaid.

YESI Ya sé, Don Fito! No, I'm just telling you.
This sounds like the story of Tepeyac—

DON FITO The Virgin Mary is not a mermaid!

YESI Oh que la chingada. That's not what I—
Here's your mezcal, Don Fito.

DON FITO Thank you.

YESI *(Trying so hard to save You.)* You need anything? Another one?
*(Quietly, aside, to You.)* I'm so sorry. He's nice, he just drinks a little.
I'm almost done here, I promise.

DON FITO *(Don Fito holds You at your waist, brings You in closer.)*
Anyway, I'm telling you.
This guy, he's carrying this mermaid.
And she's getting heavier and heavier
and by the third day, she doesn't sound like a woman.
She sounds like screaming,
like hundreds and hundreds of people
dying, crying, horrible screaming
and the man, he remembers, "Whatever you do,
don't look back at me!"
But it's impossible to carry all that weight,
all that screaming on your back
and not look.

YOU I can imagine—

DON FITO *(Don Fito inspects your hands, hard.)*
No, you can't.
Look at your hands, pelado.
What have you ever carried?
Don't look like / nothing.

YOU / You're hurting m— /

DON FITO Nothing! You'd turn back, too
if you heard all those screams,

all the screams only the water hears,
all that weight of all those things down there!
Tú no sabes, chavo!
Tú no sabes nada!

YOU   Let me / go—

    *You try to move away, but Don Fito pulls you in, back.*

DON FITO   No, no, no don't get scared, kid. I'm just telling you.
    I'm telling you this guy, this guy carrying the mermaid
    he feels all this weight, all this screaming
    and on that third day, almost by the church, he turns around, and sees
the mermaid
    but it isn't a mermaid, it's an ugly thing, una rosca de cadáveres,
    una serpiente hecha de todo lo muerto, de todo lo más horrible del agua.
    Everything down there is old and never dies and always remembers,
chavo.
    Through all of that screaming, through all of it,
    the mermaid curses the man. She tells him,
    "¡Maldito seas! ¡Me undiste, maldito! Me undiste."

YOU   You drowned me?

DON FITO   You sank me!

YOU   That doesn't make sense.

DON FITO   It's not your story, chiquitito.

    *Don Fito smacks your ass.*

YOU   What happens to the man?

DON FITO   He *(Don Fito slams another shot.)*
    Glglglgll

    *His gulping becomes louder and louder, until it's pebbles by a river and*
    *nighttime air. You leave El Tapatio, his story in your head. You drive with*
    *Yesi out to the nothing.*

## ARID, WET, DEAD, NOT

    *You and Yesi go out to the nothing close to the river at night. Nearest gas*
    *station is fifteen minutes away. Mostly billboards and sand. And that spot*
    *You kissed a boy once, and this spot. Yesi lights a joint.*

YESI   *(Light, spark, sizzle, smoke.)*
    Tchs-tchs-tchs

Sssss

Fffffff

Here, dude.

YOU  (*That high thinking, where the landscape cracks open and the brain whirs.*)
It's wild to think about how much has
changed, survived. Or not.
The land around the river, life around it.
We took a field trip once, learned about
how wet everything once was.
So, at any given point you could be
drunk out here with your friends,
and all you see is dry shrub and dirt
but you'd be standing in what was wet once.
I remember, I don't know if this is true
but I think I remember finding a little shell one time
on one of the field trips—
did you do field trips?

YESI  I guess. Yeah. We saw *The Nutcracker* one time.
And we went to a farm. It was kinda nasty. Farms smell creepy.

YOU  Yeah. Anyway, on this trip. I found a little shell on the ground
and I just kept thinking about how
everything had to have been all wet once,
more ocean than river, or desert and maybe that's what
all of this is here. An ocean that just kinda gave up being big,
gave up being an ocean. Maybe once, we gave up on being fish, y'know?

YESI  Yeah
No, dude. I don't know
what the fuck you're talking about? Hahahaha! Pinche loco, dude.

YOU  Bitch hahahaha
I'm just telling you
maybe everything eventually gets tired of being
so they become something else.
So one day, things make a choice.
Maybe the ocean saw soil erode,
mountains turn into themselves and said
me-the-fuck-too and made itself a river,
maybe water is just as willful
and maybe we were, too, maybe we were mermaids, too.

YESI  What the fuck? Maybe, though. But probably like the Jesus fish with
the legs.
Top-half fish, bottom-half person.
What the fuck even is that? Reverse mermaid?

YOU  Horrifying—
Why would anyone / choose—

YESI  People make shitty choices all the time.
Just to prove they can make them. Like, like those people crossing.
Imagine wanting to come here. Broke-ass country.

YOU  I don't think it's a choice.

YESI  Yeah. I guess so. Yeah. That's sad, then.
Fucked up to not have the choice.

YOU  Yeah. But I dunno. I look at the river and I think about what it was.
What it's become. Maybe because it wants to kill us.

YESI  Ew. Why are you like that? Cómo eres dramática, dude.

YOU  I don't think it's dramatic. Just life. (*Offers the joint.*)
Do you want any more?

YESI  Nah, not if I'm gonna start talking like you. I'm good like this.

YOU  Cool.

YESI  Cool.
. . .
You really think
the river wants to kill us?

YOU  Some part of it has to want some of us dead.

YESI  Which part?

YOU  The part that wants to be bigger, that misses stretching.
Maybe killing us is just a step in the want of the water.
Like fighting an infection.

YESI  (*In a mocking tone.*) "Fighting an infection." Oh, god.
Bruh, it sounds like YOU'RE the one that wants to die. / It's a river!

YOU  It's gotta have a deep want, no?
For the water to be an ocean, then change into a river—
Into something so delicate—
Maybe, that's what the mermaid is. Just the water, wanting.

YESI  Or it's a mermaid and it wants to eat people. It could be that.

YOU  How are you?

YESI  Just working at the bar and Albertson's. Trying to line something else
up, maybe.

My friend Io said there might be a spot opening up at Sephora.

That'd be fucking cute, to just be with make up all day. Get discounts.

I dunno. Trying to save up to move, maybe.

YOU   That'd be cool, yeah.

YESI   Y tú? How's your family?

YOU   Good. They're good.

YESI   You?

YOU   I'm good.

Well, that's not true.

YESI   You're bad?

YOU   Probably.

My head's been so fucking heavy and foggy. (*God, You want to say it, but You can't. Instead You say:* )

Somedays I just want to break it open.

I want to bash my head on a fucking rock.

Just glad to be home for now.

YESI   It's good you left, too, though, dude.

YOU   Is it? Cuz I feel like an idiot.

When I left, I thought I would arrive at myself.

I thought I'd find something up there,

some more of me up there.

And I feel like maybe the opposite happened

like I—I mangled myself into something else, into—

*Then, from somewhere, an echo of the howl, cry, bellow. A creature, far and faint, but You hear it. The water. It's calling You. It's coming.*

YOU   . . . Did you . . .

Do you hear that?

It sounds—

*A howl, cry, bellow. Closer now. Hungry.*

YESI   Coyotes, probably. Or La Llorona. It's getting late.

. . .

So, you think you've changed,

since you left?

I think you did.

YOU   Sure.

YESI   What do you think you came back as?

YOU   What?

YESI   What do you

Think you ccshhhhh

Shhhhhshshhhhh

> *Yesi's mouth turns into the river's rushing. It braids into a howl in the distance. You and Yesi leave, and nighttime emerges. At the same time, at another part of the river, a small group looking to cross the river appears.*

## ANOTHER CROSSING

> *Rustling in the bushes, a plastic bottle is crushed by an unintentional foot. Feet and breath, and the river running. La Loca, Crossing For The First Time is there along with The Other Lady With Them. They receive instructions from their coyote, Try It Again.*

TRY IT AGAIN  Cruzarán aquí, en esta parte del río.

Y de ahí, en friega hasta el centro. Les espera una camioneta.

Si se separan, o si algo pasa, siganle.

No se desanimen. Siganle.

LA LOCA, CROSSING FOR THE FIRST TIME  No, no, sabe que yo mejor me regreso.

Esto ya no me / parece—

THE OTHER LADY WITH THEM  Tenga fe en dios, y en el río.

Es lo que más nos queda, es fe.

Deme su mano, por favor.

LA LOCA, CROSSING FOR THE FIRST TIME  Que dios nos guarde.

> *A bellow, a cry, a howl. "The mermaid." Wind howl, bone dry, from the water emerged, in the distance.*

LA LOCA, CROSSING FOR THE FIRST TIME  ¿Qué fue ese ruido? Esa cosa, qué fue?!

¿Doña Martina? Doña Martina?!

> *The currents grow stronger and the water is rushing now. Try It Again and The Other Lady With Them struggling into the water. La Loca, Crossing For The First Time follows in.*

TRY IT AGAIN  ¡No tenga miedo!

THE OTHER LADY WITH THEM  *(Fighting the water that's carrying them.)*

¡El miedo nos mata!

¡Usted no tenga miedo por favor!

No tenga mie/gllllssshshshs

*And then, The Other Lady With Them goes under. For a moment everything*
*sounds like beneath the surface, as if under there with her, buoyant. For a*
*moment, everything moves like the long waiting of water, slow. The howl,*
*the bellow, the cry but this time clearer. It mourns The Other Lady With*
*Them, and carries La Loca, Crossing For The First Time to safety, this*
*cry. A splash.*

LA LOCA, CROSSING FOR THE FIRST TIME (*Their mouth pouring out*
*water, attempting to breathe, coughing. They struggle, water stinging their nose.*)
Gllshsllshhshhs

eccchhhh ehhhhccccc

¡Nos salvo!

¡El río, el río nos—

¿Doña Martina? Doña?! (*and inside the next breath, they know. They begin*
*to cry.*)
Martina . . .

TRY IT AGAIN  No se desanime. Usted corra, que ya vienen.
*La Loca, Crossing For The First Time runs. Another Officer near the river*
*watches. Eventually, static from a radio.*

ANOTHER OFFICER  Kkssshhh We had a couple head east, just crsskkkssh

We had an officer ksskshkshkskhs

The woman drownkwshksh

I'm approachingskksskskkkk

*Another Officer spots a second group coming up behind the previous one.*

ANOTHER OFFICER  Ksshshshshhs

We've got another group coming in behindkksssh

Looks about six years old and Kkkkshhhhs

They're looking like they're going to Kkksssh

*The water roars. Here is the howl, the bellow, the cry of The Drowned Thing,*
*deep and furious. The Drowned Thing appears before Another Officer, a*
*horrifying sound interrupting the radio.*

ANOTHER OFFICER  Kkkshsshsshit! Puta madresskskhhh

PLEASE SOMEONE I'Mkkkshh

GOD FUCKkkshshkshshs

*The Drowned Thing devours all the water in Another Officer. His bones crack*
*from the pressure, the force of this hunger. The Drowned Thing savors every*
*droplet that was once a man; all his insides, all their moisture. It sounds*
*horrifying. Then calm. The Drowned Thing howls, bellows, cries. Dawn*
*arrives. With it, the small mouths of the river, its town, emerge.*

## INTERLUDE: MOUTHS:

*Mmm. Mouths talking all around You.*

MOUTH ONE  Mmm. Did you hear about Rosario's kid?
He's back. A good kid. Smart. You hear?

MOUTH TWO  Mmm y lo de la sirena? Yo pensé que eran del mar. Pero cómo dijo Chavela.
Las sirenas nacen donde les de su chingada gana. You hear about the river?

MOUTH THREE  Mmm. So fucking dirty, and gross. God, I can't imagine doing that.
What they do? In all that dirt. The dirty water, God. Did you hear?

MOUTH FOUR  Mmm. My uncle, he works for la migra, pobrecito, they found him too, all dried out.
His back peeled off when they picked up his body. His skull crumbled. Did you hear about him?

MOUTH FIVE  Mmm. That's dumb, they're crossing. All those people? That's dumb.
Pendejos. Putting their kids in danger. You hear, there's more coming?

MOUTH ONE  Mmm. More water in the summer. All that rain. It's good. The ground's been too dry.
Qué bueno. ¡Que llueva, que llueva, la Virgen de la cueva! Te acuerdas?

MOUTH TWO  You hear the water at night, don't you? Weeping, maybe. The snakes been real quiet.

MOUTH THREE  La lluvia besando la tierra. El agua llenándolo todo. Quisiera nadar. Tantas ganas que tengo de agua.

MOUTH FOUR  You think the water is asking you questions? You think it's giving you answers? You think the river cares?

MOUTH FIVE  You hear what happened? On the news? That man, his baby? Imagine, wrapping a fist around the river, pulling it out your throat. Imagine.

MOUTH ONE  You hear about what happens here? Ha! That's a joke! Nothing, nothing, nothing ever happens here, except the sun.

MOUTH FIVE  Nothing ever happens here. Except the water, except every-thing. You hear everything rush in? You hear it? The water?

*The cry, the howl, the bellow. The Drowned Thing in the distance.*

ALL MOUTHS  Sssssshhhhhh

*The Mouths are rushing water. Somewhere, the cry, the howl, the bellow of The Drowned Thing.*

## IN YOUR HOTEL ROOM, EARLY MORNING WITH MARC

*You're back in your hotel room with Marc. He spent the night, so he's brushing his teeth. He's wasting so much water, You think. But this is nice, to be with someone who knows You like this. This is nice, to be with someone who adores You and asks for little besides toothpaste, which is really all You have to offer anyone right now.*

MARC  Rrrrrrssssssshhhhh

Ccrsh crsh crsh

Spppttt spptt sppt.

Grrrrllllgrrrlll

Sppt.

. . .

You sure it's cool that I stayed here? I don't know if you had anyone else / you—

YOU  I didn't. I don't.

No, it was really nice having you here.

Thank you.

MARC  My pleasure.

I was just so tired from work I knocked out immediately / after—

YOU  Sorry for hogging the bed.

Did I kick you? I've been kicking a lot, twitching.

Or cramping lately, too, at night—

MARC  Probably dehydrated.

Cramps usually mean that.

You got dehydrated legs.

YOU  What does that even mean?

MARC  Your legs probably need water.

Sorry if my alarms woke you up this morning.

I got, like, six of those shits and I still sleep through at least four, so yeah, my bad.

YOU  Are we gonna just keep apologizing all morning, or?

It's all good. Really. Been having trouble sleeping in anyway.

My body keeps wanting to get up / with nothing to do.

MARC  Probably wants to drink water

cuz you're dehydrated.

YOU  I'm kicking you out if you say I'm dehydrated one more time.

MARC  Maybe cuz you're not in your own bed.

YOU   No. Happened there, too.

    I'm just restless.

MARC   Probably cuz you're—

YOU   If you don't shut the whole fuck up!

    (*You throw a pillow at Marc. Hard.*)

MARC   Oh-kay. Shit. Just gonna put it out there, though.

    My bed's probably a lot more comfortable. It's bigger, too.

YOU   I like the luxury of a hotel.

MARC   Look at you, fancy callgirl.

YOU   Asshole.

    . . .

    Oh, I saw Xandra yesterday / she—

MARC   She told me.

YOU   / Oh. /

MARC   Yeah / she texted me to see if I / wanted to eat with—

YOU   She didn't tell me / ah, okay okay. Cool.

    I didn't know she was doing work out by the river.

MARC   Yeah, she threw herself into that shit after she broke up with Marcia.

YOU   You ever go out there with her?

MARC   No. I donate to them when I can, though.

    It's good. What they're doing.

    And now they have the mermaid on / assist, so—

YOU   (*It pours from You.*)

    I think I heard it.

    I was out by the sands out there,

    smoking with my friend Yesi.

    And I think I heard it

    and now I can't / stop—

MARC   You think it's real?

YOU   Don't you? I mean you showed me the video.

MARC   I don't think I think anything.

    I showed you that shit after you'd already heard that,

    that weird audio from your sister. You keep bringing it up, weirdo

    I'm surprised. You're always such a fuddy-duddy about / shit like this.

YOU   Fuddy- / duddy?

MARC   It's an expression!

YOU   For people old enough to have prostate problems. /

    A fuddy-duddy?

MARC  Oh god, no I just meant, you're always talking shit about /
      About the people here, about how they are, all of us.
      About how we think, and what we believe in
      so it's just surprising / to see you be so—
YOU  Whoa. No, I don't and I don't think that about you and
      *(Yes, You do, You fuckin' liar. But You don't want Marc to think that.)*
      I don't talk shit about people, but I do think that a lot of people here /
      People here get themselves stuck in—
      *(It stings, huh?)*
      They're—I don't talk shit!
MARC  Okay, maybe not like that, but you're not—
      I mean, you're not the nicest when it comes to how people here move.
YOU  I just think sometimes people here /
      They make their world so small.
      They don't know any better. They've never been anywhere else /
      They don't know anything else so, so, so /
      they just let themselves go a little.
      They / invest—
MARC  Let themselves go?
      Like—
YOU  Maybe they just don't want to see
      what they actually need to see,
      so they see mermaids instead.
MARC  Oh? And what do they need to see?
YOU  I just don't think there's any drive here /
      To fix anything, to make things / better—
MARC  What makes you different from them?
YOU  Nothing, I guess.
      / Nothing.
MARC  But you think you're different.
      You do. I'm not trying to be a dick.
      But, you do.
      Some part of you maybe even thinks you're better.
      That's it, huh? You think you're / somehow—
YOU  Wow.
      *(It's true. You hate it.)*
      Better?
      That's a really fucking shitty thing / to say—

MARC  No. That's not what I'm—
 No, I just meant. Fuck, I'm stupid.
 I don't mean to make you feel bad. / I'm sorry—
YOU  Late for that / huh?
MARC  I'm sorry. I dunno. I just—
 Just think that maybe you're—
YOU  Arrogant.
 That's fine if you think I'm an asshole
 for thinking that / people here—
MARC  That's not what I mean!
 I just meant that sometimes you talk about your life like—
 Like you walked out of some fucked-up car-wreck we're all still stuck in.
YOU  Ah.
 There it is.
 *(A tiny, ugly little pearl forms in your throat.)*
 . . .
 I don't think you're wrong.
MARC  I'm sorry.
YOU  . . .
MARC  Sorry.
YOU  . . .
MARC  I didn't mean to make it weird. I'm really sorry.
YOU  You didn't.
 . . .
 Anyway, I was thinking . . .
 . . .
 I'm gonna go out there, later tonight
 with Xandra and Yesi. To help out.
MARC  Oh. Great.
 That'll be good.
YOU  I think so.
 Alright.
 You should get ready for work.
 I gotta. Yeah,
 I gotta go to my mom's this morning. She's making breakfast.
 We got family visiting.
MARC  That's good. They'll be happy to see you.
 . . .

. . .

I'm sorry about this.

I—do you still want me to come by / tonight after /

YOU    I'll let you know, but yeah, should be good.

Yeah, I'd like to see you before I go.

If I go.

MARC    Okay.

YOU    Are you happy here?

MARC    Huh?

YOU    Happy. Here.

MARC    Happy's . . . that's not really—

I don't think about it. It's home.

I'm happy you're here now.

YOU    Yeah.

MARC    Okay, I'm gonna shower and get ready.

*Marc kisses your dumb face and heads to the restroom. The door locks. You pull up your laptop. The news.*

AN ANCHOR    —the group ran toward the Rio Grande.

That's when agents spotted a man hesitant to jump in.

Eventually, he did and struggled to stay afloat.

A CBP agent jumped in to aid the group in rescue.

The unsuccessful rescue resulted in the death of an agent

and a woman traveling with the group.

We now go to Adrian Flores for more.

*The shower turns on. The river on the computer, too.*

YOU    *(That ugly little pearl in your throat? It grows.)*

Mm . . ar . . . cc

Maaarr . . . ccc

Gl—

*Even through the screen, it calls to You.*

A CORRESPONDENT    These are the banks of the Rio Grande.

On the other side is Mexico.

The riverbed is uneven and the currents are unpredictable.

Taking one step could mean getting swept away. /

*The restroom door opens. The report continues through Marc's next line.*

Then, / US Border Patrol intervenes. The number of migrants attempting this dangerous crossing has sky-rocketed since—

MARC    Hey weirdo. You wanna get in this water with me?

*You close your laptop.*

YOU *(You exhale for what feels like the first time.)*

Sure.

Maybe I'll keep my mouth open while I'm in there.

To hydrate my legs.

MARC Dangerous.

That's how turkeys drown in the rain.

YOU That's a myth.

MARC So are mermaids.

But you sssssssssssstttttttttttt

Ssssssssssstttttttttttsssssssssshhhhhh

> *Marc's voice weaves into the shower. The water is so much louder. The shower goes, your feet follow. The shower becomes the sizzling of a pan. Kitchen sounds emerge. The sink.*

## DOS HERMANOS Y EL RIO

> *Your mami's kitchen, later that morning, huevo con chorizo sizzling. Erasmo, your godfather, is at the table. Gilberto, his brother, is watching television in the living room. Rosario, at the stove.*

ROSARIO Chhhzzzzzzkkkk

Erasmo, ya casi están los huevos.

Oye. ¿Qué vas a querer de comer tú?

YOU I'm gonna get juice. I'm not that hungry.

ROSARIO Lombriciento.

¿Estás en huelga de hambre o qué?

ERASMO Oye. ¿Y tú cuando regresaste?

YOU Been back for two days almost.

ROSARIO ¿No que acababas de llegar ayer, mentiroso?

YOU 'ama / I—

ERASMO No, sí, pos que bien. 'ta bueno.

ROSARIO *(To Gilberto, in another room.)*

Gilberto, ¿quieres frijoles con los huevos?

GILBERTO *(Seated in front of the television.)* ¿Cómo?

ROSARIO ¡Viejo sordo, te digo que si quieres frijoles!

GILBERTO Ah. Sí. Ándale.

STEFFANY *(From the bathroom, whining into a cry.)* Ahhhhuauuuauaua Titaaaa!

ROSARIO ¡Dianaaaaa! ¿Qué le haces tú a esa niña?

 Leave her alone!

DIANA *(From the bathroom.)* ¡Quiero bañarla y nomás no se deja!

 'ama, I gotta go to work soon!

ROSARIO Ay no, esa niña le corre al agua.

STEFFANY Aaahahhhhhhhuuuuaaaaaaa

 Tiiitaaaaaaaaaa!

ERASMO Esa salió buena pa' cantar.

 'ira nomás esos gritotes.

 Igual de mitotera que usted le salió la nieta, comadre.

ROSARIO Ya cállese, que nadie le preguntó a usted.

DIANA 'ama, can you come help—

 I need to get ready, please! I'm gonna be late again!

ROSARIO ¡Ya voy! Ya parezco sirvienta en mi propia casa.

 Aver, tú. *(To You.)*

 Ahí cuídame los huevos.

ERASMO Así le decía yo a mi vieja / cuando—

ROSARIO *(She hits Erasmo hard.)*

 ¡Cómo es cochino usted!

  *She goes to Steffany in the bath, leaving You in charge of the stove.*

ERASMO You okay?

YOU Just had a long night out with friends.

ERASMO Ah, puro pari. Muy bien, licenciado.

 Why you look sad?

YOU No, I'm good, / really—

GILBERTO *(From in front of the television.)* You see the news?

ERASMO ¿Los que se ahogaron en el río?

GILBERTO ¿Qué?

ERASMO Mmtskk. Nada sordo.

YOU *(It pours from You.)*

 I heard it.

 I think /

 I /

 I can hear it. Something close to the river. I think I've been hearing it.

ERASMO The río?

 Probably, yeah. Gets loud. Been raining a lot, lately.

 That río is carrying a lot.

YOU No, something else / like—

GILBERTO  *(Presiding over the television still, listening and not moving.)*
    You hear about the little girl they found?
    Se ahogó. Salió en las noticias.
YOU  *(To Erasmo.)*
    Padrino, have you been there? By the river?
    There's this sound—
    Last night, this kind of—
    Like, it's lodged / in my—
ERASMO  You're gonna burn the eggs.
YOU  Oh shit!
      *You plate the eggs.*
ERASMO  *(Erasmo looks at the plate.)*
    No, pos de cocinero no tienes nada.
    Qué bien que saliste bueno pa' la escuela.
    Yeah, it's always been something there.
    En el río.
    It's seen too much not to keep everything all pent up.
    I think that's why it keeps us here.
    Half the people here are cuz that river.
    How we got here.
    We owe it.
    We all do.
    It owns us.
    You probably don't remember,
    weren't born yet.
    How old are you?
YOU  I'm / *(Your age.)* —
ERASMO  Yeah, yeah, weren't born yet.
    But I remember, there was more water, back then.
    No se resecaba tanto el río entonces.
    And I remember, cuando Gilberto estaba chiquito y cruzaba—
    I was already here and so he—
    He got here in '82. It was easier then.
    Oye, Gilberto— ¿si te acuerdas de cuando cruzábamos antes?
GILBERTO  ¿Cómo? No te oigo.
ERASMO  Chingaos— ¿que si te acuerdas de cuando cruzábamos el río antes?
GILBERTO  ¿Cuándo?

ERASMO  Pendejo, lo que tienes de soreque también lo tienes de bruto,
    hijo 'e tu pinche madre.

GILBERTO  Que también es tu madre, animal.

ERASMO  No, pos sí, que en paz descanse.

    *Erasmo and Gilberto cross themselves.*

GILBERTO  Que dios la tenga en su gloria.

    ¿Bueno, pero qué preguntas del río?

    *Gilberto enters the kitchen.*

ERASMO  ¿Qué si era mas fácil de cruzar antes?

GILBERTO  No, pos sí.

ERASMO  Oye, pero cómo que siempre se siente algo gacho
    o triste ahí? Sí, no?

GILBERTO  Yeah, it's always been weird around there.

ERASMO  Pero no daba miedo. No, al contrario.

    Because we weren't scared. We aren't.

GILBERTO  If it's a ghost or like an old big fish
    o algo así, pues sí, es mejor no tener miedo.

    Decía mi mama antes, ella decía

    "No le tengas miedo a los muertos.

    Tenle miedo a los vivos."

ERASMO  It makes sense.

    To be more afraid of the living than the dead, no?

    Yo digo.

    Living people, they still have themselves to deal with.

    All those things rotting in their panzas.

    The dead—

    I don't think I met a dead person never.

    Maybe in dreams. Sometimes dead family talks to you.

    In your dreams.

    Según yo.

    I just know all the worst things I seen in my life, living people did them.

    Never seen a ghost kill nobody.

GILBERTO  No, pos that's true.

    Pero sí, yo me acuerdo . . .

    Este . . .

    Cuando . . .

    Válgame dios, ya se me pasó el tren.

    When I—

When did I . . . ?

Oye, when did you get here?

ERASMO I was here in '78, because that's when 'ama had already came here.

Because she brought me with her because I was the baby.

So you got here four years later.

GILBERTO Sí, that's true. I think that's true.

I'm gonna say it's true cuz then it is.

But yeah, I remember,

'apa and I would cross every so often.

To see you all here.

Me acuerdo que mi 'apa.

He would would pack our clothes for the weekend

in two plastic bags. Tie it real tight tight tighttighttight.

And when it was time, when it got darker /

He would look at the river.

Just look at all the water.

Quiet.

Real quiet.

Till he could go.

We'd go when the river said so. He could hear it, mi 'apa.

"Ya dijo el río." Así decía el. "Ya dijo el río."

So, if the river says

you go,

pos go.

We listened.

'apa would grab me real tight.

"Ándale, cabrón. Y no te me despegues."

I'd grip his hand tight tight tight.

And we'd walk into the water,

Sometimes with a . . . una . . .

Este . . . cómo se . . .

Llanta es qué? Es una tire, no? La cosa . . .

ERASMO Inner tube.

GILBERTO Sí, eso mero, sí.

Un inner tube.

Nombre. Te digo que ya se me chifla bien gacho.

Pero sí, el agua estaba canija.

Y le decía: 'apa,

'apa, tengo miedo.

Cuz I was scared a little bit. But he didn't care.

Not in a bad way. He just knew to listen to the river.

Ssshh shhh

He would just listen.

ERASMO  Always felt more alive. The river.

Always felt more like talking to it.

Sometimes, 'ama and I would wait for you

at night and we'd hear it, too.

Sh sh rsh rsh rsh *(They turn to You. They gift You this.)*

That's in you, too, licenciado.

That water. More than blood.

That's in you, too.

GILBERT  What you feel. When you go down there.

Algo pesado. That feeling.

That's the weight of our debt to that river.

What we owe it.

Something in there.

It owns us.

In the water.

In your head. Maybe ghosts.

ERASMO  Maybe just the water.

Rivers trick you like that.

Wild gets tricky.

Ask you to listen real close.

Así. Close. Bien close. Ask you to put your ear right up on it.

You should go.

GILBERTO  You should listen.

Good for your head.

You should go.

Sshh / sshh sshh /

Rsh. Rsh. Rsh.

ERASMO  Ssshhhh

Shhhhh rsssshhh

> You can't get them out of your head, their mouths. Erasmo and Gilberto's
> mouths turn into nighttime, by the river. There You are.

## BY THE RIVER

*You are by the river now, Xandra, waiting for Yesi to join. It's nighttime; time to work. To hide gallons of water and food in the bushes for those crossing. There You are.*

XANDRA  Rrssssh sssshh

Glp gulp gulp.

Sounds like it's swallowing little gulps of itself, huh?

The river?

When it's fat like that.

Hear that shit?

YOU  Little water mouths.

I can hear it.

It's taking little bites.

I could listen to it forever.

*You all listen. It feels like forever, even if it doesn't last that long. A small trance. Then:*

XANDRA  Alright, cuando llegue Yesi, if y'all wanna just take some of those jugs and y'all are gonna put them— Wait—

Pinche Yesenia . . .

YESI!

Bitch, you're late!

YESI  *(Offstage, from elsewhere and through labored breath, in a hurry.)*

Hold up!

Wait, traigo headphones.

What?

XANDRA  You're late, mensa!

*And now, Yesi enters and stresses everyone the fuck out with this explanation of why she's late. She's incredibly difficult to interrupt. She's a chismosa, so at chismosa speed.*

YESENIA  My bad, dude. Oh my fucking, god.

Dude, my brother—

You remember, Jorge? Well, he's fuckin' stupid.

So he was like, "Oh, don't go out there tonight. It's crazy."

And I was like "Shut the fuck up. We've been doing this shit."

And he was like, "No no no, you don't get it. They keep finding officers dead out there!

It's probably whatever people keep hearing in the river."

And I was like, "Shut up!" And he was like,
"Well, let me drive you down there so I know you're safe."
So, we're coming over here, and he was like, "You ever scared going
out there?"
And I was like, "Sometimes."
Cuz sometimes the Border Patrol agents get on people's asses.
And this dumbass goes, "Don't worry. I brought my piece."
So, he pulls up his shirt and he's got a gun tucked in his pants.
I swear sometimes I feel like he's the younger one, I was like,
"What the fuck are you gonna do with that?"
He was like, "I'mma kill that mermaid shit if it tries to hurt you."
And I was like, "So, you're gonna kill something you don't know is
real?"
And you could see in his eyes that like, he understood that he was
fuckin' stupid.
And who the fuck tucks a gun into their joggers? I was like "You're
gonna shoot your nuts!"
Honestly at this point, he might as well! That's the real danger.
The world having to deal with whatever dumbass kids he'll probably have!
A gun in his fuckin' musty-ass joggers!
I swear, he hasn't washed those fuckin' joggers since he bought 'em.
Pinche cochino.
Anyway, we had to stop to put gas.
Okay, so, what are we doing?

XANDRA  Setting out jugs. You can show / them—

YESI  *(To You.)* So, have you ever been out here?
It's pretty crazy. I don't know / if you heard
but they / say that—

XANDRA  Yesenia! Ya!
The water jugs. Go!

YESI  Ay, no me grites! I'm going.
*Yesi takes the water away.*

XANDRA  *(To You.)* A lot of people cross over by that side,
so you can put some water there, too.

YOU  Okay. What about this box?

XANDRA  That's granolas and Clif bars and cookies in there,
the little packs for the kids, when they come, too.
Make sure y'all tape 'em to the jugs. Tape's in the box.

YOU   Gotcha. This is—

I think it's really important that you all do this kind of work.

XANDRA   I guess, bitch. We were waiting on You to solve the immigration crisis with your degree, but—

YOU   Okay, Cesar Chavez, thanks.

XANDRA   Cesar Chavez hated immigrants.

God, no wonder You didn't finish, stupid.

Ándale, go be useful.

*Xandra leaves to join Yesi. There You are, with the water jugs.*


## A SCANNER, STATIC

*Nearby, at another part of the river, through Border Patrol radios, static.*

OFFICER IN TRUCK   Kssshsh

I think I saw them eastkssksh

Toward the back so it's the kssshsk

It's hard for the camera to catchkkkshshshk

Requesting other units kkkksshhh

OFFICER DISPATCH   *(Clearer than the first, but through radio still.)*

Ksshk Ten one.

OFFICER IN TRUCK   Kkkshshk I need the cameras to Kkkssshk

Ten thirty-three kkshhhk

OFFICER DISPATCH   Kssshk

You want me to go for you? Kshhk

OFFICER IN TRUCK   Ksshk

Yes kshsk

—er units to ksshshk

—by the bushes ksssshk

OFFICER DISPATCH   kkkshshsk

Ten one ksshk


## WITH YOU AGAIN, BY THE RIVER, ALMOST DONE.

*Back with You, Xandra, and Yesi.*

YESENIA   *(Winded, louder than she thinks she's being.)*

Dude. I'm so dumb.

I shoulda put on different shoes.

Fuckin' sand all in my shit now.

YOU  I think—

I stepped on something.

This smell keeps trailing me.

XANDRA  Yeah, You smell like shit.

I was thinking it was me.

YESI  I would say go rinse it off, in the river,

pero luego te jala de las patas and you'll die

and then I'll cry on TV and be like,

"I tried to warn him, but he didn't listen!"

YOU  Don't jinx me, Yesi. I don't need worse luck.

YESI  I know, right? Pa' que te echo más sal.

It's pretty, huh? Out here?

When it's calm?

So pretty.

XANDRA  It's beautiful.

Even with your eyes closed.

That sound. The wind.

YESI  That water.

YOU  So beautiful. Hard to imagine anything—

Anyone dying in there /

Here.

XANDRA  Because rivers and deserts aren't like that.

Fuckin' Border Patrol putos make the river dangerous,

scary, but it isn't.

This river /

We /—

YOU  (The water. It pours from you.)

Owe it.

XANDRA  It owns /—

YOU  Us?

. . .

Wait.

What did you—

YESI  Bitch, can we go soon?

I gotta babysit in the morning.

Migra's gonna roll through soon, anyway, so we should jet.

XANDRA   Yeah, for sure.

It's fresh tonight, though.

More rain's coming.

YOU   I shoulda brought a sweater. It's getting cold.

XANDRA   Fuck me! Dude!

We shoulda brought out the little blankets.

YESI   Damn, I didn't even think about it.

XANDRA   Fuck. —It's gonna get colder later. Fuck.

We shoulda—

. . .

*A truck, driving closer now, headlights.*

. . .

Shit.

There—yeah, there they are.

Pinches marranos.

Grab the bags and boxes and let's go—

*In the distance, a cry, a howl, a bellow, low.*

## A SCANNER, MORE STATIC, DEATH

OFFICER DISPATCH   Kkkkkshhhh

Nine twenty-six is reporting activity in the bushksssshsh

OFFICER IN TRUCK   Kkshhhh We need kksshshs—the subject kkshhh

—gas. Shit. My pedal'skkksshshs

*(The pig panics.)* Kkkkshhhhhs—my headlights are kkshshsh

*A cry, a howl, a bellow, hungry. The Drowned Thing appears before the officer. A horror woven from water. The officer pisses himself. He cries and tries one last call.*

OFFICER IN TRUCK   Kkkshshsh WHAT THE FUCK— GGHhssh

*The Drowned Thing reaches inside the officer and pulls out all the water from inside him through his throat. The truck flips. Officer In Truck dies.*

## BY THE RIVER, AGAIN

XANDRA   *(Breath, hurried.)* Yesi, did you get all the—

*(A loud splash, in the distance. A cry, a howl, a bellow in the distance.)* What the fuck was that?

YESI  La troca.

Dude, I think the pig got in an accident.

. . .

Don't see no headlights no more.

Do you s—

*A howl, cry, bellow. They all hear The Drowned Thing. Rage in it; a vast sadness—it pummels its way into the air. The Drowned Thing is the night now, a tarp of endless, heartbroken things wanting to breathe. You've never felt this small, mortal.*

YOU  *(That ugly little pearl in your throat.)* Oh god.

*(It grows larger.)* I ne . . . eed—

YESI  Xandra! Let's fucking go!

We g— *(crying now)*

I WANNA GO HOME!

XANDRA  *(trying not to cry, hard)*

Yesi, chill the fuck out! Let's g—

*She tries to hold a scream in her throat.*

*The Drowned Thing—it pierces, now. It pummels. It wants. You freeze. It calls to You. You call to it.*

YOU  *(The water in You quakes, and all the same your blood feels like lead.)* I nee . . . eed—

*(The water in your legs, your fingers, your arms. It wants to return.)*

I owww . . tttt . . .

Hrrggg—

*You try to run toward the river, to give it back. Xandra holds You back. You struggle.*

XANDRA  YESI, GO START THE CAR!

*(She tosses her keys to Yesi and struggles with You.)* DUDE, LET'S FUCK-ING G—

*The Drowned Thing wants. Its cry is a fist, a mouth. It howls!*

XANDRA  *(Struggling with You, with all the water in your body that wants to return.)*

WHAT THE FUCK ARE YOU DOING?! WE HAVE TO GO!

*The Drowned Thing opens itself, a horrifying braid of howls, cries, bellows. It drowns You in hurt.*

YOU  *(Your lungs lock. Your throat stops. Glottal.)* Gl—

*(Nothing. You freeze, for a second or two. Then the wind from your lungs punches its way out of your mouth!)*

GGGGGAAAAAAAHHHHHHH!!— *(The water in You stirs. You convulse. It wants to run! Your throat grieves! You almost sound like that cry, that bellow.)*

HRRRRRRGGGGGHH

G— *(You choke.)*

XANDRA  GO! MOVE!

YESI, START THE FUCKING CAR!

> *In the distance, a final howl, cry, bellow. The Drowned Thing recedes. Xandra drags You to the car. You all try your best to breathe, to be the same as before. How could you be?*

YESI & XANDRA  Ffff ffff

Hhhf hhff

Sssshhh sssssshhhh shhhhh

> *They become wind and the river rushing. The river runs.*


## AT YOUR MOTHER'S HOUSE, AFTER, WITH YOU SISTER

> *The river runs and somehow, your friends drop You off at your mother's house. You, trying to catch your breath. Your sister pours You a glass of water from a faucet.*

DIANA  Krsssshshshsh

Shshshsswhhoooo

Here. Drink.

I don't know what y'all thought you were gonna do out there.

YOU  We wanted to help.

And then suddenly, I don't know,

we couldn't—I forgot how to breathe.

I'm sorry. It was stupid.

DIANA  But you don't care, so it doesn't matter.

YOU  Is Mom asleep?

DIANA  Yeah.

YOU  I thought I woke her up.

Everything wakes her up.

DIANA  Not anymore.

YOU  Is she taking pills?

DIANA  Nah, edibles. I get 'em for her.
  They help a ton with her pain, too.
YOU  Mom's doing edibles?
  Wow. How'd you get her to agree to that?
  She's always been / so—
DIANA  She's been taking them since, like, a year ago? Year and a half?
  You want one? They're little gummies. Might help.
YOU  I'm good. Just shaken up.
  Nauseous, too.
DIANA  I haven't seen you eat since you got here.
  Maybe just blood sugar.
YOU  I haven't been hungry.
  Diana, it felt like—
  The sound / it was—
DIANA  Maybe you should put your head down. Close your eyes.
  Mom put a bunch of shit in your room. It's her storage now.
  And Steffany likes to fall asleep there cuz she's fuckin' weird,
  but I can wake her / up if you—
YOU  No, don't worry about it. No,
  I told Marc I might see him tonight, when I get back / to—
DIANA  Oh yeah. He told me
  you hung out /the other night—
YOU  (*Your throat is just a bit uglier than before.*) Oh my fucking god.
  Do all of you talk to each other?
  Nobody can take a shit here without / the whole—
DIANA  (*She bats back.*) Look, Marc and I have been friends since you all were—
  Dating? Whatever you were doing before you moved.
  It's not like we all sit around conspiring about you.
  We just talk. People talk here. People are friends here.
  Shit.
YOU  (*That ugly pearl in your throat, it grows.*)
  Don't be a fucking bitch.
DIANA  The fuck did you say?
YOU  (*Pivot.*) No no no— Oh god, I'm sorry.
  I'm telling you, this thing I keep hearing—
  My head—it's making me—
  Sorry—
  It's just weird . . . Having my sister talking to a guy I'm fucking.

DIANA  Ah, so y'all were hanging out like that?

YOU  . . . Yeah. I mean,
    He—I told him I was coming in, / and he—

DIANA  You know he's dating someone right now, yeah?
    Going on like six months.

YOU  He didn't mention anything / about a—

DIANA  Why would he? Not that it matters to you.
    You're gonna head back . . . What? In like a day?

YOU  Uh—
    He's . . . He—
    It's . . . fine.

DIANA  Yeah, it is.
    It is fine. What was he supposed to do?
    Wait for you?

YOU  . . .
    No, yeah . . .
    Actually . . .
    I've been thinking.
    I may stick around.
    Part of the reason I came back was to maybe look / for—

DIANA  Like, you're moving back back? Like moving here?

YOU  Yeah, I've been thinking,
    maybe / it would be ni—

DIANA  What'd you fuck up?

YOU  What?

DIANA  What'd You Fuck Up?

YOU  (*Bullseye. It hurts.*) Oh. Wow / um . . .

DIANA  Ugh. No.
    I'm not trying to be a bitch.
    Steffany was just crying all night—
    I'm just—
    You were so ready to get the fuck out of here when you moved—
    why—what did—yeah—did something uh—
    did something happen?

YOU  No. (*Liar.*)
    Yes, (*Fuck.*)
    just wasn't really doing too great.
    Things (*How embarrassing You are.*) just got really sad.

It would come in these really awful waves.

One day I would be fine and then this heaviness would just settle in my skin.

I could feel it in my marrow, and I'd scratch at my skin and hope my bones would just pour out, but it was just blood in there, my fingers couldn't do enough. But it's all I could think about, all the time. I just wanted to be a bag of insides pouring out, and I would drink too much and forget my head, I would just leave my head everywhere and

and sometimes I would lay there with my boyfriend, wanting to kill him, or just wishing he'd kill me,

just wishing he'd squeeze all the breath from my neck

wishing he'd pop me right open with an icepick

or that the bed would swallow us,

that the bed would kill us both—

it sounds crazy, but it felt like that and and and everything ended,

I ended every—

Yeah, I just sort of let go and got carried along with everything

and yeah.

DIANA  Mmm.

Sucks.

You shoulda said something.

YOU  I didn't want to bother you.

I just felt like I'd be something else to add to the pile.

DIANA  No, dude!—Ugh. No no.

See, this is the thing you do!

You never want to say anything until it's a problem.

You never actually want to talk about anything until it's a crisis.

You just let shit run wild until—

YOU  (*Your dumb, big mouth.*) We don't have to talk about this.

I just wanted to tell you—

DIANA  You're doing it. Right now.

You say you don't want to talk.

Then in a few weeks, or months, or years—really, whenever you feel like it—

you're gonna bring this up and we're gonna be the assholes who never asked

or who don't understand or can't help you or however you wanna tell this—but really,

really, you think we're all—
you know what, yeah we shouldn't—yeah—
Sorry. I need to— Yeah.

YOU  Are you—
Wait—are you mad at me?

DIANA  I just woke up to let you in because you did god knows what by the fuckin' river,
and I have work tomorrow morning, and I had to work a double today
and I have a kid I'm raising by myself
and since you left I've been taking care of Mom by myself
and it sucks to watch you just leave and get to have your whole fucking life elsewhere and have all the fucking fun you want to have and fuck whoever you want and pretend to be a lawyer, pretend like you're going to be some kind of hero when you come back and all of that is fine but we only fucking hear from you when it's an emergency like tonight, literally it's the only time we hear from you, but not even when we can help you. No, we hear from you when literally there is nothing for us to do to help you, that's when we hear from you, is when you're fucking drowning and Mom's been sick, and it's been scary and shitty and I get to watch her be sick and YOU, YOU get to be the one who comes back when you're in trouble when the rest of us, literally every single fucking person here is just trying to keep their goddamn heads above water and pay their bills on time and not fucking be sad about how shitty everything here feels sometimes, everyone is just doing their best to be fine with living here and dealing with our shit, because we don't have anywhere else to go when shit gets hard, because we all stayed here while you got to go.
You got to go and that's fine but now you're back and if you're here to stay fine, fine, that's fine, then stay but please start taking care of your own shit, please.
At least try because everyone here is so fucking tired.
God.
I'm—
I'm just really tired.

YOU  . . .
Mom's sick?

DIANA  (*She laughs tired.*) Haha.
Yeah.

YOU  Is there anything / I c—

DIANA  We got it.

YOU  I'm so/rry—

DIANA  We Got It.

> *Rosario enters, half-asleep, then waking.*

ROSARIO  tsscchhhh ey, chamacos.

¿'tan bien? ¿Qué pasó?

¿Por qué 'tan despiertos a estas horas?

DIANA  Por nada, 'ama. Nada.

ROSARIO  ¿Y tú?

Aver, ¿no que estabas en hotel?

YOU  Yeah, 'ama, just having a hard night.

I'm gonna go back right now. Wanted to come over. Talk to Diana.

ROSARIO  Hmmhmm.

Algo traes.

Yo te conozco.

YOU  No, de veras.

ROSARIO  Pues aquí tienes tu casa.

Y aquí estamos,

pa' cuando te quieras desahogar.

YOU  I know, mami.

ROSARIO  *(She takes your head in her hands and squeezes gently.)*

Ay hijo mio, esos ojos. Igual que los de tu abuelita.

Siempre llorosos. Pero así brillan más, ¿verdad?

Santo dios, cabezón. ¿Qué haremos contigo, eh? ¿Qué haremos?

*(She kisses your forehead.)* Bueno, criaturas. Me voy a acostar otra vez.

Que dios los bendiga. Hasta mañana.

> *Rosario kisses You and Diana goodnight and exits.*

YOU  She doesn't look sick.

DIANA  She used to.

You missed the worst of it.

YOU  I'm sorry.

DIANA  It's fine.

You look worse than she does, honestly.

YOU  Thanks.

DIANA  Yup.

Okay, I'm gonna get water and go to bed.

You need anything?

YOU  Nah.

Thank you, though.

DIANA  Yeah

> *She leaves and water pours from the faucet, loud.*

Krsssshshshsh

Shshshsswhhoooo

> *The faucet pours and pours, so loud, until You somehow make it back to your hotel, in your bed.*

## MOUTH DREAM WITH BODY COUNT

> *Your breathing pouring out, the air pouring in. Slowly, You dream every person You know here. They rise into your dream like emerging from beneath the water; a curse.*

YOU  Hhggnnrrrhhh

Ssshhh

G—

MOUTH ONE  wasshh russhh

MOUTH TWO  russhh rinsssee

MOUTH THREE  fffloahht fffhhuulll

YOU  . . . wa . . . ter?

Ggh—

MOUTH FOUR  Ssssstorm sssstill

MOUTH FIVE  gritttttttt sssssssiinkk

YOU  . . . dro . . . ne

dro . . . wn dr . . . ead

G—

MOUTH ONE  wisssssssp ssssnap

MOUTH TWO  sssstone fffffooot

YOU  . . . ppllee . . . sssee

. . . hhell . . . pp . . ppl . . .

G—

> *The howl, the cry, the bellow, The Drowned Thing calls again, from somewhere under this dream.*

MOUTH THREE  ccccoome

g—(*Mouth Three drowns.*)

MOUTH FOUR  pleeadd

g— (*Mouth Four drowns.*)

YOU  ...cccaa...n'ttt...

    ccrrr

    G—

MOUTH TWO  bbheggg

    g— *(Mouth Two drowns.)*

MOUTH FIVE  ssssiitt

    Sss g—*(Mouth Five drowns.)*

YOU  Hnnggg wr...app

    Riiii...verrrrr..unn...

    shhh

    G—

MOUTH ONE  kisssss

    g—*(Mouth One drowns.)*

ALL MOUTHS  *(Floating, their limp necks, snap.)*

    Cccome, ppleadd, pprraay, beggg, sssitt, kisss, sssinkk, ggiive /

    Cccome, ppleadd, ppraaay, beggg, sssitt, kisss, sssinkk, ggiive

YOU  Sssskkii...iiin...

    Nnn...ooo

    Sshhhs shh *(A howl, cry, bellow again—The Drowned Thing.)*

    ...nnnNooo...sss

    Ggghh—

    —

    *(Your alarm rings. You cough yourself awake.)*

YOU  ccgghh cggghhh

    ggghhhhhh

    G—

    G—

    G—

    *Your breathing turns into morning.*


## A LAST NIGHT

    *There You are in your hotel bed, Marc next to You. Above You, soothing
your aching chest and throat; your siren, as if you'd just washed ashore.*

MARC  Pssssssst

    Psssss. Hey. Hey, you okay?

    You good?

YOU  Shhii . . . ihh . . . tt
    Ggh . . . uh . . . yeah. Yeah.
    I'm sorry. I stopped—
MARC  You got sleep apnea?
YOU  No . . . I just had this . . .
    In my dream . . . everyone . . .
    This sinking . . .
    . . . like, it was like / I—
MARC  It's okay. It's okay.
    Here. *(Marc hands You a bottle of water.)*
    Drink.
YOU  *(Drink.)* That thing out there . . .
    It's . . .
    It's in me.
MARC  Yeah, I hear that.
YOU  You don't.
MARC  You know what I mean.
    . . .
    It's getting to you. All of this. Being here. I get it.
    Have you—
    Have you decided if you're going to stick around?
YOU  I don't
    know, I think
    I wish I knew what I
    wanted.
MARC  Come. *(Marc pulls You close.)*
    Kiss. *(He tries to kiss You. You pull away.)*
    Uh. Okay. Are you?
    You not feeling it tonight?
YOU  No, I'm just—
    I'm feeling sick—I think.
    Or—
MARC  Oh.
    Yeah. I'm sorry. No, I get that.
    I've been in the same space, too.
    My pops fell yesterday, and I've been stressing.
    Between work and him and all the deaths—
YOU  It's all I can think about, Marc.

Every day, all those people, their kids out there.
Their little arms wrapped around their parents,
their necks, all those people.
I know some make it but so many haven't. / It's all I—
Can—

MARC   Yeah. My cousin. He.

My cousin— I mean we weren't that close—
But you know how it is—my cousin—
He's— He was down there and I guess—
I guess he was helping.
They found his body.

. . .

YOU   Oh god.

. . .

I'm so sorry.

. . .

I didn't . . .
I'm really, really sorry, Marc.
If you . . .
If you need anything

. . .

(It pours from You.) I love you.
     You hold Marc.

MARC   (Disarmed. Poor Marc, he lets himself be held.)
I . . . I love you, too . . .
Thank you. I really needed someone to—
Yeah.
Thank you.
It's all so fucking weird and stupid—
God—
It feels like.
Damn. (Marc cracks.)
I—when they found his body—
It wasn't in the river.
It was just beside it. Like he was trash.
In the sand.
It was like—
he'd been out there for days. (Broken.)

His body was dried out, all of it.

Like the sun had eaten everything

stolen all of him from his body.

They couldn't even pick him up properly.

He fell apart, everything in him / fell apart.

YOU   Is he—was he Border Patrol?

MARC   Yeah, he'd been working a rescue / and I g—

YOU   (*Like a hideous toad, vomiting a fat, horrendous pebble, that ugly pearl, right into Marc's ear.*)

Good.

MARC   What?

YOU   (*Your throat is a cruel thing. You have gills now. You cling to Marc.*)

Good.

Good he died the way he did. Alone / like fucking trash—

MARC   (*Marc pushes You.*) Fuck you!

YOU   Those people drowning,

they're drowning because of animals like him.

Like your cousin. I'm glad he's dead. Good. Glad.

This world. It doesn't need him.

I hope it hurt. I hope it was excruciating.

Every minute he spent dying. And if you had any capacity

to actually use your fucking / head—

MARC   Nobody fucking deserves to die out there! Nobody!

You have no idea what the fuck you're talking about

and you need to / stop—

YOU   No, you don't get to be sad about innocent people drowning

and also cry about your fucking shitty cousin / who—

MARC   YOU DON'T GET TO TELL PEOPLE FUCKING SHIT!

YOU don't get to tell people how to feel about anything.

What fuckin' right do you have to—

To anything here?

God, and my cousin?! You fucking bitch!

You have been back for three days—less than that.

And you— FUCK— What the fuck is wrong with you tonight?

I wish you / would just—

YOU   Go?

You wish I would go?

Would that make it easier for you

and whoever else you're fucking right now?

Hmm? Diana told me—

She said you were seeing someone,

which you never mentioned.

Not this whole fucking time since I've been here

you never / once—

MARC  For what?!

For what?! Who owes you shit?

Who owes you anything? You don't live here!

We fuck when you visit and then you leave again.

You get to come in here and just pick all the shit you like.

And take it with you / and what—

YOU  (*You grow claws, fangs, and scales. Your skin makes poison.*)

And what is there to take from here, Marc?!

What do I take back with me? You?

You, with a whole other person you lie to at night

so that you can sleep here, next to me?

Like a dog, waiting for the next time I come around to feed you?

You, sitting here, rotting, doing what, Marc?

Doing what all of you fucking do in this shithole.

Nothing. Waiting and watching everything and everyone around you die.

And you all just shrug and rot, too, because you don't know how to do anything else.

But rot right here.

Do you know why I come home? When I feel bad?

I come home.

To pity you.

MARC  (*Marc charges at You, seizes You.*) YOU NEED TO SHUT YOUR STUPID FUCKING MOUTH BEFORE / I—

YOU  (*Soft, a blade.*) Do it. Do something. Do anything, Marc.

Do anything. Get me closer.

MARC  (*He holds You.*)

    . . .

I feel fucking sorry for you.

You—

You have nothing here.

You left and came back nothing.

*Marc kisses You. He bites down hard and draws blood; an opening.*

YOU  (*And with something like that howl, cry, bellow in your throat, You push him away.*) HHHRRRRRGGGGGGHHH!!!

GO!

GET OUT!

GET THE FUCK OUT!

GET THE FUCK OUT NOW!

G— (*Your throat catches and dries. You're almost there.*)

MARC  You should, too.

You should get out, too before

you / Sssssssssssshhhh

*Marc's mouth turns to nighttime. Marc leaves. You can barely stay upright. You might grow a tail. Fins.*


## NO SCOOBY GANG SHIT

*Nighttime, outside your hotel parking lot. There You are, on the asphalt, the river in your head runs—a madness. You're a craving thing now. You want. Yesi and Xandra's mouths are now nighttime.*

XANDRA  Crrrrr /

Crrrr /

YESI  Fssssssh

Fsssssh

XANDRA  Ffffffuck it's cold.

You okay?

YESI  It's late, dude.

You fuckin' scared us.

¿Qué pedo?

YOU  (*Your arms and legs, their small tremors.*) I want to go back.

Come with me.

I need to go back to the water

XANDRA  For what?

YOU  My head.

XANDRA  What?

YOU  (*The currents in your skull.*) My head.

I want

I want to go

I want to know everything.

YESI  You fucking serious?

   After all that shit tonight.

   You still / want—

YOU  I wonder about all the things down there

   often, about how many legs everything doesn't have.

   I want to know what happens when you drown.

YESI  Bitch, you die!

YOU  / Yes, and maybe,

   maybe suddenly you know everything.

XANDRA  Or maybe you just fuckin' die.

   When people drown, they drown.

   They die—

YOU  No.

   There's more—

   There's more than dying down there.

   Everything.

   I want to go. (*Wildness in your throat.*)

   Come!

YESI  You are fucked in the head.

   I swear, you're fuckin' wild.

YOU  No,

   we should be

   wild. In the water. (*So hard to contain all that blood in You.*)

   More. I want to / be—

XANDRA  Dead. You'd be dead! Eat, Pray, Drown!

   God, bitches go to college once and suddenly

   they got ideas about everything.

      *Far away, a splash, a cry, the howl, a bellow. The Drowned Thing is listening.*
      *You call to it.*

YOU  (*Your blood whirs, spins. It wants to rush away from You. Horses in your*
   *veins.*) There! It's coming.

   Like fists and jaws wrapped in rain.

   The rushing—

   We should go!

XANDRA  Yes,

   we *should* go.

   I got work in the morning.

YOU   To the river
      / Come!
XANDRA   We almost just fuckin'—
      No. No, we should not.
YOU   (*So close.*) I want to see, hear
      I . . . touch, I . . . please I—
      Come with me!
YESI   No, dude.
      I'm not doing no Scooby gang shit / tonight—
XANDRA   You really want this?
YOU   Water.
XANDRA   Yeah, if, if—
      If you think you should go.
      You should,
      You should go.
YOU   (*Your throat thirsts.*) I wa . . . nt the
      Gl—
      The waa . . ter . . . (*The river pounds in your head now.*)
          *Yesi and Xandra hold your head and kiss it.*
YESI   Good luck.
XANDRA   Yeah, goodl—
      Glglglgl ccrrr/ ssssshhs
YESI   Crrr crrr sshshh
      ssshhhhhhh
YOU   Thank you.
      *You run, the water in your body, vibrant, carrying You.*


## DOWN

> *You've made it to the river. There You are, the water rushing, and your mouth is nighttime. Language is nothing now for You. You, so full of want and this river's spell.*

YOU   Crrrrr
      Crrrrr
      Crrrrr
      Sssssshh sshhhh shhhh
      Ffff ffffffuck.

Ffff

You.

*You kneel in front of the river. You dip your hands in. You came to want the water. Release. Language breaks.*

YOU   I wa . . . nt

a well . . . wisssh

Pleeaa . . ssssse . . . I—

*You shove your head full force into the water. One. Two. The water stirs. A howl, a cry, a bellow. The water expels your head and hands, hard, knocks You back. God, does nothing want You?*

YOU   Gll—

WANT ME! TAKE M—

*A howl, a cry, a bellow, monstrous and vast! The Drowned Thing emerges, full of everything long gone and going!*

THE DROWNED THING   HHHHRRRRRRRRGGGGGGGGHHHHHHH HH!

bruussssssshhhhhh-sssssssstroke

Whhhhhiiiindd-whhhheeeeeept

YOU   You're—

I can hear you—

Y—

THE DROWNED THING   Flllaaahhhhhhhhht fffhhhhhhuuuullll Rrrrrhhhhhuuusshsh rrrhhhiiiinsssssse

YOU   I'm here

for you

to hear you

to give y—

THE DROWNED THING   Rrrrrhhhhhhaaaaaageee rrhhhhoollllll Ppllllhhuuuuummmeee khhhiisssssssssssss

YOU   My head.

It's full of you

of everything

you,

sad and dirt

and rocks

and dry,

and no small gods

tend to it,

my head
so full,
sand
so full of please, please
water. Please, I want
y—
THE DROWNED THING  Sssssssssstoooooone fffhhooooooottt
ssttooooorrrm ssstttttiilllllll
YOU  You called to
You
I followed
I wa . . . nt the wa . . . ter wa . . . nt
my hhhee . . . ad
full of
drown
of y—
THE DROWNED THING  Sssssiiilltt sssssliiiitt
Ssssssaaaand ssshiiiiiiifffftt
Rrrrussssssssssssssh rrrrrrrhhhhhessssssst
Rrrrrrruuuusssssh Ssssssssssssssssshhhhhhh
YOU  I want
the wet
To wed the water
You, I want to wade the wet
Te ruego
Por favor
Llevame
Llueveme
Llename
Te rrr . . ue . . gggg . . o
Por ff—
Y—rrrsrhhsh
I—sssshh
Gl—
THE DROWNED THING  Sssskiiiiin
skiiiinnnnn
Skiiiinn
HRRRRRRGGGGGGGGGGGHHHHHHHHH!

YOU  I w—
    glp you—ghhhhh
    I—
    ghghhghhhh
    Shshhshshshs gggll
    G—

*Your throat feels stupid, doesn't it? Doesn't it feel silly? To want this? Your throat. Your chest. Oh god, your lungs.*

*You plunge under the water, into the river. There You are, in the below, with The Drowned Thing, clear, clear all around You. Every Mouth joins its spell, gives it praise. You, its tribute.*

| THE DROWNED THING | MOUTHS THREE, FIVE | MOUTHS TWO, FOUR | YOU |
|---|---|---|---|
| Wash rush wind wept | | | *(It's not like in the* |
| Cold sweep flight lift | Wash wind rush wept | | *movies.* |
| Rush rinse stone foot | Fog lift sweep swift | Come plead sit kiss | *Drowning is almost* |
| Wisp snap storm still | Stone rush snap foot | Pray beg sink give | *entirely a silent act. It* |
| Breath reap tide tongue | Rinse wisp storm reap | Silt sand blood lift | *happens much quicker* |
| Silt slit soil soot | Kiss come sink plead | Wash wept rush wind | *in freshwater.* |
| Blood tint stone foot | Blood bloat full sea | Neck snap blood kiss | *Dying in freshwater* |
| Float full sea bloat | Full tint soot stream | Sea skin beg slit | *takes about two* |
| Give sink grit kiss | Slit silt beg skin | Stream full wisp rinse | *minutes. Maybe three.* |
| Sink | Plead sit pray sink | Tint stone tide reaped | *Luck. It feels counter-* |
| Sink | Sink | Full sea float still | *intuitive, doesn't it?* |
| Bloat | Sink | Sink | *You always thought* |
| Sink | Bloat | Sink | *the ocean would kill* |
| Float | Sink | Bloat | *You much faster. The* |
| Skin | Float | Sink | *body, it surprises You* |
| Sink | Skin | Float | *to discover, decomposes* |
| Sink | Sink | Skin | *much, much faster in* |
| Sink | Sink | Sink | *freshwater, too. Not that* |
| Sink | Sink | Sink | *it's happening to You* |
| Sink | | Sink | *now, but soon. Soon now.* |
| Sink | | | *Down there You realize* |
| | | | *it all so quickly.* |

*You.)*

YOU *(Drown. What You wanted most. Slowly, your body floats.)*

THE DROWNED THING *(A belly-full natural thing, a calm thing in the gut. It retreats.)*

> Hrrrrrrrgggggggghhhhhh
> Sssssshhhhhhh.

> *Then nothing for some time but nighttime. Nighttime. Then a rustling in the bushes. Small whispers. A group in the bushes.*

ANOTHER CHILD  Mami, se oye feo.

> No quiero.

FIRST TIME CROSSING  Aquí estoy. Aquí contigo.

> No tengas miedo.

TRY IT AGAIN  No se preocupen.

> Son los coyotes.

A CHILD AGAIN  Mami, tengo frío.

FIRST TIME CROSSING  ¿Y cruzamos aquí?

TRY IT AGAIN  Sí señora, aquí cruzamos. Con calma.

> Ya se ve más tranquilo todo.

> Dame la mano chiquita.

> Aver señora, usted también.

> *They step into the water with great calm, across, across, across. Gracefully. The water lets them tonight. God, the river sounds nothing like anything called a border. For a second, the border ends in the water, the border ends everywhere. Good luck.*


## EPILOGUE: MOUTHS

> *Nighttime breaks into morning. The mouths in the town, living so close to that river, close enough to hear it always, even when it's far. The river runs.*

MOUTH ONE  ¿Si escuchó, lo que pasó?

MOUTH TWO  Rosario's kid.

MOUTH THREE  In the river.

> Yeah.

MOUTH FOUR  It's sad, huh?

MOUTH FIVE  It's what happens.

MOUTH ONE  When You drown.

MOUTH TWO  Whatever the water wants.

MOUTH THREE  For You to surrender, to remember, to reach.

MOUTH FOUR  For You to fight it, but it doesn't care if You do.

MOUTH FIVE  For You to lose your body so You could long for it.

MOUTH ONE  It's like everything You want happens and somehow your body wants none of it.

    And water *(Mouth One floats.)*

MOUTH TWO  water *(Mouth Two floats.)*

MOUTH THREE  water *(Mouth Three floats.)*

MOUTH FOUR  water *(Mouth Four floats.)*

MOUTH FIVE  water *(Mouth Five floats.)*

EVERY MOUTH NOW  Water water w  a  t  e rw    a    t  e    r

    W     a    t e   r

    Ssshshhshhh

    Hhhng G— *(They float.)*

        •      •      •

# PRODUCTION HISTORIES

## THE HOUR OF FEELING
MONA MANSOUR

### *Production History*

*The Vagrant Trilogy* (comprising *The Hour of Feeling*, *The Vagrant*, and *Urge for Going*) was premiered by Mosaic Theater Company of DC (Ari Roth, Artistic Director) on June 6, 2018, directed by Mark Wing-Davey. Set Design: Luciana Stecconi; Lighting Design: Reza Behjat; Costume Design: Ivania Stack; Sound Design: David Lamont Wilson; Production Design: Paul Deziel. The cast included Nora Achrati, Michael Kramer, Dina Soltan, Hadi Tabbal, Shpend Xani, and Elan Zafir.

    *The Vagrant Trilogy* was produced off-Broadway by The Public Theater (Oscar Eustis, Artistic Director). It premiered on April 8, 2022, directed by Mark Wing-Davey. Scenic Design: Allen Moyer; Lighting Design: Reza Behjat; Costume Design: Dina El-Aziz; Video Design: Greg Emetaz. The cast included Bassam Abdelfattah, Tala Ashe, Caitlin Nasema Cassidy, Ramsey Faragallah, Osh Ghanimah, Nadine Malouf, Rudy Roushdi, and Hadi Tabbal.

## SOJOURNERS
MFONISO UDOFIA

### *Production History*

*Sojourners* was developed at the 2013 Sundance Institute Theatre Lab at the Sundance Resort; as part of the Martha Heasley Cox Virgin Play Series 2014 at the Magic Theatre (Loretta Greco, Producing Artistic Director; Jaimie Mayer, Managing Director) in San Francisco, California; and through the Playwrights Realm Writing Fellowship and Page One Residency.

The off-Broadway premiere of *Sojourners* was produced by The Playwrights Realm (Katherine Kovner, Artistic Director; Roberta Pereira, Producing Director) on January 21, 2016. It was directed by Ed Sylvanus Iskandar, the scenic design was by Jason Sherwood, the costume design was by Loren Shaw, the lighting design was by Jiyoun Chang, the sound design was by Jeremy S. Bloom, the dialect coach was Jane Guyer Fujita, the Ibibio language coach was Ebbe Bassey Manczuk, the puppet design was by Stefano Brancato, the props design was by Samantha Shoffner, and the production stage manager was Kara Kaufman. The cast was as follows:

| | |
|---|---|
| ABASIAMA EKPEYONG | Chinasa Ogbuagu |
| MOXIE WILIS | Lakisha Michelle May |
| UKPONG EKPEYONG | Hubert Point-Du Jour |
| DISCIPLE UFOT | Chinaza Uche |

*Sojourners* was further developed and produced by New York Theatre Workshop (Jim Nicola, Artistic Director; Jeremy Blocker, Managing Director) in association with The Playwrights Realm in 2017. It was produced with the same cast and crew as The Playwrights Realm, with the exception of Janice Paran as the dramaturg and Dawn-Elin Fraser as the dialect and text coach.

*Sojourners* received its West Coast premiere at the Magic Theatre in 2016. It was directed by Ryan Guzzo Purcell, the scenic designer was Eric Flatmo, the costume designer was Karina Chavarin, the lighting designer was York Kennedy, the composer and sound designer was David Molina, the dialect coach was Jessica Berman, and the stage manager was Justin Schelgel. The cast was as follows:

| | |
|---|---|
| ABASIAMA EKPEYONG | Katherine Renee Turner |
| MOXIE WILIS | Jamella Cross |
| UKPONG EKPEYONG | Jarrod Smith |
| DISCIPLE UFOT | Rotimi Agbabiaka |

The playwright would like to especially thank Mr. Essien E. Idiong and Ebbe Bassey Manczuk for their work on Ibibio translations.

## COLEMAN '72
CHARLIE OH

### *Production History*

*Coleman '72* was originally workshopped and developed in the 2021 Pacific Playwrights Festival as part of The Lab at South Coast Repertory and originally produced by South Coast Repertory. *Coleman '72* first opened in Costa Mesa, California, on April 28, 2023, with David Ivers as the Artistic Director and Paula Tomei as the Managing Director. It was directed by Chay Yew. The scenic design was by Daniel Ostling; the costume design was by Sara Ryung Clement; the lighting design was by Pablo Santiago; the sound design was by John Zalewski; the projection design was by Stephan Mazurek; and the stage manager was Darlene Miyakawa. The cast was as follows:

| | |
|---|---|
| JAMES | Paul Juhn |
| ANNIE | Jully Lee |
| JENN | Tess Lina |
| MICHELLE | Jessica Ko |
| JOEY | Ryun Yu |

## PUBLIC OBSCENITIES
SHAYOK MISHA CHOWDHURY

### *Production History*

*Public Obscenities* first opened at Soho Repertory Theater in New York, NY, on February 15th, 2023, with Cynthia Flowers, Caleb Hammons, and Eric Ting as the Artistic Directors. It was written and directed by Shayok Misha Chowdhury. The scenic design was by dots; the costume design was by Enver Chakartash; the lighting design was by Barbara Samuels; the sound design was by Tei Blow; the video and projection design were by Johnny Moreno; and the stage manager was Alyssa K. Howard. The cast was as follows:

| | |
|---|---|
| SHOU | Tashnuva Anan |
| CHOTON | Abrar Haque |
| JITESH | Golam Sarwar Harun |
| PISHIMONI | Gargi Mukherjee |
| SEBANTI | NaFis |
| RAHEEM | Jakeem Dante Powell |
| PISHE | Debashis Roy Chowdhury |

*Public Obscenities* began its run at Woolly Mammoth in Washington, DC, starting November 13th, 2023, with Maria Manuela Goyanes as Artistic Director and Kimberly E. Douglas as Managing Director. It returned to New York at Theatre for a New Audience (TFANA) on January 17, 2024, with Dorothy Ryan as Managing Director.

## SANCTUARY CITY
MARTYNA MAJOK

### *Production History*

*Sanctuary City* had its world premiere at the Lucille Lortel Theater (Caridad Svich, Artistic Director for New Play Development; George Forbes, Executive Director) in New York, on September 21, 2021, and was produced by New York Theatre Workshop. It was directed by Rebecca Frecknall, with Caitlin Sullivan serving as the remount director. The set and costume designs were by Tom Scutt, the lighting design was by Isabella Byrd, the sound design was by Mikaal Sulaiman, and the production stage manager was Merrick A.B. Williams. The cast was:

| | |
|---|---|
| B | Jasai Chase-Owens |
| G | Sharlene Cruz |
| HENRY | Austin Smith, Julian Elijah Martinez |

# WOLF PLAY
## HANSOL JUNG

### Production History

*Wolf Play* was commissioned by Artists Repertory Theatre (Dámaso Rodriguez, Artistic Director; Sarah Horton/J.S. May, Managing Directors) in Portland, Oregon, and first produced as a National New Play Network Rolling World Premiere by Artists Repertory Theatre and Company One Theatre. The production was directed by Dámaso Rodriguez, with scenic design by William Boles, costume design by Sarah Gahagan, lighting design by Kristeen Willis, sound design by Sharath Patel, and puppetry by Matt Acheson.

The cast was as follows:

| | |
|---|---|
| ASH | Tamera Lyn |
| ROBIN | Ayanna Berkshire |
| RYAN | Vin Shambry |
| PETER | Chris Harder |
| WOLF | Christopher Larkin |

*Wolf Play* received its East Coast premiere as a National New Play Network Rolling World Premiere by Company One Theatre in Boston, Massachusetts (Shawn LaCount, Artistic Director: Karthik Subramanian, Interim Managing Director). The production was directed by Summer L. Williams, with scenic design by Janie E. Howland, costume design by Karly Foster, lighting design by Kat C. Zhou, sound design by Matt Otto, and puppetry by Amanda Gibson.

The cast was as follows:

| | |
|---|---|
| ASH | Tonasia Jones |
| ROBIN | Inés de la Cruz |
| RYAN | Adrian Peguero |
| PETER | Greg Maraio |
| WOLF | Minh-Anh Day |

*Wolf Play* received its New York premiere at Soho Rep. in New York, NY (Sarah Benson, Artistic Director; Cynthia Flowers, Executive Director). The production was directed by Dustin Wills, with scenic design by You-Shin

Chen, costume design by Enver Chakartash, lighting design by Barbara Samuels, sound design by Kate Marvin, and puppetry by Amanda Villalobos.

The cast was as follows:

| | |
|---|---|
| ASH | Esco Jouley |
| ROBIN | Nicole Villamil |
| RYAN* | Quinlan / Brandon Mendez Homer / Brian Quijada |
| PETER | Chris Bannow / Aubie Merrylees |
| WOLF* | Jin Ha / Mitchell Winter |

*Wolf Play* was developed by Victory Gardens Theater, Chicago, Illinois (Chay Yew, Artistic Director; Erica Daniels, Managing Director) as part of IGNITION Festival of New Plays 2017. The initial production of 2020 was canceled during technical rehearsals due to the COVID-19 epidemic. Asterisks (*) indicate roles recast for the 2022 and 2023 production and transfer.

# A RIVER, ITS MOUTHS
JESÚS I. VALLES

## Development History

Brown University, Writing is Live, 2021
Teatro Vivo, Austin Latinx New Play Festival, 2022
Stages Houston, Sin Muros Latinx Play Festival, 2023

## Awards

Winner, Kernodle Playwriting Award, 2023
Nominee, The Venturous Fellowship, 2023
2nd Place, Latinx Playwriting Award, KCACTF
Distinguished Achievement, Jean Kennedy Smith Playwriting Award, KCACTF

# ABOUT THE CONTRIBUTORS

**Shayok Misha Chowdhury** is a many-tentacled writer and director based in Brooklyn. A Mark O'Donnell Prize and Princess Grace Award recipient, Misha was an inaugural Project Number One Artist at Soho Rep, where he directed the world premiere of his play *Public Obscenities* (one of three finalists for the 2024 Pulitzer Prize and a *New York Times* Critic's Pick). Misha was also awarded a Jonathan Larson Grant for his body of work writing musicals with composer Laura Grill Jaye; their most recent collaboration, *How the White Girl Got Her Spots and Other 90s Trivia*, was awarded the 2022 Relentless Award. Other collaborations: *Brother, Brother* (New York Theatre Workshop) with Aleshea Harris; *SPEECH* (Philly Fringe) with Lightning Rod Special; *MukhAgni* (Under the Radar @ The Public Theater) with Kameron Neal; *Your Healing Is Killing Me* (PlayMakers Rep) with Virginia Grise. Misha is also an alumnus of New York Theatre Workshop's 2050 Fellowship, The Public Theater's Devised Theater Working Group, Ars Nova's Makers Lab, New York Stage and Film Nexus, the Sundance Art of Practice Fellowship, The Drama League's Next Stage Residency, and Soho Rep's Writer Director Lab. BA: Stanford. MFA: Columbia.

**Hansol Jung** is a playwright from South Korea. Productions include *Wild Goose Dreams* (The Public Theater, La Jolla Playhouse), *Wolf Play* (NNPN Rolling Premiere: Artists Rep, Mixed Blood, Company One), *Cardboard Piano* (Humana Festival at ATL), *Among the Dead* (Ma-Yi Theatre), and *No More Sad Things* (Sideshow, Boise Contemporary). Commissions from The Public Theater, La Jolla Playhouse, Seattle Repertory Theatre, National Theatre in the UK, Playwrights Horizons, Artists Repertory Theater, Ma-Yi Theatre, and Oregon Shakespeare Festival. Her work has been developed at Royal Court, New York Theatre Workshop, Hedgebrook, Berkeley Repertory, Sundance Theatre Lab, O'Neill Theater Center, and the Lark. Hansol is the recipient of the Hodder Fellowship, Whiting Award, Helen Merrill Award, Page 73 Fellowship, Lark's Rita Goldberg Fellowship, NYTW's 2050 Fellowship,

MacDowell Artist Residency, and International Playwrights Residency at Royal Court. She is a proud member of the Ma-Yi Writers Lab, NYTW's Usual Suspects, and The New Class of Kilroys. MFA: Yale.

**Martyna Majok** was born in Bytom, Poland, and raised in New Jersey and Chicago. She was awarded the 2018 Pulitzer Prize for Drama for her Broadway debut play, *Cost of Living*, which was nominated for the Tony Award for Best Play. Other plays include *Sanctuary City*, *Queens*, and *Ironbound*, which have been produced across American and international stages, and the libretto for *Gatsby: An American Myth*, with music by Florence Welch and Thomas Bartlett. Other awards include a Guggenheim Fellowship, the Steinberg Distinguished Playwright Award, Arthur Miller Foundation Legacy Award, the Obie Award for Playwriting, the Hull-Warriner Award, the Academy of Arts and Letters' Benjamin Hadley Danks Award for Exceptional Playwriting, the Sun Valley Playwrights Residency Award, Off Broadway Alliance Best New Play Award, the Lucille Lortel Award for Outstanding New Play, the Hermitage Greenfield Prize, as the first female recipient in drama, the Champions of Change Award from the NYC Mayor's Office, the Francesca Primus Prize, two Jane Chambers Playwriting Awards, the Lanford Wilson Prize, the Lilly Award's Stacey Mindich Prize, Helen Merrill Emerging Playwright Award, Charles MacArthur Award for Outstanding Original New Play from the Helen Hayes Awards, Jean Kennedy Smith Playwriting Award, ANPF Women's Invitational Prize, David Calicchio Prize, Global Age Project Prize, NYTW 2050 Fellowship, NNPN Smith Prize for Political Playwriting, and Merage Foundation Fellowship for the American Dream. Martyna studied at Yale School of Drama, Juilliard, University of Chicago, and Jersey public schools. She was a 2012–2013 NNPN playwright-in-residence, the 2015–2016 PoNY Fellow at the Lark Play Development Center, and a 2018–2019 Hodder Fellow at Princeton University. Martyna has developed TV projects for HBO and is writing feature films for Plan B/Pastel/MGM/Orion and Killer Films.

**Mona Mansour** is a Lebanese-American playwright and television writer based in Brooklyn. Her plays include *Unseen* (Oregon Shakespeare Festival, The Gift Theater); *We Swim We Talk We Go to War* (Golden Thread); *The Way West* (Labyrinth Theater, Steppenwolf). The full-length version of *The Hour of Feeling* was at Actors Theater of Louisville's Humana Fest; an Arabic translation was presented at NYU Abu Dhabi in 2016. *Urge for Going* was presented at The Public Theater and Golden Thread. Mona Mansour was a member of The Public Theater's Emerging Writers Group. With Tala Manassah she wrote *Falling Down the Stairs*, an EST/Sloan commission. Their play *Dressing* is part of *Facing Our Truths*, commissioned by the New Black Festival. Her awards include the 2020 Kesselring, 2020 Helen Merrill Award, 2014 Middle East America Playwright Award. Her residencies include MacDowell Colony, Space on Ryder Farm, Sundance Theater Institute, New Dramatists Class of 2020. Mona writes for NBC's *New Amsterdam* and is working on a script for AMC International. In 2019, she formed the theater company Society with Scott Illingworth and Tim Nicolai.

**Charlie Oh**'s plays have been developed at Manhattan Theatre Club, South Coast Rep, The Lark, Second Stage, The Goodman, the BMI Lehmen Engel Musical Theatre Workshop, and the American Music Theater Project. His play *Long* won the Kennedy Center's Paula Vogel Award In Playwriting, placed second for the Mark Twain Prize for Comedic Playwriting, and was a 2019 Honorable Mention for The American Playwriting Foundation's Relentless Award. His play *Coleman '72* won the Kennedy Center's Paul Stephen Lim Playwriting Award and premiered at South Coast Rep in the spring of 2023, directed by Chay Yew. Commissioned by Manhattan Theater Club and the Alfred P. Sloan Foundation, and a member of Ars Nova Play Group, Page 73's Interstate 73, and EST/Youngblood. A recent graduate of The Juilliard School's Lila Acheson Wallace American Playwrights Program. BA: Northwestern University.

**Mfoniso Udofia**, a first-generation Nigerian-American storyteller and educator, attended Wellesley College and obtained an MFA from the American Conservatory Theater [ACT]. While at ACT, she co-pioneered THE NIA PROJECT, which provided artistic outlets for San Francisco youth. Productions of her plays *Sojourners*, *Runboyrun*, *Her Portmanteau*, and *In Old Age* have been seen at New York Theatre Workshop, American Conservatory Theater, Playwrights Realm, Magic Theater, National Black Theatre, Strand Theater, and Boston Court. She is the recipient of the 2021 Horton Foote Award, the 2017 Helen Merrill Playwright Award, the 2017–2018 McKnight National Residency and Commission, and is a member of New Dramatists. Mfoniso is currently commissioned by The Huntington Theatre, Hartford Stage, Denver Center, ACT, and South Coast Repertory. Her plays have been developed by Manhattan Theatre Club, ACT, McCarter Theatre, OSF, New

Dramatists, Berkeley Rep's Ground Floor, Hedgebrook, Sundance, Space on Ryder Farm, and more.

**Luis Valdez** is regarded as one of the most important and influential American playwrights and filmmakers living today. His internationally renowned and Obie Award–winning theater company, El Teatro Campesino (The Farm Workers' Theater), was founded by Luis in 1965 in the heat of the United Farm Workers (UFW) struggle and the Great Delano Grape Strike in California's Central Valley. His involvement with Cesar Chavez, the UFW, and the early Chicano Movement left an indelible mark that remained embodied in all his work even after he left the UFW in 1967. In 1978, he wrote and directed *Zoot Suit*, the play that re-examines the Sleepy Lagoon Trial of 1942 and the Zoot Suit Riots of 1943, two of the darkest moments in LA urban history. It is considered a masterpiece of the American Theater as well as the first Chicano play on Broadway and the first Chicano major feature film. Valdez's numerous feature film and television credits include, among others, the 1987 box office hit film *La Bamba*, starring Lou Diamonds Phillips. Valdez's hard work and long creative career have won him countless awards including the prestigious George Peabody Award for excellence in television, the Presidential Medal of the Arts, the Governor's Award for the California Arts Council, and Mexico's prestigious Aguila Azteca Award, given to individuals whose work promotes cultural excellence and exchange between US and Mexico. In September, 2016, he was awarded the National Medal of the Arts by President Obama at the White House.

**Jesús I. Valles** is a queer Mexican immigrant, educator, and writer-performer from Cd. Juarez/El Paso. Valles is the winner of the 2023 Yale Drama Series, selected by Jeremy O. Harris (*Bathhouse.pptx*), the winner of the 2022 Kernodle Playwriting Prize (*a river, its mouths*), and the 2022 Emerging Theatre Professional, selected by the National Theatre Conference. As a playwright, Valles received support from The Bushwick Starr, Clubbed Thumb, The Flea, The Kennedy Center, The Lortel, Manhattan Theatre Club, New York Theatre Workshop, OUTsider Festival, The Playwrights' Center, Sewanee Writers' Conference, Teatro Vivo, and The VORTEX. As a poet, Valles received fellowships from CantoMundo, Community of Writers, Idyllwild Arts, Lambda Literary, Tin House, and Undocupoets. Valles is a Core Apprentice of the Playwrights' Center and received an MFA in writing for performance from Brown University.

**Isaiah Stavchansky** is a Mexican-American writer, actor, editor, and educator. His work has been developed with The Workshop Theater, Atlantic Acting School, Mercury Store, The Williamstown Theatre Festival, The Tank NYC, and Kenyon College. He has performed at The Williamstown Theatre Festival, Chautauqua Theater Company, and The Wellfleet Harbor Actor's Theater, among other theaters. He is a graduate of Kenyon College and Atlantic Acting School Conservatory.